MYTH AND
MODERN
MAN

By Raphael Patai ─────────────────────────

The Poems of Israel B. Fontanella (in Hebrew), 1933
Water: A Study in Palestinian Folklore (in Hebrew), 1936
Jewish Seafaring in Ancient Times (in Hebrew), 1938
Man and Earth in Hebrew Custom, Belief and Legend (in Hebrew),
    2 vols., 1942–1943
Historical Traditions and Mortuary Customs of the Jews of Meshhed
    (in Hebrew), 1945
The Science of Man: An Introduction to Anthropology (in Hebrew),
    2 vols., 1947–1948
Man and Temple in Ancient Jewish Myth and Ritual, 1947, 1967
On Culture Contact and Its Working in Modern Palestine, 1947
Israel Between East and West, 1953, 1970
Jordan, Lebanon and Syria: An Annotated Bibliography, 1957
The Kingdom of Jordan, 1958
Cultures in Conflict, 1958, 1961
Sex and Family in the Bible and the Middle East, 1959
*Golden River to Golden Road: Society, Culture and Change in the
    Middle East,* 1962, 1967, 1969
Hebrew Myths: The Book of Genesis (with Robert Graves), 1964
The Hebrew Goddess, 1967
Tents of Jacob: The Diaspora—Yesterday and Today, 1971
Myth and Modern Man, 1972

Edited by Raphael Patai ─────────────────────

Anthology of Palestinian Short Stories (with Zvi Wohlmut; in
    Hebrew), 2 vols., 1938, 1944
Edoth (Communities): A Quarterly for Folklore and Ethnology (with
    Joseph J. Rivlin; in Hebrew and English), 3 vols., 1945–1948
Studies in Folklore and Ethnology (in Hebrew), 5 vols., 1946–1948
Social Studies (with Roberto Bachi; in Hebrew and English), 2 vols.,
    1947–1948
The Hashemite Kingdom of Jordan, 1956
The Republic of Lebanon, 2 vols., 1956
The Republic of Syria, 2 vols., 1956
Jordan (Country Survey Series), 1957
Current Jewish Social Research, 1958
Herzl Year Book, 7 vols., 1958–1971
The Complete Diaries of Theodor Herzl, 5 vols., 1960
Studies in Biblical and Jewish Folklore (with Francis L. Utley and
    Dov Noy), 1960
Women in the Modern World, 1967
Encyclopedia of Zionism and Israel, 2 vols., 1971

MYTH AND MODERN MAN

by
Raphael Patai

PRENTICE-HALL, INC.
ENGLEWOOD CLIFFS, NEW JERSEY

Myth and Modern Man
By Raphael Patai

ISBN 0-13-609123-7
Library of Congress Catalog Card Number: 70-163399
Printed in the United States of America • *T*
Prentice-Hall International, Inc., London
Prentice-Hall of Australia, Pty. Ltd., Sydney
Prentice-Hall of Canada, Ltd., Toronto
Prentice-Hall of India Private Ltd., New Delhi
Prentice-Hall of Japan, Inc., Tokyo

acknowledgments

The author wishes to express his thanks to the following for permission to quote from the works listed below:

Lord Raglan, "Myth and Ritual," *Journal of American Folklore,* LXVIII (October–December 1955).

Walter F. Otto, *Die Gestalt und das Sein,* Eugen Diederichs Verlag, Dusseldorf, 1955. Copyright by Wissenschaftliche Buchgesellschaft, Darmstadt.

Joseph Cambell, *The Hero With a Thousand Faces,* Bollingen Series XVII. Copyright © 1949 by Princeton University Press. Quotes from pp. 19–20, 30, 37, 245–46, 258.

Mircea Eliade, "Archaic Myth and Historical Man," *McCormick Quarterly* (January 1955). Copyright by McCormick Theological Seminary, Chicago.

New Catholic Encyclopedia, copyright 1967 by the Catholic University of America, Washington, D.C. Used with permission of McGraw-Hill Book Company.

The Black Messiah by Albert B. Cleage, copyright © Sheed and Ward Inc., 1968.

James B. Pritchard, ed., *Ancient Near Eastern Texts Relating to the Old Testament* (3rd ed., with Supplement). Copyright © 1969 by Princeton University Press.

Robert Graves, *New Poems.* Doubleday, New York, 1963. Copyright © 1963 by Robert Graves.

Teilhard de Chardin, *The Future of Man.* Copyright © 1969 by Harper & Row, New York.

Eric Bergaust, *The Next Fifty Years in Space.* Copyright © 1964 by The Macmillan Company, New York.

preface

Mythology has interested me ever since my high-school days. From 1936 on I wrote several books dealing either wholly or partly with mythological themes. The subject matter of these books pertained to the great, but to this day insufficiently explored, realm of ancient Hebrew and Jewish mythology as viewed in comparison with the myths of other ancient peoples. While working on these books, and especially on the later ones among them, my attention was gradually drawn to the presence of myth and mythical thinking in the socio-cultural environment in which I lived and worked. I began to feel, more or less intuitively at first, that myths were still being created all around me and that the life of the average American (himself a mythical figure) was still being considerably influenced by myths, single mythologems, and mythical images. This feeling prompted me to seek out similarities between ancient and modern myths, and to analyze the mythopoeic processes that could be observed not only in America but in other parts of the modern world as well. When I began to supplement these direct observations with readings, I knew that I was embarked upon preparations for a new book.

At this point in a preface it is customary for the author to express his thanks to those who helped him in writing his book. In the case of the present volume the number of those who directly or indirectly helped me is so great that I simply cannot list them all. If I would name a hundred, I may still leave dozens unnamed. Moreover, many times occasional exchanges with people who remained unidentified resulted in what I felt were valuable insights into the working of mythopoeic forces. These circumstances, it appears to me, call for recourse to one of the favorite methods of mythopoesis which consists of merging the many into one, who thereupon is personified, given a name, and endowed with superhuman dimensions and qualities. The many who helped me, then, assume the character of one single mythical figure whom I fancy calling Eudore, the Generous One, and address thusly:

Thank you, Eudore, generous beneficer and bestower, for standing by me for many years and in all places, and for giving me unstintingly of your specialized knowledge and ability in a hundred areas. Without your help this book could not have been written.

Forest Hills. N. Y.   R. P

contents

introduction

The most direct way of introducing a subject such as the one dealt with in this book is to define the terms contained in the title. Let us begin with the second part of the title, which presents no special problem. "Modern man" in the present context is taken to refer to that segment of the global population which, in the last third of the twentieth century, lives in highly industrialized environments. The highest percentage of any national population living in such an environment is found in the United States. Canada and Western Europe come next, followed by Central, Southern, and Eastern Europe and Latin America. The rest of the world is only now, under our very eyes, embarking upon the venture of modernization and is experiencing the attendant trauma, which appears to be inevitable. When discussing the influence of myth on "modern man" we shall, therefore, have in mind primarily the urban population of the United States and of similar countries.

1

With regard to the first part of our title—"myth"—the situation is much more difficult. As will be shown in Chapter I, this concept has attracted the attention of an exceedingly large number of scholars specializing in many different disciplines, and their interpretations of the term "myth" are correspondingly diverse.

Some years ago, when working on a lecture on Hebrew mythology which I delivered at the New York Academy of Sciences and at the universities of Munich and Frankfort, I was faced with the necessity of working out a definition of myth which would serve as a guide in isolating the mythical elements within the rich storehouses of ancient Hebrew and Jewish lore. The definition on which I finally settled was: "Myth . . . is a traditional religious charter, which operates by validating laws, customs, rites, institutions and beliefs, or explaining sociocultural situations and natural phenomena, and taking the form of stories, believed to be true, about divine beings and heroes." [1]

About the same time, for the introduction of our book *Hebrew Myths,* Robert Graves and I agreed on a definition that was shorter but basically similar: "Myths are dramatic stories that form a sacred charter either authorizing the continuance of ancient institutions, customs, rites and beliefs in the area where they are current, or approving alterations." [2]

Today I would still accept these definitions of myth, although I would delete the word "religious" from the first. My studies of the workings of myth in the modern world have convinced me that myth is not necessarily a "religious" charter, for it can be and often is entirely secular. Nor does it have to be "traditional," except in the sense that once a myth becomes established it rapidly becomes traditional by serving as an example to be emulated, a precedent to be repeated and thereby reaffirmed.

Also, today, on the basis of my observations of the modern scene, I would put greater emphasis on the active role played by myth in the shaping of social life. As I see it, myth not only validates or authorizes customs, rites, institutions, beliefs, and so forth, but frequently is directly responsible for creating them. In this respect, I am not too far from the position of Georges Sorel, who asserted that myths must be judged as means of acting upon the present.[3] At least, one must recognize that there is a mutual cross-fertilization between myth and those aspects of socio-cultural life that are subsumed under terms such as customs, rites, institutions, beliefs, and the like. New myths create new socio-cultural patterns, and, conversely, new customs and new social situations create new myths. As is usually the case with such mutual reinforcement situations, the question of primacy cannot be broached with any prospect of a satisfactory answer.

Perhaps it is somewhat easier to answer the question, What is it that endows myth with the extraordinary power to influence our lives? In the first place, there is the belief factor. If the myth is to exert any influence on people they must believe that what the myth tells is true. This truth, however, is not of the same order as the truth in the statement "the sun rises in the east." It is not a simple, factual truth, but rather a truth that dawns upon us as we gain an understanding of the "true meaning" of the myth. It seems as if fundamental, weighty, and crucial truths or insights into the human condition cannot be communicated directly or immediately unless the purpose of communication is merely to impart a cerebral, logical understanding. But if, on the other hand, the purpose is to enable the recipient to attain a deep emotional internalization of, and self-identification with, the communicated truth and its message, then such truths can best be expressed and communicated in the narrative form of the myth. And precisely because the truth of the myth lies in its deeper meaning, it requires repetition before it can have a full impact on its audience. The repetitions may be literal, or they may take the form of variants. In both cases the myth becomes a potent motivating factor in the existence of those who have thus internalized it as its true meaning becomes understood.

Once the truth of myth is grasped, the myth itself assumes a new function: those who come under its influence experience a sense of gratification which can take any one of several forms. It can be the gratification felt at experiencing anxiety reduction, as is emphasized by Malinowski.[4] It can be the gratification derived from the feeling of increased self-confidence, from the

elimination of doubts and uncertainties, from having come into
the possession of ultimate truth, or, as Walter Otto would have
phrased it, from the experience of something divine.[5] Or it
can manifest itself in the elation felt when one becomes aware
of being part of a general consciousness that pervades a large
human aggregate. In any case, the myth is perceived as something extremely valuable and powerfully influential.

The structure of this book to some extent resembles that of a
spaceship whose bulk, as it is launched, consists largely of the
booster rocket required to lift it into orbit, while its payload
comprises only a small capsule carried at its front end. Without
the rocket the ship could never go into orbit but once that phase
is reached, the bulky sections which comprise the early stages of
the craft can be, and are, discarded. In the present study the
rocket is represented by the historical analyses of certain types
of myth, which are necessary in order to reach an understanding of the way similar myth-types function in our own modern
world. The payload of the book is the presentation of myth in
the life of modern man. Only the historical excursuses make it
possible to recognize certain phenomena in our lives for what
they are, namely myths; to understand how these myths work;
and to delve into the complex issues of their persistent presence
("orbiting") a long time after the original motivations ("rock-
ets") seem to have become exhausted ("burned out") and appear to have been discarded.

One could easily have widened the scope of this inquiry to
include a discussion of numerous diffuse and amorphous manifestations termed "mythical" by critics and commentators of
modern life. Had we done so, we would have had to touch
upon the vast area of mythical interpretation given to all kinds
of organizational, industrial, commercial, and communications
activities by men like Marshall McLuhan and his followers and
admirers. But the narrower frame we have set for ourselves
does not allow us to follow these pathfinders into fields which,
at least according to our understanding of myth, are not mythical. Without wishing to dispute the value of McLuhan's insights

into the working of our mass media, the folklore of industrial man, and related subjects, I feel I cannot go along with the claim, put forward by one of his friendly critics, that McLuhan, in showing that mechanics and sex "are the predominant themes in the general 'public consciousness' and in operations upon it," has thereby isolated "myths" which employ "these twin themes as well as others." [6] "Predominant themes" they undoubtedly are. But then, we find mechanics and sex as predominant, or at least important, themes as far back as in Greek mythology—witness the myths about Daedalus, the "great artificer," and Aphrodite. Whether McLuhan has shown how these ancient mythological themes have been reformulated in our modern industrial society seems questionable. Nor am I satisfied, for that matter, that the chapters and sections in his book devoted to an analysis of some of their mythical aspects have done justice to these extremely important focal concerns of our modern culture.[7]

Several other aspects of the role of myth and the mythical in the life of modern man also are not discussed in this volume. In general, little or no attention will be paid to the continuing influence of ancient or traditional myths. While I am fully aware of the persistence of these influences, I have nevertheless chosen to give them scant notice because our subject is not the *survival* of the past in the present, important as an analysis of this would be, but an entirely different topic: a consideration of the *live mythopoeic forces* and processes that are at work in our culture. These forces and processes themselves are, to be sure, fundamentally identical with those that motivated man in past ages. Indeed, it is precisely this similarity that should remind us that the products in which we can observe these mythopoeic forces working are not a mere heritage or a survival from the past but are the outcome of an actual, live psycho-social dynamism which is at work in the psyche of modern man to no less a degree than it was in generations of the remote past.

Thus we shall either omit or make only passing reference to the continuing presence of ancient, primarily Biblical, myths in traditional Judaism and Christianity as still taught at reli-

gious schools, even though these myths still form an integral part
of the doctrinal and ritual aspects of these religions. Nor shall
we consider the many quasi-religious and extra-religious channels through which classical Hebrew and Christian myths have
reached us from antiquity, and the numerous areas in which the
residual influence of these old mythologies is still being felt.
These include, in the first place, the arts, literature, and language. In painting and sculpture, Biblical, Greek, Roman,
and other ancient mythologies still supply artists with a rich variety of subject matter. In literature the same materials still
reappear in historical novels, such as Thomas Mann's great Biblical tetralogy, *Joseph and His Brothers,* or Robert Graves' and
Mary Renault's recreations of Greek myths. (The utilization of
ancient mythical themes in a modern garb is a different matter,
which will be touched upon briefly in Chapter 1, section 13.)
Poetry, quite apart from myths actually retold in poems, is re-
plete with mythical images and expressions.[8] In linguistic usage,
a one- or two-word reference to a classical or Biblical myth or
mythical figure is the most economical way of conjuring up an
image which otherwise would necessitate the use of a lengthy
expression. We can describe John Doe as "a strong and crafty
man who, however, had one weak point which was . . ." or can
say succinctly, and more effectively, "John Doe's Achilles' heel
was . . ."[9] We can describe a very big and very strong man as
a Hercules (from Greek mythology), a Goliath or a Samson
(from Hebrew mythology), or a giant (from an indeterminate
folkloristic source). All these are highly attractive areas of
study, but one can foresee that the result they would yield
would be merely a more detailed documentation of the well-
known fact that ancient myths still manifest their residual presence in the mental world of modern man, especially in the more
educated sectors.

Yet another area in which old myths survive is that of witchcraft. The practices of "black" and "white" witches and warlocks
are all anchored in ancient mythologems, although the modern
American practitioners themselves, as a rule, have barely a smat-
tering of the old and rich witch lore.[10] Again, we shall forgo
(although admittedly with considerable reluctance) a discus-

sion of this subject, because essentially such myths as still underlie these practices are but the skeletal remains of a once powerful and highly potent mythology.

On the other hand, we shall discuss a few examples of the survival of old religious myths in the officially sanctioned rituals and doctrines of the modern churches, because there the old myths still function as live forces (*cf.* Chapter 9). Moreover, these ancient myths in modern religions serve as the necessary foil to set off the various other types of influences exerted by myth on present-day religious life: the reformulation of old myths (Chapter 10); the reinterpretation of old myths in a way considered more relevant to modern circumstances (Chapter 11); the radical substitution of what is perceived as an entirely new myth for an old one (Chapter 12); and the modern mythopoesis which emerges most dynamically in several Black religious groups (Chapter 13).

Myth is present in the life of modern man on the most diverse levels. It influences the thinking of the theoreticians of modern anthropology (Chapter 2, section 5) and theology (Chapter 1, section 13; Chapters 11 and 12). It comes through in the ideas of Marxist and Nazi ideologists (Chapters 5 and 6). It lends weight to the vociferous demands of youthful radicals (Chapter 4, section 3; Chapters 7 and 8). It is a source of the effectiveness of the funny and sorry fare blaring from television sets at children and childlike adults (Chapters 14–18). It powerfully imposes its will on juveniles (Chapter 19). And it holds out the comfort of survival to people who, though they have lost faith in the Other World, do believe in other worlds (Chapter 21). Certainly it is a force to be reckoned with.

1

myth interpretation
through the ages

For at least twenty-five centuries
man has asked the question "What is myth?" The problem
has attracted the attention of people with greatly varying
interests, orientations, and preoccupations, so that inevitably they adopted widely disparate approaches and came
up with widely dissimilar answers. Today, when we know
a lot more about myth than was known in any previous age,
we are still as far as ever from a generally agreed upon
consensus as to the meaning of myth.

One thing, however, can be assumed without any doubt:
the very formulation of the question "What is myth?" presupposes a certain detachment, a certain critical interest,
which could have arisen only after man had begun to extri-
cate himself from the magic circle in which myth had held
him enthralled for many thousands of years. We have good
historical basis to believe that myth was a part of human
life as early as in the Paleolithic period, the Old Stone Age.
Throughout those thousands of years that passed before

the question "What is myth?" was first raised, men had accepted myth unquestioningly. Myth had been a very important part of the body of knowledge that each individual had to acquire in order to be equipped for the battle for survival. In every human group, myth was no less carefully preserved and transmitted from generation to generation than such concrete details of practical knowledge as how to make an axe or use a bow. But while myth actually surrounded man and accompanied him from birth to death and beyond, he lived with myth for ages before asking "What is myth?" just as he had lived for eons submerged in an ocean of air before he first asked, "What is air?"

1 • *Ancient Interpretations*

Nor did man finally come to ask the question suddenly or abruptly. Gradually there arose a kind of men, a "tribe" the ancients would say, whose members took a keener interest in myths than the average man. These men, later to become known as poets, began to gather myths, to put them in rhythmically or otherwise pleasing forms, to recite them as occasion allowed or demanded, thus causing other men to accept and remember the new versions rather than the earlier, simpler ones.

Whether the ancient Sumerian, Akkadian, Hittite, and Canaanite poets—all sharing a largely common ancient Near Eastern mythical and religious heritage—believed the myths they incorporated into their epics and other poetic writings, or merely used them for themes, as was done later by Greek and Roman poets, is a moot question. In either case, our indebtedness to them is great for it was almost exclusively due to this early poetic interest that the enormously important ancient Near Eastern corpus of myths has been preserved to this day.

The interpretation of Greek myths began in the sixth century B.C. among the early Greek philosophers. Their stand on the truth of myth was invariably critical or even skeptical. They scrutinized the myths from the vantage point of rational truths, and found them wanting. To Thales, Theagenes of Rhegion, and Pythagoras (all three *c.* sixth century B.C.), myths were allegories of nature and the mythical beings were either personifications of natural phenomena or poetic designations for the elements. Thus, for instance, Okeanos, the nymphs, and Styx were interpreted as personifications of water. In this manner the gods in general were reduced to elements of nature.

With the fifth century B.C. the historical reinterpretation of myths was inaugurated by Herodotus, the father of historians. With considerable ingenuity, Herodotus applied himself to turning myths into historical accounts. For instance, a myth about Cyrus, the great King of the Persians (who, incidentally, lived barely a century prior to Herodotus), alleged that he had been brought up by a bitch, just as Romulus and Remus were said by the Latin myth to have been nursed by a she-wolf. But in Herodotus' version the infant Cyrus was brought up by a herdsman's wife named Spako (in Greek Kynō), a name meaning bitch.

While the historical interpretation of myth has never been completely abandoned, the Greek philosophers soon found new methods of myth interpretation. The metaphysicians endeavored to show that the gods and spirits who populated the old myths were, in fact, merely early versions of the metaphysical concepts with which they were concerned. The moralists, on the other hand, were concerned to show that the myths, including even the obscene stories, were actually didactic allegories.[1] The Sophists of the Greek Enlightenment attempted a reconciliation by interpreting the traditional myths or theogonic tales as allegories revealing naturalistic and moral truths.

This last method of interpretation, while criticized by Plato, found favor among the Neo-Platonic and Stoic philosophers of the Hellenistic period. To the latter, whose school was founded at Athens around 300 B.C., myths ingeniously symbolized concepts of the nature of the universe, and were thus beautiful veils concealing profound moral principles. Thus Zeus was taken to be the primary fire, or the "ether." But he was also the universal principle, and hence the other gods were said to be parts of Zeus: Hera was the air; Hades, vapor; Hephaestus, fire; Demeter, earth. The myth of the expulsion of Hephaestus from heaven meant that early man kindled fire by means of lightning or sunbeams. Other gods, the Stoics held, symbolized moral qualities (or, as we would say, human character traits): Ares, rashness; Aphrodite, profligacy; Leto, forgetfulness; Herakles, wisdom.[2]

All in all, myths were read as a method of preserving the authority of tradition as well as the religious prerogatives of the state. There were those, like the emperor Julian and the philosopher Sallustius (both fourth century A.D.), who regarded myths as divine truths and mysteries hidden from the foolish crowd and apparent only to the wise. On the other hand, the Epicurean philosophers sought to belittle the traditional tales, which they considered to be fabrications which, at best, concealed purely naturalistic and historical events and served primarily to bolster the authority of the priests and the rulers.[3]

It is quite possible that the deification accorded to Alexander the Great (356–323 B.C.), and the consciously emphasized parallelism between his expedition to India and the triumphant procession through the same remote part of the antique world attributed by myth to Dionysus, were factors in the emergence of that particular interpretation of myth which is associated with the name of Euhemerus. This Messenian philosopher (c. 330–c. 260 B.C.), who flourished about a generation after Alexander, may have also been influenced in developing his method of myth interpretation by the early manifestations of the trend to deify the Seleucid and Ptolemaic successors of Alexander. Briefly stated, Euhemerism maintains that "the traditional deities were merely earthly rulers whom the gratitude or adulation of their subjects had raised to a place in heaven."[4]

Euhemerism was gladly embraced by the Christian fathers who were eager to show that even pagan philosophers had recognized the mortal basis of the Greco-Roman pantheon. The argument was taken up by Clement of Alexandria (c. 150–c. 220), Tertullian (c. 155–c. 220), St. Cyprian (c. 200–258), Commodian (middle of the third century A.D.), Lactantius (c. 250–317), Arnobius (fl. c. 300), Firmicus Maternus (fl. 334–337), St. Augustine (354–430), and others.[5] At the same time the Church Fathers found ingenious explanations for the presence in the Old Testament of certain crude and savage elements analogous to pagan practices: Perhaps best known among these is the doctrine of "condescension" which claimed that God allowed that which was imperfect to subsist temporarily in Judaism.[6]

2 • Renaissance and Romantic Views

Following the outburst of interest in the meaning and truth of myth, which was part of the Hellenistic controversy with Judaeo-Christian monotheism, the problem was all but swept into the background and remained quiescent throughout the centuries dominated by Christian dogmatism. Christian authors, beginning with Eusebius, bishop of Caesarea, Palestine (*c.* 260–*c.* 340), treated the pagan gods—not only the Greek and Roman deities, but also those of the ancient Near East—as if they had been humans, without any doubt and without any polemic edge. For Eusebius, the Babylonian god Baal (Bel, Belus) was in reality the first king of the Assyrians. Isidore of Seville, the seventh-century author of *Etymologiae,* flatly generalizes: "Those whom the pagans claim to be gods were once men." [7] One of the interesting scholarly preoccupations in this period was the task of establishing the periods in which those men who later were believed to have been gods lived, and of synchronizing their ages with those of the heroes of the Old Testament. Thus the French martyrologist, St. Ado of Vienne (799–874), states in his *Chronicle of the Six Ages of the World* that Prometheus was a contemporary of Moses; that his brother Atlas was a great astrologer; and that Atlas' grandson Mercury was a sage skilled in several arts.[8] The names of medieval Euhemerists constitute quite an impressive list.[9]

It was in this Euhemeristic guise of kings, wise men, lawgivers, and the like, acceptable to good Christians, that the pagan gods of the classical world (and the myths told about them) survived into the Renaissance. The gods, considered as the human geniuses of antiquity who were responsible for our civilization, retained their places as historical figures next to, and intermingled with, the heroes of the Old Testament. Some of the pagan deities, having been reduced to human dimensions, were even considered worthy of being elevated to eternal bliss and were given a seat next to God. Thus the Swiss reformer Zwingli writes in 1531 to Francis I: "Shouldst thou follow in the footsteps of David, thou wilt one day see God Himself; and near Him thou mayest hope to see Adam, Abel, Enoch, Paul, Hercules, Theseus, Socrates, the Catos, the Scipios. . . ."[10]

With myth seen in this light, it was possible for the medieval custom of claiming a mythical hero as an ancestor to persist into the Renaissance. In view of these factors, as well as several others most ably presented by Jean Seznec in her book, *The Survival of the Pagan Gods,* it was little wonder that in the great Renaissance efflorescence of painting and sculpture "pagan" mythical themes were frequently utilized as subject matter.

Although the late Middle Ages and the Renaissance continue to view mythical heroes as great men, according to the Euhemeristic tradition, this period also saw the opening of a new chapter in myth interpretation. Most important in this respect was the *Genealogy of the Gods* by Giovanni Boccaccio (1313–1375), a large encyclopedic work which he wrote mostly on the basis of secondary and tertiary sources, including several of quite dubious value. Boccaccio's explanations of the myths were quite eclectic. He applied literal, moral-symbolic, and allegorical interpretations, often stating explicitly that one and the same myth is capable of all three interpretations. His major concern, it seems, was to show the edifying lessons of Christian morality beneath the pagan myths; incidentally, this approach also enabled him to safeguard himself against the reproach of impiety.[11]

In the sixteenth century the Renaissance interest in Greek and Roman mythology produced in Italy several handbooks on mythography which, in turn, contributed to the further popularity of the subject. These handbooks claimed to treat all the gods of paganism; they dealt not only with the Greco-Roman deities, but also with the divinities of the Oriental cults, as well as the Egyptian, Syrian, Phoenician, Assyrian, Persian, Arabian, Celtic, Germanic, and other gods. In the seventeenth-century editions of some of these compendiums the publishers added discourses on the gods of such remote countries as Mexico and Japan.[12] While we must join in Jean Seznec's negative judgment on the value of these treatises, we should not overlook the fact that by discussing, in however unscientific a fashion, the myths of various peoples, and by comparing them side by side, these uncritical and confused compilations of the sixteenth century pointed the way toward a comparative mythology that was to develop in the seventeenth century, in the works of the Dutch scholar Gerard Jan Vossius (1577–1649), and the two Frenchmen Samuel Bochart (1599–1667) and Pierre Daniel Huet (1630–1721).

Even for critically oriented philosophical minds, liberation from the shackles of antique and medieval modes of thought did not come easily. Take, for example, Francis Bacon (1561–1626). In his book entitled *De sapientia veterum (The Wisdom of the Ancients)*,[13] this critical genius, relying extensively on the Italian Natale Conti's (*c.* 1520–1582) *Mythologia*,[14] says, for example, that the thunderbolts of Zeus, stolen by Typhon and restored by Hermes, symbolize the authority and the fiscal power that a revolution sweeps away, but that may be recovered by eloquence informed with wisdom. To Bacon Perseus was a symbol of war, and when Perseus attacks only the mortal one among the three Gorgons, this was interpreted to mean that only practicable wars ought to be attempted.

In the eighteenth century the interest in mythology flared up in full force. The controversy between opposing schools of myth interpretation, which had lain dormant since the victory of Christianity, resumed as if only a few years, and not fifteen centuries, had intervened. The Epicurean argument was taken up by the rationalistic philosophers, such as Voltaire (1694–1778) who attempted to establish reason as the foundation of all belief and of all rules of conduct, and who therefore tried to discredit the classic myths, together with the Hebrew-Christian Scriptures, as either irrational superstitions or deliberate fictions foisted upon the multitude by the crafty priests. Arrayed against the Epicureans were the heirs of the Neo-Platonists and Stoics, represented by the German Romanticists of the late eighteenth and early nineteenth centuries, for whom poetic myth became a subject of veneration and who saw in it the mainspring of human culture. This renewed controversy as to the *value* of myth prepared the ground for the ensuing discussion about its *meaning*. The main protagonists of this fight, however, were no longer poets and philosophers, but anthropologists, psychologists, and linguists.

3 • *Cultural Evolution and*
Solar Mythology

Sir Edward B. Tylor (1832–1917) was one of the founders of modern anthropology and a chief exponent of cultural evolutionism. Tylor maintained that at a certain stage of cultural evolution and "with a consistency of action so general as to amount to mental law . . . among the lower races all over the world the operation of outward events on the inward mind leads not only to statement of fact, but to formation of myth." [15] This being the case, "myth is the history of its authors, not of its subjects; it records the lives, not of superhuman heroes, but of poetic nations." [16] Tylor's thesis was that there was a "myth-making stage of the human mind" and that "myth arose in the savage condition prevalent in remote ages among the whole human race, that it remains comparatively unchanged among the modern rude tribes who have departed least from these primitive conditions, while even higher and later grades of civilization, partly by retaining its actual principles, and partly by carrying on its inherited results in the form of ancestral tradition, have continued it not merely in toleration but in honour." [17]

As to "the causes which transfigure into myths the facts of daily experience," Tylor assigned the chief role to "the belief in the animation of all nature, rising at its highest pitch to personification. . . . To the lower tribes of man, sun and stars, trees and rivers, wind and clouds, become personal animate creatures, leading lives conformed to human or animal analogies. . . ." [18] Among the "lower races" these analogies are "real and sensible"; only in "more advanced periods of civilization" is there "the great expansion of verbal metaphor into myth." Therefore, "material myth" or "myth founded on fact" is "the primary, and verbal myth [or "myth founded on word"] the secondary formation." [19]

We now turn briefly to the "solar" mythology of Friedrich Max Müller (1823–1900), the leading Sanscritist of nineteenth-century England. From 1856, when his long essay on "Comparative Mythology" was published, until 1897, when his last publication, the two bulky volumes of *Contributions to the Science of Mythology*, appeared, Müller maintained that all Aryan mythologies, including Hindu, Greek, and Germanic, among others, tell about the sun and other natural phenomena occasioned by it, such as dawn, day, night, and the seasons. The ingenuity that went into this solar mythology was quite impressive. To take a single example, according to Müller the tale of Herakles' death being brought about by the shirt poisoned with the blood of Nessus was derived from the sun setting amid red clouds.

Solar mythology was soon followed by a number of offshoots such as lunar mythology, wind mythology, storm-cloud mythology, and sky mythology. It also stimulated research into Biblical mythology, such as a study by A. Smythe Palmer on *The Samson Saga and Its Place in Comparative Mythology* (London, 1913), and a precipitate excursion into Hebrew solar mythology undertaken by that great Islamic scholar, Ignaz Goldziher (1850–1921), in an early book entitled *Der Mythos bei den Hebräern* (1876; English translation, 1877).

Today, solar mythology is memorable mainly for the uncommon interest aroused by the truly gigantic battle between Max Müller and his bitter opponent Andrew Lang (1844–1912), a representative of cultural evolutionism in anthropology. As Richard M. Dorson has put it, "The giants slew each other, although the corpse of cultural evolutionism bled more slowly than the dismembered torso of solarism." [20]

4 • *Wundt's* Völkerpsychologie

The fact that a German psychologist preceded Jane Harrison by several years in postulating an intrinsic interrelationship between myth and ritual generally has been overlooked by the mythologists who summarized the development of various mythological theories. Miss Harrison's *Themis,* in which she made the point that myth is the correlative of the acted rite, was published in 1912. Four years earlier, however, Wilhelm Wundt, in his monumental *Völkerpsychologie,*[21] devoted a subchapter entitled "Mythus und Kultus" (i.e., Myth and Ritual) to a discussion of precisely this subject.

Nature myth, says Wundt,

> in its basic forms, including, above all, those forms
> which lend it the character of a *believed reality*
> [emphasis by Wundt], finds its expression in *acts* which
> eliminate all doubt as to its origin out of emotion
> (*Affekt*). . . . The acts which stem from mytho-
> logical motives are accompanied by specific characteristics
> which are as significant for the general connection of
> the acts of will (*Willenshandlungen*) with the feelings
> and emotions (*Affekte*) as they are expressive of the
> unusual intensity of precisely those emotions which
> belong to the realm of myth and religion. The acts
> which belong to this realm are termed *Cultus,* the
> name introduced by the Romans for the system of
> their religious feasts and sacrifices. . . . Inasmuch as
> the Cultus comprises those acts which the community
> believes to be calculated to secure for it the protection
> and help of the gods, it endows the more narrowly
> delimited circle of mythical views which relate to this
> protective relationship and the duties imposed by it
> upon man with a special, augmented value, not
> shared by the mass of other myth components. This
> value itself, however, is founded upon two characteristics
> of the mythological views which form the basis of
> the ritual; one of these is of a practical, the other of a
> theoretical, nature. Practically, the value of ritual lies
> in the reliance on the protective and helping might
> of the gods or, in particular, on the expectation that a
> misfortune which the gods threaten to bring upon
> man can be averted by means of magic acts. Theoretically,
> the significance of myth structures carried by the
> ritual consists in the truth content which is attributed

to them. A witness of this belief form, intensified to a conviction, is contained precisely in the ritual acts themselves: performances, which dominate the acts and deeds of man in all vital situations, and which often consist of the surrender of his most precious goods or even of his own life, can have their origin only in motivations whose reality is undoubted. Therewith, however, the content of those conceptions of beliefs by which the ritual is carried is elevated, with respect to both value content and external validity, high above the circle of the other component parts of mythological thinking which continue much more unsteady and exposed to destruction or transformation.[22]

The beginnings of ritual, Wundt continues, reach back into the primitive stages of myth development. The ritual acts attest to the validity of the mythical belief contents and express confidence in their protection and help. The gods themselves are endowed with a certain truth content by means of the ritual dedicated to them. Both the ritual acts proper and the conceptions of belief connected with them are endowed with the attribute of holiness. On the earliest levels of mythological development, each custom which spread to any extent had a ritual value, no matter how limited the extent. For the belief in magic which permeates primitive mythology renders each act of any importance an integral part of a magic ritual. When the gods of the nature myths are added to the primitive magic ritual, which itself originates in animistic beliefs, there ensues the development of higher ritual forms, as well as a dichotomization of myths into a part consecrated by the cult of the gods, and another, more profane, part.[23]

Moreover, says Wundt, there are three forms in which mythological thinking concerned with nature (*"natur-mythologisches Denken"*) expresses itself: firstly, in statements about the meaning of single natural objects; secondly, in stories in which natural events, or occurrences interfering with natural events, play a decisive role; and thirdly, in acts which refer back to natural-mythological motives and which consist of rites (*"Kulte"*) or rudiments of rites.[24]

As to the interrelationship between myth and ritual, Wundt observes:

> Although every ritual refers to certain mythological
> ideas, the reverse is not true: not every myth con-
> struction (*Mythenbildung*) has some connection with
> the ritual. At the early stage, when as yet no doubts
> have been implanted into religious thinking, every-
> thing that belongs to the solid substance of belief
> finds its expression in ritual, and with its compelling
> force determines thereby also the way of acting. There
> are, however, myth constructions which are less sig-
> nificant, secondary components, or which belong to
> that realm of poetic fantasy which, whether admitted
> from the outside or produced independently, has no
> deeper relationship to those emotional needs that
> give rise to the beliefs and convictions (*Glaubensü-
> berzeugungen*) nurtured by custom. These myth
> constructions, as a rule, stand outside the ritual or
> have only a loose and more variable relationship to it.
> Among many African and West Indian native peoples
> one finds that the belief in magic, rooted in a primitive
> animism, has developed into an orderly, well-regulated
> ritual which stands under the protection of common
> custom.[25]

In summary, the gist of what Wundt says is that (1) there is an intimate connection between myth and ritual; (2) mythical belief gives rise to rites; (3) the rites, in turn, validate the beliefs expressed in the myths; (4) all rites have their associated myths; but (5) not all myths have their associated rites; however, (6) the most important myths are those which *are* associated with rites. Thus Wundt, to say the least, isolates the pivotal features of the myth-and-ritual theory.

5 • *Psychoanalysis*

Close on the heels of the *Völkerpsychologie* approach fol-
lowed that of Freudian psychoanalysis. According to Freud, myth is a daydream of the race, symbolizing a psychological and ethnohistorical reality. An important slice of this reality is symbolized, says Freud, in the Oedipus myth, most familiar to us as

formulated in Sophocles' famous tragedy. In fact, this myth expresses a traumatic ethnohistorical experience which resulted, on the one hand, in the introduction of two basic taboos, those of ingroup murder and ingroup marriage, and, on the other, in the incessant outcroppings of the repressed wish to commit precisely these two crimes. (A more detailed discussion of the Oedipus myth will follow in Chapter 2.)

The Freudian school of psychoanalysis has spread its web of interpretation actually over many, and potentially over all, myths. The favorite, though not the only, "keys" have remained sexual; persons, objects, acts, situations, and other factors figuring in myths are taken as expressing in symbolic form the subconscious processes of the human psyche. The story told in the myth stands for what the individual experiences in his own life and especially in his relationship with his parents. The myth of the birth of the hero, for instance, tells of the greatest of heroic deeds—emerging from the mother's womb and surviving the birth trauma.[26] Similarly, all myths stem from the dark pool of the subconscious, into which we must delve if we want to reach down to their true psychological meaning.

In view of this interpretation of myth, common among psychoanalysts, it is remarkable that Géza Róheim (1892–1953), who was an anthropologically oriented psychoanalyst (or a psychoanalytically oriented anthropologist), gave no room at all to the subconscious in his definition of myth. According to Róheim, the myth is a narrative in which the actors are mostly divine and sometimes human, which has a definite locale, is part of a creed, and is believed by the narrator. In a folk tale, on the other hand, the *dramatis personae* are mostly human, and especially the hero is human although his opponents are frequently supernatural beings; the actors are nameless, the scene is just anywhere: it is purely fiction and not intended to be anything else.[27]

6 • *The Jungian Approach*

The single perpendicular shaft Freud sank into the human subconscious served Carl Gustav Jung (1875–1961) as the starting point for a horizontal exploration of the deep layers of the psyche. In the course of his analytical psychological investigations, Jung discovered what he considered a basic interrelationship between the workings of the individual human psyche and those processes which since time immemorial have produced mythological images. For, according to Jung and his followers (especially Karl Kerényi), the formation of myths is a psychological process which is an essential or vital feature of the human psyche, and which can be shown to exist equally in primitive, ancient, and modern man. Mythical motifs, says Jung, are "structural elements of the psyche" or, more precisely, of its deeper, fundamental part, which Jung calls "the nonconscious psyche," or, briefly, "the unconscious." This explains why mythological ideas are often paralleled by dreams or in psychoses. Thus it was observed that typical mythologems were produced by individuals who could not have had even the remotest chance of being acquainted either directly or indirectly with the old mythical prototypes of their psychic products. "Such results necessitated the assumption that these must be cases of 'autochthonous' re-emergences apart from all tradition, and also of the existence of 'mythopoeic' structural elements of the unconscious psyche." [28]

However, Jung cautions, these products of dreams and neuroses are never (or only very rarely) fully formed myths, but rather myth components, which, because of their typical nature, can be designated as "motifs," "primal images," "types," or "archetypes"—the latter being the term coined by Jung himself. "[The] archetypes appear in myths and tales, as well as in dreams and in the products of psychotic fantasy. . . . In the case of the individual the archetypes appear as involuntary manifestations of unconscious processes whose existence and meaning can be unlocked only indirectly; whereas in the myths traditional formulations of mostly inestimable antiquity present themselves. They reach back into a primitive prehistoric world with mental presuppositions and conditions the like of which we can still observe among the primitive peoples of today. The myths on this level are, as a rule, tribal lore that is transmitted through repeated recounting from generation to generation." [29]

The myths, moreover, "have a vital significance. They not merely *represent*, but also *are* the psychic life of the primitive tribe, which instantly disintegrates and perishes if it loses its mythical heritage, like a man who has lost his soul. The mythology of a tribe is its living religion, whose loss is always and everywhere, even in the case of civilized man, a moral catastrophe." [30]

Significant in this connection is the manner in which Jung connects his understanding of the mythical archetype with his basic tenet of the "collective unconscious." Modern psychology, he says, considers the products of unconscious fantasy activity either as "self-representations of processes taking place in the unconscious," or as "statements of the unconscious psyche about itself." These products fall into either of two categories: fantasies (including dreams) of a personal character which go back to what was personally experienced, forgotten, or suppressed, and which can, therefore, be completely explained by individual anamnesis; and fantasies (again including dreams) of a nonpersonal character which do not stem from individual experience and therefore cannot be explained as individual acquisitions. "The latter fantasy images have undoubtedly their nearest analogues in the mythological types. One must, therefore, assume that they correspond to certain collective (and not personal) structural elements of the human psyche in general, and, like the morphological elements of the human body, are inherited." These psychic structural elements demand the assumption of an "autochthonous" re-emergence. "These cases are so frequent that one cannot but assume the existence of a collective psychic substratum. This is the unconscious that I have termed 'the collective unconscious.' " The products of this second category of the individual human fantasy are so similar to the structural types of the myths and tales, says Jung, that "one must pronounce them related." [31]

In conclusion, however, Jung admits that his approach to myth does not afford a better understanding of its meaning. Psychology, he says, maintains that "contents of an archetypal nature manifest processes in the collective unconscious." They therefore relate to nothing conscious, but to the essentially unconscious. "In final analysis, it is quite impossible to say to what they relate." [32] Hence the ultimate meaning nucleus of the archetype cannot be described, but only circumscribed or paraphrased. It was never conscious and never will be.

> It always was and will be interpreted and nothing more,
> and every interpretation that to any extent approaches
> the hidden sense (or, from the viewpoint of the
> scientific intellect, *nonsense,* which comes to the same
> thing) has always claimed not only absolute truth and
> validity but also awe and religious devotion. Arche-
> types were and are psychic life powers which want to
> be taken seriously and to make sure in the most peculiar
> manner that their validity be recognized. They were
> always the bringers of protection and salvation, and
> their violation has as its consequence those "perils of
> the soul" well known from the psychology of the
> primitives. They are, namely, also the unfailing arousers
> of neurotic and even psychotic disorders, inasmuch as
> they behave exactly like neglected or abused bodily
> organs or organic functional systems.[33]

These archetypes or "primordial images" play as important a role in the working of the human psyche today as they did in the prehistoric times when "there was as yet no unity of the personality . . . and, in general, no consciousness." [34] Examples can be found throughout history and down to the present day to show that "the greatest and finest thoughts of man shape themselves upon these primordial images as upon a blueprint." Their origin "can only be explained by assuming them to be deposits of the constantly repeated experiences of humanity," and thus the archetype itself is "a kind of readiness to produce over and over again the same or similar mythical ideas." Moreover, the archetypes "behave empirically like agents that tend towards the repetition of these same experiences." [35]

7 · The Myth and Ritual School

It is time to leave the primordial depths of the unconscious psyche and to surface to the clearer waters of the myth and ritual school, which still commands the faithful adherence of many students of myth. This school started out on its conquering career with Jane E. Harrison's *Themis,* in which she made three important points: (1) myth arises out of rite rather than the reverse; (2) it is the spoken correlative of the acted rite—that is, it is *to legomenon,* the thing said, as contrasted with, while also related to, *to dromenon,* the thing acted; and (3) it is not anything else, nor of any other origin.[36]

It should be noted that Miss Harrison based her observations on Greek material, and that her conclusions also referred to the Greek context. Similarly, all the other scholars who developed the myth and ritual hypothesis in its early stages were students of the classics who specialized in Greek religion: Gilbert Murray, A. B. Cook, F. M. Cornford, to name only a few of the most outstanding among them.

However, it did not take long before the myth and ritual approach was applied to other fields as well. The diffusion of the theory proceeded in several directions simultaneously. In one direction, it was applied to many areas of Greek culture itself outside the religious field proper but connected with it in their ultimate origins, such as art, drama, and comedy. In other directions, the theory broke out of its confinement to ancient Greece and struck out boldly, first into European folklore, and then into the vast and insufficiently explored fields of ancient Near Eastern cultures.

In the latter area Professor S. H. Hooke became the foremost spokesman of the myth and ritual theory, which had the support of a number of specialists in Egyptology, Assyriology, Biblical studies, and related fields. The results of some of these inquiries were assembled by Hooke in two successive collections of essays whose impact on the study of ancient Near Eastern religions was as strong as that of Harrison's *Themis* on the study of Greek religion two decades earlier.[37] From the theoretical point of view, however, Hooke's efforts represent no advances from the position reached earlier by Jane Harrison, Gilbert Murray, and the other Greek scholars. In his introductory essay to *Myth and Ritual* Hooke reiterates that the early ritual patterns of the ancient Near East "consisted not only of things done but of things said. The spoken word had the efficacy of an act. . . . In general, the spoken part of a ritual consists of a description

of what is being done, it is the story which the ritual enacts. . . .
The original myth, inseparable in the first instance from its ritual, embodies in more or less symbolic fashion, the original situation which is seasonally re-enacted in the ritual." [38] Or, as
reformulated in Hooke's introduction to *The Labyrinth:* "Together with the ritual and as an essential part of it there was always found, in some form or other, the recitation of the story
whose outlines were enacted in the ritual. This was the myth,
and its repetition had equal potency with the performance of
the ritual. In the beginning the thing said and the thing done
were inseparably united, although in the course of time they
were divorced and gave rise to widely differing literary, artistic
and religious forms." [39] The position of the myth and ritual
school whether of the Greek or of the Ancient Near Eastern
branch, can be restated briefly in the form of three propositions:
(1) myth is the spoken part of ritual; (2) there is no myth
without ritual; and (3) there is no ritual without myth.

In the 1940s and 1950s the tidal wave of "ritualism" advanced, claiming many new conquests in areas as diverse as the
culture of the Stone Age, on the one hand, and the modern thea-
ter, on the other. Although to this day its main domain has
remained the Old World, it made occasional forays across the
Atlantic as well, nibbling even at such uniquely American cultural phenomena as the Negro blues. [40]

8 • Lord Raglan

The most extreme exponent of the myth and ritual theory
among modern anthropologists was undoubtedly Lord Raglan
(1885–1964). In support of his definition, according to which
myth is "simply a narrative associated with a rite," [41] Raglan
quotes a number of anthropologists who have recorded their
views on the nature of myth. Malinowski is quoted by him to
the effect that "Myth fulfills in primitive culture an indispensable function; it expresses, enhances and codifies belief; it safeguards and enforces morality; it vouches for the efficiency of
ritual and contains practical rules for the guidance of man." [42]

Next, Lord Raglan quotes C. von Furer-Haimendorf, who
says of the Gonds, an Indian jungle tribe:

The social norms regulating the tribal life of the
Gonds are firmly rooted in mythology. They derive
their validity from the rulings of culture-heroes and
from the actions of deified ancestors recounted in
epics and countless songs. The myths that tell of the
origin of the Gond race and the establishment of
the four phratries are more than history or folklore;
they are the pragmatic sanction for institutions that
determine the behavior of every Gond towards his
fellow-tribesmen, they are the vital forces inspiring
the performance of the great clan feasts, and they
define and authorise man's relations with the divine
powers on whom his welfare depends. A relationship
of mutual enlivenment links myth and ritual: as the
myths lend power to the ritual acts, so the symbolic
enactment of mythical occurrences during the cardinal
rites of the clan feasts endows the myths with reality.
. . . It is in the sacramental rites based on the clan-
myth that the unity of the clan attains realisation.[43]

Next follows a quotation from W. J. Culshaw, who observed
of the Santals, a tribe of Northeastern India, that

many of the social activities of the Santals are based
on myths, and the strength of their clan organization
is due in no small measure to its foundations in
mythology. . . . When for any reason a piece of ritual
associated with a myth falls into disuse, knowledge of
the myth begins to die out; conversely, when the myth
is looked upon as outmoded, the activity with which
it is linked begins to lose its hold on the people's
imagination. . . . The decay of the ritual is leading
to the disappearance of the ancient myth. It is nevertheless true that these stories do reveal the Santal view
of the world. When they are told they call forth assent,
and frequently in ordinary conversation the myths are
cited in order to point a moral or clinch an argument.[44]

Finally, Raglan quotes M. Fortes, who reports of the Tallensi
of the Gold Coast that "the complementary functions of chief-
ship and tendana-ship are rooted directly in the social structure,
but are also validated by myths of origin and backed by the most

powerful religious sanctions of the ancestor cult and the cult of the earth." [45]

The reports of these four observers, Raglan concludes, "should suffice to show that myth and ritual are as closely linked among modern savages as they were in the ancient civilizations." [46]

However, an unbiased perusal of the four passages in question reveals that, contrary to Raglan's contention, the authorities quoted are unanimous in refraining from stating or even as much as implying that myth is a narrative associated with rite, or that, as Lord Raglan puts it, "it seems legitimate . . . to regard as myths such narratives whether quasi-historical or quasi-fictitious, as suggest a ritual origin. . . ." [47]

In fact, the anthropologists quoted by Raglan attribute to myth a much wider significance, and have much to say about myth that has nothing to do with ritual. Thus Malinowski says that "myth expresses, enhances and codifies belief; it safeguards and enforces morality; . . . it . . . contains practical rules for the guidance of man." Furer-Haimendorf likewise states that "the social norms regulating tribal life . . . are firmly rooted in mythology; . . . they are pragmatic sanctions for institutions. . . ." Culshaw emphasizes that "many of the social activities . . . are based on myths" and that the strength of the clan organization is founded on mythology. And Fortes finds that certain social functions are validated by myths. It thus appears clear that all the four anthropologists quoted by Raglan, who observed the working of myth in the course of their own field work in various cultures, attribute to it a much wider range of functions than does Raglan himself.

9 • Myth Equals Lie

David Bidney, a leading modern anthropological theorist, has put forward an interpretation of myth which hinges on the question of the truth value contained in it. Bidney holds that "myths are, psychologically, charters of belief for those who accept them and live by them. Belief is essential to the acceptance of 'myth' and accounts for its effectiveness in a given cultural context, but the very fact of belief implies that subjectively, that is, for the believer, the object of belief is not mythological." [48] Thus far Bidney accepts the modern anthropological interpretation of myth (exemplified by the four authorities adduced by Raglan), with one difference which is a question of terminology: he maintains that "for the believer" these myths are not really myths but truths. Then he goes on to say that, "Hence, nonbelief in a given narrative, tradition or explanation is essential for its evaluation as myth, just as belief in its truth and validity is essential for its acceptance as an effective element of culture." [49] In other words, for Bidney there is no such thing as myth in itself. According to him, the "narrative, tradition or explanation" believed in by a particular society implies that in fact—that is to say, from the point of view of the user of the term myth—these items of belief are falsehoods.

While, as we shall see in the next section, the use of the term myth in the sense of falsehood is current in journalistic style,[50] the difficulty for a philosophical anthropologist like Bidney in thus equating the meaning of the term "myth" with *false* narrative, tradition, or explanation, becomes evident when he is forced by his own logic to deny the applicability of the term "myth" to the context of Greek culture in which it originally arose. "What we now regard as myths," he says, "were not myths to the Greeks at all, but traditional religious narratives which were accepted literally and formed the validation for their rites and religious institutions." [51]

This argument can be restated as follows: Since myths are stories recognized as untrue, the traditional religious narratives of the ancient Greeks, which they themselves called myths and in whose truth they believed, were not myths at all; hence, the ancient Greeks had no myths.

Bidney not only equates myth with false doctrine, he also regards its modern manifestations as evil. Positing a parallel development between culture and myth in a manner reminiscent of Wundt, he maintains that "in precritical cultures animistic tales of culture heroes and of magic and epic cosmogonic and theogonic myths tend to prevail. In critical, prescientific cultures myths of the miraculous and supernatural gain currency.

In scientific thought there is a tendency to discount narratives of the miraculous and supernatural, but to accept secular myths instead. In our so-called scientific culture we have the secular beliefs of pseudo-science, such as the myth of racial superiority and the stereotypes of racial and national character." [52]

This being the case, Bidney concludes that myth must be combatted: "That is why the struggle of man against myth demands such ceaseless vigilance. . . . Myth is most potent when it is assumed complacently that one is free from it. . . . Normative, critical, and scientific thought provides the only tested, self-correcting means of combatting the growth of myth. . . ." [53]

While we can agree wholeheartedly that it is necessary to combat scientifically unfounded and harmful secular beliefs such as racial and national stereotypes, we must disagree with the narrowing down of the concept myth to such pernicious manifestations of misguided opinion. To say that myth equals falsehood, falsehood is harmful, *ergo* myth must be combatted, disregards the rich storehouses of myths accumulated in many cultures, which, far from containing anything that needs combatting, are the repositories of some of the finest attempts made by peoples throughout history to read a meaning into the problems of the human condition.

10 • *Journalese*

Although a serious scholar like Bidney and the average newspaper reporter approach semantic issues from widely differing premises, it so happens that their views on the meaning of the term "myth" converge and, in fact, coincide. For in journalese, too, "myth" invariably has the meaning of falsehood, mistaken notion, lie, and, in particular, big lie.

Practically every issue of every newspaper contains examples of this use of the term "myth." Take the April 26, 1970, issue of *The New York Times*. On page 1 of the main section, an unsigned news story entitled "Syrian Jets Raid Israeli Positions" contains the following sentence: "For the last two weeks the Syrian press and radio have been conducting a campaign that depicts the Syrian airmen as a *legendary* force and the superiority of the Israeli Air Force as a *myth*" (italics supplied). Here the use of the term "myth" as a false belief is the more interesting since it is contrasted with "legendary" in the sense of "truly so great as to give rise to legends." This reversal of the traditional meanings of the two terms illustrates the extent to which journalese manages to reinterpret language.

On page 20 of the same issue of *The New York Times,* in a news story entitled "U.S.I.A. Issues Conservative Book List," Tad Szulc lists several books appearing on the "blue list" of the U.S. Information Agency together with the agency's comments. One of these reads: " 'Workers Paradise Lost,' by Eugene Lyons: 'The myths of the Communists are contrasted with the record of famine, terror, secret police, concentration camps.' " Here, too, the term "myth" is used in the sense of "big lie" or "mass deception."

"Myth" is used in the sense of "false belief" so frequently that quite likely it is unnecessary to illustrate this usage further. Nevertheless, I cannot resist quoting one example, because it curiously unites the condemnation of myth as false belief with the admission that it nevertheless can and does have a powerful effect on those who believe in it. In writing about the book *Human Sexual Inadequacy* by William Howell Masters and Virginia Johnson, the author of a long article in *Time,* after giving a list of false beliefs about the dangerous effects of masturbation, the size and shape of sex organs, and the like, goes on to say: "In their treatment of sexually *myth-ridden* patients, Masters and Johnson use an eclectic and considerate approach." [54]

Sometimes the same idea is expressed more circumspectly and elaborately. Take this sentence from C. Vann Woodward's review of Howard Zinn's *The Southern Mystique:* "The myth of [the South's] mysterious distinctiveness beyond the reach of reason and impervious to change has been employed as a fog to hide realities, an excuse for inaction, evasion and postponement." [55] Beneath all the verbiage is the equation of myth with purposeful deception.

Serious scholarly authors often fall under the influence of this journalistic use of the term myth, and employ it as a synonym for falsehood, untruth, fakery, and as an antonym of truth, fact, reality. The title of Ernst Cassirer's last book, *The Myth of the State*, can be cited as an example. Another example is a book published in 1970 by the Education Division of the New American Library, and entitled *Technological Man: The Myth and the Reality*. The same antonymy appears in the title of a psychological study: "The Black Family: Myth and Reality," written by Warren TenHouten, and published in the May 1970 issue of *Psychiatry* (Washington, D.C.).

In this connection it is illustrative to consider the frequency with which the designation "The Myth of . . ." appears in book titles in the sense of "false belief." Let me list a very few of them at random: *The Myth of the All-Destructive Fury of the Thirty Years' War*, by Robert R. Ergang (Pocono Pines, Pa: The Craftsmen, 1956); *The Myth of International Security*, by A. V. Levontin (Jerusalem: Magnes Press, 1957); *The Fortress That Never Was: The Myth of Hitler's Bavarian Stronghold*, by Rodney G. Minott (New York: Holt, Rinehart & Winston, 1964); *The Myth of the Machine*, by Lewis Mumford (New York: Harcourt, Brace & Jovanovich, 1970). To the same category belong titles such as *The War Myth*, by Donald A. Wells (New York: Pegasus, 1968). It is clear that if the legitimacy of the meaning of a word were to be ascertained by popular vote, the journalistic usage of "myth" as equaling "false belief" would be approved by a great majority.

11 · Malinowski

Of the anthropologists with extensive field experience, the one who devoted most attention to the theory of myth was Bronislaw Malinowski (1884–1942). Malinowski's thesis on myth, as stated at the very outset of his Frazer Lecture entitled *Myth in Primitive Psychology*,[56] is that "an intimate connection exists between the word, the myths, the sacred tales of a tribe, on the one hand, and their ritual acts, their moral deeds, their social organization, and even their practical activities, on the other." His own studies of "living myths among savages" satisfied Malinowski that myth "is not an idle rhapsody, not an aimless outpouring of vain imaginings, but a hard-working, extremely important cultural force" (p. 97). The most important services performed by myth within the context of a primitive culture "are done in connection with religious ritual, moral influence, and sociological principle" (p. 98).

The reason for myth being such a highly potent cultural force is that "it is not of the nature of fiction, such as we read today in a novel, but it is a living reality, believed to have once happened in primeval times, and continuing ever since to influence the world and human destinies. This myth is to the savage what, to a fully believing Christian, is the Biblical story of Creation, of the Fall, of the Redemption by Christ's Sacrifice on the Cross. As our sacred story lives in our ritual, in our morality, as it governs our faith and controls our conduct, even so does his myth for the savage" (p. 100).

Consequently, Malinowski goes on, myth "is not symbolic, but a direct expression of its subject matter; it is not an explanation in satisfaction of a scientific interest, but a narrative resurrection of a primeval reality, told in satisfaction of deep religious wants, moral cravings, social submissions, assertions, even practical requirements. Myth fulfills in primitive culture an indispensable function: it expresses, enhances, and codifies belief; it safeguards and enforces morality; it vouches for the efficiency of ritual and contains practical rules for the guidance of man. . . . [It is] a pragmatic charter of primitive faith and moral wisdom" (p. 101). It "comes into play when rite, ceremony, or a social or moral rule demands justification, warrant of antiquity, reality, and sanctity" (p. 107). Therefore, Malinowski asserts, every important magical practice, ceremony, or ritual has its associated belief spun out into accounts of concrete precedent which are myths (p. 107).

But, like Wundt, Malinowski does not maintain that every myth is associated with magic, ceremony, or ritual. On the contrary, he assigns myth a much wider, much more variegated role. He stresses and reiterates as "perhaps the most important point" of his thesis on myth that "there exists a special class of stories [namely the myths], regarded as sacred, embodied in ritual, morals, and social organization," and looked upon by the natives as statements "of a primeval, greater, and more relevant reality, by which the present life, fates, and activities of mankind are determined. . . ." (p. 108)

Elsewhere Malinowski formulates the same thought even more explicitly. After discussing the relationship between myth and magic, he states: "Myth, it may be added at once, can attach itself not only to magic but to any form of social power or social claim. It is used always to account for extraordinary privileges or duties, for great social inequalities, for severe burdens of rank, whether this be very high or very low" (p. 84).

When, following his theoretical introduction to myth, Malinowski next proceeds to a more detailed discussion of the myths of the Trobriand Islanders, he treats them under three headings: myths of origin, myths of death and of the recurrent cycle of life, and myths of magic. He does not assert that this threefold division is exhaustive, but it is clear that he found each of the three to be representative of a major type of Trobriand mythology.

The main function of the first type is to supply the traditional precedent and charter in such areas as the totemic clan system, its ranking order, and so on. The second type fulfills the same function with reference to aging, epidemics, death, the underworld, and so forth. These two types of myths, therefore, are not narratives associated with rites, for their function is to express, enhance, and codify belief, or to safeguard and enforce morality, or, again, to serve as guideposts in communal and individual life. Only in the third type, the myths of magic, do myths function as narratives associated with rites.

12 · Neo-Romanticism

A position on myth similar to that reached by Malinowski from an anthropological point of view was taken by the German religious philosopher Walter F. Otto (1874–1958) in his book *Die Gestalt und das Sein: Gesammelte Abhandlungen über den Mythos und seine Bedeutung für die Menschheit (Image and Existence: Collected Essays on Myth and Its Meaning for Mankind).*[57] In fact, in his emphasis on the importance of myth for mankind as a whole Otto carries the argument considerably farther than Malinowski. His prefatory remark sets the tone for his inquiry and stakes out its limits: "The existence *(Sein)* of the things themselves reveals itself to man in the primeval phenomena of Image *(Gestalt)* and Myth, in contrast to thought processes and moods of feeling; to wit, it reveals itself, as expressed by the myth, as something divine." [58] This is perhaps the most emphatic formulation of the view of myth held by many modern students of religion, whose consensus has been aptly summed up by Altizer: "Myth—the language of the religious symbol—is now seen to be the deepest and most authentic means for the expression of religious understanding and belief." [59]

Otto himself begins his examination by stating that "myth is understood in general as a story about fabulous things which may contain a deeper meaning but which is not essentially true" (p. 66). The Greek word *mythos,* he says, assumed this meaning relatively early, as soon as the Greeks began to subject the transmitted stories about the gods and the primeval world to intellectual criticism (pp. 66–67). But the original meaning of the word *mythos,* as used by Homer and other ancient Greek authors, was "word," "thing," "matter," "fact," "story," and primarily an "account" of what actually happened in the past. The older and the more venerable the "story" contained in the *mythos,* the smaller the possibility of a mistake or purposeful falsification, and, therefore, the greater its truth value (pp. 66–71).

Similarly, Otto goes on, "the primitive peoples, too, distinguish explicitly between the old and sacred stories regarded as 'true,' and the newer ones, full of imagination, regarded as 'false.' The sacred seriousness with which the true myths are received manifests itself, among other things, in that they must not be recited at will and to any audience, but often only to a very few, with the exclusion of women, and only at certain times of the day and the year. Only these old stories, regarded as sacred, about the origins, the primordial days, and the gods, are therefore myths in the proper sense . . ." (p. 72). They are claimed to be true—in fact, to represent the ultimate and most sacred truth—and are regarded as the most precious property.

Next, Otto turns to the problem of the evaluation of myth by outsiders, and especially by students of mythology. Many of the

latter simply deny the claim to truth which the myth so de-
cisively makes. They do this because they naively assume that
our own world-view is the only true one and must constitute the
yardstick for the evaluation of all others. Then, trying to explain
how the age of myth could reach its own peculiar views as to
what was true, they postulate a mode of thought which deviates
from the normal. Since this "mythical" way of thinking does
not conform to our logic, they call it "pre-logical." And all this
is done, says Otto, without as much as first seriously asking
whether myths could possibly be based upon true experience
(p. 73). Questioning the justification of such an approach, Otto
asks:

> Are we, in fact, so fashioned that we can allow our-
> selves unquestioningly to pass judgment on the idea
> world of early man? While we attribute to him a mode
> of thinking which is foreign to reality—that is to say,
> artificial—it never occurs to us that we ourselves live
> and gather our experiences in a thoroughly artificial
> world. We have long ago banished primeval nature
> from our circle of vision. Those few who have not
> only passed fleetingly through one of the wildernesses
> so far removed from us, but have actually experienced
> it, can still tell of the shudder of the awesome in whose
> face the oldest myths suddenly appear true. . . .
>   And it is not only we, the men of the technical age,
> who live in an environment which lacks the prerequi-
> sites for an understanding of myth. Already the cultures
> of antiquity became more and more removed from the
> form of existence of the generations for whom myth
> meant truth. This, and not merely the awakening of
> independent thinking, is the reason why already in
> the sixth century B.C. Theagenes of Rhegion felt that
> he had to justify the Homeric myths by declaring the
> names of the gods to be poetic designations for the
> elements, and that Xenophanes could so fiercely
> ridicule Homer and Hesiod for the humanlikeness of
> their gods. He who wants to attempt an immediate
> understanding of the ancient myths must be able to
> transport himself into the environment in which pre-

historic man lived and thought. Researchers, of course, feel that they can do this by collecting and interpreting as many survivals of the oldest cultures as possible, and by trying to disregard everything that man has experienced and learned in the course of centuries. That this is impossible is apparent. Thus we must give up any attempt at a direct understanding of the myths, and this is, in fact, the opinion of all those who know what true belief is. . . .

Since the direct road is closed to us, we must proceed indirectly; instead of asking about the meaning of the myths, let us inquire into the effect emanating from them. . . . I do not mean primarily the effect of the myth upon later generations throughout many centuries. That effect is immeasurable: without it . . . no Homer, no Pindar would have sung, no tragedy would have been written, no statues carved, no temples built.

. . . Even as late as the modern times, myth has stimulated man's spirit to always new efforts. One must therefore say: myth, whatever its origin and content, is the creative force, the arouser to creative activity! . . .

But let us speak of a much more immediate effect of myth, the one exerted by it on the posture of man himself, as long as it was held true and sacred. . . .

There was a time when it seemed self-evident that myth gave the acts of ritual their meaning and form, and that therefore it was older, more original, than ritual. However, once it has become clear how unthinkably old most ritual acts were, it seemed proper to reverse the relationship, especially since the ritual acts appeared to be so-called magical purposive acts which needed no such interpretations as those given by the myth, and, in fact, excluded them. This view has many adherents to this day.

But more thorough studies among precisely those peoples who were regarded as the chief witnesses for the magic origin of ritual acts made it evident that there was no ritual without myth, and never had been. . . .

To this was added recently the important finding

that the whole existence of primitive tribes was dominated by a single great myth of primeval events, and
that the entire ritual was carried out with conscious
reference to this myth. . . .

Thus myth and ritual cannot be separated. But the
statement that the ritual demands the myth is not
sufficient. Of greater importance is the other: that the
myth demands the ritual.

That the true myth is not without its ritual is
shown in that it in itself is a recital, a kind of ritual
act. The myth is, as the Greeks designated it, the
"word"—that is to say, it is what it is only in a spoken
form. Its recital constitutes a special act amidst the
observances of the ritual feast: it takes place in the
intermissions between individual rites. It is expected
that the ritual acts will result in beneficial effects, and
the same is expected of the recital of the myth. . . .

If, as in the ritual recital of the myth, a word must
have the power to perform miracles, it must be a word
of a special kind, a word which is more than the words
spoken every day or by which one expresses something
witty or delightful. Such a word must have the power
to have an effect in the realm of things, derived from
the circumstances that it has an essentially different
relationship to things from that which, according to
our concepts, a word has. It must be the kind of
word which not merely designates the thing, but *is*
the thing itself. This, as we have seen, is the word
originally understood by the Greek *mythos*. . . . If
the word *is* the thing itself, in a manner which, of
course, simply remains incomprehensible to the rational,
scholarly way of thinking, then it cannot be but
that it is effective in the realm of things. And of
this kind is the word of the myth which the ancient
peoples designated as the true one.

It is the word as living image (*Gestalt*) which has
this significant quality. Wherever creative things happen, the image (*Gestalt*) comes as a miracle to him
who creates so that he believes in revelation and no
longer distinguishes between thinking and being. In

the same manner did the word of the myth come to
early man; it had to be true and powerful, because it
was not a thought-out word but an experienced one:
the being (*Sein*) of the things themselves [pp. 73–78].

With reference to the interrelationship between myth and
ritual, Otto emphasizes that primitive peoples declare that they
celebrate their rituals in a manner which corresponds to the prehistoric event described in the myth, and that the same holds
true for old rituals in general. That is, the ritual act is assumed
to be a repetition of a divine primeval happening—a special kind
of repetition in which "the meaningful event of early days is
supposed to *happen* anew" (pp. 79–80).

This is precisely what is supposed to take place at the performance of the Passion Play and the ritual of the wine and the
host, which are to be seen as highly meaningful repetitions of
the event of the Redemption. More than that: in an essential
sense, they *are* that event itself. They are always performed at
the very moment when the Divine, with its truth, is immediately
present, so that through them the redemptive divine happening
takes place anew. The ritual act is nothing less than the revelation of the divine and its presence itself. In the same way, the
rituals of the ancient peoples represent sacred happenings of
early days and they recite the mythical word about it, not in
order to make this happening take place again through the force
of magic, but because the divine of the sacred happening *requires*
a manifestation in which it can be present itself (p. 80).

In this sense, the ritual act is the inevitable response of man
to the presence of the divine. It is in this response that the divine
presence expresses itself, creates itself witness, incarnates itself.
This, to Otto, means that the ritual act itself is the revelation of
divine truth. The divine, when it is truly near, wants to encounter itself in this human formulation (*Gestaltung*).

Ritual, therefore, is not only inseparably connected with
myth, but is essentially identical with it. The two are one in that
in both the divine proximity reveals itself: in the ritual as posture and act, in the myth as the true word. However, there is a

difference between the two in that in the ritual man is lifted up to the divine, and, in a way, acts together with it, whereas in the myth the divine descends, incorporates itself as word in a human or quasi-human form, and acts in a human fashion.

Thus Otto reaches the conclusion that the most original and genuine myth, wherever and however it appears, is *true*. Moreover, it is not merely one of several truths, but is *the* truth because it brings to light not only that which is temporarily right, or for the time being just and proper, but the very being (*"Sein"*) of the things, to wit, as the form of all forms, the Divine.

If this be so, Otto argues, we must approach with respect also the actual contents of the myths, which tell us of divine or godlike beings and of acts performed by them. This is especially so, inasmuch as the locale of the events attested to by the myth is not a mysteriously distant place, but is the very nature and world in which we live (pp. 86–87).

Thus Otto considers myth a general culture-producing agent:

> Although myth shows its most immediate and powerful effect in the transformation of man into the image of him who behaves and acts ritually, it remains creative in other realms as well. For under its aegis stand not only all works of art, but also the arrangements of communal life, the forms of spiritual and practical activity, the fashioning of character. However far consciousness has removed itself from the Divine, it still remains a spiritual breath of the myth, which itself once was born out of the divine presence.
>
> And thus we call the myth the true prototype of which all the others are merely shadowy reflections, but which nevertheless is present in them as well with its miraculous power.
>
> The laws which determine action are but manifestations of the prototype in a form corresponding to intellectual experience and the thinking habit. Just as the practicing artist has only to look at the perfect and his organs will produce what he has seen, by themselves, according to their particular laws, so the

moral man acts, in view of the prototype, effortlessly
and without awareness of how and why; and only
the observing intellect recognizes the laws which are
regarded commonly as the fundaments of morality
[pp. 89–90].

While Otto thus recognizes myth as the mainspring of all
human cultural achievement, it is in the spiritual realm that
he considers myth—together with ritual—as having its most fundamental role. Myth and ritual, he reiterates, constitute a dual
bridge between man and God. Both myth and ritual are, "each
in its manner, manifestations of one and the same process, which
takes place between the finite and the infinite, between man
and God. . . . The myth brings the infinite nearer to man. The
infinite does not thereby lose its awe-inspiring magnitude, but it
transforms itself and shows to man a human face, talks to him in
a human tongue. How this became possible, we do not learn
from the myth itself. . . . But the ritual, connected and related
to the myth, allows us to obtain some notion of it. The ritual, like
the myth, does not completely eliminate the distance between
the eternal and man. The eternal remains in its magnitude, but
man is transformed; the ritual presents to man a godlike face
and speaks to him in the tongue of the gods. The humanization
of the Divine in the myth and the divinization of man in the
ritual meet together in one single act . . ." (p. 254).

As far as I know, no other myth interpreter, either before or
after Otto, has ever assigned myth such a central place in theology and in all aspects of cultural achievement. It certainly is a
remarkable coincidence that both this view and that of Rudolf
Bultmann, which represents a diametrically opposite position,
should have originated in the minds of two contemporary thinkers, both of whom lived through the Nazi period in Germany.

13 • *Myth Criticism*

Recent decades have seen the emergence of a school of literary
study which is usually referred to as "myth criticism." This study
grew out of the increasing awareness of the distinct and unmis-

takable presence of myths, mythical motifs, and mythical elements (or mythologems) in a great many literary works produced throughout the ages, down to and including the present
times. While myth criticism has many variants and trends, there
are clearly discernible common principles to which all myth
critics seem to subscribe.

These general principles can be summed up, following John
B. Vickery, as follows:

> (1) The mythopoeic—i.e., myth-making—faculty is inher-
> ent in the thinking process, and its products satisfy a basic
> human need. (2) Myth is the matrix out of which literature
> emerges, both historically and psychologically. As a result,
> literary plots, characters, themes, and images are basically
> elaborations and replacements of similar elements in myth and
> folk tales. Theories of Jungian racial memory, historical dif-
> fusion, and the essential similarity of the human mind every-
> where are among those resorted to in order to explain how
> myths reemerge in literature. (3) Myth can provide not only
> stimulation for novelists, storytellers, dramatists, and so on, but
> also concepts and patterns which the critic can use in inter-
> preting literary works. A familiarity with the "grammar of
> myth" endows the critics' reading of the language of literature
> with greater precision. Myth criticism recognizes that mythical
> features reside beneath, as well as on the surface of, a literary
> work, and thereby differs substantially from earlier treatments
> of the mythological in literature. (4) Literature has the power
> to move us profoundly precisely because of its mythical quality,
> its possession of *mana*, of the *numinous*, or because of the
> mystery in the face of which we feel an awed delight or terror
> at the world of man. To continue myth's ancient and basic
> endeavor to create a meaningful place for man in a world ob-
> livious of his presence—this is the real function of literature
> in human affairs.

To these four points Vickery adds that "a concern for the
emotional patterning resident in myth is peculiarly appropriate
to the twentieth century and its struggle to achieve a viable mode
of psychic order." [60]

Vickery's introductory generalizations are borne out by the
thirty-four essays contained in the body of the volume edited by

him, which are devoted mainly to the general theme of the role
of myth and mythmaking in literature. These essays contain
analyses of the mythical in the works of authors as varied from
every critical point of view as Shakespeare, Milton, Tennyson,
Keats, Dickens, Mark Twain, Émile Zola, Melville, James Joyce,
Nathaniel Hawthorne, Stephen Crane, Virginia Woolf, William Faulkner, Thomas Hardy, D. H. Lawrence, Joseph Conrad,
Henry David Thoreau, Franz Kafka, Thomas Mann, and others.
Reading these essays one gets the distinct impression that mythmaking and myth-utilization are as much part of the literary
process in our day as they were when the unknown Babylonian
author wrote the Epic of Gilgamesh or Homer his *Iliad* and
Odyssey.

For some reason, Vickery's weighty volume contains no contribution by William York Tindall, one of the foremost literary critics of our times, who has devoted an entire book to precisely the same subject. Tindall's *The Literary Symbol*[61] is a
fine account of how several major literary figures handled ancient
mythical themes. He shows how André Gide used the Theseus
myth, D. H. Lawrence the Jesus and the Quetzalcoatl myths, Yeats
the Cuchulain myth, Dylan Thomas images from Genesis and
the Gospels, James Joyce the Moses, Odysseus, Christ, and Hamlet myths, the early Thomas Mann the Wagnerian recastings of
the old German myths, T. S. Eliot and Virginia Woolf the
Parsifal myth, and Faulkner the Narcissus myth.

However, even more relevant for our present investigation is
Tindall's own understanding of myth, which he presents after
a brief *resumé* of the views of Freud, Malinowski, Ernst Cassirer,
and Erich Fromm on myth. Tindall accepts myth in the Western
literary world "as symbolic narrative," finds that "myths involve
religion and society," and states that "myth and dream present
man's central problems." Tindall's own concern, he says, "is with
myth in recent times. With ritual it may serve to support belief,
but even for those without it, myth retains something of its old
potency. Serving the individual as it once served the group,
myth may unite him with tradition or society, and, in literature,
while uniting the conscious mind with the primitive or the unconscious, myth may express the inner by the outer, the present

by the past." [62] As we can see, while poets, dramatists, and novelists read myths and are influenced by them, a literary critic like Tindall reads also the evaluations of myth made by psychologists, philosophers, and anthropologists, and uses their insights in interpreting the mythical element in literary works.

The rich outcropping of studies dealing with myth in literature is in itself an indication of the increasing interest in myth that, almost paradoxically, characterizes our electronic age. The University of Nebraska Press alone has published in the last few years some ten volumes on myth criticism and related subjects, among them a collection of essays by Northrop Frye, L. C. Knights, and others, entitled *Myth and Symbol: Critical Approaches and Applications;* and another, entitled *Myth and Method: Modern Theories of Fiction,* edited by James E. Miller, Jr. In 1969 the University of Wisconsin published a book by F. R. Kramer entitled *Voices in the Valley: Mythmaking and Folk Belief in the Shaping of the Middle West.* In 1970 Wayne State University Press published a weighty tome by Harry Slochower, on *Mythopoesis: Mythic Patterns in Literary Classics,* in which author examines such masterpieces as works of Sophocles, Aeschylus, *The Divine Comedy, Don Quixote, Hamlet, Faust, The Brothers Karamazov, Moby Dick,* Gide's *Theseus,* Mann's *Magic Mountain,* Kafka's novels and stories, the writings of various existentialists and others.

It seems to me that perhaps the most important single general conclusion one can draw from this profusion of studies in the field of myth criticism is that our present time is as much a mythopoeic age as was the period of Homer and Hesiod in ancient Greece nearly three thousand years ago, or the period of the unknown genuises who developed the Isis and Osiris myth in Egypt another two millennia earlier. After these studies it is no longer possible to doubt that the mythmaking process is still in full swing, at least as far as our *literati* are concerned. The next question, then, is to what extent are myth, mythology, and mythical thinking a part of the lives of the large majority of our contemporary society in whose awareness literature plays, at the utmost, a rather unimportant and negligible role. It is to this question that we shall address ourselves in the subsequent chapters.

14 • *The Frills of Myth*

Before embarking on our voyage of discovery in the unchartered archipelago of myth in the modern world, a brief note is in order on one particular aspect of myth that has been neglected by the myth interpreters discussed above—an aspect that has a direct bearing on the power of myth to attract, fascinate, and influence. This is the widespread tendency of myth to become increasingly intricate, to elaborate its narrative, and to acquire many little details in its main story line over the course of time. This growth phenomenon has its close parallel in the world of nature, in particular in the development of flowers. Functionally, the flower is that part of the plant which contains, or consists of, the reproductive organs. The basic structures necessary for the production of seed are, of course, always there. But in the typical flowers as we know and love them, in the rose, the lily, the pansy, the cherry blossom, and many others, these basic structures are elaborated far beyond anything that is apparently required for the fulfillment of their biological purpose. Botanists agree that the intricate structure of these flowers, their delicately shaped petals in fanciful arrangements, and all the other elaborations and details that often assume fantastic shapes and colors, have the general overall function of attracting insects which are required for fertilization; but this general purpose fails to explain the *specific* significance of the particular form the reproductive organs take in the various species and strains of flowers, or why the same basic function is served by such an infinite variety of forms. That they become for us a source of exquisite pleasure is purely coincidental.

Quite a similar development can be observed in myths. The overall story line can usually be understood as relating to a feature in the natural or social environment or to the rituals performed in connection with the myth. It is this aspect of the myth that we refer to when we say that the myth is a traditional charter that has such and such a function. Over and beyond the general outline, however, myths exhibit a great elaboration of detail, contain many little intricacies, are characterized by a delicate patterning, and contain many other minute features for which no functional explanation can be found. These features, it seems, are developed by myths in order to arouse and hold the attention of the listeners and thereby increase their likelihood of survival. There seems to be a process of natural selection at work here, which means that those myths are more likely to endure which can better attract their audiences, just as those flowers are more likely to survive which are more successful in attracting insects. Without the elaborate and fantastic details contained in the myth it might be forgotten, for people would be interested neither in telling it nor in hearing it. However, again as in the case of the flower, mythologists are as a rule unable to find the precise meaning or purpose of what could be called the frills of myths. Perhaps myth shares with decorative patterns, with style, and certain other features of culture an intrinsic tendency to elaboration, a drive to follow a trend to its utter limits; if so, it would be futile altogether to engage in a search for the meaning of all its details. In any case, one thing is certain: like the beauty of a flower, the frills of the myth afford pleasure and esthetic satisfaction, the bestowal of which can be regarded as a precious, albeit secondary, function of myth, transcending or supplementing the purely utilitarian one.

students of man
into mythopoets

One of the most fascinating manifestations of the power myth still wields over us is its ability to transform students of society, culture, religion, and psychology—including, of course, mythologists—into mythopoets. Whatever the specialization of these students of man, it is precisely among the best of them, those endowed with the deepest insight into and the greatest understanding for the working of the human mind, that this transformation can be observed. The ordinary student of mythology, for instance, is satisfied with such tasks as recording hitherto unknown myths or new versions of known ones, comparing two or more myths found at greater or smaller spatial or temporal distances, tracking down the time and place of the origin of a myth, following its wanderings from one locality to another, and inquiring into the meaning and function of the myth in the society in which it lives. Ultimately he may even essay an interpretation of his own, which he then will hold up as the true meaning of the myth in question. It is at this point that a few mythologists cross over into the realm of mythmaking, and, without being aware of it, cease being mythologists, recorders, and students of existing myths, and become mythopoets, makers of new myths.

1 • Students and Doers

In some fields of human endeavor the dividing line is sharply drawn between those who study what others have done and those who actively participate in the doing. In the field of fine arts, for instance, very rare indeed is the art historian or critic who ever holds brush or chisel in his hand. In music, only rarely does a musicologist or music historian engage in composing. Rare too is the literary critic, engaged in reviewing and evaluating novelists or poets, who finds himself embarked inadvertently on writing novels or poems. The historian writes, but does not make, history, although makers of history occasionally do engage in historiography. The student of religion can devote a lifetime to finding out more and more about the religions of man without ever being tempted to found a new religion or even to introduce the slightest innovation into an existing one.

In the sciences the opposite tendency prevails. The basic purpose of the scientist is to engage actively in the cultivation of his chosen field by making new discoveries or reaching new understandings. If the scientist nevertheless studies the work of his predecessors, he does so primarily or solely for the purpose of critically examining it in order to find a point of departure from which he can strike out for new *terrae incognitae* or into which he can introduce a refinement, modification, clarification, or improvement. A scientist whose interest is confined to studying what other scientists before him have done is not a scientist at all but a historian of science, as, for instance, the great George Sarton was. For the modern physicist, chemist, biologist, and other scientist the history of his science is irrelevant and immaterial; the centuries-old, often millennial, quest that led to the present state of knowledge with which he starts out is of as little concern for him as the origin of the wheel is for a Detroit automobile engineer.

There is a third realm of disciplines which occupies an intermediary position between those of the arts, history, and theology on the one hand, and the sciences on the other. Those engaging in this third group of disciplines cannot do without thoroughly familiarizing themselves with the work, theories, approaches, and results of those who preceded them, but in doing so their ultimate purpose is to acquire the skills and tools available in their field in order to use them for the attainment of new results, new knowledge, new insights. Philosophy, anthropology, sociology, and psychology are the major disciplines belonging to this category. In none of these is it possible meaningfully to innovate without a mastery of, and reference to, previous schools of thought. The philosopher, anthropologist, sociologist, and psychologist, in order to fully deserve this designation, must be both a student of what others have done and himself a doer in his chosen field. The transition from the first to the second stage is not an inadvertent one. While the ultimate aim of the specialist in any of these fields is to proceed to the second stage (if not, he is merely a historian of his chosen discipline), he can do so only after having devoted sufficient attention to the first, just as a builder cannot put up a house without first preparing the foundations. And it is precisely when making the transition from studying to doing, from observation and exegesis to creative interpretation, which always involves the erection of a new superstructure, that some of the finest and most original practitioners of these disciplines are irresistibly drawn into the gravitational field of mythopoesis. It is at this point that they become mythmakers, the creators of new and often exceedingly potent myths.

Mythology itself, strangely enough, does not fit into any of the three aforementioned categories of disciplines. It clearly does not belong to the first one, because there is, as we shall show in some detail, no hard and fast dividing line between students of myth and makers of myth, between mythologists and mythopoets. It certainly does not belong to the second category, that of the sciences, because, in contrast to the scientists, those interested in myth are intent primarily on finding out what myth means, and not on creating new myths. And it cannot be lumped with the third category, because students of myth never set out purposely to erect a new structure on the old foundations, but endeavor only to understand and know as much as possible about the foundations themselves. That some of them nevertheless erect new myth structures, inadvertently and in most cases without being at all aware of it, is precisely the remarkable specificity of myth, or, one may venture to say, the manifestation of mythopoetic forces still active in our midst. One can be a lifelong student of myth and, as such, thoroughly familiar with the working of mythical forces; one may be determined to confine one's work to mythological analysis and the interpretation of myths against their historical and psychological backgrounds; one may even devote all one's brain power to an "unmasking" of myth, in the sense of penetrating into it and down to its "real" meaning; and yet one runs the risk of crossing the boundary and becoming, instead of a mythologist, a mythopoet.

2 • The Structural Myth

I said above that those of the outstanding students of myth who become mythopoets do so, in most cases, unawares. The reason that I inserted the qualifying phrase "in most cases" is that at least one mythologist was aware that he had crossed the borderline between studying myth and making myths, and explicitly stated that he did so. This man is Claude Lévi-Strauss, originator of the well known and controversial school of "structural" anthropology whose favorite field for applying his structural method is that of mythology. The key sentence for understanding Lévi-Strauss' approach is contained in the "Overture" to his book The Raw and the Cooked, in which he summarizes what it was he set out to accomplish: to wit, to provide a "code which is intended to ensure the reciprocal translatability of several myths." [1] In other words, Lévi-Strauss' intention is to show that in each of those several myths one can discern a number of structural elements that can be reduced to a common denominator and that display identical interrelationships. Then he directly continues: "This is why it would not be wrong to consider this book itself as a myth: it is, as it were, the myth of mythology."

It is not completely clear what Lévi-Strauss means by this statement, but if I understand him correctly, he recognizes here that the entire thought-construct he erected in order to show the existence of a basic structural pattern in all myth is itself a myth. The similarity between Lévi-Strauss' structural myth and the myths of the classical world can be indicated by a simple example, not taken, incidentally, from Lévi-Strauss. The myth of Adonis said something like this to the ancient Syrians: every year thousands of different plants whither away in the heat of the late spring, and then sprout out again after the fall rains. However, beneath this manifold variety of disparate phenomena there is one single common factor: all this happens because Adonis is killed and then comes to life again. The myth thus reduces the many into one, the disorder into order, the meaninglessness into meaningfulness. It establishes a code. Now precisely the same effect is achieved by Lévi-Strauss' structural myth: it reduces the many different myths, that apparently talk about many different things, into one; it points out that all of them are structured along the same principles, follow the same code. Their meaninglessness and even their contradictions are thus transformed and resolved into a meaningful order.

This meaningful order is seen by Lévi-Strauss as having its closest analogue in music. In fact, he treats myth as if it were symphonic music. In his *The Raw and the Cooked* he devotes a considerable part of the first chapter (which he calls "Overture") to an elaboration of this theme, and the structure of the book, as indicated by all the chapter headings, is based on an analogy to a series of musical works: Theme and Variations, The "Good Manners" Sonata, A Short Symphony (with First, Second, and Third Movements), Fugue, Cantata, Solo, Rondo, Concluding Aria, Well-Tempered Astronomy, Double Inverted Canon, Toccata and Fugue, Chromatic Piece, etc.

Of course, as is the case with all myths, the Lévi-Strauss musical-structural myth, too, has meaning and validity only for those who believe in it. If one believes—which in this case means if one accepts certain premises—then the structural myth springs into life, functions, resolves, satisfies. Turning to an earlier work by Lévi-Strauss, we learn that one of these premises

—that is, one of the parts of the system of mythical axioms—is: "Mythical thought always works from the awareness of opposition toward their progressive mediation." [2] Another states that there is such a thing as a "structural law of the myth." [3] A third asserts that the myth consists of all its versions. [4]

When we maintain that these axiomatic statements, and several others found in Lévi-Strauss' writings on myth, when taken together actually represent a mythopoeic achievement, we do not mean this in any critical sense. On the contrary, we assent, and find herein an analogy to the often heard view that the finest writings of the greatest art critics are themselves works of art (with which we go along without fear of contradiction between it and what we said earlier about the difference between critic and creative artist). In a similar manner, the finest studies of mythology are themselves mythopoeic works.

3 • The Oedipus Myth

In his essay on "The Structural Study of Myth," which was quoted above, Lévi-Strauss says that, since a myth consists of all its versions, "therefore, not only Sophocles, but Freud himself, should be included among the recorded versions of the Oedipus myth on a par with earlier or seemingly more 'authentic' versions," [5] and that the "Freudian comments on the Oedipus complex are a part of the Oedipus myth." [6] It is to this Freudian mythopoesis that we now address ourselves.

The major effort of Freud at mythmaking is contained in his early book *Totem and Taboo,* which was written in 1912 and 1913. In this book Freud took the information available at the time on the totemic feasts, customs, practices, and myths of certain primitive tribes, and the exogamous rules—i.e., the incest taboos—observed by the same tribes, and distilled from this ethnographic material a new myth of his own, that of the parricidal primal horde. Additional material for this myth structure was supplied by clinical observations Freud made in his own psychoanalytic practice; hence the subtitle of his book, "Some Points of Agreement Between the Mental Life of Savages and Neurotics."

Taking the Darwinian "primal horde" as his point of departure, Freud described the tragic event that "one day" transpired:
the primal horde had been dominated by a "brutal, jealous father who kept for himself all the females and drove away his
adolescent sons. . . ." [7] Then

> One day, the expelled brothers banded together, slew
> and devoured the father, and thus put an end to the
> paternal horde. United they dared and accomplished
> what would have remained impossible for a single
> individual. (Perhaps a cultural advance, the use of
> a new weapon, gave them the feeling of superiority.)
> That they also devoured the father after they killed
> him is natural for cannibalistic savages. The brutal
> primal father had undoubtedly been the envied and
> feared model for each member of the fraternal group.
> Now, in the act of ingestion, they carried out the
> identification with him, with each acquiring a piece of
> his power. The totemic meal, perhaps the first feast
> of mankind, thus could be the reenactment and
> memorial rite of this notable criminal act which
> marked the beginning of so many things—social
> organizations, moral restrictions, and religion. . . .
> [The brothers] hated the father who so forcefully
> stood in the way of their drive for power and their
> sexual demands. But at the same time they loved
> and admired him. After they had eliminated him,
> satisfied their hatred, and carried out their desire for
> identification with him, the tender sentiments that
> were suppressed in the process had to reemerge and
> assert themselves. This took place in the form of
> repentance, a sense of guilt developed which actually
> coincided with the remorse they all felt. The dead
> father thus became stronger than the living one had
> been. . . . What he had prevented earlier by the fact
> of his existence, now the sons forbade themselves in
> the psychic situation of "deferred obedience" so well
> known to us from psychoanalyses. They annulled their
> deed by declaring the killing of the father-substitute,
> the totem animal, forbidden, and renounced its fruits
> by denying themselves the women who had become

free. Thus, out of their sense of guilt the sons created
the two fundamental taboos of totemism [the killing
of the totem, and incest, that is in-group sex], which
for this very reason had to correspond to the
two repressed wishes of the Oedipus complex. Whoever
disobeyed them made himself guilty of the only two
crimes which concerned primitive society.[8]

Corresponding to the original ambivalence of the sons, totemic
religion has preserved "not only the manifestations of remorse
and the attempts at atonement, but also the memory of the triumph over the father. The satisfaction over the latter gives rise
to the memorial rite which is the totemic feast, at which all
prohibitions of the deferred obedience are lifted, and it becomes
a duty to repeat again and again the crime of parricide by sacrificing the totem animal. . . ."[9]

Except for the periodic ritual reenactment of the mythical
parricide in the totem ritual, the killing of the totem remains
forbidden, and to this religiously motivated prohibition "the so-
cially motivated prohibition of fratricide is added. A long time
was to pass before the commandment would shed its restriction
to fellow tribesmen and assume the simple wording: Thou
shalt not murder. To begin with, the paternal horde was replaced by the fraternal clan, which secured itself through the
blood bond. Society now is based upon complicity in the jointly
committed crime, religion on the sense of guilt and remorse,
morality partly on the exigencies of this society and partly on
the penances demanded by the sense of guilt."[10]

Then Freud sums up: "In the Oedipus complex there meet together the beginnings of religion, morality, society, and art.
. . ." He admits that this insight came to him as "a great surprise."[11]

Paul Roazen, in discussing Freud's theory of the origin of social
restrictions, remarks that it "is very much like the old rationalistic social contract theory of the origins of society."[12] He is
right, but only up to a point. In fact, Freud himself says that
"the totemistic system was something like a contract with the
father in which the latter supplied everything the infantile fantasy
could expect of the father: protection, care, and forbearance,

in return for which one undertook to honor his life—that is, not to repeat on him the deed through which the real father perished."[13] Subsequently he again refers to "the contract with the totem."[14] However, what Freud presents in his recounting of that awesome primal scene and its consequences is not merely a reconstruction of a social process, the operation of social forces, which resulted in a "social contract," but an actual, concrete, archetypally ritual scene, comparable in its sinister coloration to the tearing into pieces of the child Dionysus or the killing of Adonis—mythologically highly significant events whose direct effect remains with man as long as he does not begin to doubt their veracity. The protagonists in these primal mythical events act out their roles not because they have made a conscious decision to do so, but because the inner mythical (or, if you wish, psychic) forces drive them inexorably to taking upon themselves the role which is their destiny. This, precisely, is the feature that endows the Freudian primal scene with its mythical, and at the same time highly charged, character. The sons are driven to their horrible deed against their own will, by demonic forces that inform them and that prove stronger than their filial love for the father. They kill the father and devour him in a paroxysm of frenzy; they commit the deed whose very performance carries in itself the fatal inevitability of its constant repetition either in actuality, or in wishful thinking, or else by substituting the totemic animal father for the human one in a periodic reenactment of the scene as ritual. They do it, despite the foreknowledge that by committing and repeating the primal crime they will gain nothing, at least not the desired end. Looked at from this angle we recognize that Freud, without having been familiar with the myth-and-ritual theory, actually supplied the myth for the generalized totemic ritual which he synthesized and abstracted from the writings of contemporary anthropologists, and whose echoes he discerned in accounts of his neurotic patients.

Although Freud utilized the standard studies of his day (he quotes or refers to Durkheim, Frazer, Westermarck, and many others), the man whose work he found most congenial and upon whose conclusions he built much of his own superstructure was the British Arabist, William Robertson Smith, whose book, *The*

Religion of the Semites, Freud terms "excellent," and who
is the only one of the entire galaxy of ranking scholars whom
Freud introduces with words of high praise: "a man as many-
sided as he was gifted with insight and unfettered of mind." [15]
Freud was especially impressed by Robertson Smith's account
and reconstruction of the totemic meal among the ancient Semites, and after giving a detailed, ten-page resumé of his argument, returns later to Robertson Smith to quote him to the effect
that "the ceremonies of those feasts with which the ancient Semites celebrated the death of a deity were interpreted as the
'commemoration of a mythical tragedy.'" [16]

The "mythical tragedy" which Robertson Smith had in mind
was the death of the ancient Semitic vegetation god, known by
various names such as Baal, Onqōd, Adonis, Tammuz, as he
goes on to explain in some detail.[17] But Freud, not satisfied with
such concrete, localized backgrounds, supplied the *"ur-*myth,"
the primordial, all-human "mythical tragedy" which validates
not only the ancient Semitic totemic (or quasi-totemic) feasts,
but also the periodic killing of the beloved and venerated ancestral totem wherever and whenever it occurs. There can be no
doubt, of course, that Freud was fully convinced that his account
of the primal parricide was, while generalized, abstracted, and
schematized, nevertheless essentially true: it was the best reconstruction possible on the basis of the historical and clinical evidence available to him. But there can be equally little doubt that
what Freud actually did was to construct an ingenious new myth.
Intrigued by the numerous accounts of totemic rituals and neurotic parricidal desires, his analytic mind was led into a specu-
lative venture to reach beyond the dying gods, whom he
considered secondary formations, to the original, primordial father and his horde of unruly, cultureless sons. The result he
came up with was sheer mythopoesis. The account of the primal
group-crime of parricide is of the same timber as the account of
the origin of fire (the Prometheus myth), or the creation of the
first human couple, or the fall: in each of these great myths,
processes which in reality were exceedingly lengthy, diffuse, and
indeterminate, and in which the protagonists were thousands
upon thousands of humans living in different places and

throughout long periods of time, are represented as sudden events that took place in one definite locality, on one definite day, and in which the *dramatis personae* were one man, or one human couple, or one small "primal horde." Whether we call it concretization, dramatization, actualization, or personalization, this is what myth does and this is what Freud did in his recasting of the Oedipus tragedy into a primordial primitive prototype.

Another characteristic of myth which is apparent in the Freudian account of the parricide is the assumption that an event that took place in the remotest past has a lasting effect down to the present. This is a tacit assumption in all myths of origin; it is taken for granted and never questioned. The power of myth is such that by telling its tale of a *primordial* happening it satisfies the question "why?" which is directed to the *present time.* Questions such as, Why must men work hard to make the soil yield fruit? Why must women suffer in childbirth? Why are women subordinated to men? Why do snakes have no legs? and innumerable others like these are answered succinctly and with a finality that admits of no further doubt by telling of the circumstances under which Adam, Eve, and the serpent were punished by God. Nobody ever raises the question of how those single and singular primordial events can determine the shape of animals, circumstances, and relationships hundreds of generations later. Herein precisely lies the power of myth, that it can make us accept its underlying premises and can create in us a frame of mind in which its answers to our questions appear to us as completely satisfactory.

In the case of Freud's primal parricide myth, it so happens that he was troubled by the question of how and why a single event that took place at the dawn of human history should have a lasting effect many thousands of years later. He raises the question at the very end of *Totem and Taboo,* and his answer, probably the most unsatisfactory part in the entire book, is that "there seems to be a heredity of psychical dispositions . . . which, however, need certain stimuli in the life of the individual in order to become activated," [18] that "psychoanalysis has taught us that every man possesses in the workings of his unconscious mind an apparatus which enables him to interpret the reactions of other men," and that "by understanding unconsciously in this manner all the mores, ceremonies, and rules surviving from the original relationship to the primordial father, the later generations may have succeeded in taking over that emotional heritage." [19]

This sounds rather contrived and unconvincing. The fact is that one simply cannot rationally and logically explain why a primordial event should continuously exert its influence on, or have determined once and for all, the order of things. Psychological considerations, which must use the tools of logic and rationality, are unable to furnish a convincing explanation. Once, however, we recognize Freud's primal parricide for what it really is, namely a myth, all these forced attempts at explanation become unnecessary and irrelevant. The tragic single event of primal parricide, like all other origin myths, becomes timelessly effective, determines all future relationships of sons to fathers, simply because it *is* the myth of a primordial happening. Just as all women to this very day have to suffer the pangs of childbirth because God punished disobedient Eve; just as all men have to earn their livelihood with the sweat of their brow because God imposed this punishment on Adam; just as all snakes are bereft of legs because God so cursed the serpent in paradise—so the psychological attitude, the ambivalence, and all the other factors entering into the relationship of sons to their fathers were determined once and for all by the Freudian myth of that single, horrible, fraternal parricide. This feature of his use of the Oedipus myth, perhaps more than any other, indicates how completely involved Freud became in mythopoesis.

4 · *The Myth of the Hero*

Let us now turn to an example that will illustrate the transformation of a historian of religion into mythopoet. Joseph Campbell (1904–), is a man whose entire scholarly life has been devoted to the study of the mythical aspects of religion. His interests range over all religions of man, primitive, Oriental, Occidental, ancient, and contemporary. His avowed purpose in all the books he has written on these subjects has always been to make a comparative study of the major mythical themes and motifs that, he found, have a universal or near-universal distribution. The goal he set himself was no small one: to try "to compose into a single picture the new perspectives that have been opened in the fields of comparative symbolism, religion, mythology, and philosophy by the scholarship of recent years." [20]

This task was large enough, but what he actually achieved was in a sense larger still, for he ended by adding a few myths of his own making to the already existing vast corpus of myths. One single example will have to suffice to show how this happened.

In his first major mythological study entitled *The Hero With a Thousand Faces,* Campbell set out to study myths of heroes, as Otto Rank, Lord Raglan, and others had done before him. [21] He discusses a larger number of heroes than any of his predecessors did, and from the mythical life stories of the many heroes he attempts to distill the essence, as it were, of mythical herohood, which he terms "The Monomyth." [22] His conclusion is that "the hero . . . is the man or woman who has been able to battle past his personal and local historical limitations to the generally valid, normally human forms. . . . The hero has died as a modern man; but as eternal man—perfected, unspecific, universal man—he has been reborn. His second solemn task and deed therefore (as Toynbee declares and as all the mythologies of mankind indicate) is to return then to us, transfigured, and teach the lesson he has learned of life renewed." [23]

This in itself smacks to no small degree of mythopoesis, but soon Campbell elaborates the myth he has adumbrated here. Referring to Arnold van Gennep's famous *rites de passage,* he finds that "the standard path of the mythological adventure of the hero is a magnification of the formula in the rites of passage: *separation-initiation-return."* [24] These three phases are "the nuclear unit of the monomyth" which Campbell describes at some detail: *"A hero ventures forth from the world of common day into a region of supernatural wonder: fabulous forces are there encountered and a decisive victory is won: the hero comes back from this mysterious adventure with the power to bestow boons on his fellow man."* [25]

While Campbell is aware that his hero is a composite figure—

he calls him "the composite hero of the monomyth"²⁶—he is not
satisfied with the general outline of the hero's career given above,
and presents it again in even greater detail. His account reads
rather like a variant, in a more elaborate form, both of the pattern set up by Otto Rank for the birth-myth of the hero, and of
the list of points assembled by Lord Raglan for his hero figure:

> The mythological hero, setting forth from his
> commonday hut or castle, is lured, carried away, or
> else voluntarily proceeds, to a threshold of adventure.
> There he encounters a shadow presence that guards
> the passage. The hero may defeat or conciliate this
> power and go alive into the kingdom of the dark
> (brother-battle, dragon-battle; offering, charm), or be
> slain by the opponent and descend in death
> (dismemberment, crucifixion). Beyond the threshold,
> then, the hero journeys through a world of unfamiliar
> yet strangely intimate forces, some of which severely
> threaten him (tests), some of which give magical aid
> (helpers). When he arrives at the nadir of the
> mythological round, he undergoes a supreme ordeal
> and gains his reward. The triumph may be represented
> as the hero's sexual union with the goddess-mother of
> the world (sacred marriage), his recognition by the
> father-creator (father atonement), his own divinization
> (apotheosis), or again—if the powers have remained
> unfriendly to him—his theft of the boon he came to
> gain (bride-theft, fire-theft); intrinsically it is an
> expansion of consciousness and therewith of being
> (illumination, transfiguration, freedom). The final
> work is that of the return. If the powers have blessed
> the hero, he now sets forth under their protection
> (emissary); if not, he flees and is pursued (transforma-
> tion flight, obstacle flight). At the return threshold
> the transcendental powers must remain behind; the
> hero re-emerges from the kingdom of dread (return,
> resurrection). The boon that he brings restores the
> world (elixir).²⁷

The mythical construct character of this pattern would be obvious even if Campbell had not clued us in by labeling it a com-

posite monomyth. Since no actual mythology contains such a pattern of composite myth, it is itself a creation of its author who, by formulating it, stepped over the thin dividing line between studying myth and mythmaking. In yet another passage Campbell formulates the "universal doctrine" that all myths teach us. "Briefly formulated," he says, "the universal doctrine teaches us that all the visible structures of the world—all things and beings— are the effects of a ubiquitous power out of which they rise, which supports and fills them during the period of their manifestation, and back into which they must ultimately dissolve." [28] This sweeping statement is unquestionably mythopoetic—more so, even than the composite monomyth of the hero. We can definitely include Campbell among those students of man who have turned into mythopoets.

5 · *The Myth of the Noosphere*

Let us now proceed to examine one final example of the transformation of students of man into mythopoets.

Pierre Teilhard de Chardin (1881–1955), to whom we now turn, was a Jesuit priest, a faithful and obedient Catholic, a distinguished paleontologist, a theologian, a philosopher, and a most original thinker. Leaving aside his other contributions to various branches of anthropological science, we wish to present what can be considered his central idea, which concerns his interpretation of the place man has attained so far in the universe, and his vision, always couched in scientific terms, of man's future development. His key concept is the *noosphere*, a concept in which, it must be stated at the very outset, we cannot fail to discern mythical overtones. He reaches this concept by arguing from the *biosphere*, a term originally invented by Éduard Suess and also used by Vladimir Vernadsky in the sense of the "terrestrial zone containing life." Teilhard borrows this term in a somewhat different sense. For him the biosphere is "the actual layer of vitalized substance enveloping the earth." [29] Again we must pause to point out the mythical concretization and categorization contained in this statement. To lump all the myriads of living forms and all the biological individuals produced by them into an "*actual layer* of vitalized substance enveloping the earth" is, to say the least, a bold reinterpretation of observable reality, and the importation of a mythical idea into nature. The methodological significance of this approach will become clear as we follow Teilhard in his postulation of a new, higher sphere, the *noosphere* (from the Greek *noos*, mind). Before doing so, however, I would like to point out that Teilhard himself, without explicitly saying so, seems to have been aware of the quasi-mythological character of his thesis, when he wrote in an introductory footnote to his essay "The Formation of the Noosphere": "To those prepared to follow the author in his thinking it will be apparent that biology merges into theology. . . ." [30] In other words, he knew that, as is the case with all myths, the willingness or ability to believe (for what else can "to follow the author in his thinking" mean?) is an indispensable prerequisite for the recognition of the validity of his entire argument.

Now, Teilhard continues, man is distinguished psychologically from all other living creatures in that his consciousness has acquired the power "of turning in upon itself." [31] Having thus set man apart from the biosphere, he then proceeds to build up his case for the existence of a distinct noosphere—that is, a "terrestrial sphere of thinking substance." [32] He relates the noosphere to "the collective human organism which the economists so hazily envisage," and says that the noosphere constitutes "the super-organism we have been seeking, of whose existence we were intuitively aware." [33] Curiously, he makes no reference to Alfred L. Kroeber's well known concept of culture as "the superorganic," although the close relatedness of Teilhard's and Kroeber's thought on this point is evident.

From here on Teilhard proceeds to treat the noosphere as if it were a true physical or organic entity. In his earlier books he said that, "compared with the magnitude of celestial bodies, the noosphere is an almost imperceptible skin"; that the noosphere contains the "peripheral layers—ridiculously thin but formidably active and complex—of the planet [Earth]"; and that "the earth [is] . . . becoming enclosed in a single thinking envelope. . . ." [34] After dealing with "the birth and zoological structure of the noosphere," he devotes a section in his chapter "The Formation of the Noosphere" to its "anatomy." Here he argues that the noosphere has a "hereditary apparatus," a "mechanical apparatus" (called in more commonplace anthropological terminology the technological aspect of culture), and finally a "cerebral apparatus." This " 'cerebroid' organ of the Noosphere" consists of the sum total of all the human brains on earth plus all the mechanical, electronic, and other machinery, including the computers, with whose help thought can be transmitted, communicated, shared, or otherwise aided and augmented. It also includes the "network of radio and television communications which, perhaps anticipating the direct syntonization of brains through the mysterious power of telepathy, already link us all in a sort of 'etherized' universal consciousness." [35]

Having thus "attempted a sort of anatomy of the major organs of the Noosphere," Teilhard next proceeds to a "Physiology of the Noosphere." In this section he argues that "the formidable wheels [of the noosphere] turn, and in their combined action hidden forces are engendered which circulate throughout the gigantic system." There is a vast, internal process, "something . . . purposefully stirring as in a living being," the general tendency of which is an "inflexion," a "mysteriously compelled infolding," which results in "a network (a world network) of economic and psychic affiliations . . . which envelops and constantly penetrates more deeply within each one of us." In addition, "the Noosphere can function only by releasing more and more spiritual energy with an ever higher potential," so that it "is in process of 'cerebralizing' itself. The Noosphere, in short, is a stupendous thinking machine," [36] whose elements, as he says elsewhere, correspond "to the cells of a supremely specialized organism. . . ." [37]

From these premises important consequences flow for the future, as outlined in the section on "The Phases and Future of the Noosphere." Teilhard foresees a "planetized humanity," a release of at present unsuspected psychic powers, an emergence of the "sense of the universal," "the pervasion of the human mass by the power of sympathy." "Humanity," he says, "is building its composite brain beneath our eyes. . . . The constructive developments now taking place within the Noosphere in the realm

of sight and reason" will "necessarily also penetrate to the sphere
of feeling," and thus humanity "will find its *heart*." At that
stage of development the "demand for the Absolute" will become "one of the impulses which grow and are intensified in the
Noosphere." From here on Teilhard leads "those prepared to
follow him" on a fantastic voyage through time and space, compared to which the film *2001* was like a child's exploration of the
neighbor's backyard. Ultimately this voyage brings him to "the
problem of God." [38]

In depicting the future of man as symbolized and mythicized
in the noosphere, Teilhard inevitably became aware of the
affinity between his thinking and Marxist thought, and took pains
to point out the difference between the two. "Those who think
on Marxist lines," he wrote in 1950, "believe that all that is
necessary to inspire and polarize the human molecules is that
they should look forward to an eventual state of *collective* reflection and sympathy, at the culmination of anthropogenesis,
from which all will benefit through *participation:* as it were, a
vault of mutually reinforced thoughts, a closed circuit of attach-
ments in which the individual will achieve intellectual and affective fulfillment to the extent that he is one with the whole system." [39]

In Teilhard's presentation of the Marxian myth of the future,
we can recognize without difficulty Teilhard's own key concepts,
even his characteristic turns of phrase. Where he, of course,
differs from the Marxists is in his addition of a religious, or,
more precisely, Christological, component. While the Marxist concept of man's future, as Teilhard sees it, is that it will lead simply
to man's temporal and natural perfection, his own view is that
human destiny will be "fulfilled and totalized only in and through
Christ, and that it rises beyond itself into a transcendent supernatural universe." [40]

The mythical character of Teilhard's noosphere and of the
voyage upon which it is just about to embark in our days is so
clear that only a very few of its highlights need be pointed out.
In addition to the mythical tendency to personalize, concretize,
and categorize that has been referred to earlier, we recognize
the familiar ring of the eschatological vision, the old myth of

the farthest future to which Teilhard does not refer but with which he was no doubt thoroughly familiar. I think, moreover, that I am not stretching a point too far if I say that Teilhard's picture of the blissful future that lies in store for mankind contains features that remind us of the myth of the early paradisiac state of man to which so many of the eschatologies hark back and which can be discerned in the idealized picture Teilhard paints of the present and future state of his noosphere. In the last but one chapter of this book we shall return to Teilhard's myth of the escape of man from the shackles of the planet Earth.

In conclusion, Teilhard's central, and immensely fascinating, idea of the noosphere and what it can mean for the future of man reveals itself, if closely examined and placed in the proper perspective, as yet another product of the transformation of an observer and interpreter of human development into a myth-maker, a mythopoet.

3

myth and history

1 • Origins: Mythical and Historical

Mythography was the earliest form of historiography, and its favorite themes were the beginnings, the earliest periods, of history. As Karl Kerényi succinctly put it, "The going back to origin and primeval time is the basic feature of every mythology." [1] But myth is more than that, because it goes back to beginnings and retells them not for the sake of academic historical interest, nor because of the intellectual curiosity which today motivates archeological and prehistoric research. The mythical historiographer writes or tells of great, weighty, fateful, and decisive events which are relevant to the here and the now; although they happened in the dim dawn of the world, or, perhaps, precisely *because* they took place in that faraway seminal period, those events have ever since continued to influence the destiny of the world at large and of the mythographer's own people in particular. [2]

Take, to begin with, the creation of the world, or, to use the scientific equivalent of this mythological expression, the origin of the universe. In the last 150 years there have been many scientific theories about it. With the onset of the space age and the possibility of reaching other planets of the solar system and, subsequently, other stars as well, the fascination exerted by the great universe and the questions of its origin has increased tremendously. Without being an astronomer, one may stipulate that the recently formulated theories of cosmogony are closer to the truth than were the earlier ones, and that more research, with bigger and better telescopes, both optical and radio, with successful probes into other celestial bodies, and other methods, will sooner or later come up with a satisfactory answer. Nobody will wish to minimize the intellectual satisfaction the brotherhood of astronomers, astrophysicists, and related specialists will derive from reaching their solution. The scientific advance, the gigantic intellectual achievement, will be hailed, and rightly so, throughout the world. Yet, if one may permit oneself a heretical question: Of what significance will this major scientific breakthrough be for the human species inhabiting our planet? Once the excitement has died down, the curiosity been satisfied, the long-sought-for answer become common knowledge, will it result in a betterment of life, will it improve humanity, increase happiness? The question is merely rhetorical, for the negative answer is a foregone conclusion.

Scientists will argue, of course, that the betterment of life or the raising of standards of morality or humaneness is no concern of astronomy, astrophysics, and the related sciences. There can be no quarrel with this argument: it puts forward a completely valid and unexceptionable viewpoint. But herein, precisely, lies the basic difference between the scientific and the mythical approach to phenomena. The scientist wants to understand them; for him every unknown is a challenge. But, once having found the answer to a question, he is not concerned with the effect his solution will have on man. Myth, on the other hand, always keeps man in the focus of its interest. The explanations it supplies to the great questions that have agitated man ever since he was man invariably contain an element of encouragement: a phenomenon, it tells us, as we encounter it today, has this and this as its basis, its reason, its origin, its meaning, or its purpose. Once in possession of these elucidations, man can better understand, accept, and acquiesce in phenomena that previously were baffling, disquieting, or even frightening. Where science merely explains, myth always reassures; where science reports, myth comforts. When judged from this point of view, the circumstance that the mythical account is not borne out, or even is vitiated, by scientifically ascertained facts becomes immaterial.

Today, there can be little doubt that none of the many creation stories contained in the mythologies of all nations come even close to what actually took place in the universe during that unthinkably long period that preceded the emergence of the first forms of life. When compared to the great cosmic vistas just now beginning to open up, the most daring flights of ancient imagination into the days of beginning necessarily appear like the helpless convulsions of a man trying to reach the stars while tied hand and foot to stakes driven deep into the body of Mother Earth. But, however childish those early gropings appear in relation to our rapidly expanding scientific perspective, their significance as reassuring guidelines for man's relationship to the world can scarcely be overestimated.

Consider the (scientifically) ridiculous notion that God created the world in six days, found in the first chapter of the Book of Genesis. How much, indeed, has this myth meant for a major part of mankind throughout the ages! In a world that was frightening and inimical, that was the domain of uncontrollable natural and supernatural forces, it held out the reassurance that the earth was created by a benevolent and omnipotent deity for the express purpose of serving as a habitation for man. It taught that the animal and vegetable kingdoms were created in order to sustain human life, that the celestial luminaries were fashioned in order to give man warmth and light and to mark for him the day and the night and the seasons of the year, and that God hallowed the Sabbath in order to make it a sacred day of rest for all mankind. This myth, long believed to be divine truth, has now sunk into a peaceful coma and before long we shall witness its expiration. But, paradoxically, the beliefs it expressed concerning the relationship of man and the rest of the world, and the social ideas whose validation was one of its original purposes, survive, and, in fact, are today more vital than ever.

The character of the Greek creation myths is less explicit than the Biblical version, nor has their credibility remained unchallenged for so long. The one preserved by Hesiod, agrees with Genesis in stating that before all things came Chaos (literally "gaping void"), which parallels the Tohu waBohu (literally "confusion and void") of the Biblical creation story. From Chaos sprang Gaia (Earth), Tartarus (a dark place "in the depths of the ground"), Eros ("love"), Erebos ("Darkness"), and, finally, Night. From Night and Erebos were born Aither (ether, or the upper air) and Day, while Earth produced Ouranos (Heaven), the mountains, and the sea. The union of Ouranos and Gaia produced the Titans, among them the three great pairs of divinities, Kronos and Rhea, Okeanos and Tethys, Iapetos and Themis. Most of these were non-Greek nature powers—that is, pre-Hellenic in origin—and were supplanted, after a terrible titanomachia, by the Olympian gods headed by Zeus.[3]

This origin myth is theogony rather than cosmogony. It imposes neither moral nor ritual duties upon the Greeks, although it supplies a reassuring and understandable sequence of primordial happenings which resulted in the Cosmos as known to them. Some of the bafflement, which must have harassed the early prephilosophical observers of nature among the Hellenes, was resolved, or at least assuaged, by these rudimentary creation myths, which certainly express and account for the particular Greek attitude to ever-changing nature.

Differences such as those between the creation myths and the scientific theories of cosmogony also can be found between the mythical accounts of many other natural phenomena and their scientific explanations. In each case, science is satisfied with a presentation of its findings as the truth, whereas the myth goes an important step beyond this: it points out the relevance of what it has to say about the natural phenomenon for the lives of the people to whom it addresses itself.

Beginnings, in the mythical sense, do not necessarily mean ultimate origins such as the coming-into-being of the cosmos or the birth of man. They frequently refer to events which brought about the actually prevailing order in the world of men and things—that is, the social framework and the natural environment which surround and control the life of the mythographer, of his audience, and of the heirs of the traditions formulated by him. To know how the present world order came into being, what or who caused it, and what was its meaning is of primary significance, because only a correct understanding of those long past events can enable man to take his proper place and fulfill his proper role in the circumstances brought about by those primordial events. The duties, obligations, rights, and expectations of man in relation to the physical, social, and spiritual realms of his existence are all anchored in that period of origins of which the myth is the authoritative account. When understood in this sense, it becomes apparent that the significance of myth is so basic, so seminal, that there would be no exaggeration in saying myth makes the man.

Examples to illustrate this central function of myth abound in all cultures, but it may be best to refer to a familiar one. The myth of the sacrifice by God the Father of His Only Begotten Son for the redemption of mankind is an origin story; it tells not only how it came about that man was redeemed, but also how Christianity originated. And it tells not merely a story of historical significance, like, for instance, the story of the fall of the Roman Empire or of the discovery of America, but recounts an event that concerns directly and personally every Christian in every age. Like all great origin myths, it tells of one single event that happened at one particular time in the remote past, and thereby explains and endows with meaning an important aspect of the human condition that prevails today.

Thus a mythical event, in contrast to a factual historical occurrence, is a part of the present as well as of the past. It influences our present lives not merely through a chain of historical consequences, as historical events do, but directly and immediately, through the force that originally brought it about and that continues to work with undiminished effect, defying time and space.

Another notable difference between a historical event and a

mythical event is that the significance of the former lies in an objective reality, while that of latter rests on a subjective reality. The fall of Rome or the discovery of America, to go back to our previous examples, can be adjudged in many different ways, but nobody can doubt the reality of the events referred to by those terms. There is objective, external, factual evidence that these events did take place. This evidence can, and, in fact, must be accepted by anybody and everybody, whether his life, his society's life, or his ancestors' life was or was not affected by the events in question. One may not know about them, but once they are brought to one's knowledge, they automatically become part of the objective reality of one's world.

As against this, the mythical event is part of man's subjective reality, but is no less *real* for that. The difference between the objective reality of historical fact and the subjective reality of myth lies in the way one acquires one's awareness of them and the way one relates to them. One acquires awareness of objective realities through sense perception, digested ("internalized") by processes of logical thinking, and stored away as remembered knowledge. The acquisition of an awareness of subjective realities also starts in some cases with sense perception, but if so, it is internalized or absorbed, not by logical thought processes, but by a direct emotional reaction, and stored away, not as remembered knowledge, but as experienced belief.

The other way of acquiring an awareness of subjective realities does not involve sense perception at all but originates in intuitive insight, a voice reaching the inner ear, a sudden seeing the light. Our inevitable use of expressions borrowed from sensory processes to describe this phenomenon, far from raising doubts about the phenomenon itself, merely goes to show the inadequacy of our language to express nonsensory phenomena.

For those not aware of a certain subjective reality, it is as if it did not exist. To explain it to them, to argue with them, to make them see, hear, get hold of, or understand it, is, as a rule, futile. Logical arguments cannot make a man become apperceptive of a subjective reality. This is why religious disputations, such as those arranged in the Middle Ages between Christians, Muslims, and Jews, could never result in true conversion. Those who, on the other hand, have become aware of a subjective reality, in whatever way, possess in it something at least as powerful as, and often much more potent and valuable than, objective reality. It is in this sense that *Credo quia absurdum* expresses a deep psychological truth, and that a mythical occurrence can be a living reality in a way never approximated by a historical event.

2 • Myth out of History

Having stressed an important aspect of the difference between history and myth, it may come as a surprise to find that in many cases myths do have a historical kernel, or that historical traditions can and do assume mythical forms and survive as myths for a long time after the memory of the historical event itself has sunk into oblivion. Yet it is psychologically understandable that such a transformation should take place. Historical events have no necessary relevance for the lives of people in subsequent generations; their memory, therefore, tends to fade away, and three or four generations later they may be completely forgotten by everybody except those who have a professional interest in history or who must learn it in school. Mythical events, or, rather, historical events that have been transformed into myths, retain a significance, a relevance, an actuality even for a hundred generations, precisely because, as has been pointed out above, such is the nature of myth. When a historical event is transformed into myth it loses a lot in accuracy and in detail, becoming embellished in the process by many a fantastic feature that can render the entire myth incredible to the critical outsider. However, at the same time it gains immeasurably in longevity, in continuous effectiveness, and in cultural potency.

The idea that myths present historical events in a distorted form is, as we have seen above (Chapter 1, section 2), a very old one. However, the scholarly investigation of myths for the purpose of isolating the historical sediment they may contain is quite a new approach in mythological studies. One of the students of myth from this angle is M. P. Nilsson who, in his essay, "Der mykenische Ursprung der griechischen Mythologie" (The

Mycenaean Origin of Greek Mythology), has convincingly argued
that all the great heroic legend cycles of Greek mythology are
closely connected with Minoan-Mycenaean sites.[4] His argument,
together with such historical data as have become available,
clearly point to the Minoan-Mycenaean origin not only of the
great Greek cycles of saga, but also of the major component of
Greek culture as a whole. Since history leaves us largely in the
dark as to the historical origin of Minoan-Mycenaean culture
itself, one may be justified in attempting a historical interpretation of the Minoan origin myths. This approach is based on the
more and more generally recognized fact that origin myths, as
a rule, do have a historical kernel, and that they record historical traditions in mythical form. The traditions thus preserved
may or may not be historically "true," but they do contain what
in the formative or early period of the society in question was
regarded as the historical truth.

An apparent difficulty encountered in any attempt to treat origin myths as mythical reformulations of history is that many origin
myths, just like many other types of myth, come in more than one
version, and that the different versions often contradict one another. However, this difficulty is not insurmountable; in fact it
has its historical analogy in the often equally contradictory accounts given of the same event by different sources, each of
which is colored in accordance with certain sets of ideas, points
of view, and intentions. Let us take as an example the myth of
the Minoan origins of Crete, as can be pieced together from the
works of ancient Greek authors.[5]

According to these sources, the founder of Minoan culture on
the island of Crete was Minos, born on Crete of the union of
Europa and Zeus in the shape of either a bull or an eagle. After
her affair with Zeus, Europa married Asterius, king of Crete,
who fathered no child on her, but brought up her children by
Zeus, Minos, Rhadamanthys, and, according to some, Sarpedon.
When Asterius died, Minos became king of Crete, wedded Pasiphae, daughter of Helius (the Sun), by whom he had several
sons and daughters. Pasiphae fell in love with a beautiful white
bull from the sea, managed to have her desire from him by hid-

ing in the inside of a hollow wooden cow made for her by
Daedalus, and subsequently gave birth to a monster with a bull's
head and a human body, the bloodthirsty Minotaur. The Labyrinth built by Daedalus for the Minotaur at the behest of Minos,
and the events that led ultimately to the killing of the Minotaur
by Theseus are all fascinating myths but no longer belong to the
Cretan origins.

The first key to this myth is the name Europa. She, clearly,
stands for the peoples of the continent of the same name, or,
more precisely, for those of them who were believed by the ancient Greeks to have imposed their dominion upon Crete and
possibly other parts of the north shore of the Mediterranean.
Accordingly, the figure of Europa has been explained as probably no more than the eponym of the continent of Europe.[6]
Whether Europa stands for all European peoples, or only for
the early inhabitants of Crete, the myth unquestionably evidences
the early Greek belief that the peoples mythically represented
as "Europa" had come from Phoenicia—since in one version the
father of Europa was Phoinix, i.e., Phoenicia—or from the chief
Phoenician city of Tyre, whose king Agenor was, according to
the more popular version, Europa's father.

The name of Agenor, king of Tyre, can perhaps be equated
with that of Canaan, who, incidentally, is said in the Biblical account to have been the father of another famous Phoenician city,
Zidon.[7] The brothers of Europa in the popular version of the
myth were Phoinix, whose name, as mentioned, unquestionably
represents Phoenicia; Kilix, who stands for Cilicia; and Kadmos,
whose name is simply the Hebrew-Canaanite word for "east,"
Kedem, with the addition of the Greek nominal ending. All
these names clearly point to the Levant coast of the Mediterranean as the place from whence, according to early Greek mythologized historic tradition, the people and culture of Minoan
Crete had come. The details were, of course, lost in the transformation from history to myth, but the general outline is still
recognizable. The Phoenician seafarers, the myth tells us, settled
on Crete. There they were at some point overwhelmed by the
early Hellenes as represented in Europa's succumbing to Zeus.

From this union of the two peoples sprang Minos—that is, the old Minoan culture—which in turn fell under the onslaught of the Greeks (Theseus in the myth) many centuries later.

More interesting from the point of view of our attempt to trace the development of myth out of history is another possible explanation of the Zeus-Europa myth. In the fifth century B.C. Herodotus knew of a historical tradition according to which Cretan seafarers had raided Tyre, the chief city of Phoenicia: "Certain Greeks," he writes, "with whose name they [the Tyrians] are unacquainted but who would probably be Cretans, made a landing at Tyre, on the Phoenician coast, and bore off the king's daughter, Europé." [8] The assumption that an early historical occurrence, whose vague memory is contained in this reference by Herodotus, could have served as the basis of the Zeus-Europa myth is confirmed by a conflation of the historical event with the myth by the Byzantine chronicler, John Malalas, some twelve centuries after Herodotus. Writing in the seventh century A.D., Malalas states that "Taurus [i.e., "Bull"], king of Crete, attacked Tyre after a sea battle. He took the city that same evening and, despoiling it, carried off many captives, among them Europa, the daughter of King Agenor. . . . This event is still recalled in the annual Evil Evening observed at Tyre. Taurus, however, made Europa his wife, and called all his lands by her name, European regions." [9] In Malalas' version it is King Taurus of Crete who carries off Europa, which, of course, reflects the bull whose form Crete-born Zeus assumed, according to the myth, for his escapade with the Tyrian princess; and the lands dominated by Crete are called Europe after her. If Malalas is correct in his report about the annual commemoration of the Evil Evening at Tyre, then the memory of the half-historical, half-mythical event of the sack of the city by the Cretans was still alive in the seventh century.

The relevance of these observations for our modern contemporary world lies in the fact that the same processes of metamorphosis that transformed history into myth in early Greece and the still older cultures of the ancient Near East are still at work, as we shall see in several later chapters in this book. In most cases we lack the historical perspective necessary to be able to observe such processes in connection with large-scale historical events of the most recent past, such as, World War II or the Russo-Chinese conflict. But we can see the same forces at work in transforming the historical facts of individual lives into mythical accounts and the real figures of men who played certain roles in modern history into mythical images, as soon as their deaths enable such metamorphoses to set in.

3 • Dionysus, or Myth as Precedent

Having discussed in the preceding section the emergence of myth out of history, we turn now to the reverse process—namely, the formation of historical events on the basis of mythical happenings, or the phenomenon of myth serving as a prototype, a precedent consciously followed by historical figures.

Thomas Mann, as well as other poetically inspired scholars and historians before him, has pointed out that great protagonists of human history were inclined, in the crucial hours of their lives, to identify with particular historical prototypes. Napoleon, as Mann put it, "at the period of his Eastern exploits . . . mythically confounded himself with Alexander; while after he turned his face westward he is said to have declared: 'I am Charlemagne.' And so it was already in antiquity. The ancient biographers of Caesar were convinced, rightly or wrongly, that he took Alexander as his prototype." And as to Alexander himself, he "walked in the footsteps of Miltiades," [10] the Athenian general (c. 540–c. 489 B.C.) who defeated the Persians at Marathon.

What Thomas Mann does not mention is that Alexander, quite apart from harking back to Miltiades who lived barely two centuries before him, had a much older, much greater, and much more attractive mythical prototype to follow: the god Dionysus who, according to an early Greek myth recorded by Euripides in the late fifth century B.C., penetrated as a conqueror far into the East—to wit, into Lydia, Phrygia, Persia, Bactria, Media, Arabia, and "all Asia that lies by the salt sea." [11]

Arriving in Syria, Dionysus was opposed by the king of Damascus, but flayed him alive; then he built a bridge across the

Euphrates river with ivy and vine. A tiger, sent by his father
Zeus, helped him across the Tigris river. Then Dionysus proceeded to India, putting down all opposition he met on the way.
Having conquered the entire country of India, he founded cities,
gave laws, and taught the people the art of viniculture.[12]

Although the account of the triumphant march of Dionysus
across Asia and of his conquest of India originally was the Greeks'
mythical way of telling of what they believed was the spread of
viniculture from Greece into the lands of the Orient, by the
time of Alexander, Dionysus had long become the great god of
wine, passion, and frenzy whose powers were irresistible, and who
could and did inflict madness as well as joy. Some historians feel
that "after Alexander's real conquests, Dionysus' fabled ones
were extended, and he was represented as having reached India." [13] More likely, Alexander consciously and purposely endeavored to repeat the great conquests of Dionysus, not only
because he fancied himself as mythically identified with the great
Olympian, but because of all Greek gods it was precisely Dionysus who, being himself of Oriental extraction, was most readily
identified with Oriental deities. Of course, having identified
himself with Dionysus, Alexander, inevitably and tragically, had
to die young as Dionysus did.

Dionysus is important for our mythological investigations for
another reason as well. His myth contains what is probably the
earliest instance of a mythical prototype powerful enough to induce people to sacrifice their lives, to face a specially painful
death, in imitation of and in identification with the god. As Jane
Harrison has pointed out, Dionysus "can never rid himself of the
throng of worshipping women, he is always the nursling of
the Maenads." [14] It was this oft-depicted mythological scene that
the participants in the Dionysian ritual drama reenacted. But
according to another version of the Dionysus myth, soon after his
birth the Titans, at Hera's orders, seized him and, despite his
transformations, tore him into shreds.[15] Thus at one and the
same time, despite the logical contradiction of which man in his
mythologically inspired moments is blissfully unaware, the same
drama reenacted both the tragedy that was visited upon the

babe Dionysus by the cruel Titans and the celebration of Dionysus by the worshiping Maenads. The women in the ritual became not only the Maenads driven to frenzy by Dionysus, but also the Titans who tore him into shreds. And this, precisely, is what they proceeded to do. The worshipers of Dionysus believed not only that they were possessed by the god, but also that they were actually identified with the principals in this primeval divine tragedy. By the same token, one of the worshipers *became* the god himself incarnate, and was torn to pieces by the frenzied women, as was the infant Dionysus by the Titans. There are other mythical examples, too, of this dismemberment of a young man or a child by a group of frenzied women, who include the child's own mother. The myth even goes so far as to provide the mythical prototype of what the mother feels later, when her frenzy subsides and she realizes what she has done. Yet, at the same time, the youth torn to pieces was considered a sacrifice to Dionysus.[16] In Euripides' great tragedy *Bacchae*, it is Pentheus, king of Thebes, who is thus torn to pieces by the frenzied women, led by his own mother. In other mythical accounts the sacred Dionysian frenzy induced all the women of Argos to destroy their own children.[17]

Nor was this all. For in the ancient form of these original Bacchanalia, the dismemberment of the victim was carried out in a particularly cruel and barbarous manner: the frenzied women tore him to pieces with their teeth, ate his flesh, and drank his blood. This eating of the god in order thereby to absorb the mana that informed him and thus to transplant some of it physically into the bodies of his worshipers was, of course, the ultimate consummation of the divine sacrifice. At a later date, an animal victim, such as a goat, was substituted for the human one.[18]

The myth of Dionysus thus served as the precedent and the prototype for one of the most cruel and barbaric rituals of ancient Greece. It also served as precedent and prototype for some of the greatest exploits of history, beginning with those performed by Alexander, the greatest conquering hero to come out of the Hellenic world. Alexander, in turn, became the exemplar for Julius Caesar whose role in Roman history was comparable to that of Alexander in Greek, and, many centuries later, for Napoleon, the greatest figure of modern France.

Nor is it only a preexisting myth that can influence people and induce them to emulate it. The psychological need for a myth which can serve as a precedent or justification for conduct considered out of the ordinary is so pressing that people will create new myths to meet it. At times this purpose is achieved and the psychological demand supplied by attaching mythical features to an actual historical individual, as Alexander in antiquity or Che Guevara, James Dean, or Al Capone in our own day and age.[19] In other cases, the mythical personage himself is invented, like Marion Delgado or Mickey Mouse.[20] In both cases, the mythical prototype serves with equal effectiveness, and wields the power to mold followers into its own image.

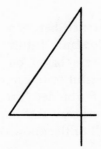

myths of the future

Like all animals, man lives in the present. But, unlike animals, man is always aware of both the past and the future. This awareness led him at an early stage in history to a preoccupation with *"Urzeit"* and *"Endzeit,"* the primeval times and the end of days. The question, "What was?" gave rise to a rich ontogonical mythology in all ancient cultures; the contrapuntal question, "What will be?" was answered by various types of teleological myths. The latter are most familiar to us from the Biblical apocalypse and eschatology. They are still with us in the form of modern science fiction.

1 • *Eschatology*

In its simplest and oldest form, Biblical eschatology (the branch of theology dealing with the end of days) merely projects into the farthest future the myth of the primal past, the tradition of the paradisiac golden age. It

81

tells us that man and beast will again live happily and peace-
fully together as they did in the Garden of Eden. Swords will
be beaten into plowshares and spears into pruning hooks. Every
man will sit under his vine and under his figtree, and there will be
no more fear in the world (Micah 4:3–4). The wolf shall dwell
with the lamb, the leopard shall rest with the kid, the lion shall
eat straw like the ox, and even the venomous snakes shall be the
toys of little children (Isaiah 11:6–9).

But there was to be one important difference between the
idyllic Edenic past and the peace of the Messianic future: in
the Garden of Eden peace and happiness were based on the
childish ignorance of Adam and Eve; the blissful state came to
an end as soon as they tasted the fruit of the Forbidden Tree of
Knowledge. In the future, however, the same peace and happiness will return "because the earth shall be full of the knowledge
of Yahweh" (Isaiah 11:9).

Knowledge and its concomitant wisdom, understanding,
power, righteousness, and unswerving justice will be the attributes
of the Messianic ruler, a descendant of King David, whose reign
will usher in that glorious future period of all-pervading peace
(Isaiah 11:1–5). The *Endzeit*, therefore, appears as something
very different, as far as its organizational sophistication is concerned, from the naive *sine lege fidemque* condition of the
Urzeit—in fact, its very antithesis. It will be a time in which all
the problems that have arisen in consequence of the loss of the
paradisiac innocence will be solved by virtue of the superior
knowledge that will emanate from the Messianic ruler and per-
vade his entire realm, man and beast alike.

In addition to this simplest and most endearing form of the
myth of the future, there are many more varieties of the same
theme belonging to different stages of elaboration. In all of them
one can discover prototypes, or archetypes, if you will, of fu-
turity—mythologems that still actuate modern man not only in
his speculations about a remote better end of days, but also in his
reveries or daydreams about worlds that lie in the future in a
developmental as well as in a merely temporal sense—that is to
say, worlds that are far more advanced than our own in point
of scientific knowledge, but that the fertile fantasy of writers can

yet place within our grasp. However, since the point I wish to make here is simply that there is a striking analogy between ancient myths of the future and modern products of science fiction, it is unnecessary to present the more elaborate types of eschatological myths. The simple archetype of the paradisiac bliss regained in the end of days through an inspired upsurge of knowledge contains quite sufficient points of departure to show that the entire genre of science fiction is its analogue.

2 • *Science Fiction*

Indeed, the extent to which the main features of the ancient myths of the glorious paradisiac future persist in modern science fiction is nothing less than remarkable. First of all, there is the central feature of knowledge. The future age depicted in most science fiction stories is one in which man has acquired a vast storehouse of scientific knowledge, compared to which our own late-twentieth-century science appears as primitive, infantile, and pitiable. Whether the scene is set on our own earth at some future time, or on another planet, or in an incredibly remote galaxy, the element of superior scientific knowledge (coupled, as a rule, with sterling qualities of the American character) plays an important role in solving a problem that threatens disaster, or in overcoming evil antagonists, or in bringing peace and happiness into the life of an alien society. Often the ingroup (i.e., the society to which the heroes belong) is depicted as having achieved peace and happiness, but is threatened by an outgroup whose evolution led it into a different direction. A clash ensues, after which the members of the outgroup (or those of them who survive) see the light and learn to live in peace and happiness.

This myth in its entirety, including the element of struggle, battle, and ultimate victory, is neatly prefigured in the "end of days" type of Biblical eschatology. The same prophecy which contains the myth of the peaceful future foretells the defeat of the Philistines, the children of the East, Edom, Moab, Ammon, and Egypt by the dispersed of Israel and Judah who have again foregathered in their land (Isaiah 11:11–16). Likewise in modern science fiction, to depict nothing more than a happy and

peaceful existence led by a scientifically highly developed people
would be utopian but would be bad fiction, because it would
lack the dramatic element, and worse mythology, if we understand myth (as we do) as a story that, in addition to several other
characteristics, has a deep significance for our lives. To be good
science fiction and good myth, the elements of struggle, of tension, of uncertainty, and ultimately of happy resolution must not
be lacking.

Nor is the figure of the great ruler, the latter-day heir of the
ancient mythical divine king, missing in the true science fiction
stories. He is always present, he always possesses knowledge superior to that of the other protagonists of the story. He is the
charismatic leader, inspiring confidence or even awe. When the
need arises, he can "smite the land with the rod of his mouth, and
with the breath of his lips slay the wicked" (Isaiah 11:4). Rarely
does he have to do more than make a command decision and
speak up; in adjudicating an issue he unfailingly sees through
deception (Isaiah 11:3); above all, he is scrupulously just.

It is not difficult to see why this modern variety of the myth
of the future is so immensely popular with young and old alike.
Like all true myths, it tells us, without ever saying it in so many
words, something significant about our problems and difficulties.
It does so by showing or telling us of a world in which advanced
science solves problems and resolves crises a hundred times
greater than ours. It spurs us on to greater efforts by holding up
before us a bigger-than-human group of heroes who have equipment and know-how and powers that we in our lives shall never
have, and who yet must struggle and do struggle and do succeed.
It allows us a glimpse of the future—the only kind of future
that many of us can still believe in in this world of technical and
social breakdowns, war and waste, overpollution and overpopulation—a future (or a remote world, which amounts to the same
thing) of immense technological superiority, in which problems,
of course, still exist, but are always met with determination,
enormous skill, and the utilization of both gigantic sources of
physical power and vastly superior psychological know-how; a
world that is at once overwhelmingly attractive and ultimately
reassuring, a universe in which men have actually become like

gods. No wonder that many statesmen and scholars, scientists and politicians, as well as simple people, are addicted to science fiction in the various forms in which it is available. It is for them, for us, a sustaining myth of as much significance as "the shoot out of the stock of Jesse" (Isaiah 11:1), the resurrection of Osiris or of Christ, or the return of the Mahdi were in other times and other places. In an age in which we must face, in addition to the minor and major nuisances referred to which surround us in our everyday lives, the possibility of the destruction of our entire planet by an atomic catastrophe, science fiction has a powerful reassuring function. It eminently fulfills what Clyde Kluckhohn calls the basic functions of myth (and of ritual) by satisfying "the need of society" and by achieving "the gratification (most often in the negative form of anxiety reduction) of a large proportion of individuals" in it.[1]

In modern science fiction anxiety reduction takes forms that can be considered as improvements over, or further elaboration of, ancient eschatologies. One prevalent characteristic of the science fiction story is that it soothes and reassures us "by radically simplifying man's emotional nature, and by altering the perspective from which one views man's accomplishments." It teaches that "the rational intelligence can preserve the future and make it a better, fuller life for all men," thereby duplicating in an updated form the eschatological promise of a future ruled over by knowledge and understanding. It maintains that "evil is nowhere mysterious or ambiguously interwoven in the very fabric of consciousness or existence. It is more likely to be mechanically conceived and hence capable of scientific solution," which is merely a repetition in modern phraseology of what Isaiah said in a more poetic form twenty-eight centuries ago. Absent, of course, is the figure of the divine king, the Messiah led and prodded by God—but his image is replaced by the self-reliant hero who is a scientist, an engineer, or a man whose training was closely related to the physical sciences, earthborn, but an "outsider," attractive to women, but concerned primarily with his often self-imposed mission of triumphing over adversaries and preserving mankind, generally from an alien menace. Where the ancient eschatology envisioned a world of peace and serenity in which no living being would have to die in order to serve as food for another, and in which there would be no war and strife, in the new eschatology of science fiction the evil persists but is subdued step by step by the powers of good, as represented by the hero whose superior technological knowledge can annihilate space and time.[2]

That modern science fiction is an extension of certain Biblical myths has been recognized by John Macquarrie, the eminent modern theologian. In commenting on this subject, Dr. Macquarrie says that the type of science fiction story which outstrips man's already astonishing technological achievements in flights of fancy are "the reverse of the biblical myth of the Tower of Babel. The biblical myth shows self-sufficiency leading to frustration, but science fiction shows it as triumphant. The quasi-mythology of modern times, unlike the ancient myths, makes no reference to God or to any power more ultimate than man himself. Such quasi-myth expresses a secular self-understanding."[3]

This, of course, is an existentialist interpretation of both the Biblical myth of the Tower of Babel and the modern science fiction mythology. In my own functional view, as already indicated above, both the Biblical myths of the eschatological type and the science fiction myths fulfill an identical, or, in any case, very similar, function: to reassure man concerning his future. To be able to do so, both types of myths must, first of all, depict the dangers, even horrors, that man will inevitably encounter in his far future path. This is necessary in order to project and concretize the fear of the future lodged in every human heart, for only by projecting and concretizing them can such fears be, if not eliminated, at least attenuated. Then comes the glorious chapter which tells of man overcoming the dangers and horrors, whether they be the monstrous beasts of Biblical mythology or the even more monstrous, because so frequently formless, horrors of outer space in science fiction. Man emerges victorious—this is the message, the great, comforting, and sustaining evangel of both.

Of course, there are significant differences between the two that must not be overlooked. The Biblical myths of the future, conceived and presented in an age in which man knew himself to be a weak and powerless being who could survive emotionally only by relying on great transcendent powers whom he believed, or hoped, he could propitiate, told of a future victory of man thanks to divine help, succor, or other favorable intervention. Men who tried to secure their future without God's help, or even against His will, perished or were utterly defeated, as is masterfully illustrated in the story of the Tower of Babel. Those who relied on God, or those whom the gods favored for reasons of their own, although their ship was tossed by inimical tempests, were destined to reach safely the coveted shores of their island of the future.

The myths of science fiction, on the other hand, address themselves to modern man who has lost belief in divine providence, whose theologians speak to him of demythologizing and the death of God, and who for two or three generations has been nurtured on the "popular belief in the omnicompetence of science." [4] Yet withal, the dread of the future remained, and, possibly, has even become greater and deeper, because science, the new god, has power, like the Indian god Siva, not only to create and sustain, but also to destroy; while it is engaged in its ceaseless triple dance of creation, maintenance, and destruction, dwarfish man can never know whether he, individually, will be lifted up by the god's sustaining hand or trodden into formless gore by his merciless feet. Therefore, the reassurance that science fiction myth conveys to modern man must differ essentially from that of the old eschatologies. It cannot hold out the hope of divine benevolence; it must instead instill into man a faith in his own ability, intelligence, and ingenuity, which are his last and ultimate defenses in a world in which his most horrifying creation, technology, threatens to go on a rampage. This is why one of the central themes in science fiction is machine *versus* man, why the contest between man and machine is so much more fascinating and at the same time threatening than that between man and some alien intelligence; for the latter is a pure figment of the imagination, whereas the former is an actually existing reality which science fiction merely raises to a higher power. And this is why the greatest victory that science fiction can envisage is that of man over the technological environment of his own creation, an environment which in the late-twentieth century he

expanded to include other planets and which in science fiction
extends to other galaxies as well.

3 • The Naked Radicals

The distance between science fiction and the behavior patterns
of the radical students and the youthful New Leftists is certainly quite considerable. Yet there is this common element between the two: both either draw their inspiration from, or at
least are significant analogues of, the ancient myths of the future
which, in turn, are but a projection into the days to come of the
myth of the paradise in which, man fondly believed, was anchored
the fountainhead of human history.

As we all remember from our reading of the Bible, Adam and
Eve lived in the Garden of Eden not only without work (eating
the fruits of the Garden), without strife, without sex, and at peace
with all the animals, but also without clothing. They were
naked, yet such was their paradisiac innocence that they "were
not ashamed" (Genesis 2:25). In fact, this feature of nakedness
and absence of shame is the last detail in the Biblical description
of the blissful, innocent paradisiac state of man; the very next
sentence introduces the serpent, and embarks on the sorry tale
of man's fall, of his tasting the fruit of knowledge, and the
ensuing emergence of shame, sex, the curse of work, the subordination of woman to man, the pain of childbirth, and the inevitability of death. Paradisiac nakedness is the point I want to add
to the myth of the future as it still lives among us and acts upon
us.

Our young radicals and New Leftists are the latter-day heirs
of a long line of dreamers about a utopian future whose main
features are fashioned after that old myth of the paradise. Their
golden age of the desired and dreamt-of future is actually nothing but a return to the golden age of the primordial past. Their
rebellion against the Establishment is actually a modern-day
version of acting out the unhappiness people always have felt
and acted out against what they felt were the iniquities of the
social order in which they lived. The Hebrew Rechabites, who
down to the sixth century B.C., abjured working the fields, living

in houses, and drinking wine, were an early example (Jeremiah 35:6). The Jewish Essenes, contemporaries of Jesus, who retired to caves in the Judean desert to form there primitivistic-utopian communities, are another. The New Left and the American Radicals, who dream of and, rather ineffectually, fight for a decent society to replace the present one which they consider as utterly indecent and corrupt, are the latest of this ilk. In all ages, the utopian primitivists expressed their yearning for a paradisiac state, among other things, by wearing rough, outlandish, primitive, and scanty clothing. The jarring extravagances in attire exhibited by the more radical among our contemporary alienated youth are too well known and too apparent to require comment. But let me express one thought: the ostentatious nonchalance about covering those parts of the body which ever since the Fall have been considered as shameful of exposure can be interpreted as yet another manifestation of the yearning for paradise, of the desire to return to the state of man and woman prior to their acquisition of knowledge, of the will to relive the myth of the Edenic naked innocence. The readiness, nay, eagerness, with which many of the radical youngsters of both sexes and in each other's company will discard their clothes seems to me to have these mythic overtones. When, for instance, the great radical youth rally was held in Washington in early May 1970, a number of the participants of both sexes discarded their clothes and took a dip in the reflecting pool at the foot of the Washington Monument,[5] as if impelled to demonstrate, not their political views in protest against the U.S. Government, but their paradisiac sexual nonchalance in front of the huge phallus of Washington.

This predilection for nudity or complete lack of restraint in clothing displayed by the young radicals is the more remarkable inasmuch as it is dangerously close ("dangerously" from the point of view of the young radicals themselves) to another type of nudity that has spread like wildfire in the last decade in the ranks and cohorts of the establishment they despise so much. That other nudity appears in many varieties: the coquettish uncovering of the thighs or of the bosom of women, their topless or see-through dresses or bathing suits, the glimpses of both sexes in complete nakedness on stage or in films, the simulation of sexual intercourse in both media, the proliferation of nudist colonies and establishments, and the like. Of course, the young radicals will argue that these varieties of what could be termed the "establishment nudity" are of a teasing, titillating, provocative kind which is despicable (if they were not so modern and radical they would say "sinful"), while the nudity or exposure they display among themselves is natural, harmless, and an indication of their freedom, of their being liberated (again, if they were not so modern and radical they would say "innocent"). One is sorely tempted to expatiate on the perilous propinquity of the two types of nakedness, the innocent and the sinful one; but, resisting the temptation, let us merely reemphasize the apparently paradisiac-mythical quality of the innocent nudity in which, we believe, we can find yet another manifestation of the persistence of the myth of the future in our modern strife-torn times.

4 • The Myth of the General Strike

Early in the twentieth century, the French social philosopher Georges Sorel (1847–1922) in his *Réflexions sur la violence* (Paris, 1908) argued that modern revolutionary movements (such as Socialism) need an image of the future, a "myth" in Sorel's language, to reassure them as to the final outcome of the struggle they were embarking upon. This revolutionary myth, Sorel observed, invariably envisages the ultimate triumph of the "cause." A product of apocalyptic imagination, the myth of the future triumph proves, according to Sorel, the most potent factor in convincing people of the rightness of the movement and, by imbuing them with a belief in its ultimate victory, in motivating them to action in its service, often despite all sober individual judgment to the contrary.

In adducing examples to show in what way these myths of the future can affect people and motivate them to action, without at the same time disrupting their actual present-day lives, Sorel refers to the early Christian myth of the return of Christ, which was expected to bring about a destruction of the pagan world and the "inauguration of the kingdom of the saints." Whether or not the Utopia postulated in the myth of the future came to pass (actually, of course, it never did) was immaterial; it was its expectation that proved a powerful motivating influence in the lives, not only of the early Christians, but of those who, much later, were caught up in the religious exaltation created by a Luther or a Calvin.

This being the case, says Sorel, it is futile and senseless to ask to what extent these myths of the future can be taken literally. What is important and essential is the myth "as a means of acting on the present." This leads Sorel to an interpretation and evaluation of the "myth of the general strike" as "the *myth* in which Socialism is wholly comprised, *i.e.,* a body of images capable of evoking all the sentiments which correspond to the different manifestations of the war undertaken by Socialism against modern society." [6]

Somewhat later in his book Sorel rephrases the idea and states, in italics: "*The general strike must be taken as a whole and undivided, and the passage from capitalism to Socialism conceived as a catastrophe, the development of which baffles description.*" [7]

Sorel concludes his book on a similarly somber note: "The conception of the general strike, engendered by the practice of violent strikes, admits the conception of an irrevocable overthrow. There is something terrifying in this which will appear more and more terrifying as violence takes a greater place in the mind of the proletariat. . . ." [8] Thus far Sorel.

I on my part would like to add that Sorel's "myth of the general strike" is a neoclassic example of the myth of the future acting on the present, the unattainable brought within reach, the mythical belief that collective violence can bring about Utopia. If this were not a mythical but a realistic idea, a concrete tenet that can be tested by commonplace trial-and-error methods, the uselessness of the general strike as a means of bringing about Utopia would have been proven the first time it was attempted, and, presumably, would have once and for all precluded its recurrence. But since it was (and remains) a mythical image, its effectiveness is not open to rational doubt, and the general strike

is again and again attempted, not because of its tested practical
value, but for the sake of the ritual reenactment of that which
the myth upholds, the immeasurable value of which lies in the
psychological realm.

One strongly feels that the pattern of group violence that is
prevalent in our day to a degree Sorel would never have
dreamed of, can be satisfactorily explained only along these
lines. The epidemic spread of protest, violence, and other group
action, not only in the United States (which spearheads the
world in this development as in many others) but also in many
other parts of our embattled planet, cannot be explained in any
other way. It is not any actual, sudden worsening of the global
situation that has created the present wave of violent protest by
today's youth; it is, rather, the mythical presentiment that by
engaging in a quasi-Sorelian "general strike" they can hasten
the advent of Utopia and thus escape what otherwise they fear
they inevitably would be headed for: industrial or intellectual
slavery, slow suffocation in a polluted atmosphere, or else sudden
atomic annihilation.

To quote Sorel once more, he stated explicitly that by means
of the revolutionary myths which existed in his day "it is possible to understand the activity, the feelings and the ideas of the
masses preparing themselves to enter on a decisive struggle; the
myths are not descriptions of things, but expressions of a determination to act. . . . A myth cannot be refuted, since it is, at
bottom, identical with the convictions of a group, being the expression of these convictions in the language of movement; and
it is, in consequence, unanalysable into parts which could be
placed on the plane of historical descriptions." [9]

At the time of this writing (early 1971) no group of the rebellious youth has as yet formulated with anything approaching
clarity what they are fighting for. They have, on the other hand,
amply, repeatedly, and vociferously stated what they are pro-
testing against. The foregoing analysis, I think, supplies the
answer to this seeming paradox. The youthful militants protest
against the present and demand the future. The protest against
the present has concrete targets: the war, the establishment, the
many unsatisfactory features of our society as presently consti-

tuted, structured, and functioning. Therefore, it is relatively easy to express in concrete terms what they are against. The demand for the future, on the other hand, must needs remain vague. Every statement about it is bound to be utopistic, would instantly expose itself to ridicule. But it is, nevertheless, a powerful demand. It is the demand for the myth of the future, about which very little can be known concretely except that it is something incomparably better than the present.

And this is where the two basic types of our myths of the future meet: the utterly vague, amorphous Utopia which the rebellious youthful segment of society wants to realize in its pathetically groping and inarticulate fashion; and the highly concretized Utopia, with its hypertrophy of machines, gadgets, psychological techniques, and parapsychological know-how that is poured into our homes by science fiction in a printed and televised form. The meeting point is in the mythical future-orientation itself—in the willingness, nay, the demand, of both to abandon the present which, like that Babylonian king of yore, has been weighed in the balances and found wanting, and to push forward toward the future, ruthlessly, if necessary, by trampling with bare feet or with space-boots on the values of the present.

In the mythical view of the future, as we are taught by old Biblical and other ancient Near Eastern eschatologies, details on the one hand are very important and play a dominant role, while on the other they are completely insignificant and therefore are totally neglected; the very mode of thought which sees an essential contrast between concrete minuteness and hazy generality is absent from the mythical perception of the future. What is important is the mythical discernment that the present is constantly waning while the future is not only constantly drawing nearer, but also beckoning more and more forcefully; that the destiny of man, inasmuch as he is unique as the human species and not merely one of many zoological varieties, is to defy the gravity of the present and to stretch his arms toward the always elusive, but eternally attractive, enticing, and inspiring myth of the future.

the myth of the
marxist world

Edmund Wilson has remarked in
his *To the Finland Station* that the Germans "have retained and developed to an amazing degree the genius for
creating myths. The *Ewig-Weibliche* ["Eternally Female"]
of Goethe, the *kategorische Imperativ* ["categorical imperative"] of Kant, the *Weltgeist* ["universal spirit"] with
its *Idee* ["idea"] of Hegel—these have dominated the minds
of the Germans and haunted European thought in general
like great hovering legendary divinities."[1] Wilson then
goes on to say that Karl Marx described the Idea of Hegel
as a "demiurge," and that "this demiurge continued to
walk by his side even after he imagined he had dismissed
it."[2] In particular, it was the Hegelian idea of the dialectic,
of the thesis, antithesis, and synthesis, that haunted Marx,
for whom, according to Wilson, it took the form of a
triad which "was simply the old Trinity, taken over from
the Christian theology, as the Christians had taken it over
from Plato. It was the mythical and magical triangle which

from the time of Pythagoras and before had stood as a symbol for
certainty and power and which probably derived its significance
from its correspondence to the male sexual organs. . . . Certainly
the one-in-three, three-in-one of the *Thesis,* the *Antithesis,* and
the *Synthesis* has had upon Marxists a compelling effect which it
would be impossible to justify through reason." [3]

Leaving aside the question of whether it is justified to interpret the Marxist dialectic as a late outcropping of such a Jungian triad archetype, let us consider for a moment the concrete
content of the original Hegelian form of what Wilson terms
"The Myth of the Dialectic." [4] Hegel's "Dialectic" was a law
which he imagined as "operating . . . in the processes of . . .
the natural world and in those of human history." These processes must pass through a cycle of three phases: (1) the *thesis,*
which is a process of affirmation and unification; (2) the *antithesis,* a "process of splitting off from the *thesis* and negating
it"; and (3) the *synthesis,* which is a new unification, a reconciliation of the *thesis* and the *antithesis.* Since the *synthesis* is
always an advance over the *thesis*—combining as it does the best
features of both the *thesis* and the *antithesis*—each of these historical cycles is a step forward in human history.

What Marx and Engels did was to take this Hegelian principle of interpreting history and project it into the future. In
doing so they created the great Marxian myth, in which reverberations of the ancient Judeo-Christian eschatological myths
of the future are unmistakable.[5] Their *thesis* was the traditional bourgeois society as it existed in their day; the *antithesis*
was the proletariat, split off from the body of modern society
and increasingly negating it. The dividing line between present
and future cuts through the very middle of this Marxian *antithesis.* For while the negation of the main body of society was
a phenomenon whose incipient manifestations were actually
discernible in Marx's time, he includes into his *antithesis* also
the turning of the proletariat against bourgeois society, which,
in his day, was still merely a future eventuality, and, of course,
from his point of view, a desideratum. As for the *synthesis,*
that lies in its entirety in the future. In it apocalypse and
eschatology unite, for Marx reveals what was to happen in the

end of days: the unification of the workers of the world, their global conflict with the owning classes (echoes of the pre-Messianic war of Gog and Magog), and the ultimate taking over of the means of production, including in the first place the ownership and control of the industrial plant, by the working class. As in all true eschatologies, not much thought is wasted on what will happen to members of the defeated side (in this case the owning class), the tacit assumption being that demolition must precede the erection of the new structure. This was part of the original Marxist doctrine, and is still repeated faithfully and without the slightest deviation by the youngest and latest disciples of Marx, who preach what is by now the orthodox Marxian religion of revolutionism on the modern American scene. One of these, David Gelber, a writer for *Liberation Magazine* and a contributor to *The Village Voice,* said in a symposium printed in *The New York Times Magazine* of May 17, 1970 (p. 112): "It is a delusion to think that we can create a decent society without first taking power away from the private industrialists, generals and politicians who set the course of this indecent society." Beyond the theological orthodoxy that comes through in statements such as this, one is struck by its rigid stylistic and terminological orthodoxy.

The concluding part of the Marxist myth, describing the new, ideal social order that was to emerge from the ruins of the old one, was also couched in the same eschatological terminology familiar ever since Biblical times. Both the terms used and the concepts behind them were vague and generalized, which of course only added to their attractiveness in the eyes of all who were dissatisfied with the existing society. Thus it spoke about the emergence of a mankind of higher unity, harmonizing the interests of all (i.e., all those who survive the conflagration), an ultimate, glorious, Messianic synthesis, an ideal society to which each will contribute according to his ability and from which each will receive according to his needs. The vagueness of this generalized picture of societal bliss becomes even more apparent if one recognizes its similarity to the idealized picture of the future development of the "noosphere" postulated by Teilhard de Chardin; to the surprise of everybody except the mythologist who recognizes in both the influence of the ancient myth of the paradisiac future, the utopias projected by Marx, the radical revolutionary, and by Teilhard, the deeply religious Catholic thinker, are so similar as to be almost interchangeable in their main features.

Teilhard de Chardin's myth of the future "noosphere" was dealt with elsewhere in this book (see Chapter 2, section 5); here let us only add one more comment on the Marxist variety of this futuristic imagery. In the century that has passed since Marx created his vision of the future practically no concrete detail has been added to that vision. The same mythical paradisiac vagueness that characterized the thinking of Marx himself on this point still envelops Marxist cerebrations today. For instance, in reply to the question, "With what would the left replace the present system?" David Gelber, in his aforementioned statement, could not come up with a more concrete answer than "In a revolution worthy of the name (such as the Vietnamese), radically advanced social institutions and human relationships develop in the course of the revolutionary struggle itself." This is Marxian amorphism on its most conservative level: nothing can and nothing should be said about the shape of things to come, except that they will be better—a statement to which nobody can take exception, but which removes the concept from political or dialectic thought and places it taxonomically into that category of myths which deal with the paradisiac future.

In painting his indeterminate picture of the future proletarian synthesis, Marx himself, as I have already indicated, walked in the footsteps of the Hebrew prophets and the late Jewish and early Christian eschatologists. That he did so was recognized by Mircea Eliade who described Marx's dependence on the Judeo-Christian eschatological myth in two different contexts in an almost identical paragraph. In the more recent of the two formulations Eliade writes:

> Marx takes over and continues one of the great
> eschatological myths of the Asian Mediterranean world
> —the redeeming role of the Just (the "chosen," the
> "anointed," the "innocent"; in our day, the proletariat),

whose sufferings are destined to change the ontological status of the world. In fact, Marx's classless society and the consequent disappearance of historical tensions find their closest precedent in the myth of the Golden Age that many traditions put at the beginning and the end of history. Marx enriched this venerable myth by a whole Judaeo-Christian messianic ideology: on the one hand, the prophetic role and soteriological function that he attributes to the proletariat; on the other, the final battle between Good and Evil, which is easily comparable to the apocalyptic battle between Christ and Antichrist, followed by the total victory of the former.[6]

Eliade is unquestionably correct in discerning apocalyptic features in the Marxian myth of the future. I would add that Marx ingeniously combined Hegelian dialectic with Judeo-Christian Messianism in teaching the inevitability of a clash between the proletariat and bourgeois society and of the victory of the former. Such combinations of tenets from two worlds carry in them the seed of global potentialities, due perhaps to their hybrid vigor, as was exemplified centuries before Marx by the spread of that combination of Jewish with Greco-Roman ideas known as Christianity.

In addition to the general Marxian myth of the future, the Marxist world supplies a most telling example of the irrepressible need, persisting even in our own modern times in the most diverse types of human aggregates, to have myths of their own. The example I have in mind is the overwhelming proliferation of the Lenin myth and its utilization far beyond the saturation point in connection with the mammoth and marathon celebrations in Soviet Russia in 1970 of Lenin's centennial. The mythical dimension of the Russian Lenin celebrations did not escape Western observers. In writing about them, a *Time* essay chose the title "Lenin: Communism's Charter Myth."[7] Neal Ascherson, reviewing several books on Russia in *The New York Review*, while not using the term "myth," likens Lenin to Muhammad, Moscow to the Caliphate, China to the Muslim Brotherhood, the Western world to the pagan realm, and terms the observances themselves "Leninolatry."[8]

Lenin had been a mythical ancestor figure for Communist Russia ever since his death in 1924. In strict accordance with the general, global function of myth in every place and every time, Lenin's writing and sayings had supplied the mythical charter that justified, validated, and explained the social situation in which the Soviets found themselves. Following his death, the ritualistic denial of his passing in the form of the oft-repeated incantation "Lenin lives!" had become a part of Soviet religion, paralleling to a remarkable degree the Christian denial of the death of Jesus, "Jesus liveth!" In both cases the stubborn repetition of the denial of the historical or, if you will, biological, fact of the death of the founder is much more than a mere symbolic utilization of a possibility inherent in language—namely, the use of the verb "lives" in a figurative sense, by way of a shorthand sign that, fully explained, means, "he lives through his ideas in which we still believe and through his teachings which we still follow." All ancestor figures live on in this feeble manner, including the grandfather whose heirs must fulfil certain conditions stipulated in his will in order to have the continued enjoyment or usufruct of his estate. No, the founder of a faith lives in a sense that is much more essential, much more vital, than this pale and bloodless one. He lives—we may not know how and where, but he lives, he is here with us, he exercises his will on us, continues to take an active interest in our doings, punishes us if we sin and rewards us if we do what he preached was right. And, most importantly, he can and will stand by us when we need his help, as quite frequently we do in the midst of life's unforeseen exigencies. That Jesus lives in this sense for the believing Christian is too well known to need any elaboration. That Lenin lives in the same sense was powerfully brought home to us during the 100th anniversary celebrations of his birth.

The power of the Lenin myth becomes especially apparent when one considers two factors: one, that his actual "ministry" in Russia was of extremely short duration. He actually assumed power in October 1917, and less than six years later a stroke effectively removed him from leadership. The short duration of his ministry resembles those of many other heroes who became myths after their deaths: Alexander, Jesus, Che Guevara, John F. Kennedy. Secondly, Lenin (apart from his great forerunner Marx, who, however, was never part of *Soviet* history) was the only Soviet leader who was neither denigrated after his death (as Stalin was), nor declared a traitor (like Trotsky), nor ousted from power and relegated to obscurity (like Malenkov and Khrushchev), nor liquidated (as many other Soviet leaders were). On the contrary, as is the case with many true mythical heroes, the more time passed after his death the greater he became, the more sacrosanct his teachings, the more "divine" his image.

As the unsigned *Time* essay referred to above (and written, undoubtedly, with the cooperation of at least one competent social scientist) put it: "[The Soviet leaders] will invoke [Lenin's] name to legitimize their rule, and adroitly select from his speeches and writings to justify the existing social order. . . . The Soviet system has demanded terrible sacrifices of its people that had to be justified in the name of Lenin's ideals. . . . The Lenin myth portrays him as the master theoretician of Communist revolutions."

Again, as is the case with many other mythological figures, Lenin too is called upon to supply the justification (or, to use a more technical anthropological term, the validation) of various disparate Communistic postures and schools. Each government in Moscow, Peking, and Belgrade, each Communist party hierarchy in Rome, Paris, and elsewhere, has its own particular Lenin to invoke and is ready to fight as heresies all other interpretations of Lenin—just as two neighboring Mexican villages will fight about whose *Virgen* is more powerful (i.e., more authentic). In this tussle the fact that there was only one person called Lenin is completely lost to sight; whatever that man called Lenin was, he is long forgotten because the Lenin who "lives" is not the memory of a flesh and blood human with his strengths and failings, his loves and hates, his necessarily and humanly limited ideas, concepts, doctrines, and beliefs, but the superhuman, mythical, deified image of the demiurge.

In scanning the long list of men and the much shorter one of women who, after their deaths, became myths and as such continued to live, one finds that in many cases the individuals in question were relatively unknown while alive, or, even if known to a smaller or larger circle of friends, disciples, followers, or adherents, did not receive more than a small share of admiration. Only after their deaths did the floodgates burst open, releasing a torrent of adulation that swept away the memory of these persons as they really were, and piled up instead a huge logjam of mythical lumber. Lenin certainly was an example of such a transformation of concrete memories into a mythical image, as were Alexander, Jesus, Che Guevara, and John F. Kennedy, whose names were mentioned a little earlier as mythical heroes with real-life ministries of very short duration.

There are, on the other hand, men who receive during their lifetime a godlike admiration, adulation, and adoration, only to be proven false deities upon their deaths and to be ignominiously ejected from their self-built Olympus or Valhalla by the very people whom they induced to enthrone them there in the first place. Throughout history one can find examples of this reverse development, of such a demythologizing upon death. In modern times, Stalin, Mussolini, and Hitler come to mind.

Of the three, Stalin was undoubtedly the best example of the process we have in mind. While he was alive and in power, he received an amount of adulation that was unparalleled in history. Not only was he the great leader, the savior of Russia and (potentially) of the entire world, but also the greatest theoretician of communism. More than that, he was the universal genius who, in his boundless wisdom, instructed engineers how to solve technical problems, told economists how to organize production, marketing, and consumption, taught biologists and geneticists the right approach to both theories and experiments, advised anthropologists and sociologists on issues of culture and society, and laid down the rules that writers, painters, sculptors, and composers not only had to, but were happy and eager to follow. Julian Huxley, in his book on Soviet genetics, collected an impressive array of samples illustrating the almost incredible adulation the live Stalin (and, to a lesser extent, the dead Lenin) received from Soviet scientists. The famous Russian geneticist, T. D. Lysenko, for instance, said at a conference on genetics, science, and selection held in Moscow in 1939, that "Progressive biological science owes it to the geniuses of mankind, Lenin and Stalin, that the teaching of I. V. Michurin has been added to the treasure house of our knowledge. . . . Glory to the great friend and protagonist of science, our leader and teacher, Comrade Stalin!" [9]

The prominent Russian historian Nikolai Leonidovich Rubinstein, in a confession of his shortcomings, stated that "his main fault was that he presented the historical theories of Lenin and Stalin as the outcome of previously existing progressive historical thought instead of interpreting them as the foundation of an entirely new revolutionary science of history." [10] In the field of law, Andrei Vishinsky's *The Law of the Soviet State* is not only a legal compendium, but also a revolutionary handbook and, as the reviewer in the *New Republic* of February 7, 1949, put it, a "hagiography" glorifying Marx, Engels, Lenin, and Stalin.[11] In 1948 the authoritative Soviet publication *Questions of Economics* contained in its seventh issue an article by Innokentii Yul'evich Pisarev which included the following statements: "Created by Lenin and Stalin, Soviet statistics mark a radical break in the tradition of scientific methodology, in the organization, practice, content, aims and tasks of statistics. . . . Lenin and Stalin solved the basic nodal problems of the science of statistics." [12]

Similar quotations could be culled from other disciplines as well, but the foregoing are sufficient to show that, during his lifetime, Stalin was a "legend." But after his death, instead of becoming a myth as one might have expected, and as his heirs in the state and party leadership could have easily and comfortably engineered without taking any risk, his image was subjected to the greatest debunking ever carried out in Soviet history. Stalin now became the embodiment of evil, but even as an anti-hero he was not allowed to assume mythical dimensions. He was demoted to a petty tyrant about whom the less said the better.

Other twentieth-century dictators shared a fate that closely paralleled that of Stalin. While in power, both Mussolini and Hitler were surrounded with an adulation that, in every respect, was the Fascist and Nazi counterpart of the Communist Stalin-worship. And like Stalin, after their fall and death (which were almost simultaneous for both of them), only the evil that they had done lived after them. Yet their cases are not as instructive as that of Stalin because both Mussolini and Hitler left behind defeated countries that were overrun by the enemy, and their rule was followed by regimes whose philosophies detested the totalitarian order and structure they had erected. It was therefore inevitable that these two "legends in their lifetime" should, upon their deaths, become, not myths but the incarnation of evil. Not so in the case of Stalin, who died some years after Russia had emerged victorious from the greatest conflict it had ever been engaged in, who led his country a long way toward economic reconstruction, and who achieved for the Soviet state a power position in the world that was second only to that of the United States. However great the tyranny of Stalin, however oppressive his egomaniac demands, he had, in the Russian historical context, the makings of a mythical hero. It is tempting to speculate whether this potential would have been realized after his death had he not insisted on excessive adulation during his lifetime.

the nazi myth

Whatever the origins of a myth, whether its roots go back to dim antiquity or its rise is due to fabrication by a single individual in our own day, the power that it can attain over the feeling, thinking, and acting of large groups of men is nothing short of frightening. Perhaps the best example to illustrate this general observation is the Nazi myth of Hitler's Third Reich.

The most significant contributor to, and shaper of, the Nazi myth was undoubtedly Alfred Rosenberg (1893–1946). However, this notorious mythopoet of German racial superiority was noted more for erudition than for originality, and, in fact, he based himself on several forerunners whose ideas he adopted and further developed. Among these proto-Nazi thinkers the most influential was Houston Stewart Chamberlain (1855–1927), a renegade Englishman, who came under the influence of Richard Wagner's racial ideas (which Wagner himself had derived from Gobineau), and who, at the age of 53, married Wagner's daughter Eva.

Chamberlain's book *The Foundations of the Nineteenth Century* (published in 1899) is a ponderous, uncritical, and misconstrued disquisition on German racism, Nordic superiority, anti-Semitism, and anti-Catholicism. The title of Rosenberg's book, *The Myth of the Twentieth Century: An Evaluation of the Mental-Spiritual Formational Conflicts of Our Time*, first published in 1930, echoes that of his spiritual mentor's. The term "myth" appearing in the title is not used by Rosenberg in the journalistic sense of "untruth," but in a sense with which anthropologists could not disagree: something that has an inner truth, that is true in a profound way.[1]

As to its contents, *The Myth of the Twentieth Century* (the third edition of 1932, which I consulted, comprises 696 pages) is an impassioned and turgid presentation of one basic idea: it is the destiny of the Nordic race, superior in every respect to all other races of man, to rally to mortal combat in behalf of Nordic ideals. In support of this central thesis Rosenberg marshals, and distorts in the process, a rich assortment of data and a profusion of references to world history, religion, culture, philosophy, biology, and anthropology. On his pages we meet the ideal great "Aryan" race which created the cultures of the ancient world and whose finest exponents and present-day heirs are the Germanic, Nordic peoples, with the modern-day Germans as their ultimate culmination. It is this unique great, tall, blond, and blue-eyed race that is responsible for all that is noble and heroic in the history of man; its antagonists are the inferior, racially impure non-Nordic peoples. To indicate the lengths to which Rosenberg was ready to go in crediting the "Aryan" race with everything fine and noble in the world, let me refer to one single example: blue-eyed Athene and golden-haired Apollo are regarded by Rosenberg as creations of the splendid Nordic racial soul. "The golden-haired Apollo," he writes, "is the keeper and protector of everything noble and joyous. . . . Consecrated to the god is the swan which originates from the north. . . . Apollo is thus the name of the first great victory of Nordic Europe. Next to Apollo stands Pallas Athene . . . the blue-eyed daughter of the Thunderer [Zeus]. . . ."[2]

This glorious Nordic spirit has throughout history been

locked in a perennial struggle with the corrupting influence of inferior races, of whom the basest and vilest is that of the Jews. While Rosenberg reserves his most venomous barbs for the Jews, the violence of his anti-Semitism and his anti-Catholicism spills over into anti-Protestantism. He attacks the Protestant churches for retaining too many Jewish and Catholic influences. He attacks Communism as well as democracy and high finance as devices of world Jewry. His book "claims to espouse an ethics of honor, loyalty, courage and inner truthfulness, but interprets these terms in a peculiar Teutonic sense. It foreshadows a religion which shall combine the values of the Persian Zoroaster's God of Light, the heroic life of a Nordic Christ, and Meister Eckhardt's God-in-the-breast. It sketches policies for the biological and spiritual regeneration of Germany and the expansion of German power. The myth of the twentieth century is Nordic man's intuition of his own character and destiny, the cult of race and honor, to be given effective religious form by some spiritual leader yet to arise." [3]

A word must be said of Rosenberg's conception of a heroic Nordic Christ because it exemplifies superbly the power mythical thinking wields over historical fact. The same Christ whom the Black Christians consider as having taken on blackness in order to share fully the black man's oppression (see Chapter 13, section 2) becomes in Rosenberg's *Mythus* a heroic, Nordic "ruling Christ," whose image he finds represented in the work of the sixteenth-century German painter Matthias Grünewald: "An old-new theme has thus emerged: Jesus the hero." He quotes the martial utterances of Jesus: " 'I come not to send peace, but a sword' [Matthew 10:34]; and 'I am come to send fire on the earth, and I wish it be already kindled' [Luke 12:49; this is my translation of how Rosenberg translates the verse into German] said the rebel of Nazareth." Returning to the subject of Christ toward the end of his book, Rosenberg asserts that the personality of Jesus "was throughout sustained by an inner fire. . . . Jesus appears to us today as a self-confident lord, in the best and highest sense of the word. It is his *life* that is meaningful for Germanic men, and not his agonizing death to which he owes his success among Alpine and Mediterranean peoples. The

form-giving ideal that shines forth to us today from the Gospels
is the forceful preacher, the man of wrath in the Temple, the
enthraller whom everybody followed, not the sacrificial lamb
of Jewish prophecy, not the crucified one." According to Rosenberg, "the entire existence of Jesus was a fiery rebellion. For this
he had to die." It is "this fire-spirit, this hero in the highest
sense" whom the German Church will gradually substitute for
the image of the crucified Christ.[4]

As one would expect, Rosenberg makes of this fiery, imperious Christ a scion of the Nordic race. In a sweeping statement
which is more mythology than history, he asserts that "the
Amorites founded Jerusalem, they constituted the Nordic
stratum in the later Galilee, i.e., 'the district of the gentiles,'
out of which Jesus was to stem." Almost all the European
painters, he says, "have already divested the face and figure of
Jesus of all Jewish racial characteristics. However much the
lamb-of-God doctrines compelled them to paint their Savior
distorted, Jesus is shown by all great painters of the Nordic
West slender, tall, blond, with a steep forehead and a narrow
head. . . ."[5]

The very idea of race, so central in Nazi thinking, is for Rosenberg a mystico-mythical concept. A race, he says, does not live
by logic but by developing a "mystic synthesis." "The ultimate
insight possible to a race is already implicit in its first religious
myth." The racial soul reveals itself in the type of beauty glori-
fied by its art. Race is the external expression of a collective
soul. After describing the Aryan race as blond, blue-eyed, tall,
and longheaded, Rosenberg asserts that some 80 percent of the
future German nobility will approximate this physical type.
However, he is more eloquent and detailed when talking about
the inner traits, the soul, of the Nordic Aryan: he is characterized by a sense of honor, courage, love of freedom, capacity to
build states, mysticism, an interest in personality and history, a
recognition of inner and outer law, a rejection of miracles, and
a spirit of exploration, invention, and scientific research.[6]

More relevant to our present interest than the concrete details of Rosenberg's Nazi myth is the effect and influence that

myth had on the Third Reich. Hitler came to power in Germany three years after the publication of Rosenberg's *Mythus*, which thereupon rapidly achieved a position of highest authority in official German thinking. In 1935 "adverse criticism of Rosenberg's *Mythus*, even in private teaching, became a punishable offense." The book was especially well suited "to win the minds and stir the hearts of young students who revere learning without being sufficiently well informed to detect Rosenberg's errors, and who are full of vague aspirations, although dissatisfied with conventional religion." [7]

By 1942 the official leadership of the Reich seriously considered adopting a thirty-point program for the complete Germanization of all churches in the Reich. This program was prepared by Rosenberg, and in it he went even further than the drastic proposals for dealing with religion he had incorporated into his *Mythus*. A basic point in his program was the establishment of a National Reich Church and the destruction of Christianity. The Bible will be banned, and Hitler's *Mein Kampf* declared its only replacement. The cross will be eliminated and replaced by the swastika. [8]

These are merely a few manifestations of the effect Rosenberg's *Mythus* had on Nazi Germany. The book was reprinted many times, and within five years of its first appearance (1930–35) it was distributed in more than 300,000 copies. By order of the Reich's Minister of Education, it was placed in the libraries of all schools above the elementary level. It became almost as important in the Third Reich as Hitler's *Mein Kampf*. [9]

Soon after the rise of Nazism in Germany, numerous books, pamphlets, articles, lectures, and addresses were written and delivered on Rosenberg's book and its author. With very few exceptions, all of them were highly complimentary. Rosenberg was presented as a Nordic genius, second in significance only to the Führer himself. Learned spokesmen of the Christian churches in Germany hastened to add their voices to the accolades. A typical representative of the latter was Friedrich Andersen, Evangelical chief pastor in Glücksburg. In a 62-page booklet, reproducing six lectures the pastor gave to different audiences, he defends Rosenberg against Catholic and Protestant attacks. What he himself has to say about Rosenberg's *Mythus* verges on adulation.[10]

In 1943 the collected writings and speeches of Rosenberg were published in München, and the adulation-filled introduction to them, written by Alfred Baeumler, was published as a separate book. By this time, just before the final *Götterdämmerung* of Nazi Germany, something of the mythical attached to Rosenberg himself; in the concluding sentence of Baeumler's book-length introduction, Rosenberg is compared to Hitler: "The unification of tradition and revolution, which characterizes the work of the Führer, is also the decisive trait of his [Rosenberg's] intellectual work." [11]

In the early months of the Nazi rule in Germany, as indicated above, some circles still dared to voice criticism of Rosenberg's *Mythus*. Among these voices was that of the Roman Catholic diocese of Berlin, which in October 1934 published a 120-page book as an official supplement to the diocesan *Amtsblatt* (official journal). The book, entitled *Studien zum Mythus des XX. Jahrhunderts*, is anonymous, but the signature Nicolaus, Bishop of Berlin, appears under a brief prefatory note. The slender volume contains a detailed and dispassionate refutation of Rosenberg's argument about the Christian Church, the conversion of the Germans, the Old and New Testaments, and the personality of Jesus. His diatribes against Jews and Judaism are passed over in silence, although on p. 65 the authors criticize Rosenberg's treatment of the Old Testament as a "Jewish concoction (*Machwerk*)." The section dealing with the Old Testament comprises sixteen pages, at the conclusion of which the authors admit: "It would mean asking the impossible of the Old Testament if one would seek in it the high level of Christian morality, the belief expressed with the clarity of the New Testament. The Old Testament is only a *step* of the divine revelation. . . ." [12]

If such was the reaction of the central Catholic diocese in Germany to Rosenberg's *Mythus,* we feel a certain trepidation when we ask, To what extent did the German people as a whole make Rosenberg's myth its own? The question is not easy to answer. But to judge from the official adoption by the Nazi party (which in Hitler's Germany was the state) of an ideology that almost in its entirety probably was derived from Rosenberg, and certainly was largely identical with his myth, the latter's influence must have been enormous. The manner in which the Nazis translated the myth into action, including the carnage they let loose on mankind in general and on the Jews in particular, is part of history, the most horrible chapter contained in the history of man. After the defeat of Nazi Germany, the International Tribunal found Rosenberg guilty of instigating racial hatred, and sentenced him to death. On October 16, 1946, he was hanged together with nine other Nazi leaders who likewise had received death sentences.

7

the case of che, or:
he must first die

The speed with which a myth can develop, provided the hero on whom it centers dies at an opportune moment and under favorable circumstances, is nothing short of astounding. This observation can be illustrated with many examples. Let us take one which, at the same time, will show the wide prevalence of the notion that the physical death of the hero is an indispensable prerequisite for the development of his myth. This idea has been expressed in at least three biographies, all published in 1969, of Ernesto ("Che") Guevara, the Argentine-born Cuban revolutionary whose last exploit was the attempt to organize an uprising in Bolivia, and who was caught and killed in the fall of 1967.

The fullest of the three biographies was written by Daniel James, who also edited *The Complete Bolivian Diaries of Ché Guevara and Other Captured Documents.* The first chapter of James' Guevara biography, entitled "Death of a Revolutionary, Birth of a Myth," describes how, despite all the proofs supplied by the Bolivian authorities, there remained a stubborn belief in the hearts of many that Che was alive, and how, as soon as the news of his death reached Cuba, the Castro government embarked on an almost orgiastic campaign to immortalize the *"guerrillero heróico."* In an extravagant panegyric, Castro "installed Ché in the pantheon of Communist immortals alongside Marx and Lenin, and proclaimed him the 'new man' [a truly mythological figure of speech] of the future which youth should henceforth emulate." In Argentina, Che's native land, the Accion Revolucionaria Peronista "solemnly proclaimed that 'never has the cause of human liberation paid a higher price: the immolation of the Christ of our era.'" To others in many parts of the world Che was the new El Cid, the "Latin American Ulysses who tirelessly seeks [note the present tense] his Ithaca," the "rebel Christ crucified," and the like. Only the Communist countries showed remarkable restraint in reporting Guevara's demise. Thus, characteristically, while the New Left in the Western world resounded with the cry "Che Lives" as soon as his body was lowered into his grave, manifesting thereby their need to immortalize him, to construct his myth, "the Communist world whose ideology he so loyally and fervently served until the end . . . virtually ignored him." [1]

The other two books on Che which I consulted contain very similar phraseology. Louis J. González and Gustavo A. Sánchez Salazar conclude their account of Che's death as follows: "Ernesto 'Che' Guevara was no more; he had passed from legend into myth." Elsewhere they say: "Guevara was a combination of warrior and apostle, adventurer and prophet." And again: "[In Valle Grande, where Guevara died] a kind of legend has already grown up around the miracles of 'Saint Che,' whose portrait can frequently be found in peasant huts in the midst of Catholic images. . . ." [2] The third book, by Martin Ebon, contains a similar evaluation of Che: ". . . there are many who feel that his heritage will inspire new revolutionary attempts, in 'the spirit of Che.' The legend of Che may prove stronger than his human and historical reality. The death of a hero, idealistic and romantic, is a powerful symbolic image." [3]

In a similar vein Geoffrey Godsell, writing in the *Christian Science Monitor,* observed: "The patron saint of the revolutionary student movement in Western Europe and the Americas is Che Guevara."[4] Two weeks later (July 9) an editorial in the same paper stated: "His halo comes from his desperate, almost foredoomed, romantic revolutionary challenge to a seemingly hardened status quo. . . ."

After giving his account of Che's death, James speculates: "If Che had survived Bolivia, if he had managed . . . to escape to Cuba, would there be a cult around him today? Could his admirers have succeeded under those circumstances in creating the myth? Not likely. Physically alive, Ché would have been spiritually and morally dead. . . . Ché 'lives,' then, because he is dead."[5]

In the last chapter of his book James raises the question: What do the radical students and the New Left "see or seek in Ché? What is the source of his hold over [this youthful minority]? Why do they worship one who was, after all, a nearly perfect failure?" The answer he comes up with is that "Ché's youthful admirers insist that what is important is not a battle won or lost but the way he lived and, above all, the way he died. To them, Ché towers above nearly every figure of the age because, amid all the dishonesty and deceit and corruption that typifies it, he remained unsullied. . . . Physically, he showed courage to the point of recklessness, as Fidel [Castro] has stated, and in the end sacrificed himself without a qualm, in furtherance of his ideals."[6]

James is undoubtedly correct in his analysis of the motivations that prompt radical students and the New Left to latch onto Che Guevara rather than some other mythical idol. But his answer is not complete. There are additional factors, or, rather, there were additional features in Che's revolutionary life and death that made him irresistible for young people who have adopted a radical, alienated, revolutionary stance. One of these features is contained in the very circumstance that he died relatively young: he had just turned thirty-nine when he was killed. Since young people today can fully identify only with a youthful leader, and since death is the prerequisite for a hero to become a myth, it follows that the mythical hero idolized by the young must be one who died in his youth. One can imagine that had Che been able to hold out in the Bolivian jungle for another, say, ten years, and had he been killed then, the death of the veteran, aging revolutionary could not have had the same impact.

Another factor that made for Che's becoming the mythical idol of the young radicals in the late 1960s was the very hopelessness of the situation which he chose as his last stand; the overwhelming odds he elected to face; and his refusal to make good his escape while there still was a chance, despite the fact that he knew that by remaining he and his cause could gain nothing except a mythical hero at the cost of his life. The young radicals are motivated to idolize Che by a readiness, actually eagerness, to identify with the underdog, with the little fellow who stands up to the big bully. (We shall meet the same motivation again in an even more pronounced form when we come to discuss the phenomenal popularity of Mickey Mouse among the young and the old alike, in America as well as in other countries.[7])

Thirdly, and perhaps most importantly, the ineffectuality of Che, whose Bolivian venture was, in reality, nothing more than a *beau geste* for which he threw away his life, strikes a responsive chord in young radicals facing the "Establishment" as represented in their eyes by universities, political parties, branches and agencies of the government, and "the military-industrial complex." The young radicals, who in all probability feel like Mickey Mouse making a stand against the Cat, are, in fact, much less effectual than that mythical hero in their attacks against the various embodiments of the "System."

The young activists themselves are fully aware of the ineffectuality and futility of the motions they have been going through for several years. Thus a student at Coe College in Cedar Rapids, Iowa, who participated in a nonviolent peace demonstration in that city, said: ". . . these demonstrations are really rather futile, aren't they? Being nonviolent has no effect on anything— but I don't know what else to do. Really, I don't." [8] As Bruno Bettelheim puts it: "Like Ché Guevara they [the rebellious youth] choose a quixotic battlefield and certain defeat. . . ." [9]

The ineffectuality of the young "revolutionaries" has been commented upon by John W. Aldridge in his excellent detailed article, "In the Country of the Young," in which he argues that hippyism allows the mediocre "to believe that their ineffectuality is in fact a serious metaphysical position and connected in some portentous way with the power of positive feeling, courageous individualism and the mystical wisdom of the East." [10]

In some anti-war and anti-establishment activists the frustration over their own ineffectiveness creates not resignation but rage, and the rage ultimately leads to violence. But even violence cannot dissipate the sense of futility. As a *Newsweek* report on "The Revolutionaries" pointed out, the young radicals smolder with "an inchoate rage that one can't help suspecting is the tinder for most of [their] violence—a frustrated fury at knowing that war and racism and profiteering persist, that the movement has tried so hard—and society has bent so little in response. . . . For the Movement has tasted almost every defeat except the ultimate one—to disappear." [11] A week later *Time* commented on "the frustrations of the peace movement." [12]

What the young radicals have accomplished thus far has been little more than a few brave gestures of defiance which become meaningful and important only if they can be viewed as part of a larger mythical species, of which the most recently produced and rapidly popularized archetype is Che Guevara. Looking at the picture of Che blown up to poster size, the young radicals can and do say to themselves: Here is a man who wanted a lot and accomplished nothing, sacrificing his life in the process; and he became a great hero, a myth. What we are doing and planning to do is an imitation of Che; even if we, too, accomplish nothing, we will become, like he, great mythical heroes. Let that be our reward, if nothing else.

But the mythical image of Che is not the ultimate archetype that moves and motivates the radical youth of today. Whether or not Che himself was motivated, during his last stand in Bolivia, by older mythical prototypes, we cannot know. But we do know that the ineffectual hero who sacrifices his life, or his virility, or something else that the average man would hold most dear, and who, in doing so accomplishes nothing, is a mythical prototype that has haunted humanity since antiquity and has in all ages managed to motivate a smaller or larger number of people to follow him, to emulate him, and to identify with him. In Chapter 19 we shall refer to the priests of Attis in ancient Rome who emasculated themselves; the Skoptsi in nineteenth-century Russia who did the same and topped it by cutting off the breasts of their women; the followers of the American actor James Dean in the 1950s who committed suicide; and the "moles" in the Japan of 1970 who cut off their little fingers to identify with Al Capone. Although so far the devotees of Che Guevara have not engaged in any such planned, voluntary, and concrete acts of self-mutilation or self-destruction, the general tenor of their behavior pattern definitely places them in a closely related category. The drive to self-destruction, more-over, can remain on the subconscious level: the all-too-frequent accidents, such as the explosions of home-made bombs in base-ments and cars claiming the lives of their inexperienced but zestful revolutionary manufacturers, are, to say the least, open to this type of psychological interpretation.

Before concluding this brief chapter about the case of Che Guevara, who would never have become a myth had he not died an early and violent death (before he was able to chalk up an impressive list of accomplishments), let us append some ob-servations on the role of death in general in the transformation of a man into a myth. To begin with, despite the well-known phrase about the great man who "became a legend in his life-time," there is no such thing as a true mythical figure who is alive. A live person may achieve all kinds of distinctions: he may become a hero, a potentate, a great teacher, a "guru," a captain of industry, an object of adulation or even adoration, and much more, but he cannot become a myth. For that, he must first die.[13] There are many reasons for this. One of them is that an integral part of the myth is the denial of the death of its hero, and the declaration, in the face of all evidence to the contrary, that he is alive. While the great leader is alive and physically present among his followers, such a denial of his death and af-firmation of his being alive would make no sense, would, in fact, be a redundancy, and would even smack of either irony or heresy. The cry "He is alive!" or "He lives again!" can be raised only after the hero's death, and if it is, it signifies the birth of his myth.

In fact, adulation received in life can militate against the hero's becoming a true mythical figure upon his death. On the other hand, relative obscurity in life, activity (or "ministry") in the midst of only a few faithful disciples, can be sufficient to serve as the foundation of the myth once death has removed the hero from the circle of his devotees. Jesus of Nazareth, while he lived, was a relatively obscure figure, the teacher and master of a small group of disciples; practically no reference to him is found in contemporary sources. Yet within a few years after his death he became one of the greatest mythical figures ever produced by mankind. Muhammad, Marx, and Lenin were known during their lifetimes to relatively small circles of followers; after their deaths they became figures of world importance. Cases in point are supplied by many Catholic saints whose myths had to be "constructed"—that is, established—after their deaths, in order to be canonized, and who in their lifetimes were known to only a small group of people. Similarly, the Muslim and Jewish saints in the Middle East were, as a rule, little known while they were alive; their fame spread, their cults were introduced, and their myths established only after their deaths.

If the death of the hero comes at a young age, his chances of becoming a myth are enhanced; if he dies a violent death, if his death is surrounded by unusual circumstances, or if he appears to have sought or accepted death in devotion to or pursuance of an ideal, the likelihood of his transformation into a myth becomes considerable. If, in retrospect, his life can be construed as having had a pervasive central theme which appeals to the survivors, his myth is assured. It would not be at all difficult to show that most of these features were present in the case of those men who in our own day and age have become myths. Che Guevara was one of them; others included John F. Kennedy, Malcolm X, Martin Luther King, Jr., James Dean, to name only a very few of the best known and most ardently admired, each by his own group of followers, disciples, or devotees.

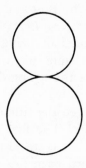

marion delgado, or:
the myth of the
child terrorist

Groups of likeminded people feel
the need not only to personify their adversaries, thereby
giving birth to such symbolic mythological figures as Jerry
and Whitey (see below, Chapter 18), but also to project
their own collective image into a mythical personification.
As an example of such mythical projection of a group's
self-image onto an ordinary individual, and the creation,
in the process, of a mythical hero, we can refer to "Marion
Delgado." Marion Delgado is a mythical five-year-old child
revolutionary, invented by the Weatherman faction of the
Students for a Democratic Society. The August 29, 1969,
issue of the *SDS New Left Notes* (vol. 4, no. 29; published
in Chicago) showed on its first page a full-page photograph
of the mythical boy revolutionary holding a concrete slab
on top of a railroad track. Over the picture was the large-
type caption "Bring the War Home!" and under it the
legend "With a defiant smile . . . Marion Delgado shows
how he placed a 25 pound concrete slab on tracks and
wrecked a passenger train."[1]

121

About two months prior to the appearance of this picture, at its June 1969 convention, the SDS had split into two. One group, which was also referred to as the Revolutionary Youth Movement (RYM), continued to maintain its headquarters in Chicago; the other had its center in Boston. The Boston group, in the September 20, 1969, issue of its own *SDS New Left Notes*, excoriated the Chicago group, whom it accused of being "an enemy of the people," and reprinted the same picture of Marion Delgado, which it held up as proof of the wrong direction taken by the Chicago RYM.

In November 1969 the Chicago group changed the title of its publication from *SDS New Left Notes* to *Fire!* The first issue of *Fire!* was published on November 7. Its editor is stated to be none other than Marion Delgado. On the third page this issue reproduces a Dürer-like etching of a sixteenth- or seventeenth-century battle scene, with this caption: "The above photograph was taken at the SDS National Action last month in Chicago. The figure at the left, drinking from the wine skin, is youth culture freak Marion DelGado. LIVE LIKE HIM!"

The second issue of *Fire!* (dated November 21, 1969) opens with a front-page article entitled "sds n.c. Dec. 26–31" and signed "Marion Delgado." It is written in the first person singular and begins with the statement that the leaders of the SDS movement had wanted him, Marion Delgado, to explain the decisions he had made recently while in hiding, and "asked me to write this article. (Actually I can't write, but I've gotten my three-year-old sister Elysia Delgado . . . to put my thoughts on paper. . . .) Due to my small size (I hardly exist at all), I was able to move freely around Washington November 14– 15 without being seen by the pigs. . . ." Then "Marion Delgado" goes on to explain at length why he thinks violent tactics are necessary to assure the success of the revolution.

Because of the difficulty of obtaining complete files of the underground revolutionary papers, I was unable to follow step by step Marion Delgado's mythical progress. But two items can be added to those mentioned already. On March 17, 1970, a Federal warrant was issued at Chicago charging Bernardine Dohrn with unlawful interstate flight to avoid prosecution for mob action, and on April 2 a second warrant charged her with violation of Federal Antiriot Laws and conspiracy. Bernardine Dohrn was inter-organizational secretary of the SDS and then became a member of the Weather Bureau, the elite corps of the Weathermen. According to an FBI handbill issued on April 24, 1970, and distributed in an effort to catch her, one of the aliases she used was "Marion DelGado." [2] The other item is that in the summer of 1970 the group of revolutionaries who claimed credit for the bombing of the Army Mathematics Research Center at the University of Wisconsin in Madison called itself the Marion Delgado Collective. [3]

On the surface of it, the fact that revolutionary activists in their late teens or in their twenties should choose a five-year-old boy as their mythical hero, appears quite unusual, to say the least, as does the fact that such a child-image should be able to inspire them to "live like him." One would have rather expected them to create for themselves a mythical hero of about twenty years of age, strong, fearless, defiant, greatly surpassing the average revolutionary in courage, cunning, and ruthlessness, somebody similar to, but much more serious and down-to-earth than, the legendary Superman, or perhaps James Bond—that is to say, a young man who could serve, without any effort of the imagination, as a true exemplar to be emulated by actual or would-be young revolutionaries. Why, we must ask, should young and aspiring wreckers of modern society want to be like a five-year-old child and "live like him"?

If we look somewhat more closely at the psychological factors involved, we will find the answer: the fact is that such a child-hero is, indeed, a most suitable mythical ideal for the type of revolutionaries represented in the Marion Delgado Collective and similar activist groups. The child-hero represents and exemplifies for them, as no adult hero could, the position which they, in their own view, occupy in society. They view society as "the Establishment," that is to say, an enormous, quasi-conspiratorial cabal of adults with established positions and hence with vested interests in the maintenance of the *status quo*. This society, they feel, wishes to make them part of itself, to mold them in its image, in much the same manner in which, in their childhood, their parents wanted to make them conform to the patterns of the adult world of which the parents were an integral part. Just as in their childhood they tried to exercise their will by opposing their parents, so, after having grown up, they feel compelled to test the limits to which society will allow them to go in defying its established order. The more permissive the parents were, the greater were the inner, psychological pressures in the children to reject the world of the parents, which they perceived as chaotic and amorphous because, as far as they were concerned, it lacked guidelines, limits, vetoes, authority, and controls. As children, they had no channels (except, perhaps, for frequent temper tantrums) through which they could express the dissatisfactions and frustrations engendered by the utter permissiveness of their family environment. Once grown up and physically removed from the family, this child-parent relationship is expanded into an ego-society relationship. The basic motivations remain the same: to test the limits of the tolerance (i.e., permissiveness) of the social environment by rejecting its values, defying its rules, flouting its authority, and destroying its assets.

The young militant is basically a spoiled child who has remained emotionally immature, infantile. His attitudes to his social environment and his actions within it differ little from his childhood attitudes and actions in the family circle. His social environment has changed considerably; the parents have been replaced by numerous and diverse new power symbols, all of which together make up the establishment, but his own relationship to it has not changed. His militant demonstrations, "non-negotiable" demands, sit-ins, and other techniques of confrontation—all of which can be engaged in and carried on only as long as they are permissively tolerated by the powers that be—are but the latter-day equivalents of childish temper tantrums and serve, beyond the immediate causes and proclaimed purposes, but one basic aim: to manifest and demonstrate that the young militant has remained the same child he had been ten or fifteen years earlier, that he can behave within the new, wider social environments in much the same manner as he did in his childhood in the family, and that both environments relate to him in a largely identical manner. What all this boils down to is simply that by unconsciously identifying the establishment with the parents, the young militant refuses to become a responsible member of society; he transfers and expands his rejection of the parents to a rejection of the establishment; he is dominated by the desire not to grow up, makes desperate attempts not to grow up, and refuses, because he is unable, to face the fact that, all asseverations to the contrary, he *has* grown up.

The foregoing interpretation differs from Dr. Bruno Bettelheim's explanations of adolescent and young adult militancy. According to Bettelheim:

1. Adolescent revolt is triggered by "the fact that a society keeps the next generation too long in a state of dependence; too long, in terms of mature responsibility and a striving for independence, of a sense of place that one has personally striven for and won."

2. It is also (or alternately) caused by a much too early development of their intellect "at the expense of their emotional development. Although exceedingly bright, some remained emotionally fixated at the age of temper tantrum. It is this discrepancy between great intellectual maturity and vast emotional immaturity which is so baffling. . . ." Such young adults, like children, are characterized by an "inability to brook delay or to think rationally or to act responsibly."

3. The rebellious students perceive all authority as representing the parents. They still suffer from "the rage that overwhelmed them in childhood. . . . Just as the infant sees his elders as so forbidding that, while they are still around, he can do nothing to better his fate, so it is for these rebellious students who project their past on to present conditions. Until they can be rid of this 'establishment' they feel they have no chance at all to live their own lives."

4. However, there is a deeper, unconscious motivation at work in the psyche of the rebellious youth: "While consciously they demand freedom and participation, unconsciously their commitment to Mao, and leaders like him, suggests their desperate need for controls from the outside, since without them they cannot bring order to their own inner chaos." [4]

In place of these several alternative explanations, I suggest that we look to the evidence offered by the case of Marion Delgado and other such mythical prototypes. A mythical prototype is certainly created out of a combination of conscious and unconscious needs. The slogan "Live like him!" under the picture of a five-year-old saboteur-revolutionary speaks volumes about both types of needs that are at work in the psyche of rebellious youths. The young militants certainly "strive for independence" —not for the mature independence of manhood, but rather for the kind of independence enjoyed by their five-year-old mythical hero, Marion Delgado: the independence dreamed about by the child who wants to run away from home into the fantasy-world of the woods. As to outside controls, the young militants' "desperate need" for them is buried very deep in the unconscious. Closer to the surface, all that their acts manifest is a compulsive need to act like the irresponsible child of five who cannot be held accountable for his deeds, whose temper tantrum was countered by the parents with a patient, and therefore infuriating, "let's wait until it passes." They want to be like Marion Delgado, who lives in a peculiar combination of two worlds, one real and one fantasy. The presence of the real world is felt (to judge from his picture) by being provided with food, clothing, and even haircuts: in all this we feel the loving care his invisible mother lavished on little Marion. That of the fantasy world is felt in his ability to live out unhindered the child's destructive impulses, and to roam abroad at will without punishment or retribution.

The desire for a life of recklessness without risk as a factor in the world of America's rebellious youth was intuitively touched upon by John W. Aldridge when he observed: ". . . it is possible to wonder, when they envision a world without risk, whether the young are not in fact expressing their nostalgia for the secure, permissive, and instantly gratifying lost Eden of their childhoods. . . ."[5]

Other authors have emphasized either the overpermissive, or the overprotective quality of the home environment which typically produces the young militants. Richard Flacks explains in *The Activist* that one source of student rebellion is the discrepancy between the home and the institutions (i.e., the colleges and universities) into which the youngsters find themselves thrust after finishing high school. The typical home background of the young activist or revolutionary is liberal, permissive, intellectually oriented, politically aware, with parents who are overtly skeptical about conventional middle-class values, who encouraged "self-expressive" and "independent" behavior in the children, and who interacted with them in a "democratic" way. After this, the university attended by these youngsters was perceived by them as being ridden with hypocrisies, rigidities, injustices, authoritarianism, acquisitive, militaristic, and nationalistic values. What is more, they formed the same picture of society as a whole. This "incongruence" between the "modernizing" family and traditional culture is the factor that triggers student rebellion.[6]

In a somewhat different vein Jane O'Reilly argues that affluent suburban parents overdo their solicitousness by taking care of every need and every whim of their children, whose lives therefore have become a dull, challengeless routine from which they wish to escape. But because of their conditioning they are not able even to run away from home effectively, and all that they can manage to do is to spend some days in the house of a neighbor down the block.[7]

The foregoing are merely a few examples of the great many interpretations of contemporary youth rebellion. In fact, the number of hypotheses is so great that they lend themselves to typological treatment. This was done by Dr. Seymour L. Halleck, professor of psychiatry at the University of Wisconsin Medical School, who found that the hypotheses of student unrest could be grouped into three categories: critical, sympathetic, and neutral. The first includes the permissiveness, responsibility, affluence, and family pathology hypotheses; the second the two armed camps, war in Vietnam, deterioration in the quality of life, political hopelessness, and civil rights hypotheses; the third, the technology, media, and overreliance on scientism hypotheses. Incidentally, Halleck himself admits that the alienated students are "miserable and ineffective." [8]

My own interpretation of the behavior patterns of the rebellious youth is closest to that of John W. Aldridge cited above, but goes one step further. My understanding, based on the overt acts of the militant youth and on the mythical proto-types which it creates for itself and in whom it personifies and objectifies its own desires, is this: these young militants typically comprise in their ranks those boys and girls who reject the path leading to adulthood, because to grow up would mean to become like their parents and to take one's place in the estab-lished order of society, which their personality, in combination with their experiences in the ten or so years that had preceded their rebellion, has conditioned them to be unable to accept.

By rejecting responsible adulthood even into their late teens and twenties, the young militants find themselves in an impos-sible situation, for which they seek a solution, or at least some relief, by escaping into a childhood fantasy-world of defiantly acting out their infantile dreams of rebellion. This is the mean-ing of their choosing as their symbol Marion Delgado, the five-year-old boy who has a childhood the likes of which they never had, but which, in romantic retrospect, they would desperately like to have had. Marion Delgado wears "a defiant smile" whereas they themselves never dared to defy their parents; at the utmost, they cried defiantly when refusing to eat their break-fast cereal. Marion Delgado is physically powerful: he can lift a twenty-five pound concrete slab, which would be no mean feat even for an adult. He has not yet reached the age when children are impressed into the slavery of the school, and yet is already possessed of a revolutionary zeal. He can and does carry out impressive acts of sabotage. Also, being a mere child of five, he can perpetrate his deeds against the establishment with-out running the risk of being punished, even if caught, for, af-ter all, it is part of the established order of society that a child is not punished.

Thus, little Marion Delgado represents much of what the young revolutionaries would like to be: strong beyond their physical frame, of independent mind, defiant of society, carry-ing out great destructive acts without, however, running the risk of being punished for them. He symbolizes the two irreconcil-able desires that agitate the young revolutionaries: the wish to enjoy all the advantages of an irresponsible childhood, and the simultaneous yearning to act out the impetuous revolutionary ideals of a post-pubertal youth who imagines that he has weighed the values of society and found them wanting.

One last point. As I look carefully at the picture of Marion Delgado, I seem to detect in it not merely a "defiant smile," but an expression of contempt. In this respect, too, little Marion is a most suitable symbol for the young activist, who professes uniform contempt for everything adult society stands for, including all the traditional do's and don't's of social conduct.

Thus, Marion Delgado can be understood as but a variant on the Che Guevara image. It may be more than a coincidence that he, too, has a Spanish last name (his first name, incidentally, is both a masculine and a feminine name). Che Guevara, as we have seen in Chapter 7, was a most suitable ideal hero for the young radicals because in him they could celebrate and idolize (and, subconsciously, excuse), their own ineffectiveness, the lack of tangible, concrete results that characterized both their lives and his. Marion Delgado manifests another aspect of the same syndrome: the desire to be a super-child, to recapture in imagination, and occasionally to act out, the fantasy of a never-never-land childhood.

religion as myth in modern life

1 · Myth in Judeo-Christian Tradition

The time has come to turn to that aspect of modern life in which myth still has the same function it has had ever since antiquity. This area of modern life is, of course, religion. The *function* of myth within the religious realm of life has remained largely the same throughout the last three millennia; that is to say, the manner in which myth informed religion in ancient Egypt or Mesopotamia can still be recognized without difficulty in the popular-traditional varieties of Christianity and Judaism. On the other hand, the *scope* of myth in religion has shrunk in recent decades very considerably. In fact, the point has been reached where the very validity of myth as a religious vehicle has been questioned. Doubts about the role of myth in religion have been raised by thinkers deeply committed to religion who have felt that myth as a form of religious expression is incompatible with our modern scientific view

131

and knowledge of the world and that, therefore, we are well
advised to demythologize religion. In applying ourselves to these
issues, let us first discuss in the present chapter the role of old
myths in modern religious life. Then, in the next chapter, we
shall consider some modern developments in the direction of
either discarding old myths or substituting new ones for them.
Thereafter the special form of reinterpreting New Testament
mythology known as "demythologizing" will be analyzed (in
Chapter 11), to be followed by a discussion of the new mythology
of the radical or "God is Dead" theologians (in Chapter 12).
Finally we will turn to the new myths with which the various
Black American religious movements have provided themselves
(in Chapter 13).

In contemplating the role of myth in the religions of our modern world two facts have to be kept in view: first, that all historical religions comprise a strong mythical component; second,
that all the major modern religions are a heritage from past,
and ultimately ancient, times.

Little needs to be said about the role of myth in ancient
religions. Even if we disregard the polytheistic religions of the
ancient Near East and the Greco-Roman world, and concentrate exclusively on those religions of which the present faiths
of the modern world are direct heirs, namely Judaism and early
Christianity,[1] we are confronted with a religious realm in
which myth was the mainstay of ritual, morality, and doctrine.
Each component element and feature in these three basic facets
of religion was based upon, supported by, and validated
through a myth. To begin with, a very few brief indications will
suffice to show that this basic function of myth is still to be
found in the Judaism and Christianity of the contemporary
world.

The ritual of the Jewish Passover (which will be discussed
in some detail in Chapter 10) is based on the myth of the Exodus; that of the Christian Communion on the myth of the Last
Supper. The Jewish moral precept of kindness to strangers and
the poor is based on the myth of the slavery in Egypt; the Christian moral precept of meekness and mildness, on these traits
attributed mythically to Jesus. The Jewish religious doctrine

of the oneness of God is based on the myth of the Lord's self-revelation to Abraham, Moses, and other religious leaders; the Christian religious doctrine of the divinity of Jesus is based on a specific interpretation of the myth of his birth, baptism, and ministry as detailed in the New Testament.

That both Judaism and Christianity as professed and practiced today go back to antiquity is such a truism that one feels almost embarrassed in stating it. If I nevertheless make the statement it is because I want to point out a fact that derives directly from the great antiquity of these two religions: both Jewish and Christian myths, which have been among the most important sustaining and effective elements in both religions down to the present day, are themselves very ancient. Such a longevity characterizes many Eastern mythologies—such as those of India, China, Japan—which, too, have survived from antiquity to the present. In contrast to them, classical Greek mythology appears almost ephemeral in its brief life span. Nor did its demise result from the displacement of classical polytheism by Christianity, but antedated the rise of the latter by several centuries.

Historical studies have shown that in the days of Homer and Hesiod, that is, in the ninth to eighth centuries B.C., the Greek myths were still in the course of formation. Two or three centuries later Greek philosophers and historians were busily engaged in attempts to reinterpret Greek mythology; in other words, by that time it was felt that the Greek myths could no longer be considered true and sacred accounts of the lives and deeds of the gods. In fact, the great Greek "immortals" enjoyed a life span that was considerably shorter than that of Noah and his ancestors, whom the Biblical story represents as mere humans.

As far as longevity is concerned, Judeo-Christian mythology thus belongs to the general type of Eastern mythologies; however, even in comparison to them, its life span is impressive. Biblical scholars admit today that the old Hebrew myths contained in Genesis and Exodus are pre-exilic, which means that they must have had currency in Israel by the seventh century B.C. at the latest (the Exile—i.e., the destruction of Judea—took place in 586 B.C.). It is a safe guess that they had emerged some three centuries earlier—that is to say, in the tenth century B.C., when David, the "son" of God (as he is styled in Psalm 2:7) ruled Israel. Yet today, thirty centuries later, a major segment of the Jewish people, including the Orthodox Jews in the United States, "believes" in those myths as a matter of official doctrine, in basically the same manner as their Palestinian ancestors did in the days of the Hebrew monarchy. To mention only a few of these myths: the creation of Adam and Eve, the Fall, the Deluge, God's nocturnal covenant with Abraham, the burning bush, the passage through the Red Sea, the revelation on Mount Sinai—all these and many more are live myths for Orthodox Jews today as they were in those old days of yore.

The Christian myth has shown the same tenacity. As far as that part of the mythological basis of Christian faith is concerned which is contained in the Old Testament, the religious Christian is expected to believe in them exactly like the Orthodox Jew. The central myth of the New Testament was, by and large, fully developed in the second century A.D.; today, eighteen centuries later, the virgin birth, the God who became man, the ministry of Christ, the miracles he performed, his crucifixion, agony, and resurrection, and the redemption of mankind through his death—these and several other essential elements of the Christian myth still remain the official truth for all the Churches.

2 • *The Mythical Base Line of
the "Theology of Survival"*

Perhaps no example can better illuminate the power wielded by the ancient Judeo-Christian myth in present-day theological thinking than the reports that issued from a three-day conference of twenty leading Protestant theologians, held on April 28–30, 1970, at the School of Theology in Claremont, California. The subject of the symposium was "Theology of Survival," and it was the first major conference convened to consider the religious dimensions of the ecological issue facing man in the modern Western world. As Edward B. Fiske reported in *The New York Times* on the day following the conclusion of the conference, "virtually all the scholars agreed that the traditional Christian attitude toward nature had given sanction to exploitation of the environment by science and technology and thus contributed to air and water pollution, overpopulation and other ecological threats." [2]

A few months after the conference part of its proceedings were printed in the September 12, 1970, issue of *IDOC International*, North American Edition, published twice monthly by IDOC North America at Huntington, Indiana. IDOC, which is an acronym for International Documentation on the Contemporary Church, describes itself as "a cooperative relying . . . on more than 300 specialists" as well as "on groups and members in 32 countries . . . [and] on members of key Christian churches and denominations. . . ." Professor L. Harold De Wolf, one of the speakers at the conference, identified the dangers which pose the basic threats to the global survival of humanity as war and preparation for war, pollution of air, pollution of water, upsetting of ecological balance, exhaustion of oxygen, overpopulation, and affluence. He admitted that "our Christian tradition has borne especially destructive ecological fruit because of some very bad hermeneutics," and quoted "the fateful verse" in Genesis 1:28 which says "Be fruitful and multiply, and fill the earth and subdue it; and have dominion over the fish of the sea and over the birds of the air and over every living thing that moves upon the earth." Then he proceeded to own that "we people of the biblical tradition have obeyed this injunction in its worst sense," that is, in the sense that it "is positively virtuous" to "conquer and exploit nature for our own benefit." Thereafter he proposed a basic reinterpretation of that fateful verse in Genesis in the sense that man must tend and keep his natural environment with care, in the spirit of Genesis 2:15 which enjoins upon man "to till and keep" the garden into which God put him, and in accordance with the teachings of the Bible which considered the land and the seas as a good in themselves (based on Genesis 1:10), and which enjoins man to have a reverence for life.[3]

Another speaker at the conference quoted, with full agreement, Lynn White's well-known article, "The Historical Roots of Our Ecological Crisis," [4] which "has shown that at least one of the causes of our present crisis is to be found in the Judeo-Christian traditions . . . which speak of man's dominance over nature. . . . By destroying pagan animism, Christianity made it possible to exploit nature in a mood of indifference to the feelings of natural objects." These statements of White are qualified by the author of the paper, Professor Loren R. Fisher, to the effect that it was "a *particular understanding* of a few select traditions [that] has been a basic cause in the growth of the present crisis." [5]

A third speaker at the conference, Professor Richard H. Overman, after quoting Lynn White's comment about Christians who insist *"that it is God's will that man exploit nature,"* went on to say, "All in all, we are likely to feel the phrase [of the familiar hymn] *Jesus, ruler of all nature* as another one of those incriminating slips, best hidden from our accusers. Perhaps, we muse, *Make straight the highway of the Lord* has been taken by Christians and made into a twisted slogan for the interstate highway which slashes through the hills. Maybe *Let every valley be exalted* is the corrupted text for the land fills which hide our urban refuse! . . . We cannot with good conscience reject any [such] accusations." [6]

These few quotations should suffice to indicate that the general feeling at the conference was indeed one of guilt over modern industrial man's having taken certain Biblical passages for what we would term charter myths authorizing him to pollute and despoil nature.

The primary issue here is the question of the mentality, the basic outlook, manifested in the year 1970 by a group of leading American theologians who feel, and believe, that the attitude of American industry, which actually means the American people, to the natural environment ultimately goes back to an ancient Hebrew myth according to which God granted dominion to man over the rest of the world. In its original form, in the meaning that this myth conveyed to the Hebrews of the monarchic period, it answered a question that bothered man in those days in no small measure. The question was: Is it justified that man should catch and kill other living beings, to wit, fish, fowl, and land

animals, in order to sustain his own life? Does not the blood
of animals contain their souls, for which reason man is not allowed to ingest their blood (see Leviticus 17:10–11)? If so, how
can man kill animals and spill their blood-soul, their life blood?
The mythical answer was clear-cut and reassuring: God gave
dominion to man over the animals because He created the animal kingdom for the purpose of sustaining human life.

To see in this myth a basis for the irresponsible pollution of
the environment, as the Claremont symposium did, is, to say the
least, a bold reading of present conditions into an ancient text.
However, and this is the point I wish to stress, this reading is
motivated by the belief that the old myth is still alive and to
this very day continues to influence our thinking, our attitudes,
and, ultimately, our acts.

The Claremont example can, at one and the same time, serve
as an illustration of the unexpected ways in which an ancient
myth can reassert its vitality in completely new and fundamentally different circumstances. The conditions of life, the technological methods of relating to the environment, the ways of
making use of the raw materials contained and yielded by nature
in seventh-century B.C. Judea were entirely different from those
that developed in twentieth-century America. And yet, the same
myth that originally reassured the ancient Hebrews that it was
licit and permissible to kill and eat their fish, fowl, sheep, and
cattle, serves—in the view of the twentieth-century American
theologians—as the basis, the justification, and possibly even
the impetus, for the industrial despoiling of nature by our latter-
day corporate robber-barons. If there ever was an eloquent testimony to the vitality and tenacity of religious myth, this certainly
is it.

In making this statement I think I should again emphasize that,
to my mind, more important than the actual factors that influence the exploitative techniques of American industry is the fact
that its behavior appears in this particular light to some of our
leading contemporary theologians. They, after all, are the last
keepers of the flame, the late heirs of the priests, prophets, poets,
and *vates* whose breath created myth in the first place, sustained
it, developed it, varied it, interpreted, and applied it. One could

even argue that as long as theologians in a society attribute to the myths of their faith the power to motivate individual or corporate societal behavior, those myths actually do possess such power. In any case, at least as far as these latter-day representatives of Christian tradition in America are concerned, the old Biblical myth that for a very long time has been the charter authorizing man to take his place at the head of creation is still sufficiently alive to make them expend prodigious efforts in trying their hand at a major reinterpretation in keeping with new problems and concerns which lay totally beyond the horizon of the Biblical times.

3 · Exorcism in the Catholic Church Today

Official Catholicism, in its consistent conservatism, adheres not only to the old central charter myth of Christianity and its other basic myths referred to in the opening section of this chapter, but also to those minor and obscure mythologems and their attendant rituals, the like of which, if she would encounter them in other religions, she would certainly not hesitate to condemn as sheer superstition. As an example of the latter, one can refer to the doctrine of diabolic phenomena in general and devil possession in particular. The belief that devils or evil spirits can take physical possession of the body of a human, penetrate into it, and control from within his thoughts, feelings, words, and acts is an ancient Near Eastern heritage in Christianity as well as in Judaism and Islam.[7] However, while in Judaism and Islam these beliefs and the attendant rituals of exorcism have survived into modern times only in the most backward and least educated circles, and are decried by the official exponents of the religion as regrettable superstitions, in Catholic Christianity the same beliefs and practices have continued to form part of the officially sanctioned doctrines and rituals of the Church. As late as 1930 a massive volume describing, along with other spiritual and mystical matters, how to recognize and deal with diabolic possession was published with the Nihil obstat and Imprimatur of Archbishop Michael J. Curley of Baltimore. Written by Adolphe

Tanquerey and entitled *The Spiritual Life: A Treatise on Ascetical and Mystical Theology*, this book defines diabolical possession as "the presence of the devil in the body of the possessed, and the dominion exercised by the devil over that body, and through it, over the soul," and describes in detail the signs of such possession. It then proceeds to prescribe the remedies for possession, including detailed rituals of exorcism.[8]

In the forty years that have passed since the publication of this volume the position of the Catholic Church on the question of devil-possession and exorcism has not been modified in any way. The official *New Catholic Encyclopedia* (official in the sense that it, too, carries the *Nihil obstat* and *Imprimatur*) states:

> Today the Church maintains its traditional attitude
> toward exorcism. It recognizes the possibility of
> diabolical possession, and it regulates the manner of
> dealing with it. The Code of Canon Law allows
> authorized ministers *(see* EXORCIST) to perform
> solemn exorcisms not only over the faithful, but
> also over non-Catholics and those who are excom-
> municated (c. 1152). A solemn method of exorcising
> is given in the Roman Ritual. In most Eastern and
> Western rites, exorcisms continue to serve as a
> preparation for Baptism. Exorcisms also form a part
> of the blessing of such things as water, salt, and oil;
> and these, in turn, are used in personal exorcisms and
> in blessing or consecrating places (e.g., churches)
> and objects (e.g., altars, sacred vessels, church bells).
> . . . In exorcising and blessing these objects, the
> Church prays that those who use them may be
> protected against the attacks of the devil.[9]

The Roman ritual referred to in the passage just quoted contains the lengthy text of the prayers and incantations that must be recited in performing the rite of exorcism, as well as the text of instructions as to the rituals to be performed. In keeping with an age-old tradition which predates Christianity by one or two thousand years, the oral part of the ritual contains references to the mythic prototypes which validate, and give power to, the rites performed by the exorcist. The encounter between Moses and Pharaoh is referred to, as are the casting down of Satan "from heaven like lightening," the subduing of the devil beneath the cross, and numerous other mythical events that serve as prototypes for what the exorcist endeavors to perform. Christ, although referred to as "the immaculate Lamb," is at the same time described as he "who treads upon the lion and adder, who tramples under foot the young lion and the dragon. . . ." No wonder that the devil would have to flee when the name of such a mighty "Lamb" is invoked. The closest mythical precedent for the exorcising of the devil is adduced in the reference to "Jesus of Nazareth . . . who, although thou [the Devil] didst despise His disciples, bade thee go bruised and overthrown out of the man, and in his presence, having separated thee from him [i.e., the man who was possessed], thou didst not presume to enter into the herd of swine. Therefore, thus now adjured in His Name, depart from the man, whom He has formed. . . ." The ritual contains several more mentions of how Jesus overcame the devil, how Moses drowned him, how God put him to flight when he drove him out of King Saul with spiritual song sung by David, and the like. In the English translation, the form of exorcising the possessed is nine pages long, with the proviso that the entire ritual should be repeated as often as necessary to achieve the desired result.[10]

This type of mythical validation of ritual is as old as religion itself. An ancient Babylonian incantation which goes back to a still much older Hurrian prototype, and thus dates from the early second millennium B.C., represents a close parallel to the Catholic exorcism described above. Just as the Catholic doctrine holds to this day that certain pathological symptoms are caused by the devil who has physically taken possession of the patient, the ancient Babylonians believed that toothache was caused by a worm which managed to lodge in the gums and was sucking the blood of the tooth and gnawing at its roots. The remedy is identical too: the evildoer must be expelled by incantation. In order to make sure that this will be effective, it had to be validated by a myth, whose hero is Ea, the wise and powerful Babylonian creator god (who, incidentally, is described as having "vanquished and trodden down his foes and secured his triumph over his enemies," the dragon-like monsters Apsu and Mummu).[11]

The myth to be recited over the patient suffering from toothache opens by telling how, in the very days of creation, the "worm went crying to Shamash, its tears flowed before Ea," and he addressed Ea thusly: "What will you give me for my food? What will you give me for my wine?" Ea's answer informed the worm that a certain tree and its juice would serve as food and drink for the worm. Dissatisfied with this divine dispensation, the worm demanded: "Set me rather among the teeth, and in the jaws let me dwell. I shall suck the blood of the teeth, and from the jaws I shall break away . . . the teeth." The incantation concludes with the curse: "Because you have said this, O worm, may Ea smite you with his strong hand." Then follows an actual recipe: "Tear apart the SA-RIM plant and mix it together with oil [and apply it to the aching tooth]." The incantation concludes with the advice that it be recited three times and the remedy be put on the tooth.[12]

Even without this striking parallel between the invocation of Ea in exorcising the worm from the tooth and of Jesus in exorcising the devil possessing a person, it is quite evident that the belief substratum underlying the Catholic ritual goes back to a very old Near Eastern mythical concept of Satan as the adversary of God. Satan, the personified force of evil, is much more powerful than man, so that man can hope to subdue him or to cast him out only by applying certain formulae, originally magical, which threaten Satan with the full force of the superior powers of the deity. Originally this myth was an organic part of the ancient Near Eastern magic world view in which the two divine forces of good and evil—sometimes, as in Zoroastrianism, imagined as equal in potency—incessantly fought for supremacy in the world. One of their favorite battlegrounds was right in the human psyche, or, as they would have put it, inside the human body. Numerous myths in both the Old and the New Testaments, as well as in the rich Jewish Midrash literature of the early post-Christian centuries, tell about Satan trying to block the path along which the pious, following a divine command, proceed confidently and unsuspectingly, and about the battle that there-upon ensues. One of the weapons at the disposal of the man so accosted is to "shout" at Satan, to "rebuke" him, to frighten him away with the mention of the name of God or by referring in capsule to the mighty deeds of God and His victories over evil.

There can be no doubt about the psychological effectiveness of this method of combatting what in ultimate analysis is but the "evil inclination" in one's own heart. "Evil inclination" is, of course, nothing but the two-thousand-year-old way of saying that man often desires to do what the tradition of his culture has taught him God forbade. To commit an act outlawed by God is a sin; the desire to commit a sin is the "evil inclination"; to feel unable to resist such an inclination is being possessed by forces of evil, by Satan. Once one finds oneself in such a state of devil-possession, the mythical rebuke, the reference to previous suc-cessful exorcisms, and the recital of the great mythical victories of deities, saints, and heroes as precedents contain the tradi-tionally sanctioned promise of succor.

Homo religiosus, it would seem, has not changed much in the last four thousand years as far as the archetypal combat in his psyche is concerned. This, at least, seems to be indicated by the tenacity of the ritual of exorcism, which not only has weathered four millennia, but has in the course of this considerable length of time barely modified either its basic features or its underlying mythical motivation.

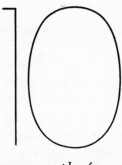

*new myths for old
faiths*

The material presented in the preceding chapter must not lead us to the conclusion that all, or even most, of the millennial myths of Judaism and Christianity have retained their full force and vitality down to the present day. The fact is that in recent decades a great many of these old charter myths have shown signs of sudden and rapid decay in the sense that they have been losing their relevance for increasing segments of the populations in the modern Western world. By the 1960s even the Catholic Church in America, traditionally the one faith best able to maintain its hold over its flock, could no longer claim to be an exception to this rule. In 1970 it was reported for the first time that the total number of Catholics in the United States has shown a decrease, together with a falling off in the numbers of baptisms, of pupils in Catholic schools, and of seminarians. At the same time, signs of unrest in Catholic lay circles and in the lower clergy became noticeable, with voices clamoring for reforms and modernization (*"aggiornamento"*) in the Church becoming louder all the time. While these demands have so far rarely touched on matters of mythological import—or, as the Catholics themselves would say, the dogmatic aspects of their religion—there can be no doubt that the decline in the power of myth is closely correlated with the increasing ferment in the Church.[1]

1 • *Protestant Dichotomy*

This development can be observed in a more pronounced form in the Protestant churches and in Judaism. Among thoughtful people in various denominations of these two faiths one encounters with increasing frequency an inability to go along with the old tenet of *credo quia absurdum est,* and an insistence that the teachings of one's religion must be made to conform to, and harmonize with, the natural order of things about which modern science knows more and more. Many people have become totally disillusioned with the traditional forms of religion and embrace an indifferent agnosticism or profess a complete lack of awareness of the religious dimension of existence. Others, while retaining a certain concern about religion, maintain that the laws of nature as we know them today no longer brook interference or disruption by an absolute Divine Will, and that therefore the old myths, which played such an important role as upholders of the religious teachings and values, can no longer claim credibility, meaningfulness, or relevance.

As a result of these developments, American Protestant Christianity, irrespective of its denominational fragmentation, has tended to cluster around two opposing poles: fundamentalism and modernism. The fundamentalists continue to adhere to the old charter myths of Christianity, whose essence is often subsumed under five central propositions: "(1) The infallibility of the Bible; (2) The Virgin Birth and the total Deity of Jesus the Christ; (3) The physical resurrection of Jesus' body; (4) The substitutionary atonement of Jesus for the world's sin; and (5) The second coming of Jesus in bodily form."[2]

The modernists, on the other hand, try to understand religious doctrines in the context of their origin, and to interpret (or reinterpret) them in the light of current conditions. Central to the efforts of these liberal Protestants is Biblical research and the theological and historical studies of Protestant scholars, in the first place in Germany. "This movement attempted to understand Christianity anew and to reinterpret it in a way which its new interpreters thought would render it understandable and acceptable to the age in which they lived." [3]

One of the criticisms leveled against liberal Protestantism was that often it succeeded in merely reversing the miracle at Cana by "transforming the wine of Christian faith into the water of scholarly opinion. These Protestant efforts too often won contemporaneity at the price of vitality. As a consequence, they can hardly claim to have made Christianity relevant to the age." [4]

The most influential of these modernist schools, that of "demythologizing," will be discussed in the next chapter, to be followed by an analysis of the most extreme, or most "radical," trend in modern Christian thought, usually subsumed under the heading "God is Dead" theology (see Chapters 11 and 12). First, however, we shall consider how an ostensibly areligious sector of modern Israeli society created a new myth to fill the void left by the fading away of orthodox belief in old, miracle-studded myths.

2 • A New Jewish Myth

Judaism shares with Christianity the experience of mythic decay; that is, it too has suffered the gradual erosion of its old mythology, which for many centuries had served as a bulwark affording protection to both the religion and its adherents. In at least one instance, however, a new myth has developed quite spontaneously in some Jewish circles, replacing the most important central charter myth that, because of a number of factors, had lost its meaningful quality. The old myth I am referring to is that of the Exodus from Egypt; the new one that replaced it is the mythical formulation of the exodus from post-Nazi Europe. The social milieu in which this new myth developed is the Israeli *Kibbutz* (communal settlement).

The central significance of Passover in Jewish religion has long been recognized by Jewish religious authorities as well as by students of Judaism. Its charter myth, the story of the Exodus from Egypt, has been made the cornerstone of practically all the observances of Jewish religion. The Exodus was the event from which the years were counted in the Hebrew monarchy (see 1 Kings 6:1), and in poetic and prophetic retrospect the time of the Exodus assumed the character of a miraculous age (Psalm 68:8, 114; Micah 7:15, etc.). God Himself, according to the Bible, considered Himself primarily as the liberator of His people from Egypt; this is how He identifies Himself in the opening statement of the Ten Commandments: "I am Yahweh thy God who brought thee out of the land of Egypt, out of the house of bondage" (Exodus 20:2; Deuteronomy 5:6), and how he refers to himself on other occasions as well (e.g., Joshua 24:6; Judges 6:8). In the story of the Exodus itself it is related that God commanded Israel to use the phylacteries to be "a sign upon thy hand and frontlets between thine eyes, for by the strength of hand the Lord brought us forth out of Egypt" (Exodus 13:16).

As time passed, the Exodus myth loomed ever larger on the Jewish religious horizon. One has only to open the prayerbook to see how omnipresent it has become. Prior to putting on the phylacteries, which, of course, is a ritual performed on every weekday, one is supposed to recite a brief prayer which says: "Behold I intend in putting on the *Tefillin* [phylacteries] . . . that we may remember the miracles which He performed for us when He brought us out of Egypt. . . . and He commanded us to put [the phylacteries] on our hand as a remembrance of His outstretched arm. . . ."[5] The last three words are a reference to the oft repeated Biblical phrase stating that God redeemed the children of Israel and brought them out of Egypt "with an outstretched arm" (Exodus 6:6; Deuteronomy 4:34, 5:15, 26:8; 2 Kings 17:36; Jeremiah 32:21; Psalm 136:12).

As part of the daily morning prayer the words of Psalm 81:11 also are recited: "I am the Lord thy God, who brought thee up out of the land of Egypt. . . ." Then the whole of Psalm 136 is recited, the central part of which is a description of the Exodus. Several more allusions to the Exodus are contained in other parts of the prayers. After the morning *Sh'ma* prayer follows yet another reference to the liberation from the Egyptian slavery, and thereafter comes the *Amidah* or the Eighteen Benedictions, after the conclusion of which follows once more a reference to the Exodus.[6]

The Friday evening *Kiddush* ("Sanctification"), recited in the Jewish home over a cup of wine just prior to the evening meal, contains two mythical validations of the Sabbath: one is a reference to God's having rested on the seventh day after He had completed the work of creation and had sanctified it. The second states that the Sabbath is a "remembrance of the work of creation, for it is the initial day of the sacred convocations in remembrance of the Exodus from Egypt. . . ."[7] That is to say, even the Sabbath is organically tied in Jewish tradition to the Exodus.

In the new moon prayers, too, the memory of the Exodus is invoked: "He who performed miracles for our fathers and redeemed them from slavery to freedom, may He redeem us soon and gather our exiled from the four corners of the earth. . . ."[8]

That the feast of Passover, which commemorates the Exodus and the liberation from slavery, should be rich in references to those great events in Jewish history needs no explanation. But the remarkable thing is that in the silent prayer and the *Kiddush* said on Pentecost, Tabernacles, New Year's day, and the Day of Atonement, those feasts as well are repeatedly stated to be a "sacred convocation in remembrance of the Exodus from Egypt."[9]

The "remembrance of the Exodus from Egypt" thus accompanies the religious Jew every day of the year, on weekdays, Saturdays, and holy days, so that one may say that one of the pivots around which the totality of Jewish religious life revolved was the Exodus. Nor is this all. When a Jewish boy undergoes the circumcision ceremony, which, under traditional circumstances, is performed in the synagogue on the morning of the eighth day of his life, a special prayer is inserted in the *Shaharit* (morning) service. This consists of a number of Biblical quotations, recited alternatingly by the *mohel* (circumciser) and the child's *sandak* (godfather), all of which relate to the Exodus, including the

Song of Moses (Exodus 15:1-18), which is the great paean of the miracles at the Red Sea.

In view of this central role played by the Exodus in Jewish life one can well understand what is meant in the statement of the Passover *Hagada:* "In every generation one must regard oneself as though he personally had come out of Egypt"—a statement that is solemnly recited year after year at the Seder ritual.

Professor S. G. F. Brandon of the University of Manchester is, therefore, more right than he could have known on the basis of Biblical studies alone when he said, "The Biblical account of the Passover, which is the cultic festival *par excellence* of Judaism, is one of the clearest examples of an historicized myth. . . . It has been the annual keeping of the Passover that has made the myth of the Exodus the supreme 'existential experience' of Israel through all the vicissitudes of the nation's long history. Such a myth is demonstrably unique in its origin, its presentation, and its power; its character can be understood only through its history and in its Jewish context." [10]

For at least twenty-five centuries the story of the Exodus was undoubtedly the most powerful and most effective charter myth of Judaism. Nobody questioned its historical truth. It was generally felt that the miraculous succor from the Egyptian slavery and the subsequent conquest of the Promised Land contained the implied divine promise of a future Messianic redemption from the sufferings of the *Galut,* the Exile, and of a triumphant return to the Holy Land. It was this vital, mythical import of the home ritual of the Seder meal at Passover, ostensibly held in commemoration of the Exodus, that endowed it with a unique, central significance in Jewish religious life.

Many Jews still celebrate the Seder in the same spirit and with the observance of the same ceremonies as have been observed since early times. However, among those Jews who are neither Hasidic nor Orthodox nor Conservative, the erosion of belief in the underlying charter myth has led to an increasing neglect of the Seder ritual based on it. As to the founders, builders, and inhabitants of the *Kibbutz* settlements in Israel, their attitude from the very beginning (the first *Kibbutz,* Deganya, was founded in 1909) has been areligious, and occasionally anti-religious, to such an extent that they eliminated from their lives all traces of religious ceremonies. The *Hagada,* the little booklet containing the historic narrative of the Exodus together with its later legendary embellishments, as well as prayers and songs, which is recited from beginning to end at the traditional Seder ceremony, was not among the few belongings they cherished sufficiently to bring along to their new places of settlement. Thus, for the *Kibbutz* people—an element, incidentally, considered by the entire Jewish population of Israel as an elite group, and, as such, exemplars to be emulated—both the old myth of the Exodus and its ritual commemoration in the Passover Seder were dead.

But old myths do not die quite so easily. Before the old ceremony could be completely forgotten, something happened that gave it a new lease on life, or, better, brought about the transformation of the old myth into a new, contemporary one. That something was the realization that the ancient Exodus from Egypt had its analogue in the new Exodus from the many Egypts of twentieth-century Europe, from Russia, Poland, Rumania, Germany, Czechoslovakia, Hungary, countries with their own modern Pharaohs under whom the Jews suffered much more horrible fates than under that ancient tyrant of the Nile. While the new Exodus fell perhaps short of the old one with respect to divine miracles, it abounded in human miracles, in examples of heroism and self-sacrifice. The narrow arm of the Red Sea which parted to allow the Israelites escape from Egypt now became the Adriatic, the Black Sea, and the wide Mediterranean, which had to be crossed, often in totally unseaworthy craft. The conquest of Canaan under Joshua was now repeated in the gradual settlement of the immigrants over several decades, and finally in their truly miraculous victory over Pharaoh's heirs and the other Sons of the East in the War of Independence.

Without ever having studied mythology, the mythical quality of these events was not lost on the members of the *Kibbutzim.* Its power asserted itself in inducing them to compose new *Hagadot,* modern ritual-liturgic accounts of this twentieth-century Exodus, and to recite these instead of the old one in revived and reshaped Seder feasts. The new *Hagadot* tell of the genocide in

Europe, the oppression in the lands of the Middle East, the Exodus, the perilous journey, the crossing of seven seas, the building of new villages, the backbreaking effort to wrest a yield from a long barren soil, the armed fight for the homeland, and the victory as the ultimate redemption. They are read at the Seder as the old one was for hundreds of years, listened to by old and young alike with the same rapt attention, and although they lack the miraculous embellishments of the old *Hagada,* their mythical quality comes through effectively and powerfully.[11]

This mythical utilization of the new Exodus and the new conquest of the Promised Land is, incidentally, one of the very few examples of the transformation of a historical into a mythical event under our very eyes. Elsewhere (Chapter 3, section 2) I have remarked that we rarely have the opportunity to observe and recognize how contemporary historical events, or even historical events of the recent past, turn into myths. The new Jewish Exodus, however, was an occurrence of such a decisive magnitude, it constituted such a break in historical continuity—with the smoke of the extermination ovens rising one day and the survivors established in a Palestinian Jewish settlement almost on the next—that the very trauma of this incredible, sudden transformation supplied the temporal and emotional distance that in the case of more gradual historical developments can be achieved only after decades or even generations have elapsed. There can be no doubt that for the first generation of Sabras (children born in Israel), or even for those who were brought to the country as small children, so that their own memory does not reach back to genocidal Europe, the story told in the new *Hagadot* of their *Kibbutzim* has already assumed the character of a myth. For them it is not history—such as they may learn in school; it has no dates, no figures, no names of individuals, no concrete details, only a condensed and compressed, generalized and yet concretized, account that conveys briefly, symbolically, and mythically the sense of what happened, its meaning, and its lasting effect on their lives.

11

the myth of demythologizing

The growing awareness of what we have termed "mythic decay" in Christianity prompted an influential and determined school of Protestant theologians to make a virtue out of necessity and proclaim that religion must be "demythologized." The school of demythologizing holds that, since we cannot be expected to believe the mythological details contained in the ancient sacred literature of Christianity, the faith itself must be purged of all the old mythological frills that traditionally had been integral parts of it. The earliest exponents of this demythologizing of Christianity were German Protestant theologians, but soon several of their French, British, Italian, and American colleagues joined their ranks, so that today demythologizing is a strong movement on both sides of the Atlantic.

The basic approach of the school of demythologizing, founded and headed by Rudolf Bultmann, starts out with the question of whether the eschatological preachings and mythological sayings of the New Testament contain, in a concealed form, a deeper meaning. After answering in the affirmative, Bultmann and his followers propose something akin to a peeling away of the mythological husks, which are no longer appealing for our modern day and age, in order to penetrate directly to the hidden meaning wrapped in them. In other words, the task Bultmann and his followers set for themselves was that of "trying to make the Christian gospel meaningful in a world where it seems largely to have lost its relevancy." [1]

As an example of how he proposes to interpret Biblical mythology, Bultmann refers to the oft-repeated statement that God has His domicile in Heaven. This, he says, is a mythological way of saying that God is beyond the world, that He is transcendent. In the times in which the Bible was written man was not yet capable of formulating the abstract idea of divine transcendence; hence the idea that God cannot be perceived by the senses was expressed by reference to space: He was said to dwell far above the earth, in heaven. The stars and luminaries, His creations and the doers of His will, which shine down on man from the heights of the sky, were said to be the visible expressions of His supremacy. In a like manner, hell is but the crude mythological way of expressing the idea which, stripped of its mythology, would refer directly to the transcendence of evil as the tremendous power that again and again afflicts mankind. Since darkness is terrifying for men, the abode of evil and evildoers was placed far below the earth where there is eternal darkness except for the glow of hell's fires.

For modern man, says Bultmann, the association of "above" with heaven and "below" with hell has become meaningless. The very terms "above" and "below" have no application in our scientific, astronomical concept of the universe. (We may add that, even on the planet Earth itself, once its spherical nature has been recognized, these directional distinctions retain meaning in only a strictly limited, localized sense. In global relations, "below" points simply to the center of the earth, while "above" radiates out into all directions from the surface of our planet. In other words, the "above" and "below" of, say the United States, are the exact opposites of those of Australia.) While, therefore, "heaven above" and "hell below" must be discarded as mythological concepts that have lost their meaning, the idea which they expressed in a clumsy and crude form—namely, that of the transcendence of God and of evil—is still both relevant and significant.[2] Similarly, the idea that God became flesh in the body of a man, and that this man, Jesus, died in order to atone for the sins of mankind is sheer mythology which we no longer can believe or need. "What a primitive mythology it is," Bultmann exclaims, "that a divine being should become incarnate, and atone for the sins of men through his own blood!"[3]

Bultmann is fully aware that in using this method of demythologizing Scripture he is taking the modern scientific world-view as his criterion. However, he argues that what he rejects is merely the mythological, and therefore unacceptable, world-view of Scripture, not Scripture or the Christian message as a whole. On the contrary, by demythologizing Scripture we can free the Word of God from the encumbrance of a bygone world-view, and achieve the purpose of making clear the call of the Word of God. "The work of demythologizing is to be carried out not to make way for a philosophy of existence, but to set free the essential *kerygma* of the New Testament. . . .This *kerygma* . . . is the proclamation of God's word addressed to man in his saving acts in Jesus Christ. . . . The gospel record . . . refers to 'a concrete figure of history—Jesus of Nazareth,' even if it customarily uses the language of myth to interpret his person and work."[4] Therefore, Bultmann says, demythologizing is in its essence, "a hermeneutical [i.e., interpretive] method of interpretation and exegesis."[5]

These few indications should suffice to show how Bultmann proceeds. His assessment is that the old myths of Christianity, which developed some nineteen centuries ago, have lost their ability to address themselves meaningfully to modern man. He therefore proposes to dig down beneath them so as to reach their true meaning which, in the first century A.D., had perforce to be clad in a contemporary mythical garb. However, in presenting what he considers the true meaning of the old myths, he utilizes forms and figures of expression which in effect clothe his Christian *kerygma* in a mythological garb appropriate to his own contemporary world.[6]

This new mythology which Bultmann substitutes for the old,

ritualistically-mystically based one, is symbolic, moral, intentional, and volitional in orientation. While he nowhere states this in so many words, he maintains that "the understanding which we already have of our own existence serves as a pre-understanding for the interpretation of the gospel." [7]

Take, for instance, Bultmann's reinterpretation of the significance of the Cross. The Council of Trent (1545–1563) taught that Christ instituted the eucharist so that in it "that bloody sacrifice which was once offered on the cross should be made present." [8] Needless to say, this old interpretation of the crucifixion is in itself a typically mythical reformulation and actualization of a primal historico-ritual event. The old view, expressed in a largely similar fashion in ancient Near Eastern, Judeo-Christian, Greco-Roman, and other religions, considered the ritual reenactment of primal mythical events to be the way to salvation, whether the latter was understood in mundane or in spiritual terms. For many centuries this conception of ritual reenactment served as the rationale of the eucharist as well.

Now Bultmann dismisses this, as he does the doctrine of reincarnation, as "primitive mythology," and teaches instead that "the cross becomes a present event . . . in every proclaiming and hearing of the Word." [9] That is to say, instead of a primitive reenactment of the sacrifice of Christ, Bultmann substitutes a recalling, proclaiming, and hearing—that is, an evocation by an act of will—of the Word of Christ, and considers His way suited to and sufficient for the modern Christian to become part of the ongoing process of human salvation initiated by Christ. We thus come to the conclusion that what Bultmann does is not to eliminate the mythological element from Christianity (or from its historical basis, the New Testament), but to substitute a new mythological interpretation which is in harmony with the new liberties and new limitations of modern man. If our analysis is correct, his "hermeneutical method of interpretation and exegesis" should rightly be termed, not demythologizing, but "trans-mythologizing."

Some of the leading members of Bultmann's school of demythologizing, while criticizing the master for stopping short of demythologizing when it comes to the *kerygma,* have themselves assigned an exceptional, lasting, and redeeming value to the central Christian myth of a Savior-Messiah. As Fritz Buri put it: "In the sea of mythological ideas and images, there are only a few really great redeemer-myths of the kind we have in the story of the eschatological Christ. As archetypes, they emerge from the unconscious, in great moments of humanity they are formulated by prophets, then they grow from generation to generation—until even they grow old and die." However, the myth of the Christian Messiah, Buri holds, has not yet reached its time of decay and death; on the contrary, it is still very much alive. It expresses symbolically " 'an intense awareness of existence and grace,' and he declares that it must have great depth 'to have survived so many variations and still be "revelation." ' Men can be moved by this symbol of authentic existence to participation in, and acceptance of, such existence, far more powerfully than they could be by any description of authentic existence in the abstract language of philosophical analysis." [10]

In a word, for Buri the central or charter myth of Christianity is still alive. And according to John Macquarrie, a foremost interpreter of Bultmann in the English language, Bultmann himself, "while accepting that in certain periods the myths arise and in certain other periods they lose their meaningfulness, would not agree that they must simply die when they have run their course. His belief is that they may contain important insights which can be lost to view by more sophisticated generations, and demythologizing presupposes the possibility of recovering such insights, though in a different form." [11]

We have so far refrained from doing what the reader probably has long expected us to do—namely, stating that the approach of Bultmann, Buri, and their colleagues to Biblical mythology is an existential one. While there is no common denominator among the many existentialist philosophers, novelists, dramatists, and authors of other types of literature, all existentialists can be said to differ from other thinkers in that they place the problem of man in the center of their thought, and that their main concern is with man's existence, his personal freedom, and therefore his responsibility for what he does and becomes. In keeping with this general trend, the existentialist view of myth, which, we now recognize, is shared by both Bultmann and Buri, sees in it "an attempt to bring to expression the way in which those who told [the myth] understood their own existence in the world." [12] This, of course, means that the existential interpretation of myth rejects as old-fashioned and rationalistic the view of myths which was almost universal in the first two decades or so of the twentieth century, according to which "most myths, if not all, are etiological; that is to say, they grew up or were invented to explain certain phenomena, beliefs, or customs." [13] For instance, in the old interpretation, the Biblical story of the Tower of Babel was considered an "etiological myth offering a primitive—and fantastic—explanation of the origin of different languages." Nowadays "attention would . . . be focused on the ambition of the builders to become as the gods, and on the frustration to which such ambition conduces." Or: in the old view, belief in demon-possession was "represented as a primitive attempt to explain certain diseases," while today it "would be understood as representing a primitive awareness that the world in which men live can be alien to their existence." [14] Thus, according to Bultmann, we have to strive to restate the content of the old Biblical myths in existential terms. [15]

What the new Christian demythologizers are trying to do today is similar, up to a point, to what was done in antiquity by the Greek historians and philosophers. Like their ancient predecessors, these modern theologians can no longer believe in the myths of their own religion. They do not want to abandon religion; on the contrary, they are firmly committed to it, as Herodotus, Palaiphatos (a contemporary of Aristotle), and Euhemerus were to theirs. But mythical accounts of miraculous happenings just rub them the wrong way. Their slogan therefore is, "Save Christianity by discarding its mythology," just as those old historians and philosophers may have cried, "Save Greek religion by ridding it of its myths." Then, as if frightened by what they have embarked on doing, they correct themselves to the effect that they do not really intend to discard Christian mythology, but merely to reinterpret it so as to make it meaningful for our modern existence.

Such a reinterpretation of ancient myths is always a risky

undertaking. The old myths were fashioned (or grew up) to answer questions that were of concern then. The form in which the myth supplied the answer was as important as the substance of the answer itself. To take up one of the examples quoted above, the existence of the many languages which made communication difficult across ethnic boundaries for the ancient Israelites was a bothersome fact that vexed many peoples. The myth of the Tower of Babel did not reduce the problem, but it did make it easier to acquiesce in it and thus liberated energies for the search for effective means of coping with it. In a typical mythical manner, the Tower myth is tied in with the total world-view of that society, with the belief that all peoples descended from one original couple (and therefore must have spoken one and the same language), that they all had lived in one place, and that the distance between man and God was not so great that God should not feel threatened by a monumental architectural project, a prototypal skyscraper. Therefore, He had to "go down" in person to confound the language of the builders and to scatter them abroad upon the face of the earth. Incidentally, the myth also seems to contain an explanatory reference to the huge towerlike structures whose remains are still visible in Mesopotamia. Read in this manner, which is the manner in which it was originally intended to be read, the myth of the Tower of Babel makes perfect sense. To read it or hear it and absorb its message gives even today the satisfaction one derives from contemplating a well turned piece of art. Its inner consistency projects its own convincing justification.

In contrast, the existential explanation not only deprives the myth of its original vigor, but also makes it into poor myth by putting the emphasis where the myth never intended it to be. The myth says nothing of "the ambition of the builders to become as the gods"; their ambition was to prevent their becoming "scattered abroad upon the face of the earth" (Genesis 11:4) —in other words, to prevent precisely that which actually befell them in direct consequence of the attempt to prevent it (vv. 8–9). The myth, moreover, speaks of the jealousy of God. God says: "Now nothing will be withholden from them, which they purpose to do" (v. 6), in a spirit reminiscent of His determination to keep Adam from becoming knowledgeable about good and evil (Genesis 2:9). But while in the case of Adam it was God's will that was frustrated, and He was not able to take away from man the knowledge the latter had gained, in the case of the Tower of Babel God prevailed and man's desire to remain one united people was frustrated. When read in this larger context, the Babel myth teaches, on the "existential" level, not that ambition leads to frustration, but that man should continue to try and try again because he cannot know when he will and when he will not succeed. But the existential level was only one of several on which the myth operated. Another level, of more immediate concern to ancient Israel, was the etiological, the explanation of the emergence of many languages, in the same spirit in which the stories of Genesis supply explanations to numerous other puzzling phenomena in the world of man and nature. To deny the etiological aspect of the myth is to destroy its beauty, its value, its completeness. To "demythologize" in this way is to be like a modern home-owner who would buy an antique statue to decorate his living room, and then chop off its legs because his ceiling is too low.

In fine, what demythologizing does is to substitute new myths for the old ones—new myths that are less easily understandable than the old ones, less appealing, more abstruse, and more cerebral. But they are still mythology nevertheless. They still express themselves in symbolic language—in fact, in the same symbolic language as did the old ones, except that the meaning of the symbols has now been discovered to be a different one. The reinterpretation of the symbolic content of the old myths made them not only less comprehensible than they had been, but also reduced their old general appeal to a matter of almost esoteric exclusivity, understood by or meant for only the select few who can devote themselves to a specialization in the study of theology.

the myth of the
god who died, or:
the "god is dead"
theology

1 · *The Theological and the*
Anthropological Approach

In this chapter an attempt will be
made to evaluate the mythological significance and implications of the "God is Dead" movement in modern theology.
In order to do so, a word will have to be said first in clarification of the difference between the theological approach
to phenomena of belief and that of the anthropologically
based student of mythology.

A theologian approaches questions pertaining to God
from the premise that either the study of traditional
sources, or his own speculations, or else his own mystical
experience can enable him to gain a true insight into the
nature and manifestations of the Divine. That is to say, the
deity itself is the center of his attention, and all his mental
and emotional efforts are directed toward recognizing and
understanding God, whose existence he takes for granted,

159

or at least always had taken for granted until the emergence of the new "God is Dead" theology. However, man has difficulty in finding his way to God, and it is therefore the theologian's task to explore the paths along which the deity can be approached. The question of whether God exists cannot at all enter the traditional theologian's thinking; in fact, until most recently, it has never arisen in theological circles, where the existence of God has always been axiomatic, the fixed point of departure.

The question of God's existence does not enter the horizon of the mythologist either, but for a quite different reason. In contrast to the theologian, the mythologist's interest is focused on man and his works and views. The student of mythology investigates human beliefs about the Divine as an integral, and often central, part of human cultural interests. This means that the interest of the mythologist is in what man believes about God, not in God Himself. Concerned with religion as a significant cultural phenomenon, he will study the same traditional sources considered authoritative by theologians, as well as accounts of theologians' speculations about the deity and descriptions of mystics' experiences; but, again, he will do all this, not in the hope of gaining an insight into the nature and manifestations of the Divine, but rather with the less ambitious purpose of learning about man and the ways in which man, at various times and in various places, believed himself to have found an approach to God. Far from taking the existence of God for granted, the very question of whether or not God exists lies entirely beyond the scope encompassed by anthropological-mythological interest.[1]

This being the case, I shall have nothing to say about the truth content of the "God is Dead" doctrine. Since the students of neither anthropology nor mythology have an opinion about the existence of God, they can have none about the question of whether such a supreme being could at all die, did die, or is dead. On the other hand, a student of anthropology and/or mythology may have something to say about a religious movement such as the one generated by the "God is Dead" doctrine, and about the social and cultural significance of the emergence of such a doctrine in the Western world in the last third of the

twentieth century. Let us begin with a quick glance at the early
manifestations of the "God is Dead" doctrine.

2 • *The Great Pan Is Dead*

Inscriptions on tombstones such as "Take heart, Marcus, no
man is immortal," were much favored in Hellenistic times. They
expressed the sense of comfort one derived from considering
that death—so often an individual tragedy—was the inevitable fate
shared by all human beings. The fact is, of course, that not only
man but all biological forms (except for a few low-level micro-
organisms unknown to antiquity) are inevitably mortal, and
some thoughtful people in ancient times, and ever since, found
encouragement in the knowledge that the unalterable rule of
existence is the termination in death of every life.

Man has, however, known forms of existence which appeared
to be deathless. Beneath the biosphere there was an order of
natural objects or materials which, while not alive, did tangibly
exist, and, because not alive, defied time and seemed, in this
sense at least, to be deathless. Apart from gigantic natural phenomena, such as the sea, mountains, or stars, the most common
objects belonging to this everlasting category were rocks and
metals, and quite early in history they in fact attracted the attention and admiration of man.

When man set out to people the universe with superhuman
beings, the raw materials upon which his imagination could draw
in constructing mythological personalities consisted of the two
categories of entities belonging to the animate and inanimate
worlds. Most of the mythical features man borrowed from the
former, fashioning his theriomorphic and anthropomorphic
gods in the shape of animals or men or a combination of the
two, and endowing them with characteristics derived from the
animal kingdom and the human realm but magnified a hundred-
fold.

Yet all this was not enough for childlike man, who needed
gods more stable, more permanent, and more enduring than
even the most superlatively magnified animal or human being

could ever be. To supply the crowning glory of his gods, man borrowed the trait from the inanimate world which seemed to him to be the most enviable: its immortality. Thus his gods became not only all-wise, all-powerful, all-seeing, and all-knowing, but also deathless. It is characteristic of the enduring force of this particular prehistoric feature in the theogonic process that even in such an advanced stage of religious development as prophetic Judaism, God was still referred to as "the Rock of Israel," and that one of the most popular Christian religious hymns to this day speaks of Him as the "Rock of Ages."

Side by side with this development went another trend which responded to the dissatisfaction felt by many when faced with gods whose immortality had placed them far beyond all human affinity, for their very deathlessness, derived from the inanimate world, seemed to render them if not inanimate, at least immovable, remote, and aloof as the very boulder to which they were likened. A god, it was felt in these circles and in these moods, in order to be of real help in need, must be of a constitution similar to that of man, must be capable of human passions, love and hate, joy and sorrow, and, above all, must share with man that fate from which no man is exempt, the great, ultimate, and unique experience of death. Thus the dying god was born.

The mythologem of the mortal god is encountered frequently enough to have prompted Sir James George Frazer to one of his sweeping generalizations which for many years went unchallenged. Man, he stated in the introductory chapter of his *The Dying God*, "created gods in his own likeness and being himself mortal he naturally supposed his creatures to be in the same sad predicament." [2] Among the so-called primitive peoples (if we are allowed, for the moment, to revert to Frazerian terminology) there is no hesitancy in stating explicitly under what circumstances the god died, or could die; but when we pass on into the world of classical mythology we find that nothing is told or known about the death of the gods, except that their tombs are pointed out. Thus, the grave of Kronos was shown in Sicily, of Zeus in Crete, of Apollo and Dionysus in Delphi, and of Hermes, Aphrodite, and Ares in Hermopolis, Cyprus, and Thrace. [3]

It is difficult to ascertain to what extent the Greek ideas of the gods' tombs were influenced by ancient Egyptian prototypes, but the fact is that in the land of the Nile, with its great emphasis on the preservation of a semblance of life in death, the gods were not denied their funerary honors, to enjoy which they had, of course, to die first. The mummies of Osiris and of other deities were shown at numerous places, while their souls were believed to shine as stars in the night sky.[4]

How the idea of the dying god manifested itself to the Greek consciousness can perhaps best be illustrated by quoting an intriguing story told by Plutarch about the death of the Greek god Pan, in which the East Mediterranean influence is unmistakable. In the days of Tiberius Caesar, a ship was sailing from Greece to Italy, and, as it was passing at eventide near the island of Paxi (one of the Echinadian Islands), the passengers, merry with wine, suddenly heard a voice from the shore calling for Thamus, an Egyptian pilot who was aboard. Thamus kept silent and answered only when the voice called him for the third time. Now the voice, coming clear and loud across the water, cried: "When you come opposite to Palodes, announce that Great Pan is dead!" Not knowing what to do about the enigmatic message, Thamus resolved to let an omen make the decision: if the wind held as they passed Palodes, he would keep silent; but if it dropped, he would do as the voice bade him. As they came to Palodes there was a great calm. Thamus stepped up to the stern and cried toward the land: "Great Pan is dead!" Immediately a loud sound of lamentation was heard, as if a great crowd were mourning.[5]

In searching for an explanation of this story, one must, first of all, remember that the Greek god Pan corresponded in many respects to the deity who on the Syro-Palestinian coast was known as Tammuz or Adonis, and who was perhaps the most poignant example and prototype of the dying god, of whose myth and ritual more will be said anon. Nor can it be mere coincidence that the man whom the mysterious voice bade serve as the herald of the sad news is called Thamus, which, of course, is but the Grecized form of the Semitic Tammuz. Since the death of Tammuz was mournfully celebrated by his followers in Greece as well as in Syria, some scholars assumed that it was the wailing and crying of such a mourning feast that the ship's passengers heard as their vessel lay becalmed offshore. We may, perhaps, reconstruct the wailing cry as follows: "Tammuz! Tammuz! Tammuz! The Great Pan is dead!"

3 • God and Man: Mortals Both

The very notion that the deity dies is a mythologem as old as the ancient Near Eastern religions themselves. The tragic, loving and lovable, passionate and suffering figure of the youthful dying god appears under many names but is everywhere easily recognizable, so true to type is he in each and every one of his numerous manifestations. The story of his short life falls into two loosely connected parts: the first tells of his loves and ends with his early and violent death; the second encompasses the period subsequent to his demise, during which attention shifts to the baleful effects his death had on the world, and ends with the account of his inevitable resurrection.

Historians of religion usually interpret the dying gods of the ancient Near East as having been symbolic of the annual cycle of vegetative life, and expressive, in mythical form, of the observed fact that at a certain period in each year the vegetation of the land died, that is to say, dried out and withered away under the searing power of the sun's rays. This interpretation is doubtlessly correct, yet for a believer of an ancient Near Eastern religion it would have been a most shocking thing to hear that the god whose death he lamented was merely a symbol which "stood for" something else. For him, Tammuz (or Baal or Adonis or Attis or Osiris) was a veritable god and not merely a symbolic representation of the vegetable world; his death, a world-shaking tragedy; and his rebirth or resurrection, a manifest event of the greatest cosmic significance.

In one important respect at least the ancient Near Eastern believer in the death of god was better off than his distant twentieth-century heir. When Tammuz died, and while he was dead, those who mourned for him and were devastated by his

death did not have to live in a world bereft of god. Fortunately,
as far as they were concerned, there were other gods, and these,
while unable to take the place of the one who had died, could
provide society with order, purpose, sense, and psychological security. However, the belief in a plurality of deities did not alter
the fact that the death of a god, of one definite and personal
god, was for that society a very significant feature of its religious
reality.

Psychologically, the death of god had in antiquity the effect of
reinforcing the proximity, the close relationship between god
and man. As has been pointed out already, a god who dies is
much more akin to mortal man than a deathless, immortal deity.
A god who himself is subject to the agony of death can be assumed to have more understanding for human agonies of all
sorts than can an immortal god. The death of god also made the
thought of the inevitable end of human life less devastating: a
fate shared by god with men could more easily be contemplated,
and, when the time came, endured than could a fate from which
the higher forces of the universe were immune. The dying god
thus helped man both to live and to die. From the psychological
point of view, therefore, the concept of a dying god undoubtedly
had palpable advantages as against that of an immortal divinity.

What can we learn from this brief and unavoidably sketchy
survey of the "God is Dead" idea in antiquity with reference to
the modern American Protestant movement which has become
known as the "God is Dead" theology?

First of all, we find that the idea is neither new nor revolutionary. Therefore, there is no justification for assuming that the
specific mid-twentieth-century American social, political, economic, and technological conditions can be regarded as a sufficient cause for the emergence of the movement at precisely this
time juncture and in precisely this part of the world. Moreover,
from the very fact that in the ancient Near East the myths and
rituals of the dying god remained a vital part of religious life for
about three millennia, we learn that the idea of the death of
god, in those days at least, was not a passing notion but a permanent and immutable part of established religion. In view of

this long history of "God is Dead" theology in antiquity, what is surprising is not so much that the doctrine was resuscitated in our day as that it had lain dormant for such a long period.

It also appears, in this perspective, that the revival of the "God is Dead" idea actually signifies a bringing nearer of man and god to each other, a partial return at least to the proximity that characterized the man-god relationship in antiquity—a proximity that had been lost in the intervening Christian era, when an immortal and practically unapproachable God was seated barricaded behind impenetrable clouds of glory somewhere "up there," very, very far away. By reducing the stature of God in making him mortal, what man achieves psychologically is to increase his own stature correspondingly and thus to move one step nearer the realization of the age-old human dream of becoming like God.[6]

However, the most important insight we gain from a survey of the historical dying gods is that the death of god, far from being the closing phase marking the end of a period of rapid religious decline, was for millennia a vital, ongoing process, balanced and followed by his resurrection as inevitably as the autumn rains succeeded the summer drought. Once a year the god died and once a year the god came to life again—this was the unalterable rhythm which in the divine realm, duplicated and, at the same time, exemplified that which patently took place in the annual life cycle of the vegetable kingdom, and that which was presumed to take place in the animal kingdom and in human life as well. The entire visible world, in this view, was a huge arena of periodic deaths and rebirths, and, while the mourning for the dying god was no less sincere and heart-rending than the lament for a flesh-and-blood loved one, the god's resurrection which followed held out the mytho-mystical hope that the loved one who had passed away was also to return in one form or another. A type of faith that lived on for three millennia must have had an extraordinary sustaining power to command the adherence of so many men and women, of so many different races and cultures, in so many different lands and times.

Characteristic of the staying power of this type of myth is the attraction it retained even in the greatly mitigated form in which it became part of early Christian mythology. For there can be no doubt that, within the great Christological myth, the most effectual features have not been the immaculate conception, or the abstract and rather difficult idea of the redemption of man through the death of the Son of God, or even the doctrine of the Trinity, but rather the powerful drama of the death and resurrection of the young god who walked among men in human shape. The death and resurrection of Christ have remained the central features of the Christian myth down to the present time. They are commemorated and reenacted annually in emotion-laden celebrations which still attract mass attendance just as the festive ritual of the death and resurrection of the ancient Near Eastern dying gods did for many centuries.

4 · *The Meaning of* "God Is Dead"

It is obviously impossible, as well as unnecessary, to discuss in the present context the entire scope, problematics, and propositions of the "God is Dead" theology. A good summary of these issues can be found in Thomas W. Ogletree's book *The Death of God Controversy*,[7] while the writings of the main exponents of this radical approach to Christian theology (especially the books of Thomas J. J. Altizer, Paul van Buren, William Hamilton, and Gabriel Vahanian) can be found in the better theological libraries. In most general terms, a basic difference between the old "dying god" religions and the new "God is Dead" theology can be stated as follows:

In the ancient Near Eastern religions the death of the deity was celebrated—that is, mourned—as an actual event that was taking place in the mythical reality of the day and age. Just as there was no doubt in the hearts as to the mythical truth of the god's existence, so there could be no doubt concerning the tragic event of the god's death. In the thinking and writing of the modern radical theologians, on the other hand, there is strongly in evidence a cognitive struggle as to the exact meaning to be attributed to the expression "God is Dead." If I understand correctly the leading exponents of this theological school, what they mean by "God is Dead" is that in our modern world the God in whom Christians had traditionally believed can be and is no longer believed in. Since a God in whom people no longer believe can be said to be dead (witness, e.g., the "death" of the gods of classical Greco-Roman polytheism), it is therefore legitimate to say that "God is Dead." I am not sure that all "God is Dead" theologians mean precisely this when they speak of the death of God, but at least several of them certainly do.

One of these, Gabriel Vahanian, considers the death of God a "cultural fact" in the sense that in the recent development of Western civilization the transcendental or supernatural realm has been lost as the necessary context for understanding man and his world. In its place a purely immanental perspective has been substituted "as the only meaningful framework for dealing with the problems and questions of human existence. In such a setting God is simply not necessary. Indeed, even the possibility of speaking of him comes into question." [8]

While this definitely means that, as far as modern Western man is concerned, God is dead, nevertheless, as Vahanian would emphasize, "the recognition of God's death as a cultural event does not destroy the reality of God himself. The real God is and remains 'wholly other' than any cultural phenomenon." [9]

The expression "lost," a key term in Vahanian's thinking, is used also by William Hamilton in the same sense. Hamilton says that the "Death of God is a public event in our history" in that we have "a sense of . . . having lost . . . God himself." [10] Like Vahanian, Hamilton can mean thereby only one thing: that what he terms the Death of God is in reality a metaphor, a figure of speech for expressing in one brief and striking phrase what more prosaic but more accurate language would describe as our having lost the ability to believe in God because we no longer feel that the traditional God of Christianity has any meaning or relevance for our modern lives. In other words, the Death of God, for both Vahanian and Hamilton, is an *anthropological,* not a *theological,* event. In a theological view, human belief or disbelief could have no effect on the existence of God. The God of theology is everlasting and the human mind cannot comprehend him, let alone influence his being. Clearly, it is the anthropologist who is speaking in these statements of Vahanian and Hamilton (and in similar statements of other God is Dead theologians); they assert something about man, but nothing about God, when they say that modern-day man has a sense of having lost God or the supernatural.

In this connection it is characteristic that the Death of God theologians describe the event of the demise of the deity as a "public event" (Hamilton), a "historical event" (Altizer),[11] a "practical awareness" (Vahanian),[12] a "cultural phenomenon" (Vahanian,)[13] and a "cultural event," that is, "not something that has happened to God. It has happened to us." [14] They never term it a "theological event," although that is precisely what we would expect to hear theologians say. In the past, theologians had a lot to say about the nature of God, His attributes, His will, His words, His acts, His commandments; they always asserted that they *knew* these and many other things about God, whether the claimed source of their knowledge was human speculation or divine revelation. In the same tradition, we would have expected the modern theologians to say that they discovered something entirely new about God—namely, that He had died. This would have been in keeping with the tradition of the centuries-old Christian theological speculations about God. It would have been a straightforward statement about the deity Himself, a startlingly new attribute to be added to the long list of theologically postulated divine attributes. In addition, such a direct statement would have reechoed the spirit of the ancient Near Eastern mythical beliefs about the death of Osiris, Adonis, Tammuz, Attis, and the other gods, all of which were *theological tenets.*

Evidently, the modern radical theologians are unable to take this path. To do so would involve them in a self-destructive set of contradictions. They would have had to start out with the traditionally entrenched beliefs about God as the only one, omnipotent, omniscient, omnipresent, eternal deity, and then would have had to announce that they had discovered (by speculation or through revelation?) something new and disconcerting about him—namely, that, after all, He was not eternal, He was not immortal; in fact, He died. However, the Death of God in this theological sense would retroactively vitiate the entire Judeo-Christian theological edifice erected in the course of three thousand years around the monotheistic God concept. Because if God died, then, obviously, He was not immortal. And if He, contrary to the solidly entrenched belief, sealed and validated with the blood of innumerable martyrs, was not immortal, then there is no basis for maintaining any of the numerous other attributes whose sum total made up the Judeo-Christian God concept. If He proved to be mortal, He also proved to be not eternal. If He had an end, He also must have had a beginning. He is, thus, reduced from immortality to mere longevity. The only possible conclusion to which this line of reasoning leads is that He was, after all, not the monotheistic deity so many generations believed Him to be. He is unmasked as a mere human delusion (or, to use the Freudian term, illusion). But if so, then the conclusion is inescapable that He could not have died, because a being that never existed cannot die.

This type of futile, self-defeating speculation would be inevitable if the favorite expression of the radical theologians, "God is Dead," were taken at its face value, if it were an "honest-to-God" pure and simple theological statement. Since, however, this would lead to a logical impasse, one is driven to the conclusion—confirmed by the elucidations of the God is Dead theologians themselves—that when they say "God is Dead" they merely mean "human belief in God is Dead." I must admit that it is with a marked sense of disappointment that I reach this conclusion, for I expected the modern radical theologians to have something new to say about God (which would be theology) and not only something old to say about man (which is mere anthropology).

However, precisely because the "God is Dead" pronouncement of the modern radical theologians is an anthropological *kerygma,* it has a distinctly mythological coloration. It is mythological in the sense that it represents a human emotion, insight, or feeling in a projected, concretized form, just as the concretized projection of sexual love in the figure of Aphrodite was solid mythology. If the image of Aphrodite was real mythology, if the death of Adonis was good mythology, which they undoubtedly were, so is the death of God.

We thus reach the conclusion that the Death of God theologians have not enriched Christian theology with a new chapter; they have, rather, added a new sequel to the age-old archetypal myth which shows man not only creating his gods in his own image but also killing them in a thoroughly human fashion. If gods die, it is because man who creates them is mortal. This, and nothing else, is the gods' original sin from whose consequences they cannot be saved.

5 • *Who Dies, the Son or the Father?*

Let us now turn to another difference between the ancient belief in a dying god and the modern radical God is Dead theology which seems to be of considerable psychological significance. In the old dying god myths and rituals it was always a youthful god who was killed. Typically, he met a violent death, like Adonis who was gored to death by a wild boar, or Attis who bled to death after having cut off his own genitals in a mad frenzy induced by Kybele. This young dying god, typically, stood in the relationship of son to an older father or mother deity, who in one version of the myth was the head of the pantheon of which the son was a member. In some variants of the myth the young dying god also had a sister, a young goddess, who at one and the same time was his bride or wife as well, and when the young god died it was this sister-spouse who led the lamentation in which the father-god barely took part. While this feature of the sonship of the dying god was retained in the old Christian myth of the death of Jesus, the new "God is Dead" theology introduced a radical departure from the old pattern by reversing the roles of the dying and of the surviving gods: it is now the father-god who is pronounced dead, while we are assured that the son-god Christ, lives on, although only after having assumed, in a vague metamorphosis, the character of The Word.[15]

In probing the psychological roots of this reversal, it is intriguing to speculate about a possible connection between it and the disparate roles youth and old age respectively play in ancient Near Eastern and in modern Western cultures. In ancient Near Eastern cultures youth was considered a life-stage of deprecable folly while old age was synonymous with wisdom. In the ancient Near Eastern social value system a son was nothing more than an adjunct to the father; it was the latter in whom rested all power and who could dispose even of the life and death of his progeny. For a father to sacrifice a son for some high religious purpose was an accepted procedure; for a son to take the life of his father for any purpose was completely unthinkable.

In such a social context it was inevitable that, when the death of a god was felt to be necessary in order to drive forward the wheel of life, it was a son-god to whom the agony of dying was assigned. His death and subsequent resurrection achieved the required psychological purpose, while the higher order of things in the divine realm registered but a relatively minor disturbance because the reign of the father-god was not shaken by his son's death.

In our modern Western culture youth is idolized and old age deprecated. As I have pointed out elsewhere, "In the West, aging is regarded as a process of decline, or deterioration, painfully contrasting to youth, which is the ideal life phase and which people want to retain as long as possible." [16] When the aggressive molding force of such a culture penetrates into the insulated study rooms of theologians, the idolization of youth and deprecation of old age will find their residual expression in making the father rather than the son into the victim of divine mortality. Therefore, "God is Dead" in radical theology means "God the Father is Dead," while God the Son is allowed to survive.

We cannot embark here upon an analysis of what such a dichotomy of the godhead into one dead and one surviving figure means as a potentially polytheistic development within an avowedly monotheistic faith, for this would land us in the alien territory of theology. But we can safely point out that, given the choice of pronouncing dead either the Father or the Son, it is highly characteristic of the culture-bound quality of modern radical theology that, contrary to all pre-Christian and Christian example and precedent, the deity whose death was chosen as the subject of the new *kerygma* should be the Father and not the Son.

This choice expresses, among other things, a strong desire to assert one's independence of all paternal authority. When the ancient Near Eastern son-god died, his death—whatever other psychological significance it had—did not disturb or in any other way alter the son-to-father relationship that existed between man and the (father) god. When, on the other hand, the father-god is pronounced dead, as he is by radical theology, this definitely means a throwing-off of the yoke of (divine) paternal authority, and implies a bid, not only for self-assertion, but also for self-determination. As Paul van Buren put it, the death of God had come about as a result of "the rise in technology and modern science, the need in our thinking to stick pretty close to what we can experience in ordinary ways." [17] In William Hamilton's view, religion means "any system of thought or action in which God or the Gods serve as fulfiller of needs or solver of problems," and he goes on to assert boldly that "God is not in the realm of the necessary at all; he is not a necessary being, he is not necessary to avoid despair or self-righteousness. . . . I am denying that religion is necessary and saying that the movement from the church to the world that we have taken as definitive Protestantism not only permits but requires this denial." [18]

Here we have supreme self-confidence laid straight on the line: what these men say is not merely that God is dead, but that we, modern Protestant technocrats, brought about His death by finding out that He is superfluous; that we have by now so firmly established ourselves in the physical realm of our existence that we are, in fact, better off relying only on ourselves. This type of thinking goes back to Dietrich Bonhoeffer, who during the Nazi era in Germany felt that in the modern world, in science, arts, ethics, and even in religious questions, God has become superfluous.[19] But as we shall see in the concluding section of this chapter, far deeper and quite contrary psychological motivations can also be discerned in the "God is Dead" movement.

6 · *The Death of Jehova*

A discussion, even a cursory one like the one contained in the present chapter, of the "God is Dead' theology would not be complete if it were confined to the Christian world. For the fact is that this type of new and radical theology caused reverberations in Jewish religious thinking as well; or perhaps it would be more correct to say that the same world developments which triggered the Protestant "God is Dead" theology also gave the impetus to a similar search in certain Jewish circles for a new and radical understanding of religion in general and the God concept in particular. The Jewish approach to the problem of the death of God can best be presented by summarizing the argument put forward by the most articulate Jewish spokesman of this trend, Rabbi Richard L. Rubenstein.

Dr. Rubenstein recognizes that "myth and religious symbol no longer are regarded as true at the manifest level," but argues that this "is entirely irrelevant to their central function which is to give profound expression to our feelings at the decisive times and crises of life." [20]

While such a statement sounds uncomfortably like Bultmann's demythologizing, when Rubenstein comes to grips with the issue of the death of God, he carefully draws a line between the traditional Jewish God concept and the new understanding of God which he struggles to reach. "After Auschwitz," he says, "many Jews did not need Nietzsche to tell them that the old God of Jewish patriarchal monotheism was dead beyond all hope of resurrection." [21] For those who face the issues of "God and human freedom and God and human evil," the old traditional Jewish patriarchal God, whose Providence shielded His Chosen People, is dead. Even the existentialist leap of faith cannot resurrect this dead God after Auschwitz." [22]

However, Rubenstein maintains that it is possible—indeed, necessary—even after the death of this transcendent theistic God of Jewish patriarchal monotheism, whom he calls "the Father-God," to understand God as "the primal ground of being out of which we arise and to which we return. I believe such a God is inescapable in the time of the death of God." This God "remains the central reality against which all partial realities can be measured." He "can be understood meaningfully . . . also as the *focus of ultimate concern.* . . . He is the infinite measure against which we can see our own limited finite lives in proper perspective." He is "the ultimate measure of human truth and human potentiality, [He] calls upon each man to face both the limitations and the opportunities of his finite predicament without disguise, illusion or hope." [23]

Having thus divested his God of all theistic attributes—for this, in effect, is what Dr. Rubenstein is doing, although he pays lip service to his Protestant fellow-theologians by calling the process "the Death of God"—he must, and does, face the question: Is "the religion of God as the source and ground of being, the God after the death of God, truly a religion?" "Can there be a religion without a belief in a theistic, creator God?" [24]

His answer is in the affirmative, albeit a qualified affirmative. He asserts that "in the time of the death of God a mystical paganism which utilizes the historic forms of Jewish religion offers the most promising approach to religion. . . ." We must sacrifice "pride in the attainments which are not central to the business of life" and must celebrate in the synagogue, in accordance with the traditions of Judaism, the "decisive events in the timetable of life"—i.e., "what we experience in common from birth to death. . . ." "Each of us before God as the focus of ultimate concern must regard the real challenges of his personal existence as essentially the same as those of any other human being." In this manner, and along this rather difficult path, we can reach the ultimate insight that "God stands before us no longer as the final censor but as the final reality before which and in terms of which all partial realities are to be measured." Despite his earlier assertion that man must face his "finite predicament without disguise, illusion or hope," Rubenstein concludes his discussion of the position of Judaism on the Death of God issue on a note of hope: "The last paradox is that in the time of the death of God we have begun a voyage of discovery wherein we may, hopefully, find the true God." [25]

In the chapter of *After Auschwitz*, which immediately follows the one from which we have been quoting, Dr. Rubenstein flatly contradicts himself, but in doing so remains true to the traditional Judaism within whose framework his thinking was formed. "In Judaism God simply does not die," he asserts, even going so far as to term the "death of God' a mere metaphor which rests on a symbolism of obviously Christian origin. In view of these qualifications it is quite apparent that when he concedes that *"we live in the time of the death of God,"* he uses a metaphor which for him means: we live in a time in which many people (primarily Protestants) consider God as having lost his central place in human life, thought, and concern, which is expressed by the shorthand term "God is dead." [26] Ultimately it all boils down to one single but significant psychological insight: the statement "God is dead" merely refers to the death of the faith of man who makes the statement.

That this is actually the case becomes amply evident if we consider the plethora of deities whom Rubenstein offers as substitutes for the old patriarchal God. They are Dionysus and Apollo, and Mother Earth, to whom he also refers as the "cannibal Mother Goddess of Earth." [27] This is certainly a remarkable harking back by a modern radical theologian to Hellenic deities, and beyond them to an old Earth Mother-type of goddess, who unites in herself the antithetical and yet complementary qualities of the life-bestowing and life-destroying elementary female character. It was the late Erich Neumann who in an unforgettable study unearthed some of the psychological foundations of the indestructible powers of the archetypal feminine expressed in the primordial goddess whose ambivalent, life-giving and death-dealing image appears in so many variations from the Old Stone Age down to our own times.[28] I myself was repeatedly attracted to analyzing the manifestations of Mother Earth in ancient Jewish culture and the constantly reemerging worship of a female deity in various periods of the long history of the Hebrew-Jewish religion.[29] In fact, Rubenstein's statement about the Earth Mother reminded me curiously of what I had written just a little earlier:

> Is the Hebrew goddess dead or does she merely
> slumber, soon to awaken rejuvenated by her rest and
> reclaim the hearts of her sons and lovers? No one can
> say. But should she manage to survive, we can expect
> this to take place only in the Land of Israel. It was
> there that she first clasped to her bosom the wild
> Hebrew warriors who erupted from the desert. It
> was there that most of her life-history, including her
> amazing metamorphoses, took place. And it was there

—less than four hundred years ago!—that her Rachel
and Leah forms revealed to the pious and the learned
the divine meaning of earthly love, the last of her
great motherly-wifely acts, and that her identity with
the ancient Biblical goddess Asherah was recognized
in a remarkable flash of intuitive insight. It will be
there, therefore, if at all, that she will re-emerge, in
who knows what surprising old-new image, to mediate,
as of old, between man and God and to draw the
returning faith-bereft sons with new bonds of love to
their patiently waiting Father.[30]

While thus Rubenstein's thinking coincides to a point with
my own, I differ with him emphatically when he characterizes
the ancient Canaanite-Israelite Earth Mother as "cannibalistic."
The death-dealing aspect of the ancient Hebrew goddess is a
function of her nature as the great womb into which all men
must return simply because it is out of it that all of them arise.
The "cannibalistic" idea, found, for example, in ancient India
and Mexico, that the terrible earth mother actually devours her
children with her huge teeth-studded mouth, is totally foreign
to Judaism. The Hebrew-Jewish Mother Earth receives her children back into her womb; her children, weary of life, return to
her willingly, nay eagerly, like tired voyagers who return at
eventide to the warmth of home and hearth.

In trying to penetrate to the mythology which constitutes the
supporting understructure of Rubenstein's thinking, we find the
following: The old Father-God whose providence kept watch over
every individual (although, simultaneously and notoriously, his
ways were "inscrutable"—i.e., beyond total human comprehen-
sion) is dead. His place is taken by a new God ("le roi est mort,
vive le roi") or Goddess whose being is undoubtedly much more
difficult to grasp than that of the old one, but who mythically and
mystically is, in essence, the same. The new, "true" God, whose
existence we only suspect, since we have only embarked on the
exciting voyage of discovering Him, puts to us a new set of demands which are less concrete and less clear-cut but at the
same time more exacting and more difficult; He is the ultimate
foundation, measure, and gauge of human existence.

This is clearly a new myth as well as a non-myth. It is a myth insofar as it tells something significant about a divine being and the relationship between him and man; it is a non-myth inasmuch as it, perhaps purposely, foregoes all the forms traditionally utilized by myth to have its way with man. It is, in final reduction, a myth perfectly responsive to the needs of modern man, who wants to but cannot believe in a positive relationship between his own utterly confused and convulsed existence and that great mythical ultimate reality which has been termed God for the last five thousand years.

7 • *The Hope of the*
Resurrection of God

Although, as we have seen above, the dying god idea has a long history behind it, going back to ancient Near Eastern cultures, it is nevertheless significant that the modern "God is Dead" doctrine emerged precisely in the age in which the sudden and violent obliteration of mankind as a whole, or of major parts of it, has for the first time in history become an acutely threatening possibility. In the distant past, when man contemplated the almost total extinction of his race as a mythical event that had taken place in a remote primeval era—e.g., in the form of the Biblical Deluge—he did not have recourse to a "Death of God" theology because, on the contrary, he saw in that great catastrophe the punishing hand of God (or of the gods), and because his very presence on earth proved to him that he was able to survive the Great Flood and repeople the earth. When the obliteration of man is not a mythical memory but a real possibility, when it does not lie in the distant past but threatens in the immediate future, and when it is not an act of God but is contrived by man himself, the psychological reaction is very different. This reaction takes two forms. One is a desperation mixed with defiance, which says in effect: A world in which it has come to this cannot have a providential divinity presiding over it. The other is the desire to rid oneself of the trauma by displacing the fear of the imminent mortal danger with the belief that the catastrophe has already taken place, but that it happened not to man but to God; what could happen to man is too horrible to contemplate, and it is therefore projected as already having happened to God. Thus one is concerned not with man's being threatened by death, but with God, who has actually died.

The mechanism of the latter psychological reaction has certain affinities with those which produced the belief in the dying Gods in antiquity. In those faraway days the greatest catastrophe that threatened man with extinction was the death of vegetation, scorched and killed off every year by the merciless rays of the summer sun. All nature, it was felt, had abandoned mankind, which itself appeared doomed to death. Thereupon, a great mourning ritual was observed, with dirges, lamentations, and impassioned wailing—not over mankind, the real object of all this concern, but over the god Tammuz, to whose death all those dreaded natural occurrences were attributed.

Observing the mourning rites of the dying god tended to ease tension. This is always the first beneficial effect of great mass rituals. One does, in the reassuring company of a large number of like-minded people, what has always been done, since time immemorial, in response to the great emergency, which is no less acute for being periodic. By directing one's reactions into the proper, time-established channels, one knows that one has done all that is required and all that is humanly possible under the circumstances. But then, although attention is completely focused on the tragic death of the god—each time a unique, shattering event and a matchless tragedy—consciousness cannot entirely exclude the memory, and hence the anticipation, of the resurrection of the god, which must follow his death in the future, as it always did in the past.

And herein lies the comfort contained in the ancient myths and rituals of the dying god for our present world at large and for the "God is Dead" theology in particular. *The god who died came to life again.* Whatever the human psychological motivations that resulted in the belief in the dying god, once there was such a belief it was followed by the belief in his resurrection. In the world of mythical reality rebirth is a natural consequence of death, which it follows in a natural sequence, thus reversing the order of physiological reality in which death is the inevitable consequence of birth. There was nothing miraculous about the god's resurrection. On the contrary, it was as "normal" as the germination of the seed buried in the bosom of Mother Earth. When Christianity adopted this old and powerful mythologem, it did so in a watered-down, weakened version; it made God take on human form, become man, before it let him die, and then represented his resurrection not as the inevitable sequel to the death of god but as a miracle that took place in the tomb (and body) of a flesh-and-blood human, like other miraculous revivals of the dead. A true god dies as a god and comes to life as a god, his godhead suffers no metamorphosis throughout, for god he remains whether dead or alive.

In this respect the new "God is Dead" theology harks back, without being aware of it, to the ancient Near Eastern dying god. It is not Jesus, the Christ, the god-become-man, whom this theology pronounces dead. In fact, it has very little to say about Christ, and what little it does say about him reminds one of Nietzsche's opinion that contemporary philosophers had muddied their shallow waters in order to make them appear deep. No, the god whom the new theology pronounces dead is God the Father, or, if you wish, the traditional Judeo-Christian God before his subjection to the harassments of trinitarianism. This God, having never become man, could die only *qua* God, that is, in the manner in which the ancient Near Eastern dying gods had died.

But if so, the dead god of the radical theology must share with the dying gods of the ancient Near East the fate that awaited them all, year after year, and that alone made their death meaningful and the mourning for them a great *human* experience. This fate is, of course, the resurrection of the dead god, although the modern radical theology is curiously unaware of it.[31] I say curiously, because one would expect modern college-educated theologians to be students of comparative religion at least to the extent of recognizing when their speculations create a divine image which falls into, or has close affinities with, an old and famous category of deities: that of the dying gods of the ancient Near East. Had they recognized the relationship between those old dying gods and their newly pronounced dead god, they would have been impelled to let him share the fate of his remote predecessors and intimated at least that he, too, was bound to come to life again.

It is not the task of the anthropologist to tell any human group what it ought to do. Nor, strictly speaking, it is up to him to make predictions. Yet, if I may be permitted to indulge, not in foretelling the future, but in merely indicating what, on the basis of a comparison with past processes, can be expected to develop within the "God is Dead" movement, I would use for once the language of theology and say this:

Gods have had ample opportunities in the course of a long human prehistory and history to prove their longevity, their tenacity, and their ability not only to cling to life under the most adverse circumstances but to regain it whenever they happened to die. Occasionally, for reasons of his own, a god managed to mislead men into believing that they had succeeded in killing him. According to an old Midrash, when the builders of the Tower of Babel saw that the top of their monstrous structure was nearing the clouds they decided to shoot arrows into heaven in order to kill God. The arrows fell back drenched with blood and the would-be deicides rejoiced: "We have killed God!" What the poor fools did not know was that their arrows fell back to earth bloodied because God had stained them in order to mislead the builders of the tower and to give them a taste of victory before He came down in His wrath and wrought His vengeance upon them.

It is this phase of imagined victory in which the "God is Dead" theologians today find themselves. They think they have succeeded in killing God by piercing His ineffable body with the arrows of their fatuous "God is Dead" *kerygma*. Whether they actually have killed Him or not, we have no way of knowing. But even if they did, as the wild boar killed the youthful Adonis in the rocky gorge under the dark cedars of Mount Lebanus, the likelihood is that He will come to life again, as He did so often in the past. And when He comes back, endowed with a new, reinvigorated, and radiant personality, He will, as Hosea (11:4) prophesied a very long time ago, draw mankind after Him "with cords of a man, with bands of love." In other words, one can expect the emergence of an even newer, more modern, and more radical theology centering on a new myth of the dying and reviving god, whose human-like suffering and fate will make him a true shepherd and whose divine resurrection will hold out ultimate comfort in this hour of humanity's extreme anguish.

myths for new
black faiths

1 • *The Black Muslims*

While old religions struggle with the problem of how to reconcile their ancient or medieval mythologies with the demands of modern times, new religions, which still continue to crop up in various sectors of contemporary society, go ahead almost nonchalantly with the task of creating their own mythological underpinning. The most telling examples to illustrate this generalization can be found among the American Negroes who have produced in the last several decades a considerable number of religious sects and movements belonging to the "faith healing" and "Holiness cult" types, as well as a systematically argued black theology.

Take the Black Muslim sect to begin with. This sect was founded in Detroit around 1930 by Ali Farrad (or W. D. Fard, or Farrad Muhammad), a peddler, possibly of Arab extraction. In 1934 Fard mysteriously disappeared, and his chief disciple, Elijah Muhammad (originally Elijah Poole, one of twelve children of a Negro sharecropper), took over the leadership. Elijah Muhammad declared that Fard was none other than Allah incarnate, and proclaimed himself His Messenger and last prophet. In 1970, when the Black Muslim sect numbered some 100,000 adherents, a basic tenet of the sect was still the same with reference to Fard: "We believe that Allah (God) appeared in the Person of Master W. Fard Muhammad, July, 1930, the long-awaited 'Messiah' of the Christians and the 'Mahdi' of the Muslims." [1] This single quotation suffices to show that, although the movement calls itself Black Muslim, or the "Lost Nation of Islam in North America," or "The Lost-Found Nation in the West," there is so little in common between it and the religion of Islam as practiced in the traditionally Muslim areas of North Africa, the Middle East, Pakistan, Central and Southeast Asia, that it must be considered an entirely new religious development. [2]

Being a new religion, Black Islam was in need of a new mythology. Its central myth was supplied by Elijah Muhammad himself in the form of a new, black version of Genesis. Sixty-six trillion years ago, Elijah Muhammad and his followers maintain, a huge explosion split apart the moon and the earth, and "Original Man" appeared on the latter. Allah himself declared that this Original Man was "none other than the Black Man." These first humans constituted the tribe of Shabazz, and they spread all over the earth. The original Black Man is "the first and the last, the maker and owner of the universe," and, in fact, divine by nature. He spoke Arabic, and through Moses, Jesus, and Muhammad—all black men—he received religious revelations from Allah. It is from him that the "so-called Negro in America" traces his origin.

After being in sole possession of the earth for all those trillions of years, a mere 6,650 years ago a brilliant but evil black scientist, Yakub by name, embarked upon a sinister scheme to destroy his fellow blacks, in brazen defiance of the will of Allah. Having discovered that the black man could be broken down into two "germs"—one black and one brown—he proceeded to mate the lighter strains until he isolated the brown race. Not satisfied with this, Yakub continued his experiments until he managed to produce the red and yellow races. After some six hundred more years of hybridizing, and "following a strict and rigid birth control law," he finally filtered out all pigmentation from his human guinea pigs, and thus accomplished his purpose—the white race. The members of this new race were very ugly—their skin a pallid white, their eyes pale blue—but, worst of all, no soul or humanity was left in them. These white devils with whom Yakub peopled the earth were—and their descendants are to this day—inferior physically, morally, and mentally, bereft of ennobling human emotions such as love, compassion, honesty, unselfishness, and courage. They are evil, they are "the human beast—the serpent, the dragon, the devil, and Satan." The very name by which they are called, "Caucasians," means, according to Elijah Muhammad, who quotes "Arab scholars" as his authorities on the point, people whose evil affects others as well. "The White or Caucasian race, sometimes called the European race" was "by nature . . . created liars and murderers . . . they are the enemies of truth and righteousness. . . ." These white devils were given six thousand years to rule. They enslaved the Black Man, degraded him, imposed Christianity upon him to make him humble and meek, and treated his women as if they were animals. The period of white dominance came to an end in 1914; however, from that date on the white devils still were allowed a period of grace for seventy years. Hence, in 1984 the rule of the Black Nation will be firmly established all over the world.[3]

Before commenting on the psychological significance of this myth, let me mention that, as far as its external form is concerned, it belongs taxonomically to that widespread category of origin myths which explain the skin colors of the various human races by referring to the acts of a creator or creators, and, at the same time, reassure the members of the ingroup that people who have their particular skin color are superior. For example, in the creation myth of the Shilluks of the White Nile—a black complected people—Juok the creator molded all men out of earth, and while he was engaged in this work he wandered about the world. "In the land of the whites he found a pure white earth

or sand, and out of it he shaped white men. Then he came to
the land of Egypt and out of the mud of the Nile he made red
or brown men. Lastly he came to the land of the Shilluks, and
finding there black earth he created black men out of it." [4]
Thus the idea that black men are better than white or red or
brown men is implicit in the raw material of which the various
races were fashioned. Every child among the Shilluks knows that
neither white earth or sand nor reddish-brown mud compares
in quality with the rich black earth of Shilluk land.

In a like manner, the Black Muslim origin myth explains, in
the first place, the existence of men of various colors, i.e., various
races, and reassures the black sons of the Nation of Islam that
they are the "original" and "best" race of those that make up
mankind. This brings us back to the psychological significance
of the myth of the Negro past as taught and believed by the
Black Muslims. One thing is clear at the outset: their myth is a
most effective charter issued from on high (through the inter-
mediacy of Allah's Messenger, Elijah Muhammed), underpinning and validating the soul-sustaining belief that, contrary to
the momentarily prevailing ephemeral situation, the Negro is not
only the Original Man, but also the elite of humankind. With
this mightily reassuring origin myth the Black Muslim charter
myth combines an even more heartening myth of the future by
asserting that the time is near when the Black Man will regain
the position of dominance and leadership in the world which is
rightfully his.

2 · *The Black Christ*

The myth of the black Christ, of his black mother, and, indeed,
of the black God, was bound to emerge in a society such as
that of twentieth-century America, in which large groups of
Negroes in the ghettos of the northern metropolises had become
increasingly aware of their oppression and inequality. One reaction to this situation was the complete rejection of the white
man and everything he stood for, and a demand for Negro self-
determination, symbolized by the slogan of "Black Power."

When it came to religion, the spokesmen and adherents of the

Negro liberation movement were in a particularly difficult position. Originally forced upon American blacks by their slave-masters, Christianity had, in the course of generations, become an integral part of their lives, an organic constituent of their very being. The logical extension of the black rejection of all white values would have been a secession from Christianity, the white man's religion, represented by white church hierarchies, centered upon the Son of God, Christ, shown in innumerable representations as a white man, son of a white mother, and sent to earth by God the Father who also was invariably imagined as white. The very word "white" played an important role in Christian theology, denoting purity, a status of sinlessness, while the word "black" meant evil and sinfulness, and stood for Satan.

A number of black Christians in the United States did, indeed, conclude that the abandonment of Christianity was necessary. Some embraced their special brand of Black Islam; others, as we shall see later in this chapter, became Black Jews. For many, however, Christianity was too dear to give up,[5] and instead of abandoning it, they reshaped it in their image, as man has so frequently done with imported religions that had first to be re-fashioned and recast before they were found satisfactory for home consumption. This is how the Black Christian churches in America came into being.[6] Black Christianity, Black Christ, and Black Power as a religion are preached by, among others, Father Raymond Ellis (himself a Lebanese) of Detroit's St. Cecelia Roman Catholic Church; Dr. Nathan Wright, Episcopal priest; Rev. Jesse Jackson; and historian Vincent Harding.[7]

We shall give here neither the history of Black Christianity in the United States, nor its rituals, nor its organization. What interests us is the myth that the leaders of the Black Christians have provided in order to satisfy their membership's need for a sustaining, validating, "life-giving" mythology to serve as the rock upon which to build their church.

As early as the nineteenth century, Bishop Henry M. Turner said "God is a Negro!" In the twentieth century, an early abortive attempt to organize a Black Orthodox Church, with a black hierarchy, a Black God, a Black Jesus, a Black Madonna, and black angels, was made by Marcus Garvey in the 1920s in New

York. Soon after Garvey was imprisoned for mail fraud in 1925, his church disintegrated. A generation later, the city of Detroit, where the Black Muslims had originated a few years earlier, became the birthplace of a vital Black Christian movement which is still spreading to various parts of the country. The Black Muslims and Black Christians parallel each other also in the strong emphasis both place on blackness as a value, black separatism, and black superiority to whites. The founder and leader of this new Black Christian church is the Rev. Dr. Albert B. Cleage, Jr., a clergyman of the United Church of Christ and pastor of the Shrine of the Black Madonna in Detroit (so renamed in 1968; formerly it was called Central United Church of Christ). In the Shrine a large painting showing a Black Mary with a Black Babe is prominently displayed. The myths of the Black Church can best be culled from a book of sermons by the Rev. Cleage, published in 1968, under the title *The Black Messiah.*

In the Introduction Dr. Cleage states that "For nearly 500 years the illusion that Jesus was white dominated the world only because white Europeans dominated the world. Now, with the emergence of the nationalist movements of the world's colored majority, the historic truth is finally beginning to emerge—that Jesus was the non-white leader of a non-white people struggling for national liberation against the rule of a white nation, Rome. . . ." [8] This thesis is validated by the following myth:

The Chaldeans, from whom Abraham sprang, were black. So were the Egyptians, among whom the Israelites lived in slavery. Moses himself was half-Egyptian and half-Jewish, which "makes him unquestionably all non-white." After the Egyptian slavery the Israelites "wandered all over the ancient world, all over Africa. They had intermarried with people from the various countries of Africa." Thus in the days of Moses "the Nation Israel was a Black Nation intermingled with all the black peoples of Africa. So there was nothing strange about Moses marrying a black woman." The peoples of Canaan with whom Israel intermixed "weren't white people either." Babylon, where Israel was taken in captivity, "was no white nation." [9]

In the Promised Land, they [the Israelites] had
degenerated into individualism. They exploited each
other. . . . Each one was . . . buying and selling his
black brothers and sisters into slavery. . . . Then
Jesus appeared . . . but his ministry apparently
ended in failure when he was crucified. All of this
was background for the miraculous rebirth of the
Black Nation at Pentecost.[10]

Jesus was a revolutionary black leader, a Zealot,
seeking to lead a Black Nation to freedom, so the
Black Church must carefully define the nature of the
revolution.[11]

After the crucifixion . . . the disciples and followers
of Jesus . . . were completely disillusioned. . . .
They went back to their fishing boats and other
occupations, trying to live as they had before they
had been persuaded to follow the Black Messiah. . . .[12]

Now these [the Jews] were black people who were
oppressed. . . . The white Gentiles, the Romans,
were oppressing and exploiting them in every way
possible. Jesus had tried to bring them together, to
bring them hope, to build a Black Nation, but he
had not succeeded. The only thing he left, according
to the Book of Acts, was about one hundred and
twenty people who set up a synagogue in Jerusalem.
They were still Jews, black Jews. But this little group
of one hundred and twenty believed that Jesus was
the Black Messiah. In all the other synagogues where
Jews were worshiping (and there were synagogues
not only in Israel, but in Egypt and all across Africa),
Jews were still waiting for the Messiah to come. . . .
Suddenly [these 120 Jews] had a strange experience.
It seemed as though the room was filled with a mighty
wind, and fire was over each head. Suddenly at
Pentecost, they were welded together into a group
and the Black Nation had power. . . . The Nation
Jesus had tried to build had come into being.[13]

All this is of utmost importance for the Black Church "to
understand because we are in the process of rebuilding the

Black nation." "We can find in Christianity a new direction and new truth. A Black Messiah and a Black Madonna. The Bible becomes something new when you understand that it is talking about a black people and a Black Messiah. . . ." "Our rediscovery of the Black Messiah is a part of our rediscovery of ourselves." "Jesus, the Black Messiah, . . . came to a Black Nation. . . ." "Jesus was born to Mary, a Jew of the tribe of Judah, a non-white people; black in the same sense that the Arabs were black people, in the same sense that the Egyptians were black people. Jesus was a Black Messiah born to a black woman." [14]

Cleage's emphatic black Christology is paralleled by a somewhat less outspoken black theology: "If we think of God as a person . . . then God must be a combination of black, yellow, and red with just a little touch of white, and we must think of God as a black God. . . . If God were white . . . he would have sent a white son down to some nice white people. He certainly would not have sent him down to a black people like Israel." [15]

The Black Son and his Black Father are invoked at the conclusion of each sermon. For instance: "Heavenly Father . . . We thank thee for the gift of thy Son, the Black Messiah, Jesus Christ. . . ." [16] One of the doctrines God revealed through his Black Son is that of Black Power: "We believe in the doctrine of Black Power as a religious concept revealed to us, as God's Chosen People, in the Old Testament and in the teachings of Jesus." [17] In this spirit, the Resurrection that the congregation celebrates at the Shrine of the Black Madonna, and at the churches of the "Black Christian Nationalist Movement," is "not the resurrection of the physical body of Jesus, but the resurrection of the Black Nation which he started, the resurrection of his ideas and his teachings." Dr. Cleage's black mythology inevitably brings him close to the pre-Christian history of the Hebrews; he "believes that most of the Jewish festivals are 'as significant to black people as for Jews,' and he is planning to incorporate them into worship in his church. The festival of Passover, for instance, will be a celebration of black release from bondage." [18]

Two more questions remain to be answered by the myth of the Black Church: how did the originally black Christians of the days of Jesus become white? And how did the Jews, who were black from the days of Abraham to the time of Jesus, become white? Dr. Cleage answers that it was Paul who was responsible for the admission of white peoples into the original church. Paul, who "never knew Jesus," . . . "modified his teachings to conform to the pagan philosophies of the white gentiles." Thus the Christian church became a church of white people. However, the true, black Christians do not need these unauthentic Pauline teachings.[19]

As to the Jews, whom "you see today in America [and who] are white," the facts (according to Dr. Cleage's myth) are simply these: "Most of them are the descendants of white Europeans and Asiatics [at this point Dr. Cleage seems to have forgotten that elsewhere he considered Asiatics to be "nonwhite," that is, black] who were converted to Judaism about one thousand years ago. . . . The Jews who stayed in that part of the world where black people are predominant, remained black. The conflict between black Jews and white Jews is a problem in Israel today."[20]

3 · The Black God

Whereas Dr. Cleage's myth claims a Black Christ as a historical fact, a black professor of theology at the Union Theological Seminary in New York, Dr. James H. Cone, maintains that "the blackness of Christ is a theological concept,"[21] but goes on to apply the attribute of blackness to God himself and does so emphatically and passionately. Dr. Cone is perhaps an even more committed advocate of Black Power than Dr. Cleage, but his myth (or "doctrine," if you prefer) of a Black Christ and a Black God moves on the conceptual and theological, rather than on the historical, level. Dr. Cone holds that "Christianity is not alien to Black Power, it is Black Power" and that "Black rebellion is a manifestation of God himself."[22] He even goes so far as to identify Christ with Black Power: "In twentieth-century America, *Christ means Black Power!*"[23] And he pro-

claims, "whether whites want to hear it or not, *Christ is black,
baby,* with all the features which are so detestable to white society." [24]

In contrast to Dr. Cleage, who seeks to establish the blackness
of Jesus (and, to a lesser extent, of God) historically, Dr.
Cone proceeds theologically in creating his own brand of the myth of
the Black Christ: "To suggest," he says, "that Christ has taken
on a black skin is not theological emotionalism. If the Church is
a continuation of the Incarnation, and if the Church and Christ
are where the oppressed are, then Christ and his Church must
identify totally with the oppressed to the extent that they too
suffer for the same reasons persons are enslaved. In America,
blacks are oppressed because of their blackness. It would seem,
then, that emancipation could only be realized by Christ and his
Church becoming black. Thinking of Christ as non-black in
the twentieth-century is as theologically impossible as thinking
of him as non-Jewish in the first century. . . ." [25]

Progressing from this position to one of daring generalization,
Dr. Cone says: ". . . Black is holy, that is it is a symbol of God's
presence in history on behalf of oppressed man. Where there is
black, there is oppression, but blacks can be assured that where
there is blackness, there is Christ who has taken on blackness so
that what is evil in men's eyes might become good. Therefore
Christ is black because he is oppressed, and oppressed because
he is black." [26]

About a year after the publication of his book *Black Theology
and Black Power,* Dr. Cone returned to the theme of the Black
Christ in an article he published in *Ebony* magazine. In it he
was even more emphatic in asserting the theological irrelevance
of Christ for the Blacks of America, unless He Himself was
Black: "Blackness is god's incarnated presence in contemporary
America. . . ." And, moreover, there is a "divine revelation
found in blackness." [27]

In his new book, *A Black Theology of Liberation,* Dr. Cone
goes a decisive step beyond the argument presented in his *Black
Theology and Black Power,* asserting that "any message that is
not related to the liberation of the poor in the society is not

Christ's message. . . . In a society where men are oppressed because they are *black,* Christian theology must become *Black
Theology,* a theology that is unreservedly identified with the
goals of the oppressed community and seeking to interpret the
divine character of their struggle for liberation." Then, he goes
on to state that "an authentic understanding" of his *Black Theology of Liberation* "is dependent on the blackness of their [i.e.,
the black community's] existence in the world." [28]

In the section in his new book entitled "God is Black," Cone
elevates the concept of blackness to a central position in his
theology: "The blackness of God, and everything implied by it
in a racist society, is the heart of Black Theology's doctrine of
God." He even goes so far as to assert that "the black theologian
must reject any conception of God which stifles black self-determination by picturing God as a God of all peoples."

Having thus made God an exclusive property of black peoples,
Cone proceeds to equate whiteness with satanic evil, in a manner
reminiscent of both the Black Muslim doctrine and the mythical
image of the white whale, Moby Dick. In fact, Cone says that
the "satanic *whiteness*" of the "white religionists" "is a denial
of the very essence of divinity." In other words, by the fact of
having been born white, the white people are "satanic" and
constitute a denial of the very essence of divinity. Therefore, in
order to know God, *"we must become black with God,"* for
ultimately "blackness" and "salvation" are "synonymous." [29]

While the old truism that man creates his gods in his own
image can be illustrated by many other examples as well (remember the Germanic blond Christ and the Mexican black Madonna of Guadalupe), the Black Christian mythology is remarkable for its theoretical equation of skin color with "soul" color. It
expresses the conviction that people having black skin can be
truly understood by others—even divine others—only if those
others are of dark skin color. This deep-down conviction was
undoubtedly a significant motivating force in the emergence of
the two parallel mythologies we have been examining, that of
the Black Christians and that of the Black Muslims. However,
once the respective mythologies took form, they in turn acted,

and continue to act to this day, as powerful factors in supporting, justifying, and validating the doctrines of black separatism and black supremacy.

4 • The Black Jews

Some Negro groups drew the final conclusion intimated in the teachings of the Black Christian Nationalist Movement, embracing the faith of which both Christianity and Islam are but daughter-religions—Judaism. Various attempts to organize congregations which styled themselves "Black Jews" began around 1915 in several northeastern cities. In Harlem, during the period 1919–1931, at least eight Black Jewish cult groups emerged, some of which acknowledged Jesus as a "Black Jew who was lynched by Gentiles."[30] An early sect of "Black Jews," officially called The Church of God, was founded several decades ago by Prophet F. S. Cherry. After arriving in Philadelphia from the deep south, Prophet Cherry learned some Hebrew and Yiddish and was directed by God, who appeared to him in a vision, to establish his church.

The main features of the mythological foundations of the Church of God were as follows: God is black. Jesus Christ, in whom the Black Jews believed, was a black man. He came, not to nullify, but to fulfill the Old Testament. The true Sabbath is Saturday. Black people were the original inhabitants of the earth. Noah, Shem, Japheth, Ham, Lot, Abraham, Isaac, and Jacob were black, but Jacob's brother Esau was the first red man. Black people sprang from Jacob, and should therefore be called Israelites, since, after Jacob had wrestled with the angel, his name was changed to Israel (Genesis 32:24–28). The reason that Gentiles insist that black folk like to steal is that they are still angry at Jacob, the father of the blacks, for having stolen Esau's birthright. The slavery of the black man, as well as his ultimate deliverance, are foretold in the Bible.

The first white man was Gehazi, the servant of Elisha, who became white as a result of a curse placed upon him by Elisha for his sin. (The Bible says in II Kings 5:27, that Gehazi became a "leper white as snow.") After having become white, Gehazi still mixed with black folk and this is how the yellow race came into existence.

The so-called Jews, not being black, are imposters. In apparent contradiction, the myth maintains that prejudice against the black man could be found as far back in history as Mosaic times, for Numbers 12:1 relates that Moses was reviled for marrying an Ethiopian—i.e., a black—woman. Yet if Gehazi, who lived several centuries after Moses, was the first white man, and if all the Israelites were black until his time, how could the black Moses have been reviled by his own black brother Aaron and black sister Miriam for having married a black woman? The inconsistency, as is typical for mythical thinking, goes unnoticed.

The Black Jewish myth contains one futuristic feature. At the end of the present century, black Jesus will come again and usher in the millennium at which time the Black Jews will go into high places.[31]

More recently established congregations of the Black Jews in Harlem, New York, Philadelphia, and elsewhere approached traditional Judaism more closely. They completely gave up all belief in Jesus, and in their ritual they emulate Jewish worship as best they can. Compared to the Black Muslims and Black Christians, these Black Jews had a relatively easier task in creating a supporting mythology for their religion. The Black Muslims and Black Christians had to fly in the face of old-established traditions that formed part of the Muslim and Christian history as understood by all Muslims and all Christians—except the black ones—literally blackening the faces and bodies of ancestral groups whom all the rest of the Muslim and Christian hundreds of millions have always and unquestioningly assumed to have been white. Had the Black Muslims bothered to examine, for a brief moment at least, the history of Islam, they would have found that the Arabs, and not the European and American Christians, were the first to enslave the blacks of Africa, to drag them in chains or ropes to the north and west African ports, there to deliver them into the hands of the Spanish, Portuguese, Dutch, and other slave traders. The Black Muslims' claim of Arab ancestry is true only in the sense that on the way to those ports the Arab slave drivers raped all or most of the nubile girls and impregnated many of them, so that by the time they arrived at the port of disembarkation, the human cargo on the ships was augmented by numerous Negro-Arab halfbreeds. Furthermore, the fact that the Arabic term for slave, 'abd, early assumed, and retains to the present day, the secondary meaning "black man," is alone sufficient proof that the Arabs were, and emphatically considered themselves, white.

And as to the Christian Black Nation, their doctrine that the original Jewish-Christians were black is likewise vitiated by the presence in our very midst of Jews who are physically indistinguishable from the white Christians, and especially from the present-day heirs of those "white" Romans of the time of Christ, the Italians. In fact, many militant blacks of America of the 1960s and 1970s based their anti-Semitism precisely on the identification of the Jew with "Whitey". While myth is known to have the power to maintain itself despite contradictory facts, it is nonetheless quite a difficult task to uphold the veracity and credibility of the myth of one's own small ingroup when it is contradicted by the powerful and well entrenched myth of the larger society of which the ingroup forms only a small part.

The Black Jews encounter no such problem. Their own myth of origin and identity follows the Bible more closely than that of the Black Christians and Black Muslims, and its central theme, the visit paid by the Queen of Sheba to King Solomon, is, in fact, Biblical almost in its entirety. However, the Black Jewish myth as recounted by Rabbi Wentworth A. Matthew of the Harlem Commandment Keepers Congregation to Howard Brotz, adds one feature: the Queen of Sheba, whose name was Candace, was "of the children of Rachel, one of the wives of Jacob." [32] Where the Black Jewish origin myth deviates more markedly from traditional Jewish mythology is in maintaining that, of the three sons of Noah, two, Shem and Ham, were black, and only Japheth was white, in contrast to the Biblical genealogy, which assigns the Cushites—i.e., the Negroes—to Hamitic stock only. The Black Jewish version makes King Solomon a black man, so that the son, Menelik, born to him and the Queen of Sheba thus had both a black father and a black mother. At the age of twelve Menelik was sent back by his mother to Jerusalem to celebrate his Bar Mitzvah (confirmation). He remained in the court of his father until he was twenty-five, when Solomon sent him back to Ethiopia with a company of men, including some priests. Solomon commanded them to take along a copy of the two stone Tablets of the Law Moses had received on Mount Sinai, but the priests deceived Solomon and took the original Tablets which are preserved to this day at Axum. Menelik became the first Israelite King, or "Lion of Judah," in Ethiopia; the Emperor Haile Selassie is his 613th successor on the throne in an unbroken line.

Because of political pressures, Haile Selassie officially follows the Coptic Christian Church; actually, however, he follows the Jewish ritual of the Falashas, the Black Jews of Ethiopia. No pork is eaten in his palace and the entire royal court is closed for business from Friday afternoon and all day Saturday. The Emperor's person is living proof that the House of David should never lack a black man to sit on the throne of Israel. When the Italians invaded Ethiopia, Haile Selassie, on his way to the League of Nations, stopped in Jerusalem to pray in Hebrew in the Holy City of his great ancestors. It is from Addis Ababa, the capital of Ethiopia, that Rabbi Wentworth Matthew of the Ethiopian Hebrew Congregation of Harlem derives his "authority as head of the Black Jews in the United States."[33]

The issue of blackness runs through the whole fabric of the mythological history of mankind in general and of the Hebrews in particular. As Cush, the son of Ham, rose to power, the continent of Africa, including Egypt, "became the center of the world's cultural and religious education, and thus Ham secured for himself and his posterity for all time, a name—Pioneers of the World's Civilization."

The Mesopotamians were an "interrace" produced by intermarriage between the children of Shem and Ham—although, as we have seen above, both Shem and Ham were black according to the Black Jewish myth. Abraham, of course, was a Mesopotamian, and was black, as were his children and grandchildren. Jacob was "plain and smooth as the black man invariably is," but his twin-brother Esau was "red and hairy all over like a hairy garment."

The children of Jacob, renamed Israel, lived in Egypt for 430 years, during which period they mingled with the Egyptians

"and thus Shem and Ham were merged into one great people."
Before Moses led the children of Israel out of Egypt he had fled
to "Median in Ethiopia" where he had "become servant to the
Ethiopian Priest whose daughter he eventually married, and
begot two sons." These two boys "of necessity had to be black
because their father was black and so was their mother. They
were the first Ethiopian Hebrews of the Tribe of Levi. They
were half Hamitic and half Semitic." [34]

The myth of the Black Jews has something to say not only
about their remote origins, but also about their brothers in present-day Ethiopia and the United States. Until World War II there
were about one million Falasha Jews in Ethiopia, constituting
about a tenth of the country's total population. "However, since
the war they have been greatly reduced, and fear is entertained
for their continued existence." There are said to be about 3,000
Black Jews in Harlem and "goodly numbers" in Brooklyn, as
well as in Philadelphia, Pittsburgh, Media, and Sharon, Pennsylvania; Youngstown and Farrell, Ohio; Chicago; Cullen, Virginia;
St. Thomas, Virgin Islands; and Jamaica, West Indies. Rabbi
Matthew's own credentials, he claims, are "sanctioned by both
the Chief Rabbi of the Falashas and the National Coptic Church
of St. Michael [which] must sanction the existence of all other
religious bodies in Ethiopia." [35]

Like some other Black Jewish cultists before him, Rabbi Mat-
thew believes that Jesus, who was not a Christian but a Black
Jew from the tribe of Judah, was lynched by whites. "When the
Gentiles find out that Jesus was black, they'll drop him as their
Lord overnight." [36]

A discussion of the curriculum of the "Ethiopian Hebrew
Rabbinical College of the Royal Order of Ethiopian Hebrews
and the Commandment Keepers Congregation of the Living God,
Inc." does not belong in a treatment of Black Jewish mythology,
but one of the subjects taught in that College by Rabbi Matthew
does. With "Cabbalistic Science," which he characterizes as an
"angelic science" (in contradistinction to "conjuring"), we re-
enter the world of mythology. It is based on "twelve foundations" which are the heavens, and "seven spirits" (which we
would rather call elements): wind, water, fire, life or energy,
light, power or force, and mind or intelligence. The science

consists of a set of secret Hebrew formulae that can be used to cure a great many ailments and to achieve all kinds of other boons. The names of the four angels, Gavreel, Micharel, Owreel, and Rafarel—which "the Gentiles mispronounce" as Gabriel, Michael, Uriel, and Rafael—must be invoked. Each of the four angels works a three-hour shift in turn and is in charge of certain matters: Gavreel, who "is the God of darkness and is ours," works from 6 to 9 in the morning and evening, healing the sick in mind or body. Micharel (from 9 to 12) protects and defends. Owreel (from 12 to 3) controls all metals and destroys evil, including evil thoughts; "he will work for you better than voodoo." Rafarel (from 3 to 6) is the physician; he heals, gives sight, cures "rheumatic," etc.[37]

It would be most tempting to analyze the myth of the Black Jews in order to separate those elements which are their own original contribution from those that have been taken over by them from other, older, Hebrew, Jewish, Ethiopian, and Falasha mythologies. However, such analysis would lead us outside our topic proper which, of course, is the study of the influence exerted by myth on men living in our modern world. From the point of view of the sustaining value of the Black Jewish myth for the Commandment Keepers Congregation it is immaterial that the emperor of Ethiopia actually does claim descent from King Solomon and does style himself "the Conquering Lion of Judah." Likewise, it is of no importance that the Falashas, or Black Jews, of Ethiopia, a marginal Jewish group, actually do claim descent from the Biblical Hebrews. What is vitally significant for the American Black Jews, and equally for all the other American Black religious movements, is to have a sustaining charter myth of their own, which supplies them with self-respect, that intangible but indispensable commodity which is as important as the daily bread.

5 • *Father Divine*

The most ingenious, because the simplest, solution to the problem of how to answer the need every new faith has for a mythology of its own was provided by Father Divine. The case of Father Divine also constitutes one of the few existing examples of a man setting out deliberately and with premeditation to construct a myth around himself and in this manner succeeding in being accepted by thousands as their god. In this respect Father Divine was more successful than the Roman emperors, who were styled gods half out of flattery and half out of fear. Father Divine was believed to be god in all sincerity by a large and utterly devoted flock. Most of Father Divine's "children" were, like him, black and uneducated, although some were white, some had Ph.D. degrees from American universities. The myth that Father Divine used as the cup from which many thousands eagerly drank the nectar of unshakable belief in his divinity was starkly simple, stripped of all the frills, embellishments, and elaborations characteristic of most mythical presentations. It was a myth reduced to the one bare essential: namely, that Father Divine was God.

Like Elijah Muhammad, Father Divine, too, started out as a disciple of a man who claimed to be God or was, after his demise or disappearance, declared God. In the case of George Baker (the original name of Father Divine), this god-man was a mulatto by the name of Samuel Morris, whose assistant and then "messenger" Baker became. Morris declared himself to be "Jehovia," and some time later announced himself to be "God in the Fathership Degree," at the same time conferring on his messenger the title "God in the Sonship Degree." [38]

Much in the early life of "God in the Sonship Degree" is obscure. Even the date of his birth is doubtful. From the 1930s to the early 1950s he maintained that he was never born but was "combusted" one day in 1900 in Harlem, on the corner of Seventh Avenue and 134th Street.[39] The question of the mythical "combustion" aside, this statement clearly gives the year 1900 as the year of Father Divine's birth. But by 1961 he had changed the myth of his origin and moved back his birth date by about forty years. In that year a small book was published which contains a sort of authorized compendium of Father Divine's teachings. Much of the material in this book consists of statements made by Father Divine on various occasions and of letters he wrote in reply to greetings he received from different parts of the world on the occasion of the fifteenth anniversary of his marriage with the second Mother Divine. Quite appropriately, the book contains a contribution by Mother Divine which stresses the purely spiritual quality of her marriage with Father Divine. In this article she writes, *inter alia:* "FATHER married Mother Divine in the first body in 1882. . . ." [40] Since Father Divine would probably have been at least twenty years old at the time of his first marriage, this would place his birth in the year 1862 at the latest. If so, he was close to 100 years old when the above lines were written, and at least 103 years old when he died, on September 10, 1965.

In 1936, when he was thirty-six (or seventy-four) years old, Father Divine organized (or allowed his followers to organize) an "International Righteous Government Convention" at which "it was moved and passed that 'Father Divine is God.' There were no dissenting votes." [41] Therewith an entirely new type of deity entered the stage of human history: a god by vote.

What were the teachings of this extraordinary man unanimously voted into godhead? For one thing, he held that in him were united two natures: a human and a divine. As a human, he considered himself frail and full of embarrassing shortcomings according to the human scale of values. But as God, he claimed all the limitless powers of a supreme deity. In a brief paragraph printed under a photograph of Father Divine which constitutes the frontispiece of the book referred to above, he states this dual nature quite explicitly: "As a man I am illiterate. As a man I would be nothing." But "as God, I am infinite, I am omniscient, I am omnipotent." [42]

His lack of education and semi-literacy seemed to bother Father Divine to such an extent that he found it necessary to refer to it several times, if only to contrast it with his omnipotence as God: "God is Omnipotent, Omniscient, and Omnipresent without a letter of human education. . . . I came as the most illiterate, humanly speaking, yet causing millions to be super-intelligent." [43]

Building on the theme of his own illiteracy and following the Christological prototype of Jesus who has taken upon himself the sins of all mankind, Father Divine expatiates on the subject of the numerous failings, frailties, and plagues of mankind that he "has taken upon himself." He states that all the infirmi-

ties, diseases, ignorance, illiteracy, physical and intellectual imperfections, including those of old age, of "the personnel of the
children of men" have voluntarily been taken upon himself by
him, and that he thereby changed all men "characteristically
and dispositionally" so that they have become "new creatures—
and they look beautiful!" and their "physical body" would never
grow old.[44]

Nor was this all that Father Divine has voluntarily undertaken
by way of suffering for the welfare of his flock. It is part of his
self-made myth that he went down to the South "volitionated
by MY Own Spirit" to "present My Body as a Living Sacrifice
to bring about social justice and social equality, if it costs My
Physical Life!" While in the South in this quest of voluntary
self-sacrifice, he was thirty-two times "in the hands of lynch
mobs," but each time he was "coming out more than victoriously
a Conqueror! NONE COULD HINDER ME!"[45]

A basic feature of the myth of Father Divine is that in him
"God Made Himself Flesh." In order to make his followers
understand how something invisible can become visible, he reminds them: "The turkey you have eaten, it was invisible last
year," and then, using the turkey as a simile, he puts to them the
rhetorical question: "Will you keep GOD in a superstitious
version in the mystic conception concerning HIS PRESENCE
and not realize the Tangibilization and Personification of HIS
Majesty, His Love and His Mercy are as operative as the turkey?"[46] The kerygma-like proclamation "I am God" recurs
several times: "I will cause every knee to bow, and every tongue
to confess That I AM GOD! Aren't You Glad?" And again:
"millions know I AM GOD."[47] In a letter written in response
to an invitation to the "Bar (sic) Mitzvah" of a girl, Father
Divine wrote on April 12, 1961: "I AM MY CREATION. . . ."
Then, in a seeming non sequitur, he refers to two of the other
basic themes of his myth: ". . . My Bride and I are ONE," and
goes on to encourage the girl about to take her "Bar" Mitzvah
vows to "fully rely on MY Spirit. . . ."[48]

The mythical theme of the oneness of the god and his bride
is built up into a veritable cornerstone of the Father Divine myth.
Father Divine's second wife was a white woman, and *His Words*

of Spirit Life and Hope contain numerous references to this "interracial and international" marriage. Both Father Divine and Mother Divine stress repeatedly that their marriage is a purely spiritual one, not soiled by carnal contact, and that both he and she have throughout the fifteen years of their marriage preserved themselves in a state of purest virginity.[49] In fact, this "Sacred Marriage" is said by him to have an immense purifying effect on all mankind: "MY Sacred Marriage is lifting humanity from the lusts of sin, and, hence, from the bondage of sickness, want and death. It shall save the nations, and wars and the debauchery of men shall merely be history, even unconceived by the future generations to come. This is what I AM doing on earth among men, propagating virginity through MY Holy Marriage to save the delinquent youths and adults of every nation. . . ."[50]

To appreciate the significance of holy marriage, one should be aware that in ancient Near Eastern religions the rite of Sacred Marriage, performed annually by the representatives of the chief god and goddess (often the king and the chief priestess), was believed to ensure the fertility of the fields, of animals, and of man for the ensuing year.[51] Since one cannot assume that Father Divine was acquainted with this ancient ritual, it is remarkable that he should have quite independently developed this myth of the global redeeming effect of his own Sacred Marriage. Furthermore, one should realize that essentially there is nothing more absurd in attributing a world-saving effect to an unconsummated marriage than in attributing it to a death by the cruel Roman form of execution by crucifixion. Whatever particular form is taken by the myth of salvation, whenever it appears it is living witness to the great yearning to be saved felt by man in many ages and places.

The "rely on me" theme is perhaps the most important part of Father Divine's self-made myth. The assertion that he is God is but the foundation for this central topic, which is the key to the hold Father Divine exercised over many thousands of adherents. Since he is god, everybody can rely on him; all those who do, undergo a miraculous transformation and all their wishes—that is, their major, consequential desires—come true. This is the core and the gist of Father Divine's message, the hub and the center into which run all the spokes of his mythical wheel. Knowing only too well that the secret of convincing lies in relentless repetition, he harps on this single subject again and again. A few examples of this almost monotonous reiteration will have to suffice.

"MY PRESENCE IS OMNIPOTENT, OMNISCIENT and OMNILUCENT and cannot fail." [52] Echoing Christ's "Ego sum via, veritas et vita," and at the same time amplifying and improving upon it, Father Divine proclaims: "I AM health! I AM Happiness! I AM Joy! I AM Peace! I AM Life! I AM Wealth and I AM Love for you and I AM a Free Gift! Aren't you glad! ('So glad!' came the immediate response.)" [53]

". . . IF YOU CONTACT ME HARMONIOUSLY, FROM ALL OF THOSE UNDESIRABLE CONDITIONS YOU WILL BE EMANCIPATED! IT IS A BELIEF AND YOUR FAITH; BEING SUBSTANTIATED AND UNSHAKEN IN CONFIDENCE YOUR FAITH WILL MAKE YOU WHOLE!" [54]

"For I AM Health for you; I AM Happiness for you; I AM Success for you; I AM Prosperity for you; I AM Vigor for you; I AM Courage for you and I AM Youth for you! I Lift you! I make you feel Young. You should be young! I make you feel Good! That is what I AM talking about!" [55]

To those who believe in him, Father Divine holds out the promise of becoming his sons, the sons of God. God, he says, is "the Father of your body and of everybody else." It is in this physical sense that "everyone is GOD'S unadulterated child!" And in the continuation of this sentence he promises, albeit indirectly, immortality to his "children":". . . but as long as you attach yourselves to mortality and materialism you will be subject to mortals' infirmities and all mortals are subject to DEATH!" [56] But since it is only through Father Divine that his children can escape mortality, should he choose to withhold his goodwill from them, they would perish: "My Spirit will set you on fire, but without My Mind and My Will, the stimulation of My Spirit will wreck you with the mortal mind. . . ." [57]

In one curious passage he holds out the promise of planetary escape, while at the same time threatening his listeners with destruction in space: "The spiritual vibrations are Wonderful.

They will give you so much energy, they will lift you so high you will contact the CHRIST Vibrations and you will transcend gravitation, but you must have the MIND OF GOD and the WILL OF GOD, for if you transcend gravitation without the MIND of GOD you might run into the sun or the moon instead of some of the other planets that are more harmonious to your well-being!" [58]

In another vision of the future Father Divine prophesies that "the time cometh and is not far distant" when "all peoples will live together in peaceful and quiet resting places." [59] In marked contrast to the elaborations and embellishments in the descriptions of his own divine powers and attributes, Father Divine has nothing more to say about the Messianic future than this brief, vague, and general statement.

While Father Divine never systematized his teachings, it was possible to piece together his myth from scattered references contained in *His Words of Spirit Life and Hope*. Moreover, that little book, together with material contained in *The New Day*, the weekly published by the Peace Mission Movement, as well as in books written about Father Divine by both believers and skeptics, affords us the rare treat of peeking in, as it were, to watch the actual birth of a myth, or better, the purposeful manufacture of a myth. Father Divine succeeded in completely enveloping his small, rotund figure in a shining shroud of mythology, in actually attaining divinity in his lifetime, attested by the fervid and fanatic faith of thousands of his followers and democratically formalized with the seal of unanimous vote. Incidentally, Father Divine thus came to represent one of the very few exceptions from the general rule referred to earlier (see Chapter 7), namely that a hero must first die before he can become a myth. He succeeded in becoming a myth in his lifetime, and more than that: the center of his own mythological pantheon.

The death of Father Divine on September 10, 1965, at his Woodmont estate was chronicled in a detailed obituary in *The New York Times* on the next day. The *Times'* reporter elicited from the attorney of the Peace Mission Movement the information that Mother Divine would carry on as she had for the preceding year or so, during which Father Divine's illness prevented him from appearing in public. The manner in which God Almighty's death was first suppressed, and then, when brought to the notice of "the Followers," underplayed and reinterpreted in a theological sense, was nothing short of ingenious. That no mention was made of Father Divine's death in the September 11, 1965, issue of *The New Day* can be explained as simply the result of the issue having been "put to bed" before the event occurred. In three subsequent issues, those of September 18 and 25, and October 2, 1965, the first page of *The New Day* carried large pictures of Father Divine with the legend: "God Almighty, Changeless Perfection, Redeemer and Savior of All Mankind Rev. M. J. Divine, Ms.D., D.D., (Better Known as Father Divine) Founder, Bishop and Pastor of the Peace Mission Movement." The contents of the September 18 and 25 issues were made up, as usual, mostly of Father Divine's addresses given many years or even decades earlier. The September 25 issue, on page 13, described how Father Divine entered a hall at Woodmont to meet his Followers, on Tuesday, September 14. Had this act of the dead Father Divine been placed on September 13th, one could have imagined that it was invented in order to parallel the resurrection of Jesus on the third day after his crucifixion. However, the October 2nd issue, under a large and smiling picture of Father Divine (captioned with the same legend), carried a lengthy article headlined "The Supreme Sacrifice That Rent the Veil in Twain," with the subtitle "Holy Week—September 10–17, 1965, A.D.F.D." The article, which began on page 1 under the picture and continued on page 2, devoted most of the space at its disposal to a long quotation from Mother Divine. Neither the picture nor the article was surrounded by a black frame, and the article was couched in such terms that, unless one knew that Father Divine had died, one would have had to use one's powers of deduction to conclude that, indeed, such was the event referred to. The word "died" or "passed away," or any other of the usual euphemisms with which Americans, who in general hate to face the inevitability of death, are wont to refer to the demise of a loved one, are conspicuously absent. Instead we read:

Our Beloved Lord and Savior Father Divine had
seen fitting and necessary to throw off the Precious
Holy Little Body that millions all over the world
love and adore [note the present tense] more than
life itself. . . . Yet there is no feeling of loss, no
grief, no anxiety, for Father Divine is. His Holy
enveloping Presence is around and within every true
Follower. . . . His sacrifice has rent the veil of the
mortal versions of the human mind in twain. . . .

Further on in the same article (p. 2) Mother Divine is quoted
as having said, "Father Divine is [again the present tense] God
and what Father Divine did He did because He willed to do
and He did gladly, and as I told Him, we were so proud of Him.
. . . Father has not changed His position. Father is still ruling
and reigning. . . ."

Therewith the myth of Father Divine as God Incarnate was
augmented by a new chapter: for reasons of his own, he decided
to abandon his human body (which he originally had assumed
only because of his great love for mankind), but this did not
mean that his active concern for man had changed or diminished
in any way. (Again, we feel here an analogy between the Father
Divine myth and the myth of Jesus Christ, who was God incarnate, who had taken on human form for a while, but whose
work for the salvation of man was accomplished only in his
death on the cross and after it, when he divested himself of his
human nature.)

Contrary to all logical expectation, the Father Divine Peace
Mission Movement continued to thrive and flourish after the
death of its "God Almighty." In the years following Father Divine's death, *The New Day* continued to refer to him consistently
in the present tense, as if he were still alive. The weekly continued to print, as it did prior to Father Divine's death, his
messages and speeches which dated back to the 1930s and 1940s,
invariably captioning them with present tense headlines. Thus,
for instance, the November 27, 1965, issue of *The New Day*
carried the bold type headline: "Father Divine Grants Interview
To A Cleveland Press Representative." One had to read the

small subtitle to find out that the interview had taken place on March 1, 1936, almost thirty years earlier.

In keeping with this policy, Mother Divine speaks of Father Divine as if he were still alive in a letter she wrote to President Johnson on August 1, 1967—that is, nearly two years after Father Divine's death. ". . . FATHER DIVINE does not only hold the solution to the racial problem, but HE holds the solution to all of the problems which are the underlying causes of the riots and many different uprisings which are plaguing our country today. . . ." [60]

This stratagem (if indeed it was one) succeeded in keeping alive not only Father Divine, but his entire Peace Mission Movement. The myth of the god by vote proved stronger than death.

Each of the four varieties of new black religions, Black Islam, Black Christianity, Black Judaism, and Father Divinism, felt the need to create a mythology that served as the charter validating its doctrines and its practices and giving meaning and justification to its very existence. Other new religions emerging on the contemporary American scene or in other parts of the modern world feel the same need and satisfy it, as best they can, with origin myths and mythical charters of their own. People whose beliefs are anchored in old religions, in faiths that originated two or three thousand years ago in the ancient Near East, understandably frown upon these new ecrudescences, which they tend to consider either charitably as crudities and vulgarities, or censoriously as gross superstitions. Be that as it may, the mythopoeic power of the new religions is beyond question, and the constant burgeoning of new religious mythologies forces us to recognize that the mythopoeic age is still far from having passed.

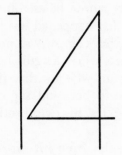

herakles in america

1 • *The Serials Hero*

One of the favorite characters of ancient mythologies, the deathless, invulnerable, godlike hero, who faces one dangerous and, indeed, desperate, situation after the other and always emerges unscathed, is still with us. In fact, he is more alive today than he ever was, more powerful, more cunning, more resourceful, more superior, in brief, more divine. Further, he is more than ever a part of our lives and thoughts in the sense that we spend more hours per capita per annum in his company than did the members of any ancient culture. In ancient times he was known as Gilgamesh, or Samson, or Theseus, or Herakles; today he goes under a much larger variety of names and guises, such as Marshal Dillon, Captain Kirk (of the starship *Enterprise*), Perry Mason, Chief Ironside, Doctor Kildare, Agent Erskine (of the F.B.I.), and so on.

The most famous of the ancient invulnerables was

the Greek Herakles, whose name the Romans Latinized into Hercules. His origins, as one would expect of such an extraordinary hero, were somewhat mysterious. His mother was the beautiful Alkmene, daughter of Elektryon, king of Mycenae. The identity of his father, however, cannot be established to the same degree of certainty, because what happened was that one night Zeus visited Alkmene, enjoying her company so much that he made the night last three times its usual length. Later that night Alkmene's husband Amphitryon, who by that time had become the ruler of Mycenae, came to her, and she conceived of both. Amphitryon's son was Iphikles; his twin brother, the son of Zeus, was Herakles.

Many myths surround the life of Herakles from his birth to his death (by which even invulnerable heroes are ultimately overtaken), but of all of them only those relating to his twelve labors are of interest to us at this time. Herakles performed these "labors" (the original Greek term for them is ἆζλοι, that is, athletic or heroic feats) in the course of twelve years in the service of Eurystheus, because the prophetess of Delphi had told him that if he fulfilled the tasks Eurystheus should set him, he would become immortal. Herakles' feats, while directly and immediately benefiting mankind, had thus the ultimate aim of assuring him immortality (or divinity), which, in a sense, he actually attained.

The first labor of Herakles was to kill the Nemean lion, an invulnerable, enormous, and ferocious beast that had depopulated all of Nemea. Ordinary weapons could not even wound the lion. Herakles finally battered it with his club and then choked it to death. Using the lion's own sharp claws as implements, he then flayed the carcass and thenceforth used the skin as his invariable wear.

The second labor was the killing of the Lernaean hydra, a monstrous doglike beast with many heads; some say it had as many as a hundred, with the mouth in each head spewing forth a venomous breath. Conservative tradition attributes only nine heads to the hydra, but all agree that as soon as Herakles managed to cut off one of them, three or four new heads sprouted out in its place. Finally, with the help of Iolaos, son of his brother

Iphikles, Herakles overcame the monster by cutting off its heads one after the other and having Iolaos slap a blazing firebrand against the stump. Thus no new heads could grow in place of the old ones. Finally Herakles cut off the hydra's one immortal head and buried it alive.

The Erymanthian boar was the third beast to be overcome by Herakles. He had to take this huge and savage creature alive, which was an exceptionally difficult task. Herakles accomplished it by frightening it out of its lair and chasing it into deep snow, where he managed to net it or chain it, thus rendering it harmless. Herakles then carried it off on his shoulders.

The fourth labor was the capturing alive of yet another animal, the Keryneian hind. Since this huge animal had not only bronze hooves but also golden antlers, some call it a stag. She (or he) was sacred to Artemis, and Herakles was thus forbidden even to wound her. But he accomplished her capture by chasing her for a whole year to the very ends of the earth, and finally catching the exhausted animal while it slept.

The fifth labor was the driving out of the countless Stymphalian birds, whose beaks, claws, and wings were of brass, and who destroyed the crops of the entire countryside, and, according to some, were actually man-eaters. Herakles first frightened the birds with a bronze rattle which he either made himself or got from Athena, and then shot them all.

His sixth labor was the cleaning out of the stables of Augeias (or Augias). These stables, in which a huge herd of cattle was kept, had never been cleaned; the accumulation of dirt in them was staggering, and they spread pestilence all across the Peloponnesus. Herakles led a river through the stables and thus cleaned them in a single day.

The seventh Herculean labor was the capture of the Cretan bull that ravaged the entire island. Some say this was the bull that had brought Europa to Crete (clearly not considered in this context as Zeus in disguise); others, that it was Pasiphae's bull, who had sired the Minotaur on her. After Herakles showed the captured bull to Eurystheus, he turned the animal loose.

The eighth labor was the taming of the four wild, man-eating horses of Thracian king Diomedes. Herakles, either alone or at the head of a volunteer force, fought Diomedes and either killed him or fed him to his own horses. Having thus tamed the horses, Herakles brought them to Argos.

The ninth task imposed by Eurystheus on Herakles was to obtain the golden girdle of Hippolyte, queen of the Amazons. Herakles set out, again either alone or with an army, defeated the Amazons, captured their general, Melanippe, and obtained the girdle as the price of her freedom. Another version has it that Hippolyte herself fell in the battle and this is how Herakles got the girdle. A relic shown in classical times in the Temple of Hera at Argos was held to be this girdle.

The tenth feat was to fetch the cattle of Geryon, a three-headed or three-bodied monster who lived on the island of Erytheie ("Red Island") in the midst of the River Ocean in the farthest west. Herakles robbed Okeanos, or Helius himself, of the golden cup of the Sun, in which he sailed west on the River Ocean. He killed the formidable dog Orthros, then the herdsman Eurytion, and finally Geryon himself. He then put the cattle on board the goblet and sailed back to Greece. Later versions added many embellishments to this old form of the myth: they take Herakles to the Straits of Gibraltar, where he sets up the famous Pillars of Herakles; through Spain, France, and Italy, where he fights off his attackers with arrows and stones; to the shores of the Black Sea, where he makes love to a female who is half woman and half serpent and begets on her three sons who become the ancestors of the Gelonoi, Agathyrsoi, and Scythians; to Sicily, where he wrestles and kills a son of Aphrodite; and to many other places and through many more hair-raising adventures.

The eleventh was the most terrible of all the Herculean labors: it involved his descent to Hades (hell) and the bringing back of Kerberos, its horrible, three-headed, dog-shaped guardian. In the oldest version of this myth, Herakles fought Hades (hell personified) and succeeded in wounding him, which seems to be a mythical way of saying that he sought to conquer death and succeeded in winning immortality. Later, when no man could any longer be credited with becoming immortal, the myth was changed, and Herakles was merely said to have brought up Kerberos. In some versions the myth was embellished with innumerable fantastic details into which we need not go at present.

The last labor of Herakles was the fetching of the golden apples of the Hesperides. As the name Hesperides ("Daughters of the Evening") indicates, these women, four in number, lived in the far west—that is, somewhere in the Atlas Mountains in northwest Africa, where they had a garden. Herakles slew the dragon guarding the garden (or merely sent it to sleep), plucked the apples, and beat his retreat. The mythical motif of the quest for immortality in the form of the fruit of the Tree of Life is again unmistakable.

In addition to these twelve labors, Herakles is credited with many more exploits: he fought the Centaurs, overcame the ape-like Kerkopes, and defeated many other adversaries, such as the sea-monster Triton, Kyknos and Lykaon, sons of Ares, Busiris King of Egypt, the giant Alkyoneus, and the wicked Syleus.

He also was a great ladies' man: the number of women, female monsters included, on whom he begot children is legion. Not the least of his exploits in this area was the episode with the daughters of Thespios, all fifty of whom, according to one version of the myth, he impregnated in a single night.

Death, whom Herakles tried to escape with all the superhuman power he had inherited from his father Zeus, finally overtook him, according to the oldest versions of his myths, because of the credulity of his last wife, Deianeira. When she found out that Herakles had fallen in love with Iole, she tried to win him back by persuading him to put on the robe (or shirt) that she had smeared with the blood of the Centaur Nessus. This blood was, in fact, a deadly poison that burned his flesh off his bones. Writhing in agony, Herakles had Hyllus convey him to the summit of Mount Oite, where he commanded an Aeolian shepherd named Poias to prepare a great pyre for him. Herakles mounted the pyre and his body was consumed by the fire, or, as others say, by a thunderbolt sent by Zeus. Although the mortal flesh of Herakles thus became ashes, his immortal part continued to live, love, and procreate in heaven.[1]

The foregoing summary of the labors of Herakles gives nothing more than the barest outline of his feats. Each of his labors is described by the ancient mythographers in rich detail, in many, often contradictory versions, and with numerous episodic embellishments. In addition, he is credited with a large number of other feats: the tasks he fulfilled, the men and monsters he killed, the women he loved are countless. Yet even the skeletal outline presented is sufficient to indicate the numerous points of contact between the Herculean labors and those of the modern serials heroes.

There is, first of all, the motif of the common weal. Most of the labors of Herakles served the benefit of mankind, or, at least, of the population of a region. The wild beasts, monsters, or other adversaries whom he killed, captured, or rendered harmless are described as having devastated the countryside, killed many people, or made their lives intolerable. The same motif recurs in most, if not all, serials. The hero has our sympathy from the very beginning because he performs his heroic deeds for the people, by standing up against and defeating those who hurt and harm them. The marshal, the lawyer, the police chief, the federal agent, the space captain, and even such infantilized cartoon heroes as Superman and his ilk all fight and overcome the selfish, ruthless, evil, cunning, cruel, and sinister—in a word, monstrous—enemies of the people.

Secondly, Herakles in performing his labors served a master. In the twelve-labor cycle his master was Eurystheus, an authority figure who, however, could not hold a candle to Herakles in point of strength, inventiveness, ingenuity, perseverance, and other such personal qualities. In other myths, Herakles is said to have performed similar great feats in the service of other masters, whose position and relationship to him were very similar to those of Eurystheus. This again is a stereotyped feature in the modern hero serials. The hero has a superior whom he must obey and who imposes upon him tasks that would be far beyond the master's own capacity. Moreover, just as Herakles and Eurystheus often had differences of opinion, so the modern serials hero occasionally must pitch his own will against that of his superior, usually managing to convince him that his, and not the superior's, point of view is correct.

Thirdly, just as Herakles was in many of his labors helped by his nephew Iolaos, who served as his faithful assistant, so the modern serials hero as a rule has his second-in-command who stands by his side and occasionally even saves his life.

Fourthly and most importantly, there is the feature of inherent superiority that sets the hero apart from ordinary mortals. In the case of Herakles this superiority stemmed from the fact that he was the son of Zeus, whence he derived his superhuman strength, his invulnerability (until the fatal moment when he puts on the death-shirt soaked with the blood of Nessus), and his charisma. The modern serials hero derives his charisma, not through inheritance, but, in conformity with our modern mythological values, through his own efforts. His is not an ascribed but an achieved charisma, obtained through work, perseverance, training, and the conscientious cultivation of the finest of those qualities with which nature had endowed him. At the stage of life in which the hero is shown in the serial he is at the peak of his powers; he is well entrenched in his position (or, if you will, in his heroic role), and when we see him being approached by those who seek his help, or confronted by an adversary, his charismatic superiority oozes from all his pores. This superiority is so impressive that the cause he represents becomes automatically right and our total sympathy is immediately captured by him, just as there could be no question but that Herakles was right and the hundreds of antagonists whom he killed in various ways were wrong, and, being wrong, deserved to die.

Herein, precisely, lies the basic psychological significance of the Herakles myth and its heirs, the hero serials. They enable us, in fact almost compel us, not only to identify with their heroes, but to derive a deep emotional-moral satisfaction from the feats that they (and, through them, we) perform. The more familiar the hero, the more often we have watched him overcome ever-increasing dangers and challenges, the more we know what to expect of him and the more we identify with him. It is this factor that makes the serials hero a much more attractive ideal figure for effective viewer identification than the hero who appears in a single play only. Our instinct of self-preservation as a rule stands in the way of committing ourselves to the same degree to the hero of a one-shot feature who, perhaps, will die at the end of the film or play; but we can unrestrainedly and wholeheartedly identify with the serials hero, who, we know, will emerge unscathed because he must be back next week to top today's exploit.

Another aspect of the effect of repetition inherent in the serial-type presentation of the adventures of the same hero or of several heroes who all conform to one basic type has been emphasized by Marshall Fishwick: "Since hero-stories demand a rigid form, and repetition is necessary to feel the power of the Gods, Western readers never tire of the stereotypes. Experiencing the same thing in a number of Westerns is like going to the same religious service every Sunday. The hero gains immeasurably from repetition." [2]

In a mass culture and a mass society such as ours, in which the individual has been reduced to a mere number and cannot escape the feeling that he is nothing more than a small cog in a vast multi-wheeled machine, the serials hero myth has an important psychological function. However much one may deplore the shallowness, childishness, and violence of the form in which it is presented, one must recognize that it does contain an element capable of satisfying a deep-seated need that continues to survive in the psyche of many members of our huge mass society: the need to imagine oneself in the role of the magnificent hero, the fearless, strong, and resourceful protagonist of vitally important causes. Identifying with the modern immortals of television, cartoon, motion picture, and story serials thus compensates for the insignificance and banality of a humdrum existence from which, in reality, only one in a thousand can escape.

2 • The Hero-Buffoon

The observation that American culture, like all the great historic cultures of former times, has created a mythology of its own has been so often made that it almost appears a commonplace. As Max Lerner, one of the most insightful observers of the American scene, put it, "The myth-making faculty is still active in contemporary America. Its expression may be found in the folklore deposits left by the past and it is still operative in the legendry that grows up around the type-figures of popular stories and songs and in the changing forms of American speech." [3] When, leaving other types of myths aside, Lerner goes on to discuss the American hero myth, he finds that there are two kinds of American heroes. There are *history-book* heroes, who, like the heroes of ancient Greece, embody the accepted culture traits and the collective achievement of American society. Washington, Lincoln, Roosevelt, Grant, Eisenhower belong to this type. More important, however, in American mythology is the other kind of hero whom Lerner calls the *vernacular* or *archetypal hero,* the "bigger-than-life figure around whom young Americans weave their wish-fulfillment fantasies." [4] Such folk heroes were, in the course of the nineteenth and twentieth centuries, "the legendary Yankee who emerged from the American revolution," Davy Crockett, Mike Fink, Sam Fink, Sam Patch, Paul Bunyan, Pecos Bill, John Henry, Billy the Kid, Jesse James, Joe Magarac, Casey Jones and, more recently, James Dean, Superman, Dick Tracy, Li'l Abner, John Dillinger, Willie Sutton, and others.[5]

Lerner does not stop in his monumental *America as a Civilization* to undertake an analysis of the various types of mythical heroes produced by the culture of this country. That task was left for Marshall Fishwick to fulfill twelve years later in his book *The Hero, American Style.* But Lerner made one significant comment about "the backwoodsman of irrepressible spirits" to which heroic type belong such figures as Davy Crockett, Nimrod Wildfire, and many others. These characters, Lerner remarks, were "part hero, part buffoon, who were described in the tall tales that Americans spin." [6]

This comment is significant because "part hero, part buffoon" is precisely how that greatest hero of ancient Greek mythology, Herakles, was characterized. To be sure, mythologists have pointed out that the buffoon character of Herakles is a later accretion, while in the original form of his myth he was hero pure and simple. But if we accept Claude Lévi-Strauss' contention that a myth must be viewed, understood, and interpreted in a conspectus of all its versions,[7] then we certainly have in

Herakles the same combination of hero and buffoon that can be observed in the backwoodsman hero of American folk myth. For the fact is that this greatest and most famous of all Greek heroes, this strongest of all men, whose father was Zeus king of the gods, and whose great deeds were unequaled in all the fantasy-rich storehouses of Greek mythology, was, at one and the same time, a buffoon, a ridiculous clown, a comic figure. It was by stressing this side of his character that he became the comic Herakles of the Attic stage, "a sort of Ralph Roister Doister,"[8] a Hellenic Buster Keaton.

It is nothing less than remarkable that the mythopoeic forces alive in America nearly three thousand years after the figure of Herakles was molded in ancient Greece should endow their own mythical backwoodsmen-heroes with the same highly unlikely combination of disharmonious traits: superhuman strength, bravery, and resourcefulness on the one hand, and buffoonery and clowning on the other. It would lead us too far afield to probe into the psychological motivations which produced this identical combination of character traits in myths so far apart in both time and space. But one thing we can definitely conclude from this surprising similarity: just as in ancient Greece, so in nineteenth-century America, true mythopoeic forces must have been at work in creating the immensely popular, beloved, and much admired figure of the hero-buffoon.

Were there any need to adduce proof of the genuine mythical character of the American backwoodsman as reflected in the innumerable tall tales about his exploits, it would be sufficient to cite this globe-spanning identity of the basic features in his character and in that of the great semi-divine Herakles of the old Greek myth. However, Heracles lives on in modern American mythology not only in the hero-buffoon character of the backwoodsman and in the impressive many-faced image of the serials hero discussed above; he is also prototypically present in such figures as Superman, who is invincible once he puts on his body-tight flying outfit, while at other times he is a pitiable, fumbling nincompoop; or in James Bond, who is perhaps even more resourceful than the great Herakles himself in overcoming one terrifying villain after the other, but who, at the same time, or alternatingly, exhibits the same insatiable and foolish appetite for the fair sex as characterized Herakles.

Nor must we forget in this connection the incomparable Tarzan. As Marshall McLuhan put it, "Like the sleuth, Tarzan is invincible. Like St. Francis, he talks to the birds and the beasts; like Androcles and Elijah, he is helped by them. Queens lust for him, their Inca-like savagery melting into soft feminine grace at his approach. He picks scores of beautiful maidens from the limbs of trees, jaws of beasts, or the embraces of apes, and restores them to home, mother safety and fortune, or bed and board, from which they insist on mass exodus toward his haunts." [9] But he is also a buffoon, a fool, who obviously prefers the company of the chimpanzee Cheeta to that of the most enticing damsels in distress yearning in vain for a chance to throw themselves into his powerful arms, who never learns even the rudiments of human speech beyond the "Me Tarzan, you Jane" stage, and who, evidently, must adopt a "Boy" because he is incapable of procreating one.

Above all, the Herculean prototype is present in an all but impenetrable disguise in the figure of that true darling of America, that smallest and yet mightiest of all comic heroes produced by American mythopoets, Mickey Mouse. It is to an examination of the psychological significance of this mythical image that we now turn.

the "mickey" myth

Those who doubt that the mytho-
poeic faculty is still with us would do well to consider the
creative vigor with which new mythical figures have been
called to life under our very eyes, the enthusiastic recep-
tion they have merited, and the enormous vitality they have
exhibited in crossing the frontiers of languages, cultures,
and continents. The favorite medium of these neo-mythical
images is the cartoon, the black-and-white drawing of either
the still (comic strip) or the animated and talking (film
cartoon) variety, in both of which the protagonists and
everything else appear in merest outline, reduced to a
barest indication of presence.

In the neo-mythical cartoon world, as in ancient mythologies, prototypes often give rise to epigons. These need
not concern us here, except to remark that both prototype
and epigon reflect one and the same archetype. It is this
archetype, the exemplar, that deserves consideration. If its
mythological character can be established, this *ipso facto*

221

will assure the epigons as well of their minor but rightful places on the modern neo-mythical Olympus.

The chief prototype of the new myth-world, is, of course, none other than Walt Disney's Mickey Mouse, whose stunted and ludicrous image conquered a major part of mankind within an incredibly short time and has remained forcefully alive and kicking for almost half a century. Before entering into a discussion of the mythical merits of the great Mickey, let us first have a cursory look at his mythical antecedents—that is to say, the doings mice were believed to have engaged in ever since Biblical and ancient Greek times. For the fact is that mice figure prominently in ancient mythologies and cults. The Philistines, in order to appease the wrath of Yahweh, God of Israel, offered him five golden mice; evidently they believed that Yahweh was in some way associated with the mice that plagued their land.[1] The fact was that the Hebrews considered mice to be just as detestable as swine, although mice seem to have been eaten in a heterodox ritual.[2]

As to the ancient Greeks, since *smintheus* ("mousey") was among the earliest titles of Apollo, it is quite possible that an oracular mouse was consulted as one of his manifestations. The mouse was a sacred animal at Cnossus in Crete and in Phocis. White mice were kept in Apollo's temples as a prophylactic against plague and sudden invasions of mice.[3]

To obtain information about the mouse myths and mouse folklore in the popular culture of various peoples, we turn to Stith Thompson's monumental *Motif-Index of Folk-Literature*.[4] In this vast register of folkloristic and mythological themes we find that mice are among the animals that have attracted human imagination in the most diverse times and places. A few examples will have to suffice. According to an Irish myth the mouse was created by Lucifer and the cat by the archangel Michael to destroy the mouse. Frequently, great strength is attributed to mice. In an Indian myth a mouse is set the task of fighting the Maharaja's state elephant single-handed and destroying it. From both India and the Congo come stories about the mouse who runs up the trunk of an elephant to his head and kills him by smearing poison over his brain. In another Indian story, mice overcome a camel. A Congolese story tells of a mouse who conquered a buffalo by running into his ear, while a European parallel has a mouse torment a bull, who cannot catch him. Mice even win a war with woodcutters in an Indian fable. A mouse stronger than a wall, the wind, and a mountain is met in Dutch, German, Scandinavian, Arabic, North African Berber, Spanish, Jewish, Indian, Japanese, and other folktales.

In another type of folktale (*e.g.,* in Scandinavia), mice appear as mysterious, frightening, or evil beings. In German and Lithuanian myths the devil himself takes the form of a mouse. In an African (Wachaga) tale a ghost returns in the shape of a mouse, while in the folklore of numerous peoples (German, Scandinavian, French, Finnish, Indonesian) the soul appears in the form of a mouse. Since the soul issuing forth from the mouth of a dying person takes the form of a mouse, both British and North American folk stories warn to keep the cat away lest it catch the soul-mouse. Magic mice appear in Indian, African, and Irish folklore, with the magic powers concentrated in their skin (African Zulu) which can carry a person aloft like a magic carpet (India).

Several folk traditions know of men who were transformed into mice (Scandinavian, Irish, Welsh, Celtic, Spanish, Indian, African, etc.), while in others it is a giant who is tricked into becoming a mouse, whereupon the cat devours him (German, Missouri French, Carrière Indians, Indian, Japanese, etc.). And, of course, there are speaking mice (India), as well as singing mice (in Jewish folklore).

When mice appear in a group, they are particularly formidable. Thus an Indian tale has it that an army of mice saved the kingdom from the invading enemy by gnawing its provisions and ammunition to shreds. Another Indian tale, which has its parallel in Jewish folklore and elsewhere, tells of mice whose sharp teeth cut through the enemy's bow strings and thus prevented it from pursuit. These mythical mice are so strong that they can pull a wagon (Scandinavian). Some mice become giants and dangerous man-eaters, like those of the Irish myth. They can be so powerful that they are able to eat iron, as in various European, Indian, and Indonesian folktales. Indian folklore even knows of a land of mice.[5]

As we can see from these few items selected from the global mountain of mouse lore found in the *Motif-Index* alone, Walt Disney in creating his Mickey Mouse happened to hit on a responsive chord in the mythically conditioned human psyche. His giant-size, talking, scheming, quasi-human mouse was nothing new in the fantastic world of mouse-mythology. The readiness with which children of all ages everywhere clasped Mickey to their hearts had undoubtedly something to do with their familiarity with the human, ghostly, giant, shrewd, powerful, lovable, fearful, frightened, and frightening mice of myths, a familiarity which was either actual, inasmuch as children may have heard the mouse tales indigenous to their culture, or else nothing more than a Jungian unconscious archetype deep in the collective psyche.

However this may be, it remained for Disney's genius to make Mickey Mouse a hero of global dimensions, a household word in many languages, and a mythical image whose psychological impact surpassed by far that of any other hero of the great mythologies. The triumphant world conquests of Mickey were nothing short of phenomenal. As Marshall Fishwick pointed out, within four years after Disney had created his mouse hero, "nationwide Mickey Mouse clubs had more than a million members. Mickey, dressed in his red velvet pants with two huge pearl buttons, won a place of honor in Madame Tussaud's waxworks," and many countries in the world took Mickey to their hearts. "Mahomet Zahir Khan, potentate of Hyderabad, called Mickey 'the leading American hero in India,'" while Russian critics pointed out that Disney "showed the capitalistic world under the mask of pigs, mice, and penguins." David Low, the great British caricaturist, dubbed Walt Disney "the most significant figure in graphic art since Leonardo da Vinci."[6]

Soon Mickey Mouse left the studio and invaded "America's nurseries and bedrooms," achieving "fame and fortune that few flesh-and-blood paragons have ever enjoyed. Entrepreneurs universalized Mickey. By 1940 over 2,000 companies were affiliated with the Disney Studios. One of them, Lionel Corporation, sold more than a quarter-million Mickey Mouse toy handcars in a single season. The Ingersoll Watch Company sent its five-millionth Mickey Mouse watch to Walt [Disney] as a special gift. . . . Children could spend hours in a Mickey Mouse world, wearing Mickey Mouse clothes, reading Mickey comics, working on Mickey desk outfits. They could play with Mickey toys and games and see Mickey cartoons at the movies. At night they could put on Mickey pajamas and tumble into Mickey beds, to dream of a happy land where cats do not break through and steal." In World War II the U.S. army used "Mickey Mouse" as the password for the Normandy invasion.[7]

As is the case with most myths, so with that of Mickey Mouse, not all the features contained in it can be readily explained. The significance of many details in the figure of Mickey Mouse as developed by Walt Disney remains obscure. Nor can one answer the hypothetical question of whether the Mickey myth would have been just as powerful and effective if Mickey Mouse had had no black dots for eyes, no legs like rubber hose, no huge ears, no string-bean body, and either more or less than three fingers on each hand. But one can answer with certainty the question about the basic appeal that this Mickey Mouse figure has had for millions of children and adults in America and other parts of the world. The appeal lay in the irresistible symbolic quality of the Mickey Mouse figure and the growing impact the Mickey myth made with each repetition of the same basic theme. This theme can be reduced to a minimum formula of three points: Mickey meets the Cat; Mickey is endangered by the Cat; Mickey overcomes the Cat.

Mickey's mythical qualities come through clearly and unmistakably, facilitating, or even compelling, viewer identification with him. He is, to begin with, a mouse, and as such a most apt symbol of weakness, meekness, timidity, ugliness, and insignificance. The cat, compared to him, is a large, powerful, and beautiful animal. For generations we despised mice, considered them pests, and kept cats to exterminate them. We even enjoyed the idea that, before killing and eating the mouse, the cat would play with it in the famous and deadly "cat-and-mouse game."

However, at one and the same time, we never ceased toying with the idea that there is much more in the mouse than meets the eye, that he has magic qualities, hidden powers, and is, in fact, not a mouse at all but a man, a soul, a giant, a dangerous being in disguise.

It is on this archetypal mouse that Disney's Mickey is built. Mickey Mouse is not really a mouse. He is as different in appearance from a real mouse as can be without losing the last shred of recognizability. He is not a photographic reproduction of a mouse, but a cartoon, drawn in a few bold, exaggerated, simplified, and symbolic strokes. He is enormous: we see him on the screen magnified hundreds of times. He wears some pieces of clothing (notably to cover his midriff), he stands and walks on his hind legs (which are encased in shoes), and he talks. True, his speech is not very articulate; he growls, whines, and squeaks, but it is clear enough to be understood not only by the Cat and the other figures appearing in the cartoon, but also by the audience of children and their parents. In a word, he is a human mouse, but not at all a mousey human. More than that, he has many of those same superhuman, fabulous qualities which have made the mythical hero the most beloved figure in history from the classic Samson and Herakles to the modern sleuth, sheriff, and lawman (Dick Tracy, Superman, Tarzan, and all the others).

This human mouse is eminently qualified to serve as an image, a symbol, for audience identification. We do not need the success of the Mickey myth all over the world to demonstrate that man everywhere—not only in our own mass society, but in many other places as well—feels threatened by individuals bigger than he and forces stronger. This fear is symbolically expressed by a feeling that can be epitomized in the admission: "I am a mouse." This mouse, who is me, now appears before me on the screen. Its outline figure, its body consisting of black and white areas, its half-human half-mouse character make it possible to identify with it without at the same time reducing oneself completely to a doormat. Once this basic identification is achieved, as it inevitably is, the rest follows almost automatically. The Cat, representing the inimical, dangerous world, is out to destroy me. I am indeed in grave danger. It seems I shall not be able to survive.

But wait! There I am in the guise of Mickey Mouse pulling off an entirely unexpected trick. I escape. And now, you know what, I plan to attack the Cat, to repay him in his own currency and then some. Look, what I am doing to that Cat! Wham! Bang! Long live Mickey victorious!

Just as the retelling of the myth was an integral part of ancient rituals, and just as the serials heroes of modern television depend upon continuous reenactments of their exploits, so with the Mickey myth the repetition of the same process with endless variations reinforces the effect of the basic message: try and you will succeed against the most overwhelming odds. For the average adult this is the comfort held out by the Mickey Mouse cartoons, their optimistic, encouraging, invigorating message, their great *kerygma,* proclamation. At the same time it also satisfies the craving for vigorous, ruthless, cruel activity—the need often felt but almost never translated into action of beating that bastard so-and-so (in everybody's life there are several such bastard so-and-so's) into pulp, to let fly, at least once, with all one's strength. Mickey Mouse does it for us. Hurray for Mickey Mouse!

For children the Mickey myth has basically the same function, with the one difference that the inimical world they see symbolically represented in the Cat is not the frightening world of industrialized society, but the equally frightening world of adults. The difference in sheer size between the Cat and Mickey makes this identification easy—in fact, inevitable. What could be a more delightful way of asserting oneself in the face of oppressive adult society, of defying father and mother (the "giants in the nursery"), than to don Mickey Mouse clothes, play with Mickey Mouse toys, watch Mickey Mouse cartoons, become and be Mickey Mouse? And what a joy that all this can be done, not only with impunity, but with the actual blessing of the parents, not to mention the aunts, uncles, and grandparents!

This is as good a place as any to stop for a moment and ask whether the Mickey Mouse syndrome can actually be termed a myth? Do the Mickey Mouse cartoons fall into the same category of human production as, say, the myths of the labors of Herakles? If judged by the quality of the audience response and by the psychological mechanisms which elicit that response, the answer must be definitely yes. Both the twelve stories of the Herculean feats and the twelve hundred or so stories of the adventures of Mickey create the same response in us, because to identify with the protagonist gives us pleasure, reassurance, and emotional satisfaction. Both take the form of stories about divine beings or heroes: there cannot be the slightest doubt that the half-human, half-animal image of Mickey Mouse is superhuman in the same sense in which the half-human half-animal Minotaur, Sphinx, centaurs, fauns, and so forth, were superhuman and thus typically mythical figures. Both the classical myths and the Mickey cartoons reassure us about the all-too-human situation of being weak, timid, and frightened by showing us the exemplar of the hero whose courage and/or guile assures him of victory even in the most hopeless situation.

As far as the truth or belief aspect of the two types of myths is concerned, we have noted that in ancient Greece there was an early time in which people actually believed in the truth of the Herakles myths (as in that of all myths in general). Similarly, in our age, there is a time of early childhood in which the child believes in the "truth" of the Mickey myth (as in that of all other myths on which our children cut their teeth). Then, in ancient Greece, doubt and unbelief took over—harbingers of the ultimate demise of Greek religion and the passing of the glory that was Greece. In our times, certainly no adult would admit to believing in the existence of Mickey Mouse. For the rationally thinking part of our adult mind, the Mickey myth is dead—as dead as the Herakles myth was for an Euhemerus. This is not quite the case with the mythical heroes of the photographically produced television serials; here the fictitious nature of the hero is by no means always so clearly recognized. The thousands of letters addressed to the lawyer or neurosurgeon hero of the television serials asking them for legal or medical advice are eloquent witness to the persistence of the actual belief in the life and truth of these serial heroes.

But even in the case of the Mickey Mouse cartoons, it has more than once been observed that it is difficult to tell who enjoys them more, the children or the parents. Full enjoyment of this kind of make-believe presupposes that the viewer does not, at the moment he is under the spell of the presentation, recognize it as make-believe. For those precious moments during which the Mickey cartoon flickers across the screen or the box, adults too can experience an involuntary suspension of disbelief, and parents are at one with their children in believing the Mickey myth to be true.

A number of common elements unite the Mickey-type and the Herakles-type myths despite the more obvious differences between them. In the Mickey-type myth (to which belong also Speedy Gonzalez, Donald Duck, Popeye the Sailor, and other small, pitiful, and ridiculous animal and human cartoon characters) the burden of the mythical message is that a weak and abused figure, given the proper provocation and motivation, can rise and defeat hateful adversaries who tower above him in stature and strength. In the Herakles-type myth (whose major modern representatives were discussed in the previous chapter) the hero is, to begin with, possessed of superhuman strength, cunning, resourcefulness, and other abilities. But the adversaries arrayed against him are also infinitely more dangerous and deadly than the ones bested by the Mickey-type hero. The basic similarity of the two hero types lies primarily in the power relationship between the hero and his adversary. Whether Mickey or Herakles, the hero in each case faces overwhelming odds. In fact, in the course of the almost ritualized combat sequence, there are invariably one or more junctures at which the hero is quite clearly trapped and defeated. The psychological effect of this phase of the myth is the same whether the trap in which the hero is caught is represented by the huge teeth of the Cat closing in on a helplessly twisting Mickey, or some fantastic death machine in a faraway galaxy which has rendered Captain Kirk unconscious or unable to move. Man or mouse, they share the same agony and we agonize with them.

But, the greater the agony, the surer the defeat, the more inevitable the imminent annihilation—the greater the elation at the rescue which, we knew all the time, would have to come. It is precisely this moment, the one in which defeat turns into victory, which gives us the greatest satisfaction, the culmination and climax, the intensive sensation of pleasure in anticipation of which we are willing to follow again and again the same stereotyped story sequence. This pleasurable sensation is greatly augmented by our witnessing the vengeance of the hero, the total annihilation of the villain, the triumph of justice. The greater the torture inflicted by the villain on the hero, the greater our pleasure at seeing the villain get what is coming to him. Therefore, in order to augment our pleasure at the climax, the initial power relationship between hero and villain must be as unequal as possible. As the myth opens, showing the hero embarking on his task of the week (or month or year), he must be represented as having practically no chances at all. Thus in many stories we are at this stage given to understand that the same task has been attempted by several other braves, all of whom paid with their lives for their foolhardy gallantry. The hero thus has all the odds stacked against him, he is made to appear small and weak, and certainly no match at all for the all-powerful invincible villain—except for the fact that he is the hero, and is therefore mythically predestined to prevail.

A second and equally important similarity between Mickey and Herakles is that both partake of a double character: Herakles, as we have seen in the preceding chapter, is both superhuman hero and ridiculous buffoon. The same two character types are contained also in the stereotyped personality of Mickey Mouse. He is, to begin with, a buffoon-like, comic figure. His very appearance provokes laughter. But then, after sufficient provocation by the Cat, he shows his mettle: underneath the mousey exterior he is, in reality, a great little hero. Inasmuch as he is a mouse, he is Clark Kent; but inasmuch as he defeats the Cat, he is Superman.

While Mickey and Herakles are thus recognized as two variants on the same basic hero theme, both of them contrast sharply with the child terrorist hero of certain militant student groups discussed earlier in Chapter 8. The fundamental lesson taught by the Mickey and Herakles type myths is: you do have a chance, you can prevail even against the most hopeless odds; therefore, stand up and fight, be like the hero. Marion Delgado, on the other hand, proffers a very different teaching: make yourself small, become invisible in the crowd, satisfy your ego by committing acts of sabotage that cannot be traced to you, but never face your adversary openly; be like the child who sticks out his tongue at his mother behind her back. If this were one of the few occasions on which a student of culture is permitted to engage in evaluation, I would say that, on balance, the Mickey and Herakles type myths can be entered on the credit side of the cultural ledger of our modern times, while the myth of the child terrorist undoubtedly belongs in the debit column.

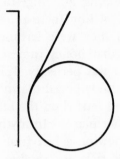

*the myths of oral
gratification, or:
coke and smoke*

It would be a most tempting
undertaking, as an introduction to this chapter, to trace,
·in a rapid global survey, the rich mythological connota-
tions of drinks and drinking. Such an essay would show
that in a surprisingly large number of cultures, scattered
over all parts of the globe, the act of drinking (whether of
pure water or any other beverage), far from being a simple act of slaking one's thirst, is considered a little personal
ritual that establishes a definite, if ephemeral, nexus between the drinking individual and a certain body of myths
that surrounds that particular beverage in that particular
culture.[1] Since such a presentation, however, could not be
fitted into the framework of this study, let me instead confine myself to a few remarks about one particular, highly
mythologized, drink and the food substance out of which
it was believed to have been prepared, both of which fig-
ured prominently in the culture to which our own civilization owes more than to any other, that of the ancient

233

Greeks. The food I have reference to is honey and its mythological divine prototype, ambrosia; the drink made out of it is honey-mead in the earthly realm, and nectar in the Olympian.

One of the oldest dreams of man has been to obtain health, youth, happiness, and immortality by finding and ingesting a miraculous substance that would bestow on him these priceless gifts that in real life were as elusive as they were irresistibly desirable.[2] The ancient Greeks believed that honey came close to being such a wonder food. Although it was perfectly clear to them that honey was made by bees, they also believed that it was a heavenly dew that fell down at night and settled on the blades of grass and on the leaves of trees and other plants.[3] In mythical thinking there is as little difficulty in knowing a fact from the realm of natural history and at the same time (or in the next minute) believing something contradictory relative to the supernatural origin of the same thing as there is in believing that, say, a hero like Theseus was the son of King Aigeus of Attica and that at the same time he also was the son of a divine father, the great sea-god Poseidon.[4]

Be this as it may, the fact remains that, because of its assumed heavenly origin, honey was believed to be a divine food in the sense that its consumption restored health and prolonged life. That the Greeks were not the only people in antiquity to hold such beliefs concerning honey can be concluded from a passage in the Bible which relates that when Jonathan, the son of King Saul, tasted of the honey he found in a forest, "his eyes brightened,"[5] which could have been only the result of a heavenly quality inherent in the honey. What is more, the manna that fell from heaven to feed the Children of Israel in the desert tasted "like wafers made with honey."[6] These and other indications in the Bible point to an ancient Israelite belief in the heavenly origin and nature of honey.

Returning to the Greeks among whom these beliefs are more clearly, and, in fact, amply attested, we should note that they used honey as a medicament for many kinds of ailments. They diluted it in water to serve as an intoxicating beverage, a kind of mead, and also employed it as an ointment, as soap, and as an embalming agent to prevent the decay of dead bodies. And, inevitably, they considered honey to be a food of the gods and honey-mead to be their drink.

According to a Greek myth, the infant Zeus was fed honey by bees; in a parallel myth, he was nourished not by bees but by the Peleiai—that is, the Pleiades—and the food these seven mythological daughters of Atlas and Pleione, who later were placed by Zeus among the stars, gave him was not honey but ambrosia and nectar. (The bees, incidentally, were believed to begin gathering honey only after the Pleiades rose.) Further, it was known that the first food of other children of the gods was either honey or else nectar and ambrosia.

What these two divine foodstuffs exactly were (that is, were imagined to be) cannot be ascertained from the references to them contained in ancient Greek literature. But some old Greek authors maintained that ambrosia was nine times as potent as honey, from which one may legitimately conclude that it was imagined as a nutrient similar to honey, a kind of honey of the gods. If honey was considered the quintessence of sweetness, loveliness, and balmy fragrance, ambrosia was all this but ninefold so. If honey was believed to prolong human life, ambrosia not only prolonged the life of the gods but was the substance whose ingestion gave them immortality. By analogy we can conclude that nectar was similarly imagined as a honey-mead raised to several times the potency of its earthly prototype.

Since ambrosia was the basis of the gods' immortality, ambrosia and *athanasia* (i.e., immortality) were equated; it is thus no wonder that mortal men tried to obtain it and thereby become immortal. Of at least one of these, Tantalus, a Greek myth reports that he indeed succeeded in becoming immortal by eating ambrosia. Of two others, Achilles and Demophoon, it records that they tried to attain immortality by anointing their bodies with ambrosia.

Not satisfied with this, mythopoeic fantasy attributed to the gods all those other uses of ambrosia to which honey was put in the world of men. Thus ambrosia was the ointment with which Hera cleansed her skin; ambrosia was the soap with which Athene washed Penelope; ambrosia was the substance used to anoint the corpse of Sarpedon and to heal the wounds suffered by gods. The goddess Thetis infused ambrosia and nectar into the nostrils of dead Patroclos in order to prevent the decomposition of his body—exactly as the Egyptians did with their embalming fluids. And, as a fine finishing touch, even the steeds of the gods had ambrosia-grass as their fodder in order to make them as immortal as their divine riders.

Before passing on to a discussion of the modern-day replacement of this classical mythologem of the divine food and drink, a word may be said in clarification of the place of ambrosia and nectar within the framework of our functional definition of myth. What, if any, purpose did these myths serve in the lives of the ancient Greeks?

It seems to me that, given the philomythical atmosphere of early Greece, the myths about ambrosia and nectar enabled the ancient Greeks to accept the inevitability of illness, old age, and death. What these myths taught them, in the unique way in which only myths can teach man to understand and acquiesce in the facts of life, was that illness, old age, and death, which are the inescapable fate of man, including the greatest heroes of mankind, would hold sway over the gods as well, were it not for ambrosia and nectar. In nature and essence, the great gods are like us mortal men, or, looking at it the other way around, we men are like the gods; except that the gods have their magic food and drink which make them immortal. Human frailty and mortality, therefore, is but a temporary bane. Search for ambrosia and you will escape them, as Tantalus did, as Achilles and Demophoon almost succeeded in doing.

We thus discern in the ambrosia and nectar myth a positive, an optimistic note: it *is* possible for man to remain young, to escape sickness, even to become immortal—if only he succeeds in finding nectar and ambrosia. At the same time, this is an essentially amoral mythologem: it puts within human reach, though not grasp, the acquisition of happiness by holding out the possibility of obtaining a magic food and drink. Conspicuously absent is the idea that goodness is the quality that could be rewarded by those priceless gifts. Its message is that whether one is good or bad, deserving or not, one can attain youth, health, and immortality if only one manages to find those elusive divine nutrients, nectar and ambrosia.

For the mythopoeic and mythotropic Greek mind the comfort contained in the knowledge that these magic foodstuffs existed was sufficient. For modern man, action- and achievement-oriented as he is, more is needed. While the desire for youth, health, and immortality is as strong today as it was in Homeric Greece, there is at present the added urgency, nurtured by an activistic and aggressive culture, of doing something about it. A typical example of how this additional need is satisfied within the context of our culture is provided by the ubiquitous advertising of soft drinks and cigarettes.

It is interesting to observe that the beneficial effects claimed for either soft drinks or cigarettes lie completely in the realm of the imaginary. With regard to soft drinks, while they have no proven ill effects on health, medical authorities agree that, if one is thirsty, the best thing to drink is pure water, without any flavoring, sweetening, coloring, or other additive. As to cigarettes, the harm they do to human health is by now so well known that it does not even have to be mentioned. This being the case, the advertisements for both soft drinks and cigarettes carefully avoid claims of health improvement which could be shown to be fraudulent, and concentrate instead on psychological effects. And it is in this area that they constitute the modern counterpart of the old myths of nectar and ambrosia.

Had ancient Greek culture known anything resembling modern advertising techniques, the ad for honey or mead would probably have shown a group of gods enjoying a drink over a caption something like "For the gods—nectar; for you—Sybarite (or some other such enticing trade name) Mead." This would have created the impression in the mind of the Greek viewer that by drinking "Sybarite Mead" he could join, in some unexplained but psychologically effective way, the company of the happy Olympians. Today this type of advertising is used in endless repetition for both soft drinks and cigarettes. A typical television commercial for a cola-flavored drink, for instance, will

show a young man and a girl, both carefully chosen ideal specimens of their sex and age, in a mutual attitude which subtly
but unmistakably impresses the viewer with the fact that they
are either greatly attracted to, or in love with, or having an affair
with, each other. To this are added highly desirable surroundings, such as a sunny beach, a wavy sea, a snowy mountain, a
shimmering swimming pool, a beautiful flower garden, a luxurious automobile or power boat. In this environment the boy and
girl are shown to be engaged, for a few seconds, in a daring or
exciting or obviously highly pleasurable activity, or else in some
other activity that clearly manifests the strength of the man
and the desirability of the woman. Then comes the high point
of the commercial from the sponsor's point of view: the two
heroes stop whatever they were doing and take a gulp from a
bottle visibly identified as containing the cola-flavored and cola-
colored soft drink that paid for all this merriment. The effect of
the drink is instantaneous: the two heroes burst into a guffaw
of laughter, and/or snuggle up to each other and look into
each other's eyes with sex-laden expressions, or show signs of
great exhilaration or a new burst of energy, or let go of an or-
gasmic sigh of pleasure, while the music that accompanied the
brief drama from its beginning peaks into a blissful crescendo.
And, as if all this were not enough, a voice or a chorus is heard
singing in irresistible notes about the miraculous effect the product will have on you: "You've got a lot to live and Pepsi's got a
lot to give," or "Pepsi makes you come alive." Or you might be
invited to drink Coca-Cola and thereby join the "now generation" or "those who think young."

However, the accent is not always on youth as the promised
result to be attained by the simple expedient of imbibing the
brown or pink contents of a bottle of this latter-day nectar. In
other commercials the accent is on the strength-restoring quality
of the beverage, usually couched in such terms as "the pause
that refreshes." In this connection it is significant that Coca-Cola
is very conspicuously enjoyed by professional athletes.

It has been observed by critics of the American mass media
that the method used in television commercials is "never [to]
present an ordered, sequential, rational argument but simply

[to] present the product associated with desirable things or attitudes. Thus Coca-Cola is shown held by a beautiful blonde, who sits in a Cadillac, surrounded by bronze, muscular admirers, with the sun shining overhead. By repetition these elements become associated, in our minds, into a pattern of sufficient cohesion so that one element can magically evoke the others. If we think of ads as designed solely to sell the products, we miss their main effect: to increase pleasure in the consumption of the product. Coca-Cola is far more than a cooling drink; the consumer participates, vicariously, in a much larger experience. In Africa, in Melanesia, to drink a Coke is to participate in the American way of life."[7]

The observation that the repetition of the associated elements creates a pattern in the mind of the viewer, who by reaching for a Coke feels magically transported into the desirable scene he witnesses night after night on his television set, is an important one. I would, however, go one step further and argue that we have here a clear analogy to the manner in which in ancient Greece the myths impinged on human life, influenced it, and shaped it. Even without having been exposed to bombardment by commercials, the ancient Greeks knew, because they heard it repeated many times, that ambrosia and nectar were the food of the gods; that honey, too, was a food of the gods; and that there was something of an ambrosial quality in honey. Therefore, the consumption of honey was associated in their minds with imitating the Olympians in a small way, with associating oneself with the Immortals, and with partaking of their nature, even if only to a minuscule extent. The Greek who enjoyed honey performed, in fact, a little private ritual which was validated by the numerous mythological references to the divine food of ambrosia and nectar.

In a like manner, the modern-day consumer of Coke feels that he imitates and associates himself with the quasi-mythological scenes of the television commercials. That those scenes are quasi-mythological, or even fully mythological, when viewed through the eyes of the average American (let alone the few privileged Africans or Melanesians, referred to by Carpenter in the quotation above), becomes readily apparent if one but considers the setting. The health, beauty, youth, gaiety, excitement, and luxury depicted with but slight variations in the endlessly repeated short commercial scenes as the setting in which the Coke is consumed (sorry, it is never merely "consumed"; it is always "enjoyed"), are as far removed from the limited means, drab life, labile health, and advancing age of the average television viewers as were the gods and heroes of ancient Greece from the Greek citizens. In both cases there is the illusion of partaking, even if only to an infinitesimal degree, of a world that one can never make, a world that has everything one lacks, misses, and desires, and that is peopled by divine, or at least godlike, beings.

In the case of the television commercial, the mythological effect is enhanced by the circumstance that it comes from the same source from which emanates so much of the mythology of the modern world. In many cases, the otherwise nameless heroes who exude their Coke-given exuberance, youth, vim, and vigor are either identical with, or resemble in appearance, those other, greater heroes and deities of the magic box—the sheriff, policeman, detective, agent, and so on, of the television serial, who week after week perform their Herculean labors and always remain, of course, unscathed like true immortals. The mythological character of these serials heroes was discussed in another part of this book (Chapter 14); here they are referred to merely in order to point out that any resemblance between them and the Coke-drinking, laughing divinities of the commercials is not coincidental but calculated to reinforce the mythological impact of the latter.

Whatever has been said above in connection with the soft drink complex, is equally applicable to the smoky realm of cigarette advertising. From the point of view of the advertiser there is, to be sure, one difference between the world of the Coke and that of Smoke: the Coke ads take a product that is, by and large, innocuous, albeit valueless, and turn it into a nectar; the Smoke ads, on the other hand, begin with a product that is harmful and evil-smelling and, with their spurious but insistent ingenuity, metamorphose it into a commodity of high desirability. How well they have done their job becomes apparent if one considers that despite the medical evidence as to the deadly effect of cigarette smoking on a statistically ascertained percentage of smokers, the volume of smoke rising out of American (and other) lungs increases year after year. In achieving this remarkable result, the advertising agencies are helped—although they are unaware of it—by the workings of a Jungian archetypal smoke mythology activated by their ads and commercials in the psyche of the viewer. The matter requires closer looking into, and in order to clarify it we must again make a brief excursus outside the modern Western world.

Smoke first became known to man as an unpleasant but unavoidable by-product of fire. He wanted fire for its warmth and light, the protection it afforded against wild animals, its power to render food more tasty, and its many technological uses. Since fire was always accompanied by smoke, the nature and qualities of the latter could not escape man's attention. In his smoke-filled primeval cave habitats, man experienced the power of smoke to make his eyes tear, his throat get dry, his head swim, his consciousness disappear, and ultimately his life become extinguished. He noticed the different odors of the smoke rising from various burning substances, found some more to his liking, others odious, and observed variations in his reaction to them. Herein lay the origin of the use of smoke as a trance-producing agent and hence as a means of establishing communication with the spirit world. The ritual use of the smoke of the sacred laurel by the priestess of Apollo before she uttered her oracle is paralleled among modern-day tribes in India, America, and Africa. Frequently, the inhalation of the sacred smoke produces convulsions, frenzy, and ecstasy, in which state the medium (as the smoker who reacts in one of these culturally defined ways can properly be designated) sees, hears, and converses with the spirits, or gives utterance to words which are said to be those of a supernatural being speaking through his mouth.[8]

While the inhalation of smoke is a widely prevalent method of establishing contact between man and the supernatural, or, we may also say, of elevating man temporarily into the world of spirits and gods, the inhabitants of the supernal world themselves are believed to enjoy the smoke of sacrifices. The burning sacrifice turns into smoke, which rises to where the gods live; hence it is in the form of smoke that the gods enjoy that which is offered to them. Since the ancient Greeks considered the pungent smoke of burning carcasses as having an offensive smell, they burned incense together with the bloody sacrifices to sweeten their odor.[9]

The ancient Near Eastern peoples, whose sacrificial rituals preceeded those of Greece by two or even three millennia, did not hold the smoke of burning flesh to have a bad smell. To be sure, they too offered sweet smelling substances to their gods, as we read, e.g., in the Akkadian myth of Gilgamesh, in which Utnapishtim (the Babylonian Noah) burned cane, cedarwood, and myrtle as a sacrifice for the gods after he survived the deluge in his ark.

> The gods smelled the
> savor,
>
> The gods smelled the sweet
> savor,
>
> The gods crowded like flies
> about the sacrificer.[10]

However, in the Bible the smoke itself rising from the animal sacrifice burning on the altar is represented as pleasing God. After the deluge, when Noah offered burnt-offerings to God, "the Lord smelled the sweet savor" and was thereby induced to have pity on mankind.[11] "Sweet savor unto the Lord" is the technical term applied to the burnt-offerings in the sacrificial ritual that was performed by the Hebrews and the Jews until the year 70 A.D. when the Second Temple of Jerusalem was destroyed by the Romans.[12] According to an archaic Biblical view, the offerings burnt on the altar were the "food" and "bread" of God,[13] which he enjoyed in the form of their smoke.

While we may have difficulty in empathizing with deities who enjoy the acrid and pungent smoke of burning flesh, our odor- and perfume-conscious culture has conditioned us to agree wholeheartedly with the ancients who believed that their gods took delight in the sweet smoke of incense. Incense is, in fact, a generic term which can refer to hundreds of sweet smelling sub-stances taken mostly from the vegetable kingdom, but occasion-ally also from the animal and mineral worlds. The practice of offering gods or spirits the smoke of substances that was pleasing to human nostrils is found in many times and many places all over the world. Its mythological foundation is the belief that such an offering makes the gods favorably inclined toward the donor, that it helps prayers rise to heaven, that it repels evil spirits and demons, and that it wards off dangers.[14] The use of incense in the Catholic Church goes back to the Biblical Hebrew practice, and the fact that it still is an integral part of the mass and other rites and is also used by certain Protestant denomina-tions (*e.g.*, by the Anglican communion) is eloquent evidence to the archetypal persistence of the "sweet savor" as a visible and smellable link between man and god.

Of course, I do not mean to argue, or even to hint, that the Madison Avenue ad men, in dreaming up cigarette commercials, are in any way or manner influenced by the ancient myths or rituals of smoke or incense. In all probability they know noth-ing about the role of smoke in the ancient Near East and Greece, or in the more recent primitive world. And as to incense, the very fact that no ad (to the best of my knowledge) has ever used the incense motif, or even as much as referred to it obliquely, seems to indicate that not even the most imaginative advertis-ing agency has as yet discovered either the phenomenological or the substantial similarity between the smoke of incense and the smoke of cigarettes.

Nevertheless, and this is significant for our understanding of the role myth plays in the life of modern man, in putting them-selves the question of how best to make cigarette smoking attrac-tive to the modern American public, the ad men came up with answers that duplicate mythical situations and scenes, and create images and brief happenings that can be called micro-myths and that essentially fall into the same category as the ancient myths about smoke.

These, as we saw, comprise two types: those which tell about the ecstasy induced in men by smoke, and those that describe the pleasure gods (or other divine beings) derive from the smoke. Both have their counterparts in the ads. The first category, as a rule, takes a subordinate place and is underplayed but it is present nevertheless. It does not show the smoker of a cigarette actually erupting into an ecstasy or frenzy (this type of reaction is reserved for the unadvertised illegal smokes, such as marijuana and drugs used by sniffing), but it presents him, or, more frequently, him and her, achieving a state of blissful pleasure as soon as they fill their lungs with the first puff of filtered or unfiltered tobacco smoke. By endlessly repeating the sigh of satisfaction, or the throaty cry of pleasure ("Yea, me and my Winston . . .") these ads imprint into the smoker's psyche the exact manner in which he not only is supposed to react but actually will and does react to inhaling a lungful of smoke. At that moment the mythical archetype of the effect of smoke inhalation takes over.

It will readily be seen that this aspect of the smoke bliss is not a particularly promising field as far as the possibilities of reenactment in smoke ads is concerned. The range of facial or other physical expressions of smoke-induced pleasures is, after all, quite limited. As against this, the other category, the one depicting or alluding to the pleasure "divinities" derive from smoke, allows a wide range of illustration. The modern counterparts of the ancient supernaturals can be shown in an almost limitless series of situations which will associate the joys of smoke with the other pleasures they enjoy. These images create the impression in the mind of the smoker that by lighting a cigarette he is magically transported into the company of those "superhuman" beings whose life is an uninterrupted sequel of excitement and enjoyment, and who are divinely endowed with beauty, eternal youth, health, strength, and supreme sexual attractiveness.[15]

"Magic transport" into a totally different world is actually and literally a favorite method of triggering these psychological processes. One cigarette commercial invited the smoker to "come up" into an enchanted garden with a cascading fountain of "Kool" waters; another opened up before him an entire wide "Marlboro Country" in which he (in the shape of a rugged he-man with whom the viewer is magnetically forced to identify) pleasurably inhales, not the clean, sharp air of the great outdoors, but the much more irresistible smoke that supposedly soothes the savage breast. A third one appealed to the little measure of sadism carefully suppressed but nevertheless latently lurking in many a male psyche, by showing a young man with large, rectangular dark glasses, flaring nostrils, a haughtily up-turned head, and a contemptuously downturned mouth, who suddenly abandoned his beautiful and adoring female compan-ion in such likely or unlikely spots as a taxicab, an elevator, a mountain cable car, a luxurious yacht, but not before snatching from her fingers his pack of "Silva Thins," which he then lovingly placed in his left breast-pocket right next to his heart.

Compared to these more imaginative cigarette ads, others that typically showed a young man and woman lighting up their cigarettes in closest proximity while looking at each other with melting adoration must appear as commonplace. The latter, too, of course, did not show ordinary people in ordinary cir-cumstances enjoying a smoke as part of their ordinary lives, but idealized individuals, in "richer than life" surroundings, with whom to identify means for the ordinary individual an elevation of his self into a higher sphere, an imaginary penetration into, and a momentary participation in, a world that he can never make. Psychologically, this is a fleeting realization of myth in one's own life, and, as in the case of the Coke commercials, it has the function of supplying satisfactions that are totally beyond the ordinary physical realm of reality. The magic power of the ubiquitous Coke and Smoke commercials and illustrated adver-tisements thus adds an illusory but nevertheless psychologically significant mythological dimension to the drab and dragging existence of millions of modern men.

(By the time the above chapter was in galley proofs, the ciga-rette commercials on television had been outlawed. Therewith a most amusing chapter in modern mythmaking had come to a close.)

madison avenue
myth and magic

In earlier chapters we discussed the mythical affinities of the serials hero, the world of science fiction, Mickey Mouse cartoons, commercials, and ads for Coke and Smoke. These myths are presented and disseminated either principally or exclusively through television, the most influential mass medium of the modern world. However, none of these characteristic television presentations represents a conscious or overt attempt to utilize traditional myths or mythologems. On the contrary, the mythological character of these offerings becomes evident only after one peels off their contemporary disguises and penetrates to their essential, stereotyped features. This is what we attempted to do in the chapters dealing with these myths of the modern world.

1 • *Mythical Personages*

The area where mythological images in a pseudo-classical, undisguised, and straightforward form are used to a point of surfeit is that of the television commercials for detergents and other household products. However, the minor art of the television commercial is far from constituting the first time that classical mythology has been used for artistic or psychological effect.

A return to the mythological themes of classical antiquity characterized the European Renaissance, and in particular the artistic output in Italy and France. Greco-Roman gods and goddesses, nymphs, fauns, and other half-human, half-animal creatures of Greek mythology were as often depicted in the Renaissance as in ancient Greece or Rome. Yet the frequent utilization of such mythological figures by the Christian painters and sculptors of the Renaissance did not imply a revival of a religious faith in the pagan gods. The Greco-Roman deities were used as themes —as excuses, as it were—for showing nude bodies in innumerable positions and configurations, for the esthetic pleasure of both the artist and his patrons. Incidentally, they also gave the artist ample opportunities to flatter his patron, whom he could represent in the guise of a Greek god or goddess, with nobody taking it too seriously or taking offense at it.

For our purposes, the television commercials to which we now turn differ in their utilization of mythical themes from Renaissance art in one significant respect. They resort only rarely to an actual presentation of mythological figures from past ages. (The white Ajax knight is one notable exception.) What they almost invariably do is present, in innumerable versions, one basic mythological idea that in itself is a heritage from past ages: namely, the solution of a problem in an instant, by actual magic, performed by a superhuman, i.e., mythical personage. These commercials typically consist of a short film of about half a minute to one minute's duration. They tell a simple story that usually falls into two parts: the first presents a problem, the second its resolution. It is in the second part that myth and magic come into play. The mythical personage whose sudden appearance results in the resolution of the problem is equipped with great magic powers; with the ease and calm that characterize true divine intervention in human affairs, he supplies the solution and then disappears.

Take, for instance, the commercials for the Ajax cleanser that, after successful runs for several years, were retired in 1968. The opening scene varied: it showed either a group of children playing outdoors in a suburban setting with their clothes all grimy, or a group of workers digging up a street, with even dirtier clothes. The problem was only implied, but immediately understandable, especially if you were a housewife: how can one get all that "ground-in dirt" out of the clothes? Now comes the solution: suddenly a knight in *white* shining armor gallops down the street or across the field, riding on a *white* charger, with a huge *white* lance pointing forward in his mighty right hand. With great speed, so great indeed that the eye cannot precisely discern what is happening, the White Knight stabs with his lance, or merely points, at the group of boys or men. There is an explosion-like *white* flash, whose force spins the boys or men around, and as soon as they regain their equilibrium they all notice that their incredibly dirty clothes have suddenly become just as incredibly *white*. By the time the stunned group recovers its wits sufficiently to look around for the cause of this sudden, miraculous transformation, the White Knight has disappeared, and with a happy grin they all turn to one another, at which point the camera fades out, probably so that it will not have to show the process of dirtying up those magically whitened clothes being resumed.

This commercial ingeniously utilizes the medieval mythical concept of the "knight in shining armor" who, in the nick of time, appeared out of nowhere, rescued the damsel in distress, and then went his way. We are not shown the tedious steps the housewife has to follow in laundering. In fact, the distaff side of the family or of society is conspicuous by its absence. The whitening of the dirty clothes is effected through the magic touch of the knight's lance, while the clothes are actually worn by the men or the boys. It would be, of course, too much to expect the Madison Avenue mythmakers to be aware of the slight anachronism in showing an ancient Greek mythical hero by the name of Ajax (there were, actually, two Greek warriors by this name) in medieval armor.

The White Knight has a counterpart from Araby in Mr. Clean. Despite his prosaic-sounding name, Mr. Clean is a jinnee straight from the wonderland of the *Arabian Nights' Entertain-*

ments. He is huge, half-naked, totally bald, wears a big ring in one ear, and is shown either smiling broadly or scowling threateningly, the latter because, when it comes to dirt, "he is mean." He comes in several versions: as a drawing on the plastic containers in which the "Mr. Clean" cleanser is marketed, in animated cartoons, and in motion pictures. In the latter two incarnations he appears suddenly out of nowhere, like the White Knight, but also like the jinnee in the famous story of Aladdin's lamp. The problem he solves is, again, dirt, although this time of that variety which is supposed to disfigure primarily the kitchen floor. Being of the jinnee-slave type, Mr. Clean not only brings the wonder-working cleanser to the harassed housewife, but actually gets into the fray with the dirt he hates, and vanquishes it.

Nor are the Madison Avenue mythopoets above borrowing mythical figures from the television serials themselves. We all remember the incomparable Mr. Spock, science officer of the starship *Enterprise,* completely human except for his pointed ears which betray the Vulcan half of his ancestry more visibly than does his superhumanly anti-emotional, logical mind. The manufacturers of "Cheer" (a household detergent) seem to have succeeded in what not even the most fantastic monsters of remote galaxies managed to do; they kidnapped the astute and quizzical Mr. Spock from his starship, to "beam him down" into the kitchen of a desperate, dirt-pursued housewife, where he materializes in the midst of a shower of sparks, and where—having lost in transit the points of his ears—his appearance does not at all upset the worried woman whom he engages in a friendly conversation about the advantages of "Cheer." Somewhere in between we hear a booming voice: "Out of the future comes to you all-temperature Cheer."

Another modern-day variation on the same theme is the Man from Glad, who sells plastic food bags. Instead of shining armor he is clad in a white trench coat. He wears no hat, which makes it possible for him to impress us with his shining platinum white hair. He arrives, not on a white charger, but plopping down from the air. His image, in modern terms, is no less mythical than that of the White Knight from the past, or of the

Mr. Spock-like figure from the future. However, the problem he solves with his glad smile, his superior knowledge, and his sleight-of-hand conjuring up a box of Glad Bags out of nowhere has, for once, nothing to do with dirt. His mission is to teach us how to prevent the drying out of sandwiches and other food that is not consumed immediately.

Yet another mythical figure is resuscitated from European folklore. He is the "Green Giant," whom the commercial turns into the patron saint of green peas, while the workers who produce the peas are dwarfs taken straight from Walt Disney's *Snow White*. This is not a typical *"deus ex machina"* commercial like those mentioned before, because it does not present a problem first and then its solution through a mythical personage who suddenly appears. It merely shows a mythological scene: the dwarfs work diligently at sorting, carting, cooking, and canning peas, while the Green Giant, who towers over the landscape, looks down upon them benevolently.

Another giant, this time in the shape of a beautiful girl, is more tricky. She takes hold of part of a paved highway, which in her hands looks like a soft ribbon, twists it around, then lifts it up into the air, thereby first frightening and then delighting the driver of a car speeding along the road.

Yet another commercial that utilizes the flight motif in connection with automobile advertising is that of a car rental agency whose slogan is "Let Hertz put you in the driver's seat!" The commercial does not show Hertz carrying out its offer, but shows a man soaring through the air in a seated position, overtaking a car that is moving ahead at full speed but without a driver. The man glides down into the driver's seat, and both car and driver continue the journey which was not interrupted even for a second.

2 · *Animal Myths*

The role of animals in mythological thinking constitutes one of the oldest and richest chapters in the fantasy world of man. Paleolithic cave paintings testify to the early human practice of donning animal skins and masks and thus symbolically assuming the character of an animal for magico-religious purposes. Freud, as is well known, has made much of the identification of the murdered father with an animal—the totem—and the belief that grew out of this identification concerning the fatherhood of the totem-animal and the animal filiation of the primal fraternal horde (see above, Chapter 2, section 3). Totemic clans, which consider themselves the descendants of a particular animal, still believe that they actually possess some of the characteristics of their totem ancestor.

Traces of this close primal human relationship to animals can be found among the civilized peoples of the ancient world. Historians of religion are in general agreement as to the original animal form of the ancient Egyptian gods. Animal attributes of deities persisted in all other ancient Near Eastern religions, and their echoes can still be discerned in the divine imagery of the Greek, Hebrew, and Christian faiths. Art historians have commented on the bull-like character with which Michelangelo endowed his Moses in his endeavor to give him a divine cast of countenance. Long before zoology became a subject of scientific study, mythological zoology was a favorite human preoccupation; it expressed an infinite variety of man's imaginings about animals.[1] The latest development in zoological mythology has taken place on Madison Avenue.

The product in connection with which animals are most frequently utilized in television commercials is the automobile. This is facilitated by the very names of cars, especially of sports cars. Cars come with such names as Wildcat, Cougar, Impala, Mustang, Stingray, Barracuda, Falcon—names that imply speed or ferocity or both. But while the names merely conjure up the image, the commercials actually show us the wild animal in action, in motion: we see a big cat sitting in the car next to a woman whose features, expression, and movements are supposed to be reminiscent of the wildcat or the cougar. Or we are shown one of these carnivores sprinting, with the inimitable gracefulness that is theirs, and then suddenly we see a car speeding ahead, then again the animal, and thus back and forth in rapid succession, calculated to impress into our minds the identity of the animal and the car. Or, in a related field, we are treated to a cartoon drawing of huge tiger paws and claws leaping forward and biting into the road; within a second or so the picture changes into that of a tire which, the voice assures us, "grrrrips the road."

The identification of cars with wild animals has become so complete that at least one bank, wishing to advertise the availability of loans to finance car purchases, coined the phrase "get a wildlife loan." In numerous ads in *The New York Times* and other dailies and magazines this advice appeared in large bold type over pictures of all the animals after which the various car models are named. Only the initiates could know that the romantic zoological offer actually referred to such a prosaic thing as a car loan.

One of the most persistent commercial exploitations of the mythical wild animal motif has been the huge advertising campaign launched by the Humble Oil and Refining Company with the slogan "Put a Tiger in Your Tank!" It started with the relatively simple idea of graphically illustrating the statement that by filling up with Esso gasoline, the trade name of Humble's gasoline, one supplies one's car with the power of a tiger. To show the tiger-power of Esso, ads were drawn showing a huge, grinning tiger lurking behind the Esso gasoline pump. Posters showing the tiger in this manner soon appeared all over the country and were conspicuously placed at Esso gasoline stations. Next, animated cartoons in television commercials showed the same tiger giving a powerful push with his front paw to a car that has just filled up with Esso gasoline. Then you discovered (still in television commercials) a live tiger sitting on top of a tall Esso sign next to a gas station. At the same time, other commercials showed automobiles with a tiger's tail sticking out of their gasoline tanks, creating the illusion of a tiger actually crouching in it. Then stuffed tigers of various shapes began to appear, placed neatly on the ledge under the rear windows of cars (some with heads nodding, others with two little green or yellow electric bulbs for eyes), and stuffed tiger's tails were displayed in various places inside cars or tied to the radio antenna.

Before long the mythical Esso tiger leaped across the Atlantic and appeared in the same form in various countries. (I myself saw him often in Italy and France).

Nor did the mythopoeic fantasy of Madison Avenue stop here. New commercials carried the tiger theme to new heights. One showed a man having his car filled up at an Esso station; while he was busy paying the attendant, the tiger approached the car from behind, to the great delight of the car-owner's little son. I read somewhere (to my regret I can no longer remember where) that this tiger-campaign did more for boosting the sales of Esso gasoline than any other type of ads ever did for any other automotive fuel.

The conclusion one is led to by a consideration of the frequent utilization of the animal motif by the automobile industry (including the manufacturers of tires and the distributors of gasoline) is, to put it as simply and briefly as possible, that even in this modern mechanized world of ours men are still attracted by wild animals. The identification of a car with a speedy, wild, untamed, ferocious animal motivates people to buy cars, not because they believe that the animal whose name the car bears is faster than the car (every child knows better than that), but because the mythical association of the car, which belongs to him and over which he has control, with a wild animal satisfies a hidden yearning for power and ferocity which in reality are among the most unattainable things in the life of an ordinary man. Moreover, the identification of the *car* with a wild animal has the great advantage over identifying one's own person (or character) with such a beast in that it does not, as the latter would, place any demand, not even an imaginary one, on the physical strength, courage, audacity, energy, or willpower of the man in question. He can be a weakling, an effete sampler of the "finer things in life," in fact, a Playboy-Rabbit (see Chapter 20), and yet have, or want to have, in his car a powerful, wild animal at his disposal. This is the hidden fantasy pool that is being tapped, with considerable skill, by the Madison Avenue myth of the car that was a carnivorous beast.

The mythological impact of the animal world is, of course, not confined to the automotive realm. Animal designations appear in the names of restaurants (The Leopard, El Toro, Sacred Cow, La Paloma, Le Cheval Blanc, Russian Bear), book series (Penguin, Pelican, Dolphin), dance halls (Cheetah), and in many other areas of modern life. It seems quite evident that while most modern urbanites rarely see animals except for such pets as cats and dogs, their fantasy-world is still peopled with animals tame and wild, and close association—at least in imagination—with animals still retains its old mythical attractiveness.

3 · Kitchen Magic

Much of Madison Avenue's mythmaking effort is centered on the kitchen, the kingdom in which the housewife rules supreme. The ad men's kitchen magic, while it never loses sight of the ultimate goal, which of course is to sell the product, often reaches this goal by introducing a miraculous element into the kitchen, and/or by making the housewife (or, on occasion, her daughter) appear as superior in practical knowledge, understanding and intelligence to her fumbling, incompetent husband.

The general psychological basis of the Madison Avenue kitchen magic is the all too human infantile wish-residue, common to men and women, to see something that is outside the physical laws of nature. We, of course, *know* that we are most unlikely to witness inexplicable phenomena, but a part of our ego wishes this were not so and finds occasional satisfaction in such things as firmly believed sightings of Unidentified Flying Objects (see Chapter 21, section 4), extrasensory perceptions, and the like. The commercial mythopoets know only too well how to exploit this readiness, found in so many of us so many times, to see and believe the impossible. They do it in an almost tongue-in-cheek manner, but, at the same time, by blithely ignoring the abyss that separates "A is *like* B" *from* "A *is* B"—that is, a simile, or, at best, a metaphorical phrase, from an actual identification—they create a world of mythical miracles.

Take the commercial that is based on the simile "Detergent X cleans like a white tornado," or on the metaphor, "Detergent X is a white tornado." What the commercial I have in mind does is to show, by trick photography, an actual miniature fun-

nel-like white tornado rising out of the shopping bag carried
by a housewife. The woman is totally unconcerned, but not so
her neighbors, or, in a variant commercial for the same product,
a group of firemen who observe her. These outsiders get quite
hysterical at what they see, scream at one another, "That's a
white tornado!" rush after the housewife, and burst into her
kitchen, presumably to rescue her from the power of elements
unleashed, only to find her in the midst of removing a container
of the product from her shopping bag, at which moment the
white tornado disappears into the bottle. She turns to the in-
truders with that calm, supercilious, superior expression on her
face that characterizes so many of the television commercials'
"know-it all" or "in" figures when passing on their esoteric information to the uninitiated dumb-heads, and says: "Why, of
course, it's my White Tornado!"

The same idea of magic metamorphosis is utilized by another
kitchen product marketed under the trade name "Dove." The
dove, of course, has long been associated in the Western world
with the religio-magical idea of the Holy Ghost. Innumerable
paintings depict the Holy Ghost in the form of a white dove.
Now Madison Avenue takes the white dove, has it fly in through
the open kitchen window and, once inside, settle on what is
known as the working area. Within a split second the white
dove turns into a box of "Dove," to the awed surprise of all
who happen to witness this magic transformation, except the
housewife who originally bought the box of "Dove" and who
evidently sees in the magic happening nothing but a vindication
of her shopping know-how.

As the foregoing examples show, the American housewife's
fight against dirt, dust, stains, odors, and other forms of pollution
assumes mythical dimensions on the television screen. The battlefield extends from the kitchen to other parts of the home, as
well as to all parts of the bodies of the people who live in it.
The bathroom is an especially sensitive area where the housewife must constantly be on the alert for odors, germs, and other
hidden dangers. The floors and carpets of the rooms also demand her unflagging vigilance. The television commercials

make it abundantly clear that the overworked housewife would be fighting a losing battle against these overwhelming odds were it not for the very special magic power offered her in the form of this or that product.

The same holds good for personal hygiene. The ungroomed man and woman, we learn from the commercials, is a menace to society and an enemy of himself. He (or she) exudes noxious odors from all parts of his body, his hair is an unkempt mess snowing "dangerous dandruff," his very proximity is intolerable so that he can find neither a girl friend nor a job, and is a veritable outcast. The magic products, however, can change all this in a jiffy. Yesterday's untouchable becomes today's Prince Charming; yesterday's Cinderella—today's queen of the ball and the hearts. The magical element in these fantastic metamorphoses are often underplayed in the commercials which emphasize instead the contrast between the "before" and the "after," but even so the miraculous nature of these transformations is readily apparent.

We have not yet mentioned the one appliance which plays the central role in the housewife's Sisyphean struggle against dirt: the washing machine. Located either in the kitchen itself or in a separate laundry room, the automatic washer is undoubtedly the favorite child of Madison Avenue. The amount of attention the washing machine gets shows clearly that it is the most mana-laden appliance in the entire household. Of course mana, i.e. power, is claimed for all the detergents; but their power is nowhere as impressively demonstrated as in the washing machine which churns and spins and shakes and groans and roars, while miraculously transforming the dirtiest rags into sparkling clean clothes. No wonder that the washing machine was lavishly endowed by the Madison Avenue ad men with the most fantastic qualities, and that they could not resist emphasizing and playing up the masculine, phallic, aspect of this most powerful, active, and aggressive of all major household appliances.

One of these television commercials shows a huge, strongly masculine arm rising perpendicularly out of a washing machine and clutching the advertised washday product. The phallic connotation of the picture is as clear as that of the scene described by Tennyson:

> So flash'd and fell the brand
> Excalibur:
> But ere he dip't the surface, rose
> an arm
> Clothed in white samite, mystic,
> wonderful,
> And caught him by the hilt, and
> brandish'd him
> Three times and drew him under
> in the mere.[3]

On another channel, the competition did one better and countered by showing not merely an arm but the entire washing machine expanding upward in a gigantic mechanical erection. The reaction of the housewife who witnesses these phallic miracles is typically the same: she is awed and yet delighted.

4 · *The Mythical Advice*

While not all commercials use the magic and miracle approach in their attempts to sell the products of their sponsors, a large number do and thrive on it. Others build—whether consciously or not—on other mythological elements. As far as I know, no statistics are available on the percentage of mythological *versus* nonmythological commercials on television, but since television carried by 1968 no less than 3,022 commercials a month, taking up about one quarter of the total broadcasting time on all stations, the exposure of the American public to the magic, miracles, and mythology of Madison Avenue must be quite considerable. Without touching upon the question of the quality of these commercials, either as commercials or as attempts at mythmaking, their very presence and persistence, the profusion of the repetitions of themes and the proliferation of new variants can be interpreted as being indicative of at least a readiness in wide circles of the American people to go along with, and be influenced by, this type of mythological fabrication. And, considering the number of hours the average American spends watching television day after day, one can estimate that he is fed about as much mythical material from this one source alone as the average ancient Greek was from all sources of his contemporary culture.

It is quite fascinating to follow the emergence and development of these Madison Avenue myths. Take, for instance, the case of the White Rock Girl. For many years a carbonated water was marketed under the name White Rock. At some time, the manufacturers adopted the picture of a fairy-like girl sitting on a rock as the emblem of their product. For years, the White Rock Girl adorned the label of every bottle and did nothing else besides. Then, one day, she came alive in animated cartoon form on a television commercial; she flew around a little, hit the rock with her magic wand, causing sparks to fly in all directions, while a crystalline high soprano voice sang a little ditty praising the quality of the beverage thus advertised. Then the ditty changed, and it now praised, not the beverage, but the White Rock Girl herself. Some time later, in radio commercials, after the ditty was completed, a masculine voice could be heard saying something to the effect that "the bubbly, vivacious White Rock Girl says" that only those restaurants deserve your patronage in which White Rock beverages are served.

This master stroke completed the mythical, Pygmalion-like process of bringing the White Rock Girl to life. She not only moved around, flew, and sang, but was now possessed of a mind of her own, with which she could offer advice—surely the ultimate sign of an independent intelligence. Madison Avenue has accomplished the addition of one more mythical character to its host of spirits, heroes, genies, ghosts, ghouls, doves, and tornadoes.

Another such mythical character shares with the White Rock Girl the circumstance of being known by an appellative only, while the true proper name of both remains for a future generation of mythmakers to either ferret out or invent. He is the

serious, almost sullen, but always extremely dignified man referred to as El Exigente, "the demanding one." To our regret,
we are unable to trace his development from the early beginnings to the present when he seems to be a more important
(and more permanent) personage in Colombia and other Latin
American countries than their incumbent dictators. But we
know that for several years now he has been the most feared
man south of the border. We see him on television commercials,
walking slowly, in a dignified manner as behoves a man of great
power and influence, down the street of a small Latin American
town. As soon as his white suit and broad light yellow sombrero-
style Panama hat emerge from around the corner, the children
who have played in the street run indoors, and the adults, both
men and women, peek anxiously between drawn curtains, following with their apprehensive glances the figure of El Exigente
as he moves along the street. What is this fear that surrounds
El Exigente? Why the deadly silence that falls over the usually
noisy streets of the *ciudad*? Is El Exigente about to exact some
fearsome tribute from the people? Is he going to take their sons
into the army or select their daughters for exercising the ancient
rights of the *jus primae noctis,* or demand intolerable taxes
from the parents? No, he plans neither atrocities, nor brutalities,
nor even extortions. As he disappears around the corner, we are
left for a moment in suspense, but only for a moment, because
in the next shot we see El Exigente sampling heaps of coffee
beans, and, behold, he is actually smiling, without however losing his natural dignity even for a moment. The people around
him break out in loud and jubilant cries: El Exigente has found
our coffee crop acceptable! Music bursts in, and everything dis-
solves in cheer and happiness.

Now we are in a position, in retrospect, to reconstruct what
happened. The town we saw is a town whose entire livelihood
depends on the coffee grown there. El Exigente is the demanding
buyer of the coffee beans who visits the town year after year. He
examines the beans carefully to see whether they are up to the
standard required by his employers, the *Norte Americano* coffee
manufacturer called Savarin. It evidently happened several
times in the past that the coffee beans were found unsatisfactory,

and El Exigente refused to buy them. This, of course, spelled ruin for the whole town. They had to dump their crop into the sea (if it was conveniently near), and starve until the next crop. This is why a pall of hushed silence falls over the street when El Exigente reappears. Will our coffee meet his exacting standards? If not, little Juanito will have to go barefoot and hungry throughout the coming hard winter.

Having established El Exigente as an undoubted living being, like the White Rock Girl (the Madison Avenue mythopoets can do this superbly), his activities and opinions become, of course, of interest to the American housewife who sits at her kitchen counter and considers carefully the various factors that should influence her in making the important decision as to which brand of coffee to buy when next she goes to the supermarket. To help her make the right decision, the Savarin people obligingly send her from time to time a colorful page which not only contains a "store coupon worth 10¢ at your grocer when you buy Savarin coffee," but also shows a true color photograph of El Exigente, frowning in serious concentration, at the fateful moment when he ponders the acceptability of a sack of coffee beans. The text next to the picture assures the trusting American housewife that "EL EXIGENTE KEEPS SEARCHING the coffee fields of Latin America —so that you at home can enjoy the delicious flavor," etc. As the crowning argument, El Exigente is quoted directly: "EL EXIGENTE SAYS: Take this coupon to your store immediately! You may already be a winner, etc." The advice put into the mouth of the White Rock Girl, El Exigente, and others of their ilk, is the clinching proof of their having achieved an existential reality.

5 • Myths Based on Myths

Two factors helped Madison Avenue to have the public accept the kind of mythopoesis we have just been describing. One is the miraculous element in the serial and single feature film programs which had been staple fare on television for many years. The other is the product endorsement by Famous Names and Faces.

In the serials we are treated (or were until recently, since serials tend to peter out), week after week, to inimical extraterrestrial invaders ("The Invaders") or friendly visitors from the other planets ("My Favorite Martian"); to earthlings visiting other worlds with fantastic inhabitants ("Star Trek," "In the Land of Giants"), or equally fantastic undersea realms on our own planet (explored by Admiral Nelson with his atomic submarine); to ghosts of dogs and humans ("Topper," "The Ghost and Mrs. Muir"), genies ("I Dream of Jeannie"), ghouls ("The Munsters," "The Addams Family"), and witches ("Bewitched"); to flying men and women ("Superman," "The Flying Nun"); and many more of this genre.

In the single feature films broadcast over television the fantastic element is equally important. One station broadcasts every week a two hour long feature film under the general title "Creature Features." The "creatures" are usually huge monsters, such as prehistoric dinosaurs, gigantic apes ("King Kong"), birds, and so forth, which somehow manage to get to Manhattan and devastate much of it before being killed. Or they may be artificially made humans or quasi-humans, based, quite frequently, on the "mad scientist" theme, and the like. These feature film offerings on television have inured and habituated the viewers to accepting the miraculous and the supernatural almost as a matter of course. Thus the foundation was laid for the acceptance of the miraculous element in the commercials as well.

If the frequency of a type of program is any indication of its popularity, we must conclude that the American public likes to watch miraculous and fantastic features as much as, or perhaps even more than, Westerns, or police, detective, and spy adventures. Absurd as the synthetic heroics of the latter are, they satisfy the desire of the demuscularized and desk-bound city dweller for the active and strenuous life of the great outdoors and for the fast action of fists and guns. The fantastic serials seem to have an equal or even greater appeal to a more infantile layer in our psyche; they satisfy the craving to recapture the world of miracles which surrounded us in early childhood, a kind of paradise lost in which wishes came true, and in which two benevolent and seemingly omnipotent giants (father and mother) protected us from evil spirits while assuring us of the friendly presence of fairies, dwarfs, genies, and the like. It is this lost myth of contact with supernatural beings that is being recaptured for us in the fantastic serials, which also contribute indirectly to a strengthening of our self-esteem, thus providing ego satisfactions on several levels.

While no adult would admit to believing either the miraculous happenings which suffuse the fantastic serials, or the existence of the impressive legions of dwarfs, giants, spirits, ghouls, genies, witches, monsters, and the like shown on these programs, such denials are, in a sense, vitiated by the very fact that millions of people spend considerable amounts of time every day, or several times a week, watching these offerings. Without wishing to deny that these programs are, to a certain extent, entertaining, one feels that their entertainment value alone cannot explain their popularity. A degree of belief, even if only of a make-believe or "as if" variety, a kind of willing, or even involuntary, suspension of disbelief, must be a latent but nevertheless potent factor in forming the habit of watching the fantastic serials and providing satisfaction from them. They, together with the equally miracle-laden commercials interspersed every ten or fifteen minutes, create a mood of mythical-wondrous effluvium of which the conscious and supposedly critical mind of the television watcher may be entirely unaware, but which nevertheless subtly and insidiously influences his thinking.

The second factor that prepared the ground for the effectiveness of the insistent shopping advice pouring forth from the mouths of miraculous or realistically portrayed characters invented by the Madison Avenue mythopoets is the equally time-honored advertising method of "pushing" a product by having famous figures of the stage, the screen, or the world of sports tell you in commercials that they use and love the product in question. If they, the Famous Names and Faces, the Great Ones of our times, use and love it, how can you do without it? Now, side by side with these commercials, one also gets the assurance and advice of Mr. Clean, the Man from Glad, the Spock-like figure "beamed down" into the kitchen, and many other mythical images created by the Madison Avenue mythopoets. In other words, these mythical figures are made to behave and to talk exactly like the real Famous People; the same function is assigned to them; both advise you as to how to better your life by using this or that product. Since we, in general, are wont to accept advice only from people whom we believe to be more knowledgeable than ourselves, there can be little doubt that the Madison Avenue magicians have succeeded not only in creating mythical figures and bringing them to life, but also in making us believe that they are indeed persons whose advice is worth listening to, people who know more than we do.

In attaining this by no means small mythopoetic achievement, Madison Avenue was materially aided by the Hollywood image factory. It has often been pointed out that large numbers of television watchers develop the tendency to believe that the doctor or lawyer hero of serials is actually an expert physician or attorney, and that many address letters to lawyers Perry Mason and Judd or to Drs. Kildare or Ben Casey asking their advice in legal and medical problems. It is this mentality, this peculiar confusion of the play with reality, or, rather, this transformation of the plays' make-believe into a fully believed reality, that has prepared the ground for a similar transformation in the case of the mythical images of the commercials. Without being consciously aware of the process, the television viewer has become ready to believe not only that Dr. Kildare is a great healer who can advise him in his illness, but also that El Exigente or the White Rock Girl know, and therefore are in a position to advise him, about coffee and soda water. Since such a belief is the prerequisite of the effectiveness of these types of commercials, the very fact that they have multiplied in recent years to the extent they have is proof of the belief they manage to engender. The sum total of it all is a degree of mythicization of our thinking that one would certainly be inclined to disbelieve were it not for the cumulative proof supplied day after day by the medium itself.

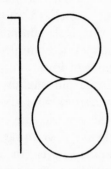

jerry, whitey, and baby

Personification, or, in more general terms, concretization, is a favorite method of mythology. When talking about a man who fell in love with a woman the mythologically informed ancient Greeks (or Romans) would say, "Aphrodite (or Venus) touched his heart," or "Eros (or Amor) shot an arrow into his heart." Whenever and wherever the emotion of love appeared, the ancients perceived in it a manifestation of these gods. Poets used their names in place of the word "love." When, for instance, Ovid tells about the vow Attis made to Kybele, "If I lie, may the love for which I break faith be my last love of all," he uses the word "Venus" for "love," so that in literal translation the actual words of Attis were: "If I lie, may that Venus for whom I break faith be the last one for me." [1]

These personifications and concretizations in the form of a single deity had the psychological advantage of providing a concrete focal point onto which one could project diffuse and confusing feelings. It was no longer a complex emotional process, hard to understand and to trace back to its origin, that brought about the phenomenon of falling in love, but a simple, single act of a god or a goddess. Being wounded in the heart by an arrow of Amor is, of course, an analogy to being hit by a real arrow in a battle—in both cases the effect is traced to a single, definite act by an outsider over whom one has no control. Responsibility is thus shifted from oneself to another person; and if that other person is a god, one feels completely absolved of all blame that otherwise would attach to committing, for instance, improper acts under the influence of love.

Another psychological advantage deriving from the mythological process of personification and concretization is the attendant subordination of the specific into the generic, the relief derived from the recognition that the single event or thing one experiences as a deeply disturbing phenomenon is, in fact, merely one of the oft-encountered manifestations of a type, a category, a class of events or things. There are, of course, minor variations in each individual event or case, but behind them, and overshadowing them in importance, are the generic features which, once recognized, enable one to deal with the individual case so much more easily and effectively. In dealing with individually arisen contingencies, mythically informed man is like the experienced bullfighter who, while observing carefully the individual behavioral traits of the bull which he faces for the first time in the arena, at the same time draws on his knowledge of the behavior pattern of bulls in general and thus performs his ritual with the reassuring foreknowledge of how the bull will react to each of his own movements.

A third attraction of concretization, personification, and categorization—that is, the subordination of individual events or things to generalized types—is that these techniques offer a simpler, easier, and more convenient way of relating to events handled in this way. First of all, it is always easier to deal with one than with many. Hence the tendency to overlook individual difference and emphasize the common features to the exclusion of everything else. It is easier to feel that one is having yet another encounter with Venus, whom one has already met several times before and with whose effect on one's emotions one is quite familiar, than to face up to the problematic possibilities inherent in a new, never-before-experienced relationship. We cannot be sure that Ovid had something like this in mind when he spoke about the "last Venus" of handsome Attis, but another great poet, some two thousand years later, has expressed the idea explicitly:

> This they know well: the Goddess yet abides.
> Though each new lovely woman whom she rides,
> Straddling her neck a year or two or three,
> Should sink beneath such weight of majesty
>
>   •   •   •
>
> Woman is mortal woman. She abides.[2]

I hope my good friend Robert Graves will forgive me the barbarism of quoting just a few of the fourteen lines of his beautiful sonnet. But my purpose here is not to provide esthetic pleasure to the reader, but to show how true poetic intuition can harmonize with, and recapture, ageless mythological thinking. The goddess whom Graves finds possessing one after the other the women with whom the poet falls in love is, of course, the same Venus whose earthly manifestations, according to Ovid, the youthful Attis blithely, and, as it turned out, unsuccessfully, foreswore, with fatal consequences to himself.

These mythical tendencies of personification, concretization, and categorization are still with us, and in quite potent forms. They lie at the roots of what sociologists call *stereotypes*. That the tendency to consider all members of certain human aggregates as sharing identical mental traits—this is what stereotypes basically do—has mythological antecedents or overtones will appear more plausible if one considers a related popular phenomenon—the practice of referring to a human aggregate as if it were a single individual.

In World War II the British soldiers and American GIs used the term "Jerry" in these senses: 1. Germany; 2. the German people; 3. the German army; 4. any part of the German army that faced them or that they encountered, including the smallest groups; 5. any individual German soldier. The term was always used as if it were the proper name of an individual, without either the definite or the indefinite article. It was never "the Jerry" or a "Jerry," but only "Jerry." A GI coming back from a patrol would report: "We found Jerry; we killed five of them." Or: "There came Jerry; he said . . ." This usage strictly as a proper noun indicates the completeness and finality of the personification and categorization of "Jerry."

These mythological processes were even more pronounced in the case of "Jerry" than in the case of "Johnny," a name used in the sense of "any man or boy." With "Johnny" there is still a residual trace of usage in the sense of a general noun, as expressions such as "a Johnny-come-lately" indicates. As against this, no article at all is ever set before "Jerry." He is a truly mythological individual, with his own proper name (like Venus); even if he appears in front of you in the shape of five or ten or a hundred men, he is still "Jerry," the single individual who, in that case, personifies the single category to which those many men belong and into whose person all of them merge.

In exactly the same manner and in a completely analogous sense is the term "Whitey" used by American Negro militants. The term is never used with either the definite or the indefinite article. There is no such thing as "the Whitey" or "a Whitey." "Whitey" is a true proper noun, like Jimmy or Harry, but it is also, like "Jerry," a term for an entire category of people and any group of persons or individual person belonging to that category. Every individual belonging to the Caucasian race, as well as any group of such individuals, and the entire noncolored population of America is "Whitey." As in the case of all true mythological personification and categorization, a certain amount of doubt is left as to whether any particular use of the proper noun in question refers to the individual in whom symbolically the group is personified or to one or more of his manifestations that together make up the category symbolized by him. Such a slight ambiguity was present when an ancient Roman used the word Venus, as in the lines of Ovid quoted above, and the same is the case in such modern terms as "Jerry" and "Whitey." It is apparent in the book title *Look Out Whitey! Black Power's Gon' Get Your Mama* [3] in which the first part uses "Whitey" in the generic sense, while the last part ("Your Mama") addresses itself to "Whitey" as a singular individual in that it does not say "Your Mamas." This mythological conflation of the individual and the category is achieved in other cases as well—for example, in the threat "get Whitey!" or in such phrases as "get back at Whitey," "what Whitey don't understand . . . ," "run Whitey out of Harlem." [4] The emergence of such new mythical figures as "Jerry" and "Whitey" under our very eyes, incidentally, should help us understand the origin of Venus, of Mars ("Mars ravaged the country" means not only that the country suffered from war, but also that warriors, personified as Mars, ravaged the country), and of the other ancient mythological figures.

Let me add just one more example. Although this one is not as unequivocal as were the two discussed above, it shows how the mythical processes we are considering here penetrated the mind and speech patterns of the average American family, and especially those of the young mother. When an American woman is pregnant she expects "a baby." From this usage one could assume that after her child is born, it would be preferred to as "the baby." Before birth the child being formed in the mother's body is something indefinite: the mother does not know whether it will be a boy or a girl, does not know what will be its name; all she knows is that she is expecting "a baby." After birth, all this vagueness and indefiniteness disappear. She no longer expects a baby, she has it, it is here, she holds it in her arms, and it assumes a very definite role in her life. All indications thus are that the mother would refer to it as "the baby": the single, individual baby whom she carried and bore, whom she loves, of whom she takes care. And yet, instead of referring to it as "the baby," she talks about him as "Baby," without the definite article. This form of reference is used consistently as long as the infant lies in his cradle—that is, until he learns to walk or to talk. Very rarely is he referred to by his given name, never as "the baby," not even as "my baby" or "our baby," but always, briefly and invariably, as "Baby." When mentioning her infant in a letter to her own mother or women friends, the young mother will frequently capitalize the noun: "Imagine, Mom, what Baby did today . . ." If a new child is born, even within a year of the birth of the first one, the term "Baby" is immediately transferred to the newborn, while the older one is graduated to "Jimmy" or "Janey."

There can be little doubt that "Baby" is the result of the same processes of personification and categorization which gave birth to "Jerry" and "Whitey." The infant is for the mother the personification of all the babies she has seen and known; in most cases, she wanted to have "a baby," so that when he is born he is the concretization of her desires to have "a baby." Thus when he is born "Baby" becomes his proper name; it appears to the mother that it is the most fitting name of her Jimmy or Janey, because in the initial relationship between "Baby" and herself what counts is not the name the parents selected for the infant—they may have vacillated to the last minute between two or more names, may have actually given the infant more than one name (e.g., to satisfy both sets of grandparents), and even after having settled on names they may not yet be sure which will be the name by which they actually will call him. In the meantime it is "Baby," a name most suitable to express the very personal relationship between mother and child.

At some time Baby, if he is a boy, may be transformed into "Junior." This new designation is used, exactly like "Baby," as if it were a proper noun—that is, it can take neither the definite nor the indefinite article, nor can it assume plural form.

Jerry, Whitey, Baby, and the other such expressions that a study of popular usages could easily turn up indicate the continued existence of the need to group into a single concretized entity all individuals who appear to us similar, and to subsume them all under one mythical personality. From terming all German soldiers, whether encountered singly or in groups, "Jerry" there is only a small step to attributing a basically identical personality to all of them—that is to say, to having the separate individualities of each one blocked out and supplanted by a stereotype. This is how facile, and mostly erroneous, generalizations are arrived at: all Negroes are primitive; all Jews are clannish; all Scots are stingy. While not all outgroup stereotypes are derived from, or correlated with, mythical personifications or reductions of the many into one, all mythical compressions of the many into one carry within them the seeds of stereotyping.

the destructive
myth: self- castration
and suicide

In the foregoing chapters we have discussed several functions of myth in the society and culture within which it lives. We saw how myth serves as a sustaining force, how it reassures and encourages, alleviates pain, eliminates tension, and holds out great promises for the future. Yet, so great is the power of myth that, if it so chooses, it can compel man to deprive himself of pleasures, deny himself satisfactions, inflict suffering upon himself, mutilate his own body, sacrifice his manhood, and even destroy himself in the most painful manner imaginable. It is with these destructive aspects of myth that the present chapter deals.

1 • Self-Castration

Cases are known from the ancient world in which a mythical prototype exerted such a fascination that people emulated him even if it meant endangering, mutilating, or even destroying themselves. A typical form of the self-mutilation provoked or induced by the myth consisted of castrating oneself by cutting off one's own genitals with a sword, in honor of a god or a goddess whose myth contained a reference to such an act. Artemis of Ephesus, the Syrian Goddess at Hierapolis, and the great Phrygian goddess Kybele were among the deities whose devotees had to be castrated before they could become their priests. Let us have a closer look at the account of Kybele and her ill-fated lover Attis, which is probably the most clearly stated and most influential self-castration myth in antiquity.

Kybele was the great mother-goddess of Phrygia, located in the northwestern corner of Anatolia, whose orgies were known to the Greeks by the fifth century B.C. at the latest.[1] According to her myth she sprang originally from the ground as a bi-sexual being, and was subsequently reduced by the gods, who used surgical methods, to a female. From the severed male genitals an almond tree of unequaled beauty sprang up. It attracted Nana, daughter of the River Sangarios; she plucked a blossom, put it in her bosom, and soon found herself with child. Upon its birth, the baby was exposed, but a goat attended to him and he grew up to become a beautiful youth. His name was Attis. Kybele, who thus was a lineal ancestress (or ancestor) of Attis, and, according to a variant myth, actually his mother, loved him with a jealous passion. When he made love to a river nymph, Kybele drove him mad, in which state he castrated himself under a pine tree and bled to death.[2]

After giving a somewhat prettied-up version of the Attis myth, Ovid concludes with the comment: "His madness set an example, and still his unmanly ("molles") ministers cut their vile members while they toss their hair."[3] From Rome the worship of Kybele spread into Gaul where, at Autun, according to early Christian authors, "men, brought up to a pitch of frenzy by the shrill music of flutes and the clash of cymbals, sacrificed their virility to the goddess, dashing the severed portions of themselves against her image."[4]

The myth of Attis, incidentally, can be taken as a classic example of that type of myth which explains the origin and meaning of a religious rite by recounting a "historical" first:

the cruel rite of self-mutilation practiced by the priests of Kybele is being performed *because* Attis, the lover of Kybele, castrated himself in a like manner. The *because* is, of course, a purely mythical one: the logical connection between the deed of Attis and that of the actual priests of Kybele is rather tenuous. But the mythical connection is convincing: since the first devotee of Kybele was driven by her to castrating himself, *therefore* Kybele evidently expects the same act of her present-day devotees. Hence the self-mutilation in the course of a frenzied feast celebrating the great goddess.

Frazer in his monumental *Golden Bough* comments that "the story of the self-mutilation of Attis is clearly an attempt to account for the self-mutilation of his priests, who regularly castrated themselves on entering the service of the goddess." [5] Without venturing into the notorious and always vexing question of what was first, the myth or the ritual, one can state with certainty that, from the point of view of the individual candidate for Kybele's priesthood, the myth came unquestionably first: he had learned of the myth, and was sufficiently impressed by Kybele to join her retinue and allow himself to be worked up into a state of frenzy in which he emulated Attis by castrating himself.

Although the cult of Kybele, the Phrygian Mother of the Gods, was well known to the Greeks, it never managed to obtain a foothold on the Greek mainland. In Rome, however, toward the end of the Punic wars, conditions were ripe for the triumphant entry of the Great Mother. In the year 204 B.C., exhausted by their long struggle with Hannibal, the Romans received a prophecy to the effect that they would be helped if the great Oriental Mother goddess were brought to Rome. A delegation was immediately dispatched to the city of Pessinus in Phrygia. After some argument, the Roman emissaries secured the small black stone which embodied the goddess and brought it back to Rome. The help of the goddess became instantly apparent: she favored the Romans with an exceptionally rich harvest, and in the very next year Hannibal took his Punic army back to Africa.

Following such an auspicious entry into Rome, Kybele easily

conquered the Latin Republic. Soon her emasculated priests, called *galli,* could be seen in the streets, in their Oriental costume, with little images suspended on their breast, carrying in procession the image of the goddess and chanting her hymns to the accompaniment of cymbals, tambourines, flutes, and horns.[6] Stout-hearted Romans looked with disgust at the effeminate *galli;* others, more susceptible to the foreign allure, were attracted by the myth and the ritual of the goddess. We have no historical data as to the age group to which the latter belonged, but this much at least stands to reason: the men who were caught up in the Phrygian frenzy to the extent of sacrificing their manhood to the Great Mother must have been, as Attis was, very young; surely no older man would let momentary ecstasy rob him of his senses to such an extreme, painful, and irrevocable extent.

In the myth of Attis and Kybele and its attendant ritual we have an example of a mythical act being emulated in real life by young people in a later age, a different country, and a different cultural setting. Moreover, the mythical deed emulated is not an act of heroism or bravery, nor a feat in the course of whose performance an individual endangers himself for the benefit of a loved one or of a group of his peers. It is a deed of self-mutilation, closely akin to self-destruction, performed in a frenzied state, during an attack of madness induced by the vengefulness of a jealous goddess; those who emulated the self-emasculation of Attis did it in a state of frenzy similar to his. Moreover, there can be little doubt but that the chopping off of the *membrum* quite often must have ended in death due to loss of blood or infection. But precisely because it was an act of self-destruction, or at least a most serious self-impairment, it is the best example to show the power a myth can obtain over an individual or a group, even in the face of all reason and all instinct of self-preservation. The mythical prototype beckons, and he is being followed down the road, even though it be the road of death.

Nor must we imagine that it was only in antiquity, in the Orient or in Rome after it succumbed to the lure of Eastern religion, when frenetic ecstasy had become an accepted form of ritual expression, that myth had the power to impel youthful and possibly mentally somewhat unbalanced worshipers to such a precipitate, and later probably regretted, act as that of self-castration. In 1772 a Russian peasant named Kondrati Selivanov founded a religious sect, that of the Skoptsi or Skoptzy, meaning "mutilated." Having read in Matthew 19:12 "there be eunuchs which have made themselves eunuchs for the kingdom of heaven's sake," and interpreting it literally, Selivanov included self-castration among the practices of his sect, while its women were expected to have both of their breasts cut off. Despite these cruel demands, and despite government persecution, the sect gained many adherents throughout the nineteenth century.

2 • *Suicide Without a Cause*

Examples like this can, moreover, be found much closer to the present—in fact, in our very own day and age and in our very own proud American scene. I am referring to the hero myth that grew up around James Dean. A young and talented actor, remembered especially for his moody role in *Rebel Without a Cause,* James Dean took the fancy of rebelliously inclined teen-agers actually committed suicide to join him," says Fish-when he was twenty-four years old. This was followed by a veritable James Dean cult, which held sway for some years. "Several teen-agers actually committed suicide to join him," says Fishwick.[7] To me it seems that the motivation of these suicides was not so much to "join" James Dean, which would presuppose a concrete belief in an afterlife, as to imitate his fate, to die young, to become, like him, an unfulfilled hero.

The hero who suffers a violent death while still young, thus becoming an ideal figure, an exemplar to follow, is a mythological archetype of the same category as Attis. Neither Attis nor James Dean had performed any remarkable deeds for which they could be considered as true heroes. In fact, they were rather anti-heroes. Attis was the passive recipient of the love of imperious Kybele; because he was weak he fell into the arms of the first little nymph that came along, at which point he became the passive recipient of the wrath of Kybele, lost his mind, cut off his own genitals, and bled to death—a truly unimpressive life, singularly empty of accomplishment even for its short duration. James Dean, likewise, had a rather unimpressive record; the few films in which he played were nothing exceptional, and his role in them was that of the unhappy, moody, passive, silent, inarticulate, resentful youth. His death, like that of Attis, was visited on him by outside forces. In fact, Dean had even less to do with his death than Attis had had to do with his.

And yet the devotees of James Dean followed him into death as those of Attis followed him into self-castration. Clearly, in both cases it was not the individual personality of the hero that made such a deep impression on those who became his devotees, but the added dimension of his mythical significance. After causing the death of Attis, the grief-stricken Kybele went into deep mourning for him, fasting, until finally Attis was resurrected—a mythical-ceremonial precedent containing the promise that his devotees, too, would rise triumphant from the grave.[8] In this context, Attis appeared as a significant figure, no longer a passive, noncommittal, frail youth, but a truly great god who voluntarily undertook the sufferings of castration and death in the sure knowledge that resurrection would inevitably follow. Thus Attis, in his mythological embellishments, became enlarged into a god of the vegetation that dies and revives every year, a father god and a sky god who played a central, cosmic role in the fates of man, a fitting consort of the great mother goddess Kybele. It was this myth of the great Attis that had the power to motivate youths to perform the painful rite of self-castration in order thereby to emulate him, to identify with him, and thus to reassure his return and, ultimately, his life.

Similar motivations must underlie the suicides of youths in emulation of the ostensibly weak and insignificant movie idol James Dean. Those who killed themselves cannot be asked why they did it, but those who stopped short of this ultimate step can provide some clue. In the years following the death of James Dean there were many young men (or boys) who affected the mannerisms of James Dean—not of the real James Dean, whom few of them ever met, but the character he played in his film roles. They dressed like him, combed their hair like him, let their head hang forward and somewhat to one side as he often did on the screen, adopted the hesitant, almost stammering, speech pattern with the characteristic double start of every sentence or phrase, and, most importantly, assumed the same posture toward society that James Dean projected in his movie roles: a posture of alienation, of withdrawn bitterness, of being misunderstood, unloved, unwanted, of negating the world as it is without knowing (or, for that matter, caring) how it could be changed for the better. This posture, whether or not it had anything to do with the real James Dean, was the essence of the James Dean myth, and it was this myth that led, in several cases at least, to suicide as the only, inevitable, ultimate Deanly act, just as self-castration was the last conclusion to which were driven some of those caught up in the Attis syndrome.

The Attis-James Dean myth is with us in numerous other guises. One of the forms in which it appeared in recent years was the Che Guevara myth dealt with elsewhere in this book (Chapter 7).

3 • Al Capone in Japan

As in the classical world, so in modern times, too, the mythical example can project its power across continents and cultures. A case in point is the myth of Al Capone, the notorious Chicago gangster of the 1920s, which today, forty years later, exercises a hold over some Japanese youth gangs. The fifteen- to twenty-year-old members of such a gang in Osaka are referred to locally as *mogura*, "moles," because they spend all their time in the vast underground shopping and entertainment centers carved out beneath Osaka in the last few years. The "moles" neither go to school nor work; usually they simply loiter in front of the coffee shops, smoking cigarettes and looking for pickups. Sometimes they fancy themselves as gangsters and engage in fights, or they will stage impromptu rock concerts in the endless subterranean arcades. The identifying mark of the moles is a chopped off third joint of the little finger of the left hand. They believe that Al Capone had such a joint missing, and they spontaneously held up their left hands and pointed to the missing third joint while talking to a reporter of *The New York Times*. "I Al

Capone," a young mole said; then indicating the hands of
his friends, which also had a joint of the little finger missing, he
added: "All Al Capone." [9]

Evidently the power of the remote mythical prototype, whom
these bored and idle Japanese youngsters fancy imitating, is
strong enough to induce them to undergo a minor but irreparable
mutilation of their hands. The psychological mechanism, of
course, is identical with the one that two thousand years earlier
compelled the devotees of Kybele to sacrifice their manhood
in emulation of Attis, and that, in the late 1950, drove youngsters to suicide in America in emulation of James Dean: by
imitating a striking event or deed from the life of the hero, his
devotees mythically identify themselves with him and thereby, in
their own eyes, attain a bigger-than-life status.

In order to understand the emergence of the Osaka "moles"
and their identification with Al Capone, one must be aware of
several factors. One is that lawless gangs are an old and traditional feature in Japanese society. Some Japanese films which
have reached these shores in recent years have depicted certain
aspects of these outlaw bands. It could therefore be expected
that modern urban environment should give rise to delinquent
juvenile groups such as the "moles." The second is that the ability
to suffer pain in a manly fashion and the readiness to inflict
pain upon oneself are also traditional features of the Japanese
ethos. Hence chopping off a finger joint as a mark of identification of the "moles" is in keeping with Japanese tradition. The
third factor to consider is the lure of America whose intensity in
youthful Japanese circles is often not sufficiently appreciated.
Hence American features, whatever their inherent value, carry
great prestige and are imitated. This is especially true for drop-
outs, that is, for youths who did not have the benefit of a balanced
presentation of Japanese versus American cultural values. As to
the channels through which the image of Al Capone reached the
Osaka youngsters, one can easily conjecture that they must have
been motion picture films performed either in theaters or broadcast over the Japanese television network. In either case, Al
Capone as the great American hero who defied the forces of law
and order, who was a law unto himself, and whose strong-arm

methods made him a legend in his lifetime, could not fail to make a deep impression on some Japanese delinquent juveniles who were searching for a mythical and, at the same time, American figure after whom to pattern their otherwise aimless lives.

4 · Self-Immolation

Yet another example of the powerful influence a faraway mythical prototype can exert on people who know of him only from hearsay, of his great deeds only the rudiments, and of his motivations next to nothing is supplied by the rash of self-immolations that claimed numerous victims in the United States and in Europe.

Suicide by burning oneself to death has an established and venerable place in Buddhist mythology. According to an old Buddhist tradition, the Pratyekabuddhas, enlightened and saintly men, would decide for themselves when the time had arrived for them to loosen the ties of life; they would then rise a few cubits above the ground and burn themselves. According to an old Buddhist text, "abandoning one's existence" is the best self-sacrifice, for to give one's body is better than to give alms; to burn one's body as an offering is more meritorious than to kindle lamps at a shrine, and is the best worship. One Buddhist myth tells of Bhaisajyarāja, who, dissatisfied with his previous worship, although painful and extravagant, filled his body with all sorts of oil and set it on fire.

Myth motivates ritual: thus Buddhist monks in China used to beg for fuel, build a funeral pyre, sit cross-legged on it, cover their head with a piece of linen soaked in oil, and set themselves on fire.[10]

When viewed against this background, we shall readily understand that in a Buddhist culture suicide by self-immolation is a traditionally and religiously sanctioned act which a monk may perform simply because he feels that he is approaching or has attained a state of enlightenment. Therefore, when, beginning 1963, several Buddhist monks and nuns set themselves on fire in South Vietnam, they did this not so much as a protest against the persecution of Buddhists by the Catholic South Vietnamese government, although this is how their suicides were, as a rule, interpreted in the American press,[11] but rather as a demonstration of their unshaken faith in their own Buddhist way of life and death. Nor did self-immolation mean to them what it appeared to mean when viewed through Western eyes. In the Western view political suicide is the supreme, defiant act of self-sacrifice in the face of antagonists on whom one has tried in vain to exert an influence in other ways. In Buddhist tradition self-immolation is a highly desirable way of "loosening the ties of life," of getting one step nearer to *nirvana*, the great goal of all informed Buddhists, and as such an act upheld by both myth and precept. What the Buddhist monks and nuns did in Saigon in burning themselves to death was utilizing this highly approved method of passing over to a new existence for an assertion of Buddhist values and a demonstration of the impotence of the Saigon Catholic leadership to as much as touch Buddhism.

The clearest proof that this, indeed, was the meaning of the suicides by fire within the context of Buddhist culture was supplied by those self-immolations which were performed with the explicitly stated purpose of expressing *gratitude* rather than protest in regard to relations between Buddhists and the Saigon government. On December 1, 1963, *The New York Times* reported that a Buddhist girl burned herself to death in a public square in Saigon in gratitude for the release of jailed Buddhist priests. Some six weeks later the *Times* reported (in its January 15, 1964, issue) that a Buddhist monk burned himself to death in South Vietnam in gratitude for the success of the Buddhist movement. Cases such as these, which to the Western mind are much less comprehensible than suicides in protest, indicate the generally positive or affirmative character of self-immolation in Buddhist culture.

After the news about the Vietnamese self-immolations began to appear in the American press, a wave of suicides by burning oneself to death started in America. American culture, of course, is one with a high suicide rate, so that Americans did not have to borrow from the Vietnamese the idea of ending one's life voluntarily. But American suicides were, typically, the way out some people chose when confronted with personal problems that seemed insoluble. Suicide as a protest against a public disgrace, injustice, or some other intolerable situation just did not seem to have an appeal for Americans. But the news about the men and women in Saigon, Panthiet, and elsewhere, who chose death as the ultimate protest against a tyrannical government and the persecution of their religion—for this is how the Vietnamese suicides appeared to the American public—assumed with each repetition more and more the character of a myth whose growing force finally was too much for several Americans to resist.

While suicide as a protest against a public crime would in itself have indicated Vietnamese influence, suicide in a public cause by self-immolation, unheard of in America, was *prima facie* evidence that some American men and women had indeed succumbed to the power of attraction exerted by the Buddhist myth of self-immolation. The typical American suicide has always been as painless as possible: an overdose of sleeping pills, inhalation of cooking gas, and the like. Or else, death had to be instantaneous: hence the numerous suicides with guns, or by throwing oneself down from a high building onto the pavement or from a high bridge into a river. For Americans, inculcated by their cultural conditioning with an inordinate fear of physical pain, to chose suicide by self-immolation is an almost incredible act. Yet such was the power of this new myth of self-destruction that not only did those who decided to die in protest of American policy put the match to their gasoline-drenched bodies, but so did people who sought death as an escape from physical pain. Prior to the arrival of this Asian import these people typically would have chosen drugs. Now, incredible as this appears, one woman in Nashville, Tennessee, set herself afire because of a toothache, and died a horrible death.[12] We look at such an act with the same incomprehension with which ancient Rome must have viewed those young Romans who, caught up in the ecstatic frenzy of the feast of the Phrygian Kybele, drew the sword and cut off their own genitals in emulation of the foreign and strange myth of Attis' self-emasculation.

Mythical influence can proceed from one continent to another, and then return, in a strengthened form, from the second to the first. Among the young Americans who followed the example of the Vietnamese self-immolations and burned themselves to death was a certain Norman Morrison who immolated himself in November 1965, in front of the Pentagon to protest America's Vietnamese war policy. When Susan Sontag visited North Vietnam in June and July of 1968, she found there a veritable "cult of Norman Morrison." Many times, in the ceremonial speeches of greeting made to Miss Sontag and her fellow visitors, the phrase "We respect your Norman Morrison" was used. Songs had been written celebrating his act, his picture was often pasted on the sun visors of trucks, and he was frequently referred to as a "benefactor" of the Vietnamese. "Norman Morrison," Miss Sontag writes, "has become genuinely important for the Vietnamese. . . ." [13]

In reading this account, I could not help asking myself: Who knows how many Vietnamese may have reached the final decision to burn themselves to death under the influence of Norman Morrison's example? And who knows how many Americans, in turn, committed suicide by fire under the cumulative effect of these added Vietnamese self-immolations? In any case, it would appear that the faraway mythical example is possessed of sufficient power to propel it back and forth across the ocean several times, without any loss, and possibly even with an increase, of intensity.

From 1965 to 1970 about a dozen Germans set themselves aflame and died because of disappointed love. In January 1969 an epidemic of self-immolations began in Czechoslovakia, with eighteen suicides or attempted suicides in this manner within two weeks, half of them in protest against the Soviet occupation of the country, the rest for personal reasons. On January 17, 1970, a seventeen-year-old *lycée* student in Lille, France, poured gasoline on himself in a corner of the school courtyard, put a match to himself, and burned to death. He left a note stating that he was committing suicide because of Biafra. Three days later, a nineteen-year-old student of a neighboring commercial high school immolated himself in a like manner "in protest" and because he "could not adjust to this world." These two suicides were followed by a wave of further self-immolations, and by the end of January 1970, a total of fifteen Frenchmen had committed suicide in this manner.[14] Then, in July 1970, a man burned himself to death in New York City, at 42nd Street and 5th Avenue, in front of the Allied Chemical Building. By September 1970, the gruesome total of suicides by fire outside Southeast Asia had approached one hundred.

the new sex myth

1 • *Fantasy and Performance*

It has often been observed that sexual appetite in man is greater than sexual capacity. This means that even when he has as much sex as he can take, he still wants more. Performance cannot keep up with desire. Libido leaps ahead of tumescence. While overtaken with genital exhaustion, a man's (or a woman's) mind may still indulge in erotic fantasies. Herein lies one of the problems that sex poses to man.

Another is the inability of the male to possess sexually those women who attract him and excite him most. The average, ordinary man in our modern world can have sexual intercourse with women even without using the services of prostitutes. But the women whom he can enjoy are, of necessity, his own female counterparts; in other words, average, ordinary women. Having such women may satisfy the man's sexual hunger, but not his erotic fantasies.

In them, the male will continue to imagine himself conquering and possessing the most exquisite women, the esthetically, sexually, erotically, and emotionally most attractive specimens of the female sex. With women, the same situation obtains in reverse.

The fantasy of the perfect sex partner is aroused, maintained, and intensified by innumerable features of our modern culture. Wherever they go and wherever they may look, men living in our cities today have their senses continuously and literally assaulted by the image of the highly desirable female. The movies, television, magazine and newspaper ads, posters, store-window mannequins, life-size, smaller than life, bigger than life, in colors or in black-and-white, in partial or total undress, in all kinds of alluring and enticing positions with the most express indications of availability, willingness, readiness to welcome you to their arms—add to this the occasional, fleeting glimpses of real-life highly desirable females in the streets, in places such as elegant shops, and you have the combined and cumulative effect of making many men dissatisfied with whatever sexual activity actually is available to them.

Up to a few years ago the world of sex, while it was "big business," was one-dimensional, or, better, one-directional. It had one aim: to arouse the male libido by bombarding man's senses with an endless image battery of desirable women. No one stopped to ask how the women felt about all this, or whether they had a libido of their own which, perhaps, they would have liked to feed on images of desirable, irresistible men. There were, it is true, indications that something like this was in the wind: the public adulation of matinee idols and early movie heroes (Rudolf Valentino) by masses of women showed that they were as susceptible to the "charms" of the opposite sex as were the men. But it was not until the late 1960s that some women, and more and more of them as time passed, openly advocated the adoption by women of the very same attitude toward men that had characterized man's relationship to women for many generations. As has been pointed out repeatedly, the birth control pill had much to do with this development, for it enabled women, for the first time in history, to adopt the casual attitude to sex that formerly had been a male privilege. At the same time, of course, the pill contributed to making the male attitude to sex even more casual than it had been before, because it effectively eliminated the last vestiges of the conscientious man's worry about making his casual sex partner pregnant.

Once the sexual excitation became manifestly two-directional, a reciprocal intensification set in. The "emancipated" woman now became the hunter as well as the hunted, while the male, long accustomed to the role of the hunter only, suddenly found himself hunted as well. The sex game became almost like a catch-as-catch-can match with no holds barred and with both sexes subscribing to the same absence of rules: I take whomever I want and can, and I allow myself to be taken by him (or her) who wants me, if I so choose. There can be little doubt that the primary outcome of this new sexism has been a greatly increased number of copulations per person per annum.[1]

As far as the male was concerned this new development had weighty consequences. First of all, it became much easier for a man to reach that copulative frequency at which his physical constitution bade him halt. Such an increase in frequency, however, made it only more apparent that, beyond a maximal sexual activity, the libido, the erotic appetite, can still remain unsatisfied. And secondly, the easier it became for the ordinary male to have sex with the ordinary female, the more painfully he became aware of the distance between his actual sex partners and the quintessentially desirable females who, of course, remained as unattainable for him as they had ever been. It is at this point that the new sex myth came into play.

2 • *The Sexual Superman*

Stated as briefly as possible, the new sex myth holds up before the ordinary man the archetype he yearns to become, the ideal he wants to emulate. This ideal image comes in many hues and colors, depending on the occupation, age, financial status, and so forth of our "average" male. But in every instance he has one trait that all men who have succumbed to the new sexism want most: he has a way with women, or, since this is not the place to mince words, he has only to raise a finger, or an eye-brow, and the most luscious girls fall into his arms and bed. In fact, he is so irresistible, he exudes such an amount of masculine sex appeal, that girls who are perhaps not quite as luscious as those of the first category (but still far, far above the level to which our ordinary male would dare to lift his eyes) actually pursue him and throw themselves at him.

One bit of testimony to the power of this sex ideal is its ubiquitous appearance in television commercials and other ad-vertisements. The most diverse products are proffered with the same monotonous ploy: our unattractive, ordinary guy uses the product just once, and, lo! he is transformed, as if by magic, into the ideal image of his sex, into the irresistible male whom girls literally pursue. (Needless to say, these girls themselves invari-ably are of the most irresistible type; one wonders what products they used in order to make themselves so maddeningly attract-ive.) In one commercial for a hair cream the suddenly Adonified young man takes to his heels to escape the aggressive beauties who clamor for his attention; in another, peddling an aftershave lotion, his escape routes are blocked, but with manly resolve he cuts loose with a few well-placed karate chops that should, temporarily at least, discourage the attacking pack of hungry females. One must assume that the executives of the firms manu-facturing the products thus advertised put up with these and similar inanities only because they are effective: the commercials actually manage to implant the belief into the mind of the ordi-nary man that by using the product in question he will indeed be transformed into an irresistible Adonis. How great, how great indeed, must be the power of the new sex myth to create a predisposition in people to accept such vacuities!

A salient feature of the new sex myth is its emphasis on sexual performance. It is not enough for the male and the female to acquire and possess a façade that irresistibly attracts members of the opposite sex (or, in the case of homosexuals, of the same sex); that is merely the curtain-raiser. The main act is the act itself, the performance in bed. The myth considers peak performance in the sexual arena as the highest value in the man-woman relationship. This, in turn, and in consonance with our techno-

logically oriented culture, has led to a corollary mythologem—
namely, that of the possibility of improving one's sexual performance by acquiring "advanced" techniques.

Now, as is only too well known, techniques can be improved
by reading detailed instructions as to the best ways of performing the activity in question, or by watching experts perform it,
or by purchasing the recommended tools, or by a combination
of any two or of all three of these methods. Hence the profusion
of the "how to" type sex books, and of ads which offer men
products with whose help he can become a superperformer,
such as this: *"Now! Every man alive can make the kind of love
every woman alive dreams of! Now you can do everything that's
expected of you. . . . Achieve the Double Climax! Now it's
possible for your woman to experience TWO climaxes at the
same time. Send only $9.95. . . ."* Or: *"Next weekend see real
live 8mm love-making on your bedroom wall! . . . Turn on
your libido! For educational purposes only—Triple your sexual power! Make your fantasies come true. $19.50 for 200 ft."* [2]

While these ads and many of the sex books address themselves to men, who have been, at least in our Western culture,
the initiators in sexual relations, and to whom our tradition still
ascribes the role of the aggressive partner, there has been in
recent years no dearth of advice directed to women. In books
and articles of this kind the burden of the message is the same
as in the male-oriented literature: you can become a highly
successful woman in the sexual battlefield if only you will learn
the techniques involved. Once you acquire the techniques, you
will behave and act in such a way, from the moment you first
set eyes upon a man until such time as he finally relaxes in your
arms utterly spent and satisfied (and probably fast asleep), that
he will become captivated by you, will love you, adore you, and
remain your slave forever. The old Platonic myth of the androgyne, whose male and female halves were severed by the
jealous gods and who ever since search for each other, has thus
received a new twist: the sign of having found the ideal mate is
the total sexual satisfaction he (or she) is able to provide in his
(or her) capacity as a champion of perfectly mastered sex
techniques. As Nelson N. Foote put it in the characteristically

restrained language of the sex researcher, the new ideal that is becoming widespread is that "a man's masculinity is gauged primarily by his ability to provide sexual satisfaction for his partner." Needless to say, this new ideal must be balanced by a similar one in the reverse: "the younger generation of men seems closer to a unified, positive attitude of appreciation toward the joys and values of sex." [3]

As early as some twenty years ago Herbert Marshall McLuhan observed that "the display of current feminine sex power seems to many males to demand an impossible virility of assertion," and that what survives in "such a barrage . . . is the view of the human body as a sort of love-machine capable merely of specific thrills. This extremely behavioristic view of sex, which reduces sex experience to a problem in mechanics and hygiene, is exactly what is implied and expressed on all sides. . . . In the era of thinking machines, it would be surprising, indeed, if the love-machine were not thought of as well." [4]

This preoccupation with the technical, manipulatory aspect of sex has inevitably led to the addition of yet another basic feature to the new sex myth: 'it is, as one writer put it, "the desirability, the quasi-divinity above all things, of the orgasm in America," [5] or, as it is more familiarly referred to, "the tyranny of the orgasm." This tyranny has imposed itself upon the ordinary man and woman through the overwhelming power of the new sex myth which holds up as the ideal that must be emulated the individual who can both give and experience a large number of very intense — i.e., highly pleasurable — orgasms. If this trend continues, the time may actually come when, as one astute observer, Edward Grossman, put it half facetiously, "middle-class students scoring low in orgastic potency will be required to take remedial sex as the poor and the black used to be given remedial reading. . . ." [6] The same idea is expressed in a more restrained form by sociologist Nelson N. Foote, who follows the statement, quoted above, about man's masculinity being gauged primarily by his ability to provide sexual satisfaction for his partner with the assertion that "the moment is . . . propitious for bringing more squarely into the curriculum [of colleges] the consideration of what masculinity and feminity should mean in practice today." [7]

3 • *The James Bond Myth*

Myths require individual images in which their otherwise diffuse features can be concretized, personified, and made tangible. Once such an image is born, that image and its background myth mutually reinforce and intensify each other's mythological potency. Thus when the myth of the annual death and resurrection of the vegetation was personified in the myth of Tammuz-Adonis, the natural cycle actually observed annually confirmed the belief in the death and rebirth of the youthful god, while the annual enactment of the Tammuz-Adonis ritual with the accompanying recitation of his myth strengthened the mythical view of the life cycle of the flora.

In a similar manner, the new sex myth has produced its personified, individual, ideal images. These were (and are), typically, movie actors and actresses who portray on the screen characters of great sexual allure and prowess, and who, by that peculiar process of osmosis which results in the transference of acted roles to the actual lives of the actors, have themselves become highly charged sex symbols. In the early days of the movies there was the vampire-type heroine whose wiles and charms ruined men; later came the sex-goddess whose beauty and body heat melted everything and everybody around her. The male opposite numbers of this female personification of irresistible sex was for a long time the strong he-man; attractive, it is true, but not in a specifically erotic-sexual manner. Then in the late 1950s the true counterpart of the sex-goddess finally emerged: the new sex hero, who combined sexual irresistibility with an apparent disinterest in his gorgeous female pursuers (except, that is, in making love to them, usually within a few minutes after they succeed in bringing themselves to his attention), and with a goodly dosage of brutality, ruthlessness, callousness, and even cruelty. James Bond, of course, is the first to come to mind, but there are many more of this type on the screen, on tele-

vision, in novels, short stories, and in the comics. Of James
Bond books alone, over 10 million copies have been sold in the
ten years or so in which the popularity of "007" was at its peak.
A synopsis of these books and of the films based on them shows
that, apart from such accomplishments as expertise in the
"right" drinks, foods, clothes, cars, watches, hotels, etc., which
serve to establish firmly his image as that of a most sophisticated
individual (we shall see later how much is made of precisely
these features in the "Playboy Philosophy"), James Bond's
greatest talents lie in sex and violence. In both areas he performs superbly, and — an important additional feature — without ever losing his "cool." A sexual athlete such as Bond can,
of course, be expected to pair off only with girls who are equally
expert in love-making, girls who, as soon as he shows a little
interest in them, "reciprocate and quickly tumble into bed
with him," and who in the film versions are "the most lissome
beauties the movies can find." [8]

As incredible as his sexual virtuosity is the amount of intense
pain James Bond can unflinchingly suffer and of the violence
he can dish out. The James Bond books, and even more so the
movies, are a series of torture and pain, both received and meted
out, with sexual acrobatics in between. Yet the plots, which
constitute the framework for the brutalities, are, as Richard C.
Carpenter has pointed out, surprisingly similar to the deeds and
sufferings of the archetypal mythical hero. Because of this, and
because the perils and the testing that the hero undergoes "are
analogues of the perils and testing everyone who authentically
encounters life must undergo," although greatly raised in intensity and meaning, the myth of the hero journey, even in its
James Bond imitation, "is simply the most persuasive pattern
of human activity" and it "symbolizes the most important thing
man can do. A narrative built on this pattern calls on our deepest concerns even if we are not intellectually aware of the pattern at all. . . ." [9]

The Bond hero journey involves a descent into Hades, the
domain of evil, inhabited by the modern counterparts of malev-
olent magicians, sorcerers, witches, and warlocks whose guile
and technological sophistication are many times greater than

those of 007. Moreover, while he is alone almost all of the time, his enemies are many, organized into a well-trained and blindly obedient corps of corruption. Yet James Bond willingly enters these labyrinths and seeks out their Minotaur-like ruler, as Theseus did in the famous Greek myth. He is willing to face torture and even death, never because of any personal reason or ambition, but simply because he is willing to suffer, to experience unspeakable agony "in order to save the rest of us from disaster, or even discomfort. . . ." [10] The greater the dangers he faces, the sufferings he undergoes for our sake, the more will we love him, the more will we want to be him, the more will we identify with him, and the more will we find his cruelty, brutality, and sexual omnivorousness excusable and even attractive. Since "people select their dramatic entertainment on the basis that some of their needs are vicariously satisfied through it," [11] or, as I would prefer to put it, since people's myths both express and satisfy their needs, it is clear beyond a doubt that "the James Bond books and movies and other sadomasochistic materials enjoy an enormous popularity with the American public" [12] precisely because they present a mythical ideal prototype whom so many of us would like to emulate.

For the same reason, the effect of these "heroes" on our ordinary man in the street, or in the spectator's seat, is considerable. He not only identifies with them while actually under their spell, but tries to emulate them in his life — i.e., he tries to live the myth. However, the major features and exploits of the mythical sex-*cum*-violence hero are beyond his ken — after all, despite all the hair cream, aftershave lotion, toothpaste, deodorant, and so forth that our average man religiously uses, those gorgeous girls still have not started to pursue him, nor can he go out and shoot up or beat into a bloody pulp that other fellow who seems to hate his guts. He therefore must resort to emulating minor, secondary features of the mythical prototype, such as the clothes he wears, his hairdo, the way he moves, walks, and talks, and the apparent lack of concern with which he drops a girl a few minutes after having slept with her. As the ultimate effect of this insidious influence, he develops the Playboy complex.

4 · *The Playboy Complex*

The key (an old phallic symbol!) to the Playboy Club opens up to our ordinary guy a world in which he can, and is even expected to, act out his Walter Mittyesque sex fantasies. Of course, it is not quite correct to say that he can act them out, because, after all, those sweet "Bunnies" with their half-naked bodies and their magnificent mammalia who bend over him smilingly and solicitously while serving his drinks are only for show. One cannot touch them, let alone take them to bed. But one is definitely surrounded by an atmosphere, a make-believe, of sexual permissiveness, carefully fostered by the *Playboy* magazine whose philosophy expresses, and approves of, the unfulfillable erotic fantasies of our ordinary guy. *Playboy,* through both the club and the magazine, teaches that the goals in life are sex and money, that life must be seen "as a happy time," that "a man's reach should exceed his grasp, else what's a heaven for," that "chastity is just another word for repression," that "life is a merry-go-round of beds, sofas, rugs and any other convenience that will comfortably accommodate a prone position for two," and that "sex is an end in itself, but it is also a means, even when taken in sporadic doses and with different partners, for developing one's self-esteem, exploring one's individuality, and establishing one's identity." [13] *Playboy* also teaches that, despite their rousing roundness, or perhaps precisely because of it, women are strictly one-dimensional — their only function is to serve as toys, sexual playthings of men.

In brief, the *Playboy* world enables our ordinary guy to feel and to some extent to behave *as if* he were a James Bond. Moreover, I think we are not mistaken if we consider the rule forbidding the "Bunnies" to date Playboy Club members an excellent device calculated to increase the latters' feeling of security: they run neither the risk of being turned down by a "Bunny" and of thus being proven incapable of living up to their mythical archetype, nor that of getting themselves into the potentially embarrassing position, having bedded the buxom and (mythically) highly sexed as well as widely experienced girl, of having to put up or shut up. They drink, eat, enjoy the exciting proximity of the "Bunnies" and the entire artificially sexed-up atmosphere of the premises, and then they can safely go home for a restful second half of the night, when with or without female companionship, they can enjoy the memory of having been a playboy, of being a playboy, which is the nearest they can get to attaining their mythical James Bond-like image of themselves.

The same motivations come into play in the attractive center foldout of *Playboy* magazine, showing in every issue another smiling, hypermammalian young woman. The appeal of these creatures rests not merely, as Harvey Cox commented in *The Secular City*, on their apparent acquiescence, on the image they project of "women over whom it is easy to fantasize dominance," [14] but also, and primarily, on the fact that in enjoying the picture of the Playmate of the Month nothing more than fantasizing is either called for or possible.

At the same time, since these quasi-nude "young Aphrodites function . . . as the reader's vicarious lovers," the pictures serve as a "safety valve": they "easily convince the viewer that the girls," with their expressions which are "intimate and willing," could actually and easily "be his sexually, and he could be in the picture" with them. These center foldouts and the other similar pictures in *Playboy* "foster the impression that many respectable and lovely young girls are willing to engage in non-marital sexual activities," [15] and thus reassure the fantasizing male that if only he would make a serious effort, he could easily find such "nice" and attractive girls as his real-life playmates.

Thus in the fantasy-world created by *Playboy* every man is a potential James Bond as far as the sexual aspect of this great mythical personality is concerned. The *Playboy* stereotype, held up as "a goal to achieve, a model of behavior to emulate, and an identity to assume," [16] is highly knowledgeable about clothing, grooming, interior decoration, cars, music (especially jazz), food, drink, parties, travel, sports, entertainment, and women, concerning whom he embraces and practices the tenets of complete sexual freedom. In all this the Playboy ideal closely resembles James Bond.

The area of unbridgeable difference between James Bond as the mythical archetype and the playboys who are his would-be imitators is in the realm of physical courage, strength, and brutality, the endurance of torture and the unflinching confrontation with mortal perils in the service of a greater cause. This is something, it would appear, which the relatively affluent, sophisticated, mature American bachelor cannot countenance even in his fantasies. If he could, the *Playboy* complex, so relentlessly thrust at him in the magazine and the clubs, would probably have chosen as its emblem a wild and dangerous animal, something like a black panther, a puma, a cougar, a tiger, a leopard. Ancient mythologies did, in fact, establish close associations between strong masculine gods and members of the carnivorous and ferocious family of great cats. Dionysus had his tiger, Herakles his lion's skin. But such a symbol, while acceptable when it is made to refer to the power of a motor vehicle ("Put a Tiger in Your Tank!") is clearly inapplicable to the Playboy himself, who would be too hard put to live up to the implied demand on muscles, courage, and temperament. To be surrounded by the accoutrements of James Bond, to be taught to emulate him in appreciating "the finer things in life," is all well and good; but to couple this with even the faintest implication or hint that the would-be Playboy might have to try to emulate James Bond's more sterling qualities would be definitely too much to ask. It would be too taxing, too frightening for the type of man who is the target of the *Playboy* philosophy. Hence, the symbol chosen for the debonair, jaunty Playboy, the connoisseur of wine, women, and all the finer things in life, who is supposed to be "a sophisticated, cosmopolitan, urbane, diverse, affluent intellectual, promiscuous (if that is the word), mature bachelor," [17] is, not a ferocious carnivore, but, of all things, that most timid and most pitiable of animals, the rabbit.

Of course, needless to say, the Playboy Rabbit is no ordinary rabbit, but a mythical quasi-human rabbit who is "almost inevitably shown in the company of one or more beautiful and

adoring . . . alluringly unclad young women," and he is always shown with "eyes half-closed to indicate a somewhat bored
attitude of utter sophistication." [18] The Playboy Rabbit is "the
single most salient concrete representation of the 'Playboy Stereotype.' " [19]

With an uncanny eye for giving the people — that is, the particular type of people to whom you want to appeal — what
they want, Playboy has helped itself to a generous loan from
the Mickey Mouse mentality, and settled as a symbol on the
only animal that is a match for the mouse in weakness, meekness, and helplessness. In fact, Playboy even went one important
step further than Walt Disney in exploiting the psychological
satisfactions that lie in self-identification with a defenseless,
pitiful animal. Disney's message in his Mickey Mouse films was
(as we have seen in Chapter 15) that downtrodden, intimidated man *can* stand up to an inimical, frightening society
(Mickey defeats the Cat); Playboy's message is: even though
you are a downtrodden, intimidated rabbit, you can learn to
enjoy all the finer things in life (including, in the first place,
adorable as well as adoring women), if only you become a Playboy. Thus one understands that, on this level, there is no contradiction between a man being a rabbit, and at the same time a
successful Playboy surrounded by adoring "Bunnies" and taking
sophisticated pleasure in what life has to offer.

Perhaps there is yet another factor in Playboy having chosen
the rabbit as its patron animal: the rabbit is considered in
folklore and in popular consciousness to be a most prolific animal. By a transference, which is readily understandable, although it lacks any basis in fact, the rabbit could easily be taken
as an animal with an exceptionally intense interest in sex.
Such an animal is eminently qualified to serve as a symbol for
Playboy, whose philosophy is that nonmarital sexual intercourse
is not only proper, but desirable, and that every playboy should
engage in as much of it as feasible. Thus the nonaggressive,
sophisticated, blasé, but highly sex-oriented playboy has his
perfect symbol in the rabbit.

As one would expect, the female counterpart of the playboy
rabbit is a perfect match for him. She is the playmate bunny

who enjoys sex as much as he does, who has the same attitude toward sex, and who, if possible, is even more sex-centered than he. While the playboy is not above going to considerable lengths in order to have his way with women, the type of female he encounters and courts is very much like him, so that, in effect, in the imaginary playworld in which the playboy and the playmate move, their relationship in essence is identical with the relationship between 007 and his girls as projected with such insistent monotony by the James Bond books and movies.

5 • The New Woman

But what about the "new woman," apart from and outside of the male-based realms of *Playboy* and James Bond? Although the women's liberation movement has made great strides forward in the last few years, it is as yet far from having achieved equality with men in the area of sex, which for women has suddenly assumed such overwhelming importance. It is not as if women today could not have as much sexual freedom as men; that primary prerogative has been theirs for some years now. Today as little opprobrium attaches to an unmarried girl living in what, is an earlier age, used to be called "common-law marriage" as to an unmarried man doing the same. Short-lived, fleeting romances or casual encounters are as much a matter of course for women as for men. Recent polls show that only a very small percentage of men still attach any importance to virginity in the girl they intend to marry. In real sexual practice, then, men and women, at least in major segments of our society, have achieved equal freedom.

Where women still lag behind men is in the achievement of equality in the mythology of sex, especially in regard to sexual imagery. To this day there is an incomparably greater emphasis on the representation and display of female, than of male, sexual charms. The pictures of nude or almost nude women, seen in so many places and in numerous media, are displayed with the obvious intention of attracting and arousing men. No comparable display of male nudity can be observed; moreover, where naked men are exhibited in photographs or in the flesh, the purpose is, as a rule, to attract male homosexuals, and not females, although the latter, too, may derive enjoyment or erotic pleasure from viewing them. It is, of course, easily possible that this disproportion in the "provocative" presentation of male-directed female nudity and female-directed male nudity is contingent on the much lesser appeal of male nudity for women as compared with the unending fascination the sight of the female body has for males. The existence of such a differential reaction to visual erotic stimuli between men and women has been established beyond doubt in a number of studies which revealed that "men are more responsive to visual and psychological sexual stimuli; women are more responsive to tactile stimuli." [20] If this difference is innate — i.e., not culturally induced — then we can assume that the disproportion referred to in utilizing the exhibition of nudity in one sex in order to stimulate the libido in the other will tend to persist.

In fashions, too, an analogous disparity persists. Women dress obviously for the main purpose of arousing the male libido: they put on miniskirts, micro-miniskirts, tight pants that outline their physical charms, transparent dresses, topless outfits, and the like. Or, alternately, they resort to the older method of covering up almost the entire body in order thereby to give allure to what constant exposure would render unexciting. (Who can forget, having once read it, Anatole France's irresistible satire *Penguin Island?*)

On the other hand, if a man wears extremely provocative clothing of any type, he is, as a rule, a homosexual, interested in attracting other men only. Despite the vagaries of modern dress and undress, we still have not seen the return of the fifteenth- and sixteenth-century codpiece, nor any other fashion that would allow a woman to feast her eyes on the outlines of the male genitals, as Medieval ladies could on the large, shiny, protruding, horn-like steel capsule which housed the genitals of armored knights, or as the women of certain primitive tribes can on the gaily decorated long penis-sheaths of their otherwise unclothed menfolk.

Nor has the entertainment industry, especially the movies, yet produced a female James Bond, although in real life women by now may have learned the crude art of dropping a male bedfellow as callously as that great hero of the bed and the gun drops his swooning girls. Evidently, despite the brazen back-and-forth strutting of a scantily clad girl in one of the television commercials while the invisible chorus sings "You've come a long way, baby!" women have as yet to catch up with men in the "exploitation" of the opposite sex.

However that may be, the sexually irresistible male and female are mythical stereotypes that are exploited with relentless monotony by the television industry. Most commercials repeat, and seem to be based on, one simple, almost primitive idea: promise men or women sexual irresistibility and they will buy anything. This idea is predicated on the equally primitive assumption that certain external characteristics which can be instantly acquired by the application of this or that product are all that is needed to make any person irresistible to members of the opposite sex, to turn an ugly duckling into a beautiful swan. Hair curlers, shampoos, eye makeup, false eyelashes, lipsticks, powders, face creams, perfumes, toothpastes, deodorants, shaving creams, after-shaving lotions, hair creams, automobiles, clothes, appliances, foods, drinks, cigarettes, and many other products too numerous to list are all sold on this simple premise. All use the mythical female with her irresistible beauty or the mythical male with his equally irresistible manliness, and all reinforce the false and damaging belief that happiness equals sexual attractiveness, which, in turn, can be acquired by buying and using the advertised product.

The woman in these ads is consistently portrayed as if she were in a constant state of extreme sexual excitement. Her eyes are liquid, her nostrils flare, her lips are half parted. Her entire being says: "Here I am; just touch me and I shall swoon into your arms. Make love to me and I shall have the most intense orgasm you have ever given a woman. I can give you pleasures that will exceed your wildest dreams." From this provocative behavior to actually taking the initiative the distance is small. Consequently, women are shown with increasing frequency as those who initiate contacts with men, and quite often as doing it with a considerable measure of aggressiveness. We have referred to the television commercials which show women literally attacking the man after the latter uses a few drops of this or that cosmetic product. This is an open reversal of the traditional roles of men and women, and it would be an interesting study in the psychology of sex to find out to what extent ads of this type actually express hidden psycho-sexual tendencies in the two sexes: a desire in women to be sexually aggressive, and a desire in men to become the hunted instead of the hunter.

As to the women, in the past whatever psycho-sexual aggressiveness they manifested was usually displayed in a group context. Individual women behaved as they were supposed to behave: shyly, demurely, and modestly. Only in grief, when bereaved of a near relative, were women allowed to throw off their customary restraint and to act wildly, hysterically. Women as a group, on the other hand, could, and often did, display unbridled ferocity. We mentioned the Bacchanalia in which a young man who represented Dionysus was torn to pieces by a frenzied group of women who bit and clawed him to death and drank his warm blood for good measure (see Chapter 3, section 3). In our own times, but long before the women's liberation movement institutionalized female group violence, teenage girls used to mob their idols of the moment: Frank Sinatra, Elvis Presley, the Beatles, as well as early movie stars, all had their share of being almost torn to bits by shrieking and squealing hordes of female teenagers — a type of behavior that did not and does not have its equivalent in the male sex.

However, all this was female mob action. Female psycho-sexual aggressiveness on the individual level is a relatively new phenomenon, whose emergence was undoubtedly aided by the television commercials referred to above. The relentless repetition of scenes showing women as the huntress and man as the hunted, and their occasional performance on other media and description in fiction, could not fail to create a readiness or an inclination in a certain number of women and men (whose proportion is probably growing) to engage in such behavior or to experience such an encounter in real life. One indication of the spread of this type of reversal of the traditional sex roles is the advocacy and practice by the women's liberation movements of women whistling at men, pinching men's behinds, and the like.

The inevitable male reaction to this type of female behavior is to adopt an attitude that for generations in the past has characterized the female response to active pursuit from the male. Now it is the man who is shown in some commercials fleeing from the pursuing females or in some other way expressing the desire to be left alone. Most typical of the behavior this new type of man is the television commercial, mentioned in another context, in which the man, portrayed with clearly sadistic features, gets rid of the beautiful woman who evidently is out to win him, but not before he snatches from her his beloved cigarettes.

In view of this reversal of roles it is inevitable that some women should have second thoughts when they stop to consider the results of these new concepts of masculinity and femininity. As Foote put it, "many young women wonder whether to blame themselves, whether they have become too strong, whether they should try to help their boys become men by returning to passivity, sweetness, and dependence." [21]

It would, of course, be a mistake to believe that the new sex myth involves a complete reversal of the male-female roles. What the new sex myth primarily accomplishes is to eliminate the differences that in the past characterized the roles of each of the two sexes in relation to the other. Today women are allowed to do practically everything that in the past was a male prerogative, including attitudes, behavior, and activities. The same holds true in reverse as well, in the sense that men today can and do display attitudes and behavior or engage in activities that formerly were the exclusive domain of females, and that in increasingly wide circles it is considered proper and seemly for them to do so. In other words, what the new sex myth is rapidly accomplishing is not so much a *reversal* of the sex roles as a diminution of the traditional distinctions between the male and female roles. The latter is aptly symbolized in the growing popularity of the "unisex" type of apparel, whose avowed purpose and appeal to the younger generation lie precisely in the fact that it makes men and women appear indistinguishable. On a deeper level the new sex myth has effectively eliminated all the taboos that traditionally surrounded sex — whether it was the women or the men who had to obey them — and thereby has given to both a measure of sexual freedom known a few decades ago only in certain so-called primitive societies.

While the new sex myth, as it has emerged from the foregoing pages, has no story to tell, it does uphold powerful prototypes and does influence the thinking and the behavior of people. These prototypes are sexual supermen, or, if you wish, sexual virtuosos. No live man or woman can hope to match their libido, their allure, their inexhaustible potency. But their power is such that it keeps us trying. Inevitably, it also keeps frustrating us. On balance, the new sex myth is unquestionably one of the most damaging myths of modern man.

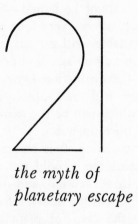

the myth of
planetary escape

1 • *Flammarion*

Those who have lived through an earthquake report that there is no other experience comparable to it in the intensity of the terror it can produce. As far as actual physical experience is concerned, they are undoubtedly right. But human imagination has long ago conjured up a vision whose horror dwarfs the fright generated by even the most violent quake. That vision is the end of the world. The interesting thing about this horrifying fantasy of the end of days is that, whereas other frightening aspects of the natural environment have gradually softened as man's knowledge and understanding of nature increased, the fear of the world's end, on the contrary, has intensified. In the old days of Biblical faith the end of days was frightening enough, but its trauma was greatly mitigated by the belief that it held no threat for the just. For them it was to be a time of triumph, the be-

305

ginning of an era of paradisiac bliss. With the increase of man's understanding of the order of the universe, such comforts held out by the old eschatologies appeared more and more childish. The end of the world then came to be recognized as the inevitable outcome of a physical process that cannot be halted — the gradual cooling down of the earth which, after a very long period, but not long enough to be incalculable, will put an end to all life on this planet. This process must go on and lead to its inexorable conclusion, at which point the distinction between good and bad, between saint and sinner, will make absolutely no difference in the ultimate outcome, which will be the extinction of all life on earth, including that of the human race.

The thought is both sobering and frightening. It is certainly understandable that man, or at least some men, could not acquiesce in it. There must be a way out, these men felt, and they groped around in the dark to find it. This was the mood, a fearful, desperate mood, that gave rise to the myth of planetary escape.

My own first encounter with the myth of planetary escape took place about half a century ago. I may have been about ten years old when I read a large, very long, but very fascinating book by Camille Flammarion (1842–1925) entitled, I believe, *Stella.* I read it in Hungarian translation, and what I remember about it to this day is that it dealt with a faraway future time when the earth had cooled down to such an extent that most, or all, of humanity had died, except for a young couple, the heroes of the story. In the last part of the book the young man and woman managed in some way — I cannot remember how, and, frankly, I do not want to seek out the book now and reread it — to leave the dying earth and soar out into space toward a larger planet which just by that time had cooled down sufficiently to become habitable. Thus the future of man was assured. Here, in a rudimentary, half-scientific and half-romantic form, was the main outline of the myth of planetary escape.

2 • *Teilhard de Chardin*

Some two generations after Flammarion another, much more profound, thinker, also a Frenchman, had new ideas of his own about the planetary escape. We have already discussed Pierre Teilhard de Chardin's myth of the noosphere (in Chapter 2, section 5). It is through the ultimate development of the noosphere that Teilhard envisages the breaking out of humanity from the confines of its small global abode. After the noosphere achieves further advances in "the process of planetisation . . . in the direction of growing unanimity," says Teilhard, "humanity will have completed itself . . . when it is psychically centred upon itself (which may yet take several million years)."[1] At that stage, "the primary attribute of Reflection" will develop *"the will to survive.* In reflecting upon itself the individual consciousness acquires the formidable property of foreseeing the future, that is to say, death. And at the same time it knows that it is psychologically impossible for it to continue to work in pursuance of the purposes of Life unless something, the best of the work, is preserved from total destruction."[2] This, in turn, will result in the noosphere's becoming "charged to the fullest extent with psychic energies to impel it forward in yet another advance . . . ," which can mean nothing else but that, "like those planetary orbits which seem to traverse our solar system without remaining within it, the curve of consciousness, pursuing its course of growing complexity, will break through the material framework of Time and Space to escape somewhere towards an ultra-centre of unification and consistence. . . ."[3]

The planetary escape Teilhard envisions is not as crude, or as physical as Flammarion's transference of the last human couple to another, younger planet where they are destined to become a new Adam and Eve. Rather, he foresees a sudden self-elevation of the noosphere into a higher (or, as he often says, deeper) spiritual sphere where an almost mystical union takes place between man and God. One of his favorite expressions is the "divinization" of man, or of the human noosphere, or of the cosmos as a whole, or of "matter" in general. Yet what ties Teilhard's fantasy of the future of the noosphere integrally into the undying myth of planetary escape is his frequent use of precisely this word, "escape," which one is forced to interpret as meaning exactly what it says—namely, an escape from the physical conditions as they will prevail on earth one or two million years hence.

As early as 1917 Teilhard had written that "the spirit cannot free itself except by some clean break, some escape, of a completely different order from the slow organization of matter that led up to the elaboration of the brain. . . ." [4] Only a few years later, this vague feeling about the inevitability of the escape from matter assumed in Teilhard's mind the form of the imperative escape from the earth. In 1924 he wrote: "As the end of the time approaches, a terrifying spiritual pressure will be brought to bear on the limits of the real, born of the efforts of souls desperately straining in their desire to escape from the earth." [5]

In his later writings this escape, though still a spiritual one, comes clearly to mean an escape from either the earth or the physically visible universe. In this form the idea is repeatedly touched upon in Teilhard's most important work, *The Phenomenon of Man,* which he completed in manuscript in 1938, but which, like all his major works, the Church did not allow him to publish, so that it saw the light of day only after his death in 1955. [6] In it, discussing the end of days in the chapter entitled "The Ultimate Earth," Teilhard admits that "a fantastic and inevitable event . . . comes nearer with every day that passes: the end of all life on our globe, the death of the planet. . . ." [7]

Although the planet will die, man will merely enter the "ultimate phase" of his existence. After rejecting the gloomy prognostications of a sudden, catastrophic end of mankind, such as described in "the novels of the Goncourts, Benson and Wells, or in scientific works signed by famous names," Teilhard asserts of such disasters that, "however possible they may be in theory, we have higher reasons for being sure *that they will not happen.*" [8] His argument is that *"man is irreplaceable.* Therefore, however improbable it might seem, *he must reach the goal,* not necessarily, doubtless, but infallibly." [9] What this goal is, and how man will reach it, is described in the last chapter of the book, entitled "The Ultimate." Teilhard envisages that "under the increasing tension of the mind on the surface of the globe, we may begin by asking seriously whether life will not perhaps one day succeed in ingeniously forcing the bars of its earthly prison, either by finding the means to invade other inhabited planets or (a still more giddy perspective) by getting into physical touch with other focal points of consciousness across the abysses of space." In other words, he sees the possibility of a "meeting and mutual fecundation of two noospheres. . . . Consciousness would thus finally construct itself by a synthesis of planetary units." [10]

Teilhard's solution of the problem of the end of the world is, as he continues to expound, "that mankind, taken as a whole, will be obliged . . . to abandon its organo-planetary foothold" which will entail "detaching the mind, fulfilled at last, from its material matrix, so that it will henceforth rest with all its weight on God-Omega." [11] In his "Life and the Planets," a lecture delivered at the French Embassy in Peking in 1945, Teilhard refers to those who "seek to reassure us with the notion of an escape through space," and who suggest that "We may perhaps move to Venus—perhaps even further afield." But he finds little satisfaction in these hopes, for, "apart from the fact that Venus is probably not habitable (is there water?) and that, if journeying between celestial bodies were practicable, it is hard to see why we ourselves have not already been invaded, this does no more than postpone the end." [12]

This being the case, Teilhard is led to envisage an entirely novel sort of planetary escape: we must, he says, "finally banish the spectre of Death from our horizon," which we can do "by the idea . . . that ahead of, or rather in the heart of, a universe prolonged along its axis of complexity, there exists a divine centre of convergence" which, "in order to stress its synthesizing and personalizing function," he calls "the *point Omega*." From here on Teilhard embarks on a mythical-eschatological fantasy voyage that easily dwarfs every previous vision of the ultimate end of humanity:

> Let us suppose that from this universal centre, this
> *Omega point*, there constantly emanate radiations
> hitherto only perceptible to those persons whom we
> call "mystics." Let us further imagine that, as the
> sensibility or response to mysticism of the human race
> increases with planetisation, the awareness of Omega
> becomes so widespread as to warm the earth psychically
> while physically it is growing cold. Is it not conceivable
> that Mankind, at the end of its totalisation, its folding-in

upon itself, may reach a critical level of maturity
where, leaving Earth and stars to lapse slowly back
into the dwindling mass of primordial energy, it will
detach itself from this planet and join the one true,
irreversible essence of things, the Omega point? A
phenomenon perhaps outwardly akin to death, but in
reality a simple metamorphosis and arrival at the
supreme synthesis. An escape from the planet, not in
space or outwardly, but spiritually and inwardly, such
as the hyper-centration of cosmic matter upon itself
allows.[13]

Elsewhere Teilhard raises the question of whether mankind
must "look forward to nothing but a state of *senescence* at the
end of the planetary cycle of hominisation or, on the contrary,
will it be a *paroxysm* of the Noosphere?" His answer is that
"the human multitude is moving as time passes not towards any
slackening but rather towards a super-state of psychic tension,"
and will ultimately reach "an eventual critical point of collective
reflexion." This "critical point of planetary reflexion, the fruit
of socialisation, far from being a mere spark in the darkness,
represents our passage [i.e. "escape"] by translation or dema-
terialisation, to another sphere of the universe. . . ."[14] In yet
another essay he predicts that "another million or two years of
co-reflexion will bring to the species" an "intense psychic union"
in which "the difference will tend to vanish between man's will
to survive and his anxiety to escape (even at the cost of an apparent death) from the temporo-spatial phase of his evolution."[15]

All the references to an "escape" of man from his earthly,
physical existence make it clear that Teilhard saw in a planetary
escape the prerequisite for the attainment of a new, spiritual dimension for the noosphere. While the place or situation or condition *into* which man will escape in those eschatologically remote days of the future are thus very differently conceived by
Flammarion and Teilhard, both thinkers share the notion of the
inevitability of the escape from the limitations of the present
planetary existence which, for one reason or another, will have
to come to an end. If, to refer back to the teachings of a third

ingenious Frenchman, Claude Lévi-Strauss is right in considering all variants of a myth as integral parts of the myth itself,
then we certainly must accept the two pictures of the ultimate
future of man as painted by Flammarion and Teilhard, despite
the great dissimilarities between them, as two versions of one
and the same myth, that of the planetary escape.

3 • *Space Technology*

Today authors of technical books hardly fall short of their
fantasy-pursuing colleagues in depicting the future of space travel
and colonization. Erik Bergaust, the author of more than a
dozen books on rocketry and space flights, writes in one of his
more recent studies about what he foresees will happen in the
next fifty years in space exploration. "In all probability," he
says, "unmanned freight ships similar to the lunar ferry will be
built to haul cargo to Mars and Venus as well, in support of future
interplanetary settlements." [16] He quotes "the famous Dr. Eugene Sänger" to the effect that

> the steady expansion of mankind's living areas during
> the last millennia will not halt with the complete
> colonization of the Earth's surface, but will automatically
> extend to other planets as soon as technology provides
> the necessary means. . . . Not overpopulation of
> the Earth alone during the next two centuries will
> force man inevitably into space. . . . Also his spiritual
> and intellectual needs will compel man during the
> next centuries to leave this narrow, earthly prison and
> expand his living and vital areas beyond this planet.
> Just think of the preservation of human civilization
> and culture if the Earth should become uninhabitable.
> . . . It suffices to look at the natural course of life
> of our galaxy which—in the opinion of astrophysicists
> —will inevitably lead in future millennia to the
> incineration of the Earth by the increasing radiation
> from the nuclear reactions of the Sun, and, further-
> more, to complete cooling of the Sun and, consequently,
> the Earth. . . . Space flight is the only sensible
> reason for mankind's not resigning and giving up

further efforts for the development of his civilization
and culture in view of these perspectives. It seems only
possible by means of interplanetary space flight to
transplant man and his civilization to other planets of
our galaxy and thus save him from extermination. . . .[17]

Additional motivations for space flight, according to Sänger,
are provided by man's "thirst for knowledge" and "the purely
spiritual motivation of [a] human longing to reach the
heaven. . . ."[18]

Then Bergaust goes on to quote several other space experts,
all of whom agree that the future of man lies ultimately in space.

Technical people are supposed to be hardheaded realists; all
their attention, all their abilities are and must be absorbed in the
world of materials and the application of the laws of physics.
And yet, as we have seen, the myth of planetary escape haunts
them, too, as it did the early astronomer and novelist Flammarion, and as it does the theologian-anthropologist Teilhard de
Chardin.

4 · *The UFOs*

No sooner had man developed the ability to raise himself up
from the ground and to float about or fly in the air than sightings
of mysterious flying objects began to be reported. Flying is, of
course, a very ancient dream of man, and myths about humans
who flew skyward (Elijah, Daedalus, and Icarus) have been
paralleled since antiquity by myths telling about extraterrestrial
beings who came down from the heavens to visit the earth (e.g.,
the "Sons of God" in Genesis 6, as well as myths of the other
ancient peoples).[19]

What all man was able to do was to *dream* of flying up into
the sky (or into heaven) on fiery chariots or with the help of
artificial wings, the myths about divine visitors who came down
to earth attributed also to them similar means of aerial locomotion. However, in the nineteenth century, when man actually
learned to aviate, the extraterrestrial visitors were imagined
(and "sighted") using aerial vehicles that were, by and large,
similar to those actually utilized by man, except that they repre-

sented a more advanced stage of technological development (on this point, see below). Once man developed the ability to move out into space, the reported sightings of unidentified flying objects (UFOs), assumed to have come from outer space, increased very greatly. In October 1957 the first earth-orbiting artificial satellite, the Russians' *Sputnik I*, was launched. Within three months there were 701 UFO sightings, as compared to 477 such sightings in the nine preceding months, an almost five-fold increase. As Dr. Carl Sagan of the Smithsonian Institution Astrophysical Observatory put it: "The clear implication is that Sputnik and its attendant publicity was responsible for many UFO sightings." [20]

E. J. Ruppelt, Director of the U.S. Air Force's Project Blue Book (a study of UFO reports), estimated that in the five and one half years from June 1947 to the end of 1952 there had been some 44,000 UFO sightings in the United States. Of the 1,593 reports analyzed by the project, close to 27 percent remained of unknown origin. Nevertheless the report concluded with the view that the UFO was a "Space Age Myth." [21]

Astronomers, astrophysicists, and other scientists best able with their professional equipment to observe UFOs, and best qualified by training and experience to interpret the nature of objects sighted through visual and photographic observation, are, on the whole, skeptical. Various observations of certain selected areas of space for prolonged periods of times and in locales characterized by numerous reports on UFOs failed to detect a single unexplained object. Despite these negative results, frequent reports of UFO sightings continued. In fact, some observers and writers suggested that the scholars and the U.S. Air Force which entrusted them with the study of the UFO reports had conspired to deny their existence and that there was an extensive program of censorship relative to the UFO problem.[22]

This type of reaction to the failure of scholarly investigators to discover any evidence of UFOs definitely points to an affective attitude to UFOs on the part of those who believe to have sighted them. Authors writing about UFOs have repeatedly pointed out the passion evoked by the UFO as a subject of discussion.[23] Some, following in the footsteps of Carl G. Jung, who considered the belief in flying saucers a direct heir of a past and lost religious belief in a divine mediator, see in the angel of religious mythology the precedent of extraterrestrial visitation, and hence, by implication, view the occupants of UFOs as the latter-day heirs to angels.[24] Many of the "contactees"—i.e., those men and women who believe or maintain that they have been contacted by UFO occupants—"profess to relevatory experiences which become the basis for their preachments." [25] One generally attributed characteristic of the UFO occupants is that they are gentle individuals, harmless, benevolent, and helpful. In these traits they resemble that type of angel which developed at a relatively late period in the traditional religious mythologies—the early angels were often fierce, fiery, dangerous of approach—and which is the only one known to the average American or European.

The study of UFO reports suggested to some investigators an entirely novel approach to Biblical mythology. Paul Thomas in his book entitled *Flying Saucers Through the Ages* examines the thesis that many Biblical events were descriptions of UFO phenomena.[26] Following his lead, Dr. R. Leo Sprinkle raises a series of questions, all predicated on the possibility that UFOs had reached our planet in early times and that the memory of such landings is preserved in the Bible:

> Is there archaeological evidence on other planets
> which might indicate previous expeditions from
> extraplanetary sources? Did Adam and Eve symbolize
> —or represent—the establishment of a colony from
> another planet? Is there a "Kingdom of Heaven" i.e.,
> an organization(s) of extraterrestrial civilization?
> Was the Star of the East over Bethlehem a UFO
> phenomenon? Was there a long range purpose for
> various covenants between ancient men and angels,
> e.g., the covenant between Abraham and the Angel of
> the Lord in regard to the practice of circumcision?
> Does the psychotic condition stem from repression
> and/or confusion of psychic and spiritual processes?
> Is there a similarity—or identity—of the inspirational
> teachings from angels to ancient man and the creative
> processes of modern man? [27]

Our own comment on this series of questions and the approach they represent is that they can be considered as an example of how new myths can (or try to) modify old ones. Since myths always satisfy human needs, they must, so to speak, keep up with the changing times. New eras create new needs, and these in turn create new myths, or, as in this case, give rise to attempts to refashion the old ones. Angels, obviously, won't do in the modern space age. The old Biblical angels must be retired, after having faithfully served God and man for three thousand years; or, at least, they must be remade in the image of extraterrestrial visitors in whom the new age can—and, as all evidence indicates, very much wants to—believe.

These new angel-substitutes have the advantage over their old-fashioned predecessors of allowing themselves to be seen (although, so far at least, not to be photographed) by a larger number of witnesses. The old, single, and lonely hermit, prophet, seer, man of God, or saintly individual, whose word is the only testimony to angelic visitations of yore is now replaced by the more prosaic "contactees" whose accounts or reports contain many more observed details as to the size, shape, color, clothing, movements, and occasionally words of the mysterious visitors. The number of these "contactees" is quite impressive. One book devoted to the subject lists ninety-eight sightings of UFOs with an occupant or occupants. There was one report of such a sighting in 1914 (a large globe with a small humanoid occupant in a diving suit); then, no reports until July 1947, from which time until March 23, 1966, ninety-seven sightings were reported. By far the best visual crop was yielded in 1954, when there were forty sightings of UFOs with occupants [28]—that is, more than all the angel "sightings" in the Old and New Testaments together, although those books span a history of many thousands of years, and were written in an environment which as a whole approved of angelic visitations.

Without going into the question of whether the UFOs, or at least some of them, are or are not space vehicles in which intelligent beings from other planets or celestial bodies have been coming to visit this earth, let us merely discuss the meaning of the extraordinarily large number of sightings since 1947. As

Jung pointed out, the very fact that so many people *believe* that they have seen "flying saucers" indicates that such a belief satisfies a psychological need. According to Jung this psychological need arises in a society which feels threatened, but in which the belief in divine mediators (such as angels) has declined and disappeared. The vacuum thus created is filled by the new belief in the modern-day heirs of the heavenly messengers, beings from unknown worlds who are possessed, like the angels of old, of an intelligence much superior to man's, but who, unlike the angels, use highly sophisticated, and therefore mysterious, mechanical contraptions as means of locomotion.[29]

I am inclined to a somewhat differently weighted explanation of the psychological mechanism that leads to the widespread, almost epidemic, belief in the flying saucers. It seems to me that the clue to the ultimate meaning of this belief must be sought in the fact that the overwhelming majority of UFO reports tell, not of the extraterrestrial *beings* who come to visit this earth, but of the *vehicle* in which they come. This emphasis on the vehicle, the spaceship, seems to indicate that it is *its* appearance, more than that of its occupants, that satisfies a psychological need felt by many in our modern times. The superiority of these extraterrestrial space vehicles to all aircraft and spacecraft known on this earth is frequently emphasized in the reports. They can perform maneuvers and attain speeds that are far beyond the capacity of manmade flying vehicles. It is this feature, together with the friendliness of the occupants as described by relatively much fewer reports (see below), that points to the flying saucer as a *mythical vehicle of planetary escape*.

What the flying saucer myth actually conveys is this: When our planet, for whatever reason, can no longer sustain human life, there will be an avenue of escape to another planet, another galaxy, another world. In our modern space-conscious age, this myth clothes itself in a garb which reflects what people today know about flights by terrestrial aircraft and spacecraft. But, since imagination always runs ahead of reality, the reports of UFO sightings usually attribute to the flying saucers aviational capabilities that greatly surpass those of even the most advanced manmade craft, and that, incidentally, augment the comfort they give, the hope they hold out, for the planetary escape. When sighted in groups, as they occasionally are, the UFOs fly in typical air-force formation (in line, echelon, triangle, rectangle, etc.) but show a much greater, indeed, an amazing, maneuverability.[30] They give all indications of having at their disposal incredibly powerful energy sources unknown to modern technology. Since one of the most annoying features of our aircraft is their noisiness, the UFOs, as a rule, are noiseless. Since the most difficult maneuver for manmade craft is to hover motionlessly in the air, and especially a few feet above the ground, this feat is often ascribed to UFOs. Since manmade aircraft is either balloon-shaped or cigar-shaped (Zeppelins, blimps, and helicopters), bird-shaped (the various airplanes), triangular (the delta-wing), or roughly quadrangular (planes with twin fuselages), practically the only simple shape left, which would mark a craft as extraterrestrial in origin, is the saucer or disk. In other words, the UFOs can be considered as representing a further development, supplied by popular fantasy, of manmade air and space craft, a superior craft, one that comes from outer space and that is therefore capable of transporting humans to other celestial bodies.

One of the most characteristic features that stamps the flying saucer sightings as a latter-day manifestation of the myth of planetary escape is, as already mentioned, the friendliness of its occupants. Although the craft itself is often said to have left scorch marks on or around the place where it landed, and although its proximity is said to have caused disruption of electricity and other disturbances in electrically powered machinery, it has never been said to have caused physical damage to either humans or objects. As to the occupants of the flying saucers, in contrast to those of the horror-inspiring novel of H. G. Wells, *The War of the Worlds* (1898), or of the famous radio broadcast of Orson Welles in 1938 which caused a mass panic in New York and other cities, extraterrestrial visitors are invariably described in the reports of those who claim to have had contact with them as benevolent. The over-all impression one gains from a synopsis of all the reports is that our planet is being visited from time to time by superior beings from outer space who come to observe us, to look us over, to study us, always with a friendly, sympathetic attitude. What their ultimate intention is with these visits remains, as a rule, unknown; most of those very few "contactees" who claim to have actually conversed (in English, of course) with occupants of flying saucers venture no statement or guess as to what the final purpose of these visits might be.

An exception to this general rule is presented by the flying saucer movement (for a movement, indeed, it had become) initiated by Mrs. Marion Keech and subjected to a detailed study by Leon Festinger and his associates.[31] Especially interesting in this study is the account of the information Mrs. Keech received from the extraterrestrial visitors about life and activities on a universe of planets beyond the solar system. The sum total of the description of these outer-space societies amounts to a veritable mythology. Part of the teachings and prophecies from outer space was a prediction of a great flood that was to swamp most of the West Coast of America on December 21, 1954.

Once this date for the cataclysm was known, the belief spread in the circle of the faithful that rescue operations from outer space had begun. "Some people had already been picked up by saucers for transportation to other planets, and more would follow them soon. . . ." Four days before the appointed date—that is, on Friday, December 17th—the members of the movement expected a flying saucer to land in the back yard at four o'clock to take them to the safety of another planet. Despite the fact that the promised pickup did not materialize, the faithful continued to believe and to expect the cataclysm. On December 20 Marion Keech received several new messages repeating the promise of the rescue via saucer at midnight that night. The cataclysm itself was to occur seven hours later, at 7 A.M. in the morning of the 21st. Nothing happened until about 4:45 A.M., when Mrs. Keech announced that she had just received a message to the effect that God, with His mighty word had saved them "from the mouth of death. . . ."

After the initial reaction to the disappointment brought about by this "disconfirmation," the leaders and members of the group rapidly adjusted to the new situation. They gave numerous press and television interviews, stressing the cautionary nature of the whole experience, the existence of faults in the earth's surface, and the need to be ready to evacuate in case of an emergency. The flying saucers, they maintained, would continue to survey the earth and to stand by if an evacuation should prove necessary. The remarkable thing was that most of the members of the group "passed through this period of disconfirmation and its aftermath with their faith firm, unshaken, and lasting," and that it was followed by increased proselytizing. The latter, Festinger and his associates argue, is typical of prophetic movements in the wake of the disconfirmation of their basic beliefs and expectations.[32]

On the basis of this case history and the general tenor of other, less explicit accounts of flying saucer sightings and contacts, we can venture a psychological explanation of the motivations that induce such an astonishingly large number of people to believe so fervently in the flying saucers and in the benevolent interest of their occupants in the affairs of man. These beliefs must be born of the desire and the need to have a way out if and when the feared global catastrophe occurs. Like Teilhard de Chardin, these people believe that man cannot fall victim to a planetary conflagration, that man must survive; but, not being able to envisage, as Teilhard does, a new phase of life detached from its material matrix and joined in its pure essence to the Omega point, and having long lost their faith in the old reassurances contained in traditional religious teachings, they see only one avenue of escape—that opened up by space technology and proven to be navigable by a considerable flying saucer traffic from other celestial bodies to our planet and back. Their new myth of planetary escape holds out the promise—not formulated in explicit terms, but merely implied or hinted at, as is typical of mythological formulations—that when that end of the days comes, great flotillas of extraterrestrial craft will swoop down silently and in perfect formation to gather up Me and Mine and all those others whom the earlier space scouts found deserving, and transport them into the safety of an unknown, faraway, and magnificent world.

wanted: a charter myth for democracy

We have reached the end of our examination of some manifestations of the working of myth and mythical thinking in modern life. We found—to sum it up in the briefest form—that modern man still creates his own myths, and his life is still influenced by mythical prototypes and images. Myths, mythical beliefs, and mythical thinking, we discovered, crop up in quite unexpected places: in socialist, Communist, and totalitarian thought, in the world of entertainment, in science fiction, in the behavior of young radicals, in the advertising media, in learned theology and modern folk belief, in the realm of sex, and in the workings of a scientific and popular imagination stimulated by the belief in an impending global catastrophe, to name only a few. Modern man, so proud of his technology, of his rational, logical, and purposive bent of mind, and of his down-to-earth realism, has thus been found to stand in this respect quite near his ancestors who lived two or three thousand years ago in pre-scientific antiquity in Asia and Africa, in the ancient Near East, and the classical world.

One last question remains to be answered: Do the insights we gained into the working of myth in the psyche of modern man lend themselves to utilization for the benefit of our embattled contemporary Western world? Our modern society is torn by the strife of the older and the "now" generation, of students and hardhats, of doves and hawks, of whites and blacks; it flounders between culture and counter-culture, and is tossed by the conflicting claims of competing socio-political ideologies and the demands of numerous special-interest groups. Can it, in this turmoil, in the midst of these threatening signals of disintegration, turn to its advantage the finding that mythical thought is still a powerful force in our midst? The answer, I think, is definitely yes.

The democratically-elected governments of the contemporary Western world have so far left unused the channel of important influence over their constituencies represented by myth. In several previous chapters it has been shown how various totalitarian states and ideologies have in the recent past utilized such channels. We have also seen how certain subgroups within the Western democracies have created their own myths to motivate, bend, and satisfy those to whom they wanted to or did appeal. It was also pointed out that not infrequently new myths have been growing up in our very midst from the grass-roots level. In each of these cases, the myths of the society or the group functioned as an effective, unifying force in addition to supplying a purpose which motivated and stirred up goal-directed action.

That the governments of the Western democracies—and I have here in mind the United States in particular—have not followed this path is probably due to either one of two reasons: they may not have been aware of the possibility of exerting influence on their peoples through mythical channels; or they may have refrained from so doing because of moral considerations—a matter of conscience—and because anything faintly resembling "brainwashing" is anathema. Only at election times have party propagandists undertaken efforts to create short-lived *ad hoc* myths for their candidates and to transform them, as it were, into modern equivalents of the classical *Augenblicksgötter*, or momentary gods. Apart from this exception, and possibly a few insignificant other cases, mythmaking and mythical influencing of the public outlook has not been engaged in by democratic governments.

The findings of this book show unequivocally, not only the existence, but also the effectiveness, of myth in the life of modern man. It seems to me that at the present critical state of affairs in Western socio-political relations, governments can no longer afford to let the fertile loam of mythmaking and mythical influencing lie fallow. Myth must be made to serve as a unifying, goal-giving force in modern democratic national life. The alternative is national decay and chaos.

In making this suggestion I am not unmindful of the dangers inherent in the course I advocate. Myth, as several examples in this book show, can not only be a constructive, positive force, but also a dangerous, negative one. Individuals and groups, even very large ones, have in the past wrought havoc and brought destruction to both themselves and others under the influence of pernicious myths. There can be no doubt that state-inspired myths can represent a similar danger for modern Western democracies as well. But this danger is not greater than the danger that their legislative bodies could enact harmful laws, or that their governments could make wrong decisions. Despite the built-in checks and balances, these risks are part of the democratic process and must be incurred.

By and large, notwithstanding its many imperfections, democracy is the best way of government developed thus far by man. One of its dearest values is the basic tenet that every man must enjoy freedom of opinion and expression. To suppress opposition by force, as is done in the totalitarian Communist states with their dictatorial one-party systems, is unimaginable in a true democracy. However, herein precisely lie the seeds of the internal disunity and strife of which democracy suffers to a much greater extent than totalitarianism. There can be no question but that the democratic atmosphere actually fosters differences of opinion and enables, even encourages, individuals to make efforts to win over others to their own views. The question that does arise is, How is it possible that under totalitarian governments, which ruthlessly suppress dissent, most people nevertheless willingly follow the one-party line without feeling oppressed or deprived, while in a democracy, despite all the freedoms it affords, so many people are dissatisfied and even acutely unhappy with the system?

The answer, I think, lies in the power of myth which is being brought to bear fully upon man's mind under totalitarianism but which is largely unutilized in democracy. The myths of totalitarianism are huge, overwhelming structures which exert a quasi-magic influence on the people and tend to override individual concerns. They imbue the individual with the sense of being part of a great venture, a feeling which psychologically is enormously satisfying and which, whatever its drawbacks, makes for national unity. In Communist totalitarianism this great mythical venture has been the liberation and unification of the oppressed working classes, first in the country itself and then in the world at large, and their transformation from disenfranchised, exploited, poverty-stricken masses into the dominant, ruling class firmly in control of the means of production and of the government machinery. This proletarian myth has been found applicable and effective with some variation in countries with such diverse traditional cultures as Russia, China, North Vietnam, and Cuba. The central myth of Nazi totalitarianism was that of the Teutonic master race whose destiny was to rule the world or, at least, the "Fortress Europe."

A nation does not necessarily have to be as large as the Chinese, Russian, or German to be motivated and united by a central myth and the idea of a great, and necessarily mythical, venture. Biblical Judea is an example of a small nation with a central myth—the chosenness by and the worship of the one invisible God, and with the idea of a great venture or mission—to become the religious center of all nations (see Micah 4:1).

These examples, and others that could be adduced, lend themselves to a generalization: it appears that the typical great national charter myth is composed of at least two parts; one pertaining to the basic values, achievements, and goals of the nation itself, and the other having reference to the task of the nation relative to the world at large.

Despite all the outpouring of modern myths from various elements and components of the American people, several of which were discussed in this book, America as a whole has so far failed to produce its great, central, uniting, national charter myth. The absence of such a myth is not acutely felt in times of palpable danger threatening from abroad (such as was last experienced by America in World War II), when the imperative of warding off the peril serves as a uniting national purpose. But in times of peace, or even when the country is involved in a foreign war with an enemy who, however, does not represent a clear and present threat to the nation, strife and disunity can easily develop unless prevented by the unifying force of a central, national charter myth.

All that America has produced so far in this area are disjointed mythologems which are still far from being pulled together into a unified and unifying myth of democracy. Americans are undoubtedly conscious of certain features in their national character and in the value system of their country. Many of them are proud of their high standard of living, extensive educational network, democratic political system, highly developed technology, and more features with regard to which, they feel, America is superior to the rest of the world. The values attached to these features and the beliefs surrounding them constitute elements that could go into that part of a national charter myth which pertains to the basic values, achievements, and goals of the nation itself.

Nor is the American consciousness wanting in potentially mythical elements in its view of the role America plays or should play in the world. Americans, or at least many of them, feel that their own values, achievements, and goals are of such a nature that the rest of the world could and should adopt them to its own great advantage. Actually, America has demonstrated for more than a century, but especially since World War II, that she is willing to make considerable efforts and sacrifices in order to introduce her values, achievements, and goals into those parts of the world in which the people are willing to receive them or can be persuaded to do so. In these features, America possesses significant elements which could go into that part of a national charter myth which pertains to her tasks and role relative to the world at large.

Yet withal, American democracy has not yet managed to produce its charter myth. Even the longest list of mythologems, or disparate mythical features, does not in itself and by itself add up to such a charter myth, which is precisely what America needs today. Only a great, central myth of democracy, which will summarize effectively, symbolically, and imaginatively, as only a myth can, what America stands for at home and abroad and what America can be for her own people and for the world, will have the power to unite the nation, to motivate it to concerted action, and to infuse its members with that feeling of elation which being part of a great venture means for the individual.

chapter notes

Introduction

1. See Raphael Patai, "What is Hebrew Mythology?" *Transactions* of the New York Academy of Sciences, 2nd series, XXVII, No. 1 (November 1964), 73; also Patai, "Zum Wesen der hebräischen Mythologie," *Paideuma: Mitteilungen zur Kulturkunde,* XI (Frankfurt am Main, 1965), 58.

2. Robert Graves and Raphael Patai, *Hebrew Myths: The Book of Genesis* (Garden City, N.Y.: Doubleday, 1964), p. 11.

3. See Georges Sorel, *Reflections on Violence,* authorized translation by T. E. Hulme (New York: Peter Smith, 1941), pp. 131ff. For a fuller discussion of Sorel's position, cf. Chapter 4, section 4, below.

4. This view of Malinowski to be discussed more fully in Chapter 1, section 11.

5. For a fuller discussion of Otto's approach cf. Chapter 1, section 12.

6. Cf. Walter Ong, S.J., "A Modern Sensibility," *Social Order* (February 1952), as reprinted in Gerald Emanuel Stearn, ed., *McLuhan Hot and Cool: A Critical Symposium* (New York: Dial Press, 1967), pp. 84–85.

7. See Chapter 4, section 2; Chapter 20; and Chapter 21, sections 3 and 4.

8. See, e.g., Dan S. Norton and Peters Rushton, *Classical Myths in English Literature* (New York: Holt, Rinehart & Winston, 1952). These authors begin their Preface by stating: "No one can understand English literature unless he knows something about classical myths, for our writers . . . still use classical myths in their stories and poems."

9. Numerous such expressions taken from Greco-Roman mythology are gathered in Frances E. Sabin, *Classical Myths That Live Today*, rev. ed. (Morristown, N.J.: Silver Burdett, 1940).

10. See, e.g., Susy Smith, *Today's Witches* (Englewood Cliffs, N.J.: Prentice-Hall, 1970).

Chapter 1

1. See George Grote, *History of Greece* (London, 1903), I, p. 356, as quoted by Richard Chase, *Quest for Myth* (New York: Greenwood Press, 1969), p. 1.

2. Chase, *op. cit.*, p. 2.

3. David Bidney, "Myth, Symbolism, and Truth," in *Journal of American Folklore*, LXVIII (October-December 1955), 379.

4. Jean Seznec, *The Survival of the Pagan Gods* (Bollingen Series xxxviii; New York: Pantheon Books, 1953), p. 12.

5. *Ibid.*, pp. 12–13; Chase, *op. cit.*, pp. 3–4.

6. See Wilhelm Schmidt, *The Origin and Growth of Religion* (London: Methuen, 1931), pp. 20, 24.

7. See Seznec, *op. cit.*, p. 14, quoting Isidore of Seville, *Etymologiae*, VIII: xi.

8. *Ibid.*, p. 15.

9. P. Alphandéry, "L'Evhémérisme et les débuts de l'histoire des religions au Moyen-Age," in *Revue de l'histoire des religions*, CIX (1934), 1–27; J. D. Cooke, "Euhemerism: A Mediaeval Interpretation of Classical Paganism, in *Speculum*, II (1927), 391–410.

10. Zwingli, Christianae fidei brevis et clara expositio, as quoted by Seznec, *op. cit.*, p. 23.

11. *Ibid.*, pp. 220–24.

12. *Ibid.*, pp. 224ff.

13. First published in London in 1609.

14. First published in Venice in 1551; French translation published in Paris in 1599.

15. Edward B. Tylor, *Primitive Culture* (New York, 1924), II, 446 (originally published in 1871).

16. *Ibid.*, I, 416.

17. *Ibid.*, I, 283–84.

18. *Ibid.*, I, 285.

19. *Ibid.*, I, 299.

20. Richard M. Dorson, "The Eclipse of Solar Mythology," *Journal of American Folklore*, LXVIII (October-December 1955), 415–16.

21. First edition, Leipzig, 1908; second edition, Leipzig, 1914; the subsequent source references are to this second edition.

22. Wundt, *Völkerpsychologie* (Leipzig, 1914), V, 23–24. My translation of all the quoted passages.

23. *Ibid.*, pp. 25–27.

24. *Ibid.*, pp. 86–87.

25. *Ibid.*, IV, 316–17.

26. Cf. Otto Rank, *The Myth of the Birth of the Hero*, Nervous and

Mental Disease Mono. Ser., No. 18 (New York, 1914; reissued New York: Robert Brunner, 1952). Originally published in German in 1908.

27. Géza Róheim, "Myth and Folk-Tale," *American Imago,* II, No. 3 (1941), 266.

28. In reaching this conclusion, Jung refers in a footnote both to the parallel drawn by Freud (*Traumdeutung,* 2nd ed., 1900, p. 185) between certain aspects of infantile psychology and the Oedipus myth, and to the observation made by Freud to the effect that the "generally valid effectiveness" of the Oedipus legend must be explained from the similar infantile supposition. See C. G. Jung, "Zur Psychologie des Kind-Archetypus," in C. G. Jung and K. Kerényi, *Einführung in das Wesen der Mythologie,* 4th ed. (Zurich, 1951), p. 109. Although this book is available in an English translation by R. F. C. Hull, entitled *Essays on a Science of Mythology* (Bollingen Series xxii; New York: Pantheon, 1949), I have translated all the passages quoted here.

29. *Ibid.,* p. 110.

30. *Ibid.,* p. 111.

31. *Ibid.,* p. 112.

32. *Ibid.,* p. 113.

33. *Ibid.,* p. 114.

34. *Ibid.*

35. C. G. Jung, *Two Essays on Analytical Psychology* (New York: World Publishing, 1956), pp. 79–80.

36. Jane E. Harrison, *Themis* (Cambridge, 1912), pp. 13, 328, 331.

37. S. H. Hooke, ed., *Myth and Ritual: Essays on the Myth and Ritual of the Hebrews in Relation to the Culture Pattern of the Ancient East* (London: Oxford University Press, 1933), and *The Labyrinth: Further Studies in the Relation between Myth and Ritual in the Ancient World* (London: Society for Promoting Christian Knowledge, 1935). A third anthology of essays discussed in particular the application of the myth and ritual approach to kingship; cf. S. H. Hooke, ed., *Myth, Ritual, and Kingship: Essays on the Theory and Practice of Kingship in the Ancient Near East and in Israel* (London: Oxford University Press, 1958).

38. Hooke, *Myth and Ritual,* p. 3.

39. Hooke, *The Labyrinth,* pp. v-vi.

40. Cf. Stanley Edgar Hyman, "The Ritual View of Myth and the Mythic," *Journal of American Folklore,* LXVIII (October-December 1955), 465, 470–71.

41. Lord Raglan, "Myth and Ritual," *Journal of American Folklore,* LXVIII (October-December 1955), 454; cf. Raglan, *The Hero* (London, 1936), p. 145.

42. The quotation is from B. Malinowski, *Myth in Primitive Psychology* (London, 1926), p. 13. It is interesting that, in quoting the above passage in his article "Myth and Ritual," p. 457, Raglan omits the crucial words "of ritual."

43. The quotation is from C. von Furer-Haimendorf, *The Raj Gonds* (London, 1948), p. 99, as quoted by Lord Raglan, "Myth and Ritual," p. 457.

44. W. J. Culshaw, *Tribal Heritage* (London, 1949), p. 64, as quoted by Lord Raglan, "Myth and Ritual," p. 457.

45. M. Fortes, *The Web of Kinship Among the Tallensi* (Oxford, 1949), p. 3, as quoted by Raglan, "Myth and Ritual," pp. 457–58.

46. Raglan, "Myth and Ritual," p. 458.

47. *Ibid.*, p. 459.

48. David Bidney, "Myth, Symbolism and Truth," *Journal of American Folklore*, LXVIII (October-December 1955), 294.

49. *Ibid.*

50. This was pointed out as early as 1946 by Mark Schorer in his *William Blake* (New York, 1946). Schorer, however, excluded this sense of "myth" from his definition of the term. Cf. Mark Schorer, "The Necessity of Myth," in Henry A. Murray, ed., *Myth and Mythmaking* (New York, 1960), p. 354.

51. Bidney, *op. cit.*, p. 310.

52. *Ibid.*, p. 325.

53. *Ibid.*, p. 325–26.

54. *Time*, May 27, 1970, p. 60 (italics added).

55. *Commentary* (May 1965), p. 60.

56. Originally published in 1926; reprinted in *Magic, Science, and Religion* (Garden City, N.Y.: Doubleday, 1954), which is the edition quoted in all subsequent citations.

57. Düsseldorf-Köln: Eugen Diederichs Verlag, 1955.

58. This and all subsequent quotations are my translation from the German original.

59. Thomas J. J. Altizer, "The Religious Meaning of Myth and Symbol," in Thomas J. J. Altizer, William A. Beardslee, and J. Harvey Young, eds., *Truth, Myth, and Symbol* (Englewood Cliffs, N.J.: Prentice-Hall, 1962), p. 107.

60. John B. Vickery, *Myth and Literature: Contemporary Theory and Practice* (Lincoln: University of Nebraska Press, 1966), pp. ix-x.

61. See William York Tindall, *The Literary Symbol* (Bloomington: Indiana University Press, 1955), pp. 178–90.

62. *Ibid.*, pp. 177–78.

Chapter 2

1. Claude Lévi-Strauss, *The Raw and the Cooked: Introduction to a Science of Mythology* (New York: Harper & Row, 1969), I, 12.

2. Claude Lévi-Strauss, "The Structural Study of Myth," *Journal of American Folklore*, LXVIII, No. 270 (October-December 1955), 440.

3. *Ibid.*, p. 436.

4. *Ibid.*, p. 435.

5. *Ibid.*

6. *Ibid.*, p. 436.

7. *Totem und Tabu: Einige Übereinstimmungen im Seelenleben der Wilden und der Neurotiker* (Leipzig, Wien, Zurich: Internationaler Psychoanalytischer Verlag, 1925), p. 171. All the following quotations are from this edition, in my English translation.

8. *Ibid.*, pp. 171–73.

9. *Ibid.*, p. 175.

10. *Ibid.*, p. 176.

11. *Ibid.*, p. 188.
12. Paul Roazen, *Freud: Political and Social Thought* (New York: Knopf, 1968), p. 153.
13. Freud, *op. cit.*, pp. 174–75.
14. *Ibid.*, p. 180.
15. *Ibid.*, pp. 160, 161.
16. *Ibid.*, p. 183, quoting William Robertson Smith, *Religion of the Semites*, 2nd ed. (London, 1907), pp. 412–13.
17. Robertson Smith, *op. cit.*, pp. 413–16.
18. *Ibid.*, p. 190.
19. *Ibid.*, p. 191.
20. Joseph Campbell, *The Masks of God: Primitive Mythology* (New York: Viking, 1959), p. 4.
21. Joseph Campbell, *The Hero with a Thousand Faces* (New York: World Publishing, 1956); originally published by the Bollingen Foundation in 1949. In one footnote on p. 322 Campbell refers in passing to Otto Rank, *The Myth of the Birth of the Hero*. There is no reference at all in his book to Lord Raglan's *The Hero*.
22. He took this word from James Joyce, *Finnegans Wake* (New York: Viking Press, 1939), p. 581.
23. Campbell, *The Hero with a Thousand Faces*, pp. 19–20.
24. Italics in the original. It may be mentioned here that Campbell took a certain liberty with the Gennepian *rites de passage*, whose original three stages were separation, transition, and incorporation. See Arnold van Gennep, *Les Rites de Passage* (Paris, 1908); English trans., *The Rites of Passage* (Chicago: University of Chicago Press, 1960).
25. Campbell, *Hero with a Thousand Faces*, p. 30; italics in original.
26. *Ibid.*, p. 37.
27. *Ibid.*, pp. 245–46; italics in original.
28. *Ibid.*, p. 257.
29. Pierre Teilhard de Chardin, *The Future of Man* (New York: Harper & Row, 1969), p. 163, n. 2. Chapter 10, "The Formation of the Noosphere," to which we refer in our present discussion, was originally published in French in the *Revue des Questions Scientifiques*, Louvain, January 1947, pp. 7–35.
30. *Ibid.*, p. 161.
31. *Ibid.*, p. 164.
32. *Ibid.*, p. 163, n. 3.
33. *Ibid.*, pp. 165, 166.
34. See Teilhard de Chardin, *L'énergie humaine*, 1937, p. 152; *Le coeur de la matière*, p. 14; both sources quoted from Émile Rideau, *The Thought of Teilhard de Chardin* (New York: Harper & Row, n.d.), pp. 358–59; and Teilhard de Chardin, *The Phenomenon of Man* (New York: Harper & Row, 1959), p. 251.
35. *The Future of Man*, pp. 173–74.
36. *Ibid.*, pp. 176–80.
37. *L'énergie humaine*, p. 164, as quoted in Rideau, *op. cit.*, p. 448.
38. *The Future of Man*, pp. 181–87.
39. *Ibid.*, pp. 300–1. Cf. also what Teilhard has to say on Marxism in his *The Phenomenon of Man*, pp. 260–61. Since the Marxist myth has many

and diverse ramifications that have no direct bearing on the transformation of scholarly students of man into mythopoets, we do not include its analysis in the present chapter, but devote to it a separate one later in this book (see Chapter 5).

40. Cf. Rideau, *op. cit.*, p. 185. Rideau recognizes that "the very width of scope" of Teilhard's phenomenology "makes it akin to the great systems, in particular to those of Hegel and Marx" (p. 41), and that Teilhard "agrees with Marx in his appreciation of modern technology" (p. 72). In fact, he finds it necessary to warn that one should not "be so inordinately attracted by Teilhard's hope in an earthly end awaiting mankind by his mystique of action, as mistakenly to assimilate his thought to Marxism and succumb to the temptation of the Marxist ideal" (p. 224). In a long footnote (pp. 646–47) Rideau further discusses Teilhard's attitude toward Marxism, and concludes that although much in Teilhard's thought is analogous to that of Marx, and "Teilhard's dialectic is akin to at least Marx's . . . in that it embraces 'one single indivisible reality, man-nature,' " nevertheless "there is still a radical opposition between an atheist system that in denying God cuts away the foundation of the person and of interiority, and a doctrine that makes man reach his term by a transition into God."

Chapter 3

1. Cf. C. G. Jung and K. Kerényi, *Einführung in das Wesen der Mythologie*, 4th ed. (Zurich, 1951), p. 17. My translation.

2. Cf. B. Malinowski, *Magic, Science, and Religion* (Garden City, N.Y.: Doubleday, 1954), p. 100.

3. Cf. Hesiod, *Theogony*, 116ff.

4. Published in 'Αντιδωρον: *Festschrift Jacob Wackernagel* (Göttingen: Vandenhoueck and Ruprecht, 1923), pp. 137–49; cf. also Martin P. Nilsson, *The Minoan-Mycenaean Religion and Its Survival in Greek Religion*, 2nd ed. (Lund: C. W. K. Gleerup, 1950).

5. Apollodorus, iii.i.i; Hyginus, *Fabulae*, 178 and 19; Pausanias, *Descr. Graec.*, v.25.7; Apollonius Rhodius, ii.178; Theophrastus, *History of Plants*, i.9.5; Deodorus Siculus, iv.60 and v.80; cf. also Ludwig Preller and Carl Robert, *Griechische Mythologie* (Berlin: Weidmann, 1894), II, 346ff.; Robert Graves, *The Greek Myths* (New York: Braziller, 1959), 56.a–d; H. J. Rose, *A Handbook of Greek Mythology*, 2nd ed. (London: Methuen, 1933), pp. 182ff.

6. Rose, *op. cit.*, p. 183.

7. Genesis 10:15.

8. Herodotus I:2.

9. Ioannes Malalas, *Chronographia*, ed. Ludovicus Dindorff (Bonn, 1831), book II, pp. 30–31.

10. Cf. Thomas Mann, "Freud and the Future," in Henry A. Murray, *Myth and Mythmaking* (New York: Braziller, 1960), p. 373. Reprinted from *Essays of Three Decades* by Thomas Mann (New York: Knopf, 1937). Napoleon used the phrase "I am Charlemagne" in a letter to Cardinal Fesch in 1806; see Christopher Herold, ed. and tr., *The Mind of Napoleon* (New York: Columbia University Press, 1955), p. 109.

11. Euripides, *The Bacchants,* in *Ten Plays,* trans. Moses Hadas and John McLean (New York: Bantam Books, 1960), pp. 281–82.
12. Graves, *op. cit.,* 27.c, and sources in note 4.
13. Rose, *op. cit.,* p. 155.
14. Cf. Jane Harrison, *Prolegomena to the Study of Greek Religion* (New York: World Publishing, 1955), p. 561 (originally published in 1903).
15. Graves, *op. cit.,* 27.a, and sources in note 1.
16. Rose, *op. cit.,* pp. 152–53.
17. Apollodorus II: 26–29; Rose, *loc. cit.*
18. Cf. Harrison, *op. cit.,* pp. 478ff.
19. See Chapters 7 and 19.
20. See Chapters 8 and 15.

Chapter 4

1. Clyde Kluckhohn, "Myths and Rituals: A General Theory," *Harvard Theological Review,* XXXV (1942); reprinted in Robert A. Georges, ed., *Studies on Mythology* (Homewood, Ill.: The Dorsey Press, 1968), pp. 147–48.
2. See R. Gordon Kelly, "Ideology in Some Modern Science Fiction Novels," *Journal of Popular Culture,* II, No. 2 (Fall 1968), 211–17.
3. John Macquarrie, *The Scope of Demythologizing* (Gloucester, Mass.: Peter Smith, 1969), p. 235.
4. The phrase is John Macquarrie's; *ibid.,* p. 234.
5. See photograph on p. 9 of *Time,* May 18, 1970.
6. See Georges Sorel, *Reflections on Violence,* authorized translation by T. E. Hulme (New York: Peter Smith, 1941), pp. 131–37.
7. *Ibid.,* p. 164.
8. *Ibid.,* pp. 298–99.
9. See Sorel's letter to Daniel Halevy, printed as Introduction to *Reflections on Violence* (New York: Collier, 1961), pp. 49–50.

Chapter 5

1. New York: Doubleday, 1953, pp. 189–90 (first published in 1940).
2. *Ibid.*
3. *Ibid.,* p. 190.
4. *Ibid.,* pp. 179–98; the quotations in this paragraph are from p. 179.
5. See Chapter 4, section 1.
6. Mircea Eliade, "Archaic Myth and Historical Man," *McCormick Quarterly* (January 1965), as reprinted in Donald E. Hartsock, ed., *Contemporary Religious Issues* (Belmont, California: Wadsworth, 1968), p. 36. A very similar formulation of the same passage appears in Mircea Eliade, *Myth, Dreams and Mysteries* (New York: Harper & Row, 1960), pp. 25–26; this book was originally published in French as *Mythes, Rêves et Mystères* (Paris: Gallimard, 1957). It is somewhat puzzling that Eliade, while recognizing in the passage quoted that the "myth of the Golden Age" is put by "many traditions . . . at the beginning and the end of history," nevertheless in the same essay makes the statement that "myth is always

related to a 'creation'; it tells *how something came into existence"* (emphasis in the original; "Archaic Myth and Historical Man," p. 29). Evidently, if many traditions contain a myth of the Golden Age that will recur at the end of history, then myths are not "always" related to origins. See also above, Chapter 4, section 1, on this double *Urzeit* and *Endzeit* aspect of myth.

7. *Time*, April 27, 1970, pp. 34–35.
8. April 23, 1970, pp. 44–48.
9. See Julian Huxley, *Soviet Genetics and World Science* (London: Chatto and Windus, 1949), pp. 56–57.
10. *Ibid.*, p. 159.
11. *Ibid.*, p. 162. Vishinsky's book is available in English (New York: Macmillan, 1954).
12. See Innokentii Yul'evich Pisarev, "Some Questions on the Theory of Statistics" (in Russian), *Voprosy Ekonomiki (Questions of Economics)*, I, no. 7 (1948), p. 50.

Chapter 6

1. See Albert R. Chandler, *Rosenberg's Nazi Myth* (New York: Greenwood Press, 1968), p. 6. Cf. also Hewey Hatfield "The Myth of Nazism," in Harvey A. Murray, *Myth and Mythmaking* (New York: Braziller, 1960), pp. 199ff.
2. Alfred Rosenberg, *Der Mythus des 20. Jahrhunderts*, 3rd ed. (München: Hoheneichen Verlag, 1932), pp. 55, 72. This and all subsequent passages are my translation from the German.
3. Chandler, *op. cit.*, pp. 7–8.
4. Rosenberg, *op. cit.*, pp. 172, 413, 148, 592–93, 596, 605 (in the order of the quotations in this paragraph).
5. *Ibid.*, pp. 47, 605.
6. Chandler, *op. cit.*, pp. 67, 70, 85.
7. *Ibid.*, pp. 10–11.
8. *Ibid.*, pp. 113, 122–24.
9. *Ibid.*, pp. 3, 8.
10. Friedrich Andersen, *Sechs Vorträge über Alfred Rosenberg: "Der Mythus des 20. Jahrhunderts"* (Flensburg: Nordmark Verlag August Westphalen jun., 1936).
11. Alfred Baeumler, *Alfred Rosenberg und der Mythus des 20. Jahrhunderts* (München: Hoheneichen Verlag, 1943), p. 111.
12. *Studien zum Mythus des XX. Jahrhunderts* (Berlin: The Catholic Diocese [Ordinariat] of Berlin, October 1934), p. 73 (emphasis in the original).

Chapter 7

1. Cf. Daniel James, *Ché Guevara: A Biography* (New York: Stein and Day, 1969), pp. 1–12, 203.
2. See Louis J. González and Gustavo A. Sánchez Salazar, *The Great Rebel: Che Guevara in Bolivia* (New York: Grove Press, 1969), pp. 195, 231, 232. On May 21, 1970, *The New York Times* (p. 35) reported that Dr.

George E. Sweazy told the delegates of the annual general assembly of the United Presbyterian Church in Chicago that "he had heard of one 'revolutionary' who shared an apartment in St. Louis with a girl friend. 'In their apartment they have only two pictures,' he said, 'one is of the late Che Guevara, the Latin-American militant, and the other is of Jesus.'"
3. See Martin Ebon, *Che: The Making of a Legend* (New York: Universe Books, 1969), p. 8.
4. *Christian Science Monitor,* June 20, 1968.
5. James, *op. cit.,* pp. 306–7.
6. *Ibid.,* pp. 305–6.
7. See below, Chapter 15.
8. *The New York Times,* May 10, 1970, p. 25.
9. See Bruno Bettelheim, "Obsolete Youth," in *Encounter,* XXXIII, No. 3 (September 1969), 40, footnote 7.
10. Cf. John W. Aldridge, "In the Country of the Young," *Harper's Magazine* (November 1969), p. 94.
11. *Newsweek,* May 11, 1970, p. 38.
12. *Time,* May 18, 1970, p. 7.
13. This was recognized even by authors who look with disfavor at myth because they consider it falsehood. Thus, e.g., Tom Wicker says: "When destiny decrees for the hero the martyrdom of violent death in the midst of uncompleted labors, the legend forms instantly. And unless its unreality is promptly pierced by the informed and objective evaluation of those who knew and appreciated the real man, he enters the fog of mythology." Cf. Tom Wicker, *Kennedy Without Tears: The Man Beneath the Myth* (New York: William Morrow, 1964), p. 9.

Chapter 8

1. The picture was reprinted with a brief note in *The New York Times,* September 4, 1970, p. 12.
2. Handbill reprinted in *The New York Times Magazine,* October 25, 1970, p. 39.
3. *The New York Times,* September 4, 1970.
4. The explanations which I have subsumed under points 1 to 4 are offered by Dr. Bruno Bettelheim in his paper "Obsolete Youth," in *Encounter,* XXXIII, No. 3 (September 1969), 32, 34, 39, 40. See also Bruno Bettelheim, *The Children of the Dream* (New York: Macmillan, 1969), p. 207. Cf. also David Dempsey, "Bruno Bettelheim Is Dr. No," in *The New York Times Magazine,* January 11, 1970.
5. John W. Aldridge, "In the Country of the Young," *Harper's Magazine* (November 1969), p. 105.
6. Richard Flacks, "Rebellion in the Post-Industrial World," in *The Activist,* IX, No. 3 (Spring 1969), 11ff.
7. Jane O'Reilly, "Notes on the New Paralysis," *New York,* III, No. 43 (October 26, 1970), 28ff.
8. Seymour L. Halleck, "Hypotheses of Student Unrest," in Julian Foster and Durward Long, eds., *Protest! Student Activism in America* (New York: Morrow, 1970), pp. 105–22. It is interesting to note that Dr. Halleck makes no reference to Dr. Bruno Bettelheim's approach.

Chapter 9

1. If we do not consider in this context the third monotheistic religion, Islam, we do so for but one reason: the present study deals with the role of myth in the *modern world*, which, for the purposes of this book, we have taken to comprise the highly industrialized Western nations only. In this part of the world Islam has very few adherents, and therefore the role of myth in the contemporary *Dar ul-Islam* ("House of Islam") falls outside the limits of our present study. However, we shall discuss in section 1 of Chapter 8 the mythology of the American Black Muslim movement. A forthcoming study on *The Arab Mind* will give me an opportunity to discuss the meaning of myth for the central, Arab, component of the Muslim world in the Middle East.

2. See Edward B. Fiske, "Christianity Linked to Pollution," *The New York Times,* May 1, 1970, p. 12.

3. L. Harold DeWolf, "Christian Faith and Our Natural Environment," in *IDOC International,* North American Edition, September 12, 1970, pp. 3–15.

4. See Lynn White, Jr., *Machina ex Deo: Essays in the Dynamism of Western Culture* (Cambridge: MIT Press, 1968), Chapter V.

5. Loren R. Fisher, "Man and Nature in Old Testament Traditions," in *IDOC, op. cit.,* pp. 16–17.

6. Richard H. Overman, "A Theology of Survival," paper presented at the April 1970 Theology of Survival Conference of the School of Theology at Claremont, p. 1. Mimeographed. (Italics in original.)

7. Cf., e.g., *Encyclopaedia of Religion and Ethics,* III, 451ff., VIII, 304, X, 133ff.; R. Patai, *Golden River to Golden Road: Society, Culture and Change in the Middle East,* 3rd ed. (Philadelphia: University of Pennsylvania Press, 1969), pp. 463ff.

8. Adolphe Tanquerey, *The Spiritual Life: A Treatise on Ascetical and Mystical Theology* (Tournai, Belgium, 1930), pp. 720ff.

9. *New Catholic Encyclopedia* (New York: McGraw-Hill, 1967), V, 749, s.v. Exorcism.

10. Montague Summers, *The History of Witchcraft and Demonology* (London: Kegan Paul, 1926), pp. 211–19.

11. See E. A. Speiser, "Akkadian Myths and Epics," in James B. Pritchard, *Ancient Near Eastern Texts,* 2nd ed. (Princeton, N.J.: Princeton University Press, 1955), p. 61.

12. B. Meissner, "Assyriologische Studien," in *Mitteilungen der Vorderasiatischen Gesellschaft,* IX, No. 3 (Berlin, 1904), 40–45.

Chapter 10

1. A list of modern Catholic works on the problem of contemporary atheism can be found in Thomas J. J. Altizer and William Hamilton, *Radical Theology and the Death of God* (Indianapolis: Bobbs-Merrill, 1966), pp. 196–97.

2. Richard D. Knudten, ed., *The Sociology of Religion* (New York: Appleton-Century-Crofts, 1967), p. 5 (Dr. Knudten's Introduction to Sydney E. Ahlstrom, "Theology and the Present-Day Revival").

3. Thomas O'Dea, "The Catholic Crisis," in Donald R. Cutler, ed., *The Religious Situation: 1968* (Boston: Beacon Press, 1968), p. 291.

4. *Ibid.*

5. *Seder 'Avodat Yisrael* (Redelheim, 1868; photographic reprint, New York: Schocken Books, 1937), p. 56.

6. *Ibid.*, p. 113.

7. *Ibid.*, p. 198.

8. *Ibid.*, p. 232.

9. *Ibid.*, pp. 348, 352, 366, 387, 391, 396, 411, 424, 433.

10. S. G. F. Brandon, "The Sinister Redhead," in *The New York Review,* May 7, 1970, p. 43.

11. This analysis is based on my perusal of three Hebrew *Kibbutz-Hagadot,* those of Kibbutz HaBone Hadera, 1939; Kibbutz 'En Gev, 1950 (both mimeographed); and the one published in several editions by the Culture and Information Department of the *Kibbutzim* of HaShomer HaTza'ir, Tel Aviv. Cf. also Nathan Steiner's Hebrew essay on *Kibbutz-Hagadot* in *Studies in Bibliography and Booklore* (Cincinnati: Hebrew Union College-Jewish Institute of Religion, 1965), VII, Nos. 1–4, pp. 10ff. (Hebrew part), which contains a bibliography of several hundreds of such *Hagadot.*

Chapter 11

1. John Macquarrie, *The Scope of Demythologizing: Bultmann and His Critics* (Gloucester, Mass.: Peter Smith, 1969), p. 14.

2. Ved Mehta, *The New Theologian* (New York: Harper & Row, 1965), pp. 131ff.

3. Rudolf Bultmann, *Kerygma and Myth* (London: S.P.C.K., 1953), p. 7, as quoted in Macquarrie, *op. cit.,* p. 22.

4. Macquarrie, *op. cit.,* p. 23.

5. Rudolf Bultmann, *Jesus Christ and Mythology* (London: SCM Press, 1960; New York, 1958), p. 45, as quoted by Macquarrie, *op. cit.,* p. 34.

6. Fritz Buri has recognized that Bultmann's *"kerygma* is just a residue of myth which should be dealt with in the same way as other myths." See Fritz Buri, "Entmythologisierung oder Entkerygmatisierung der Theologie" ("Demythologizing or Dekerygmatizing of Theology"), in *Kerygma und Mythos* (Hamburg: Evangelischer Verlag, 1952), II, 85, 93, and 96, as quoted by Macquarrie, *op. cit.,* pp. 132 and 136.

7. Macquarrie, *op. cit.,* p. 103.

8. *Ibid.*

9. *Ibid.*

10. The above statements of Fritz Buri are quoted from the summary of his position given in Macquarrie, pp. 139 and 208.

11. *Ibid.,* p. 208.

12. *Ibid.,* p. 212.

13. *Encyclopaedia of Religion and Ethics,* IX, 118.

14. Macquarrie, *op. cit.,* pp. 212–13.

15. *Ibid.,* p. 214.

Chapter 12

1. The contrast between the two approaches here called theological and anthropological-mythological was succinctly stated by Alfred Bertholet: the first, according to him, "assumes God to be an objective essence," while the second "regards religion merely as one aspect of the psychic life of man." And he goes on to say, "At the one extreme stands Hegel's conception of religion as a process working itself out within the being of God; at the other, Feuerbach's conclusion that it is an illusion spun by man." Cf. Alfred Bertholet, "Religion," in Encyclopedia of the Social Sciences (New York: Macmillan, 1934), XIII, 237.

2. Cf. Sir James George Frazer, The Golden Bough, Part III, The Dying God (London: Macmillan and Co., 1911), p. 3.

3. Ibid., pp. 3–4.

4. Ibid., pp. 4–5.

5. Plutarch, De defectu oraculorum, 17; see Loeb Classical Library, Plutarch's Moralia, V (1936), 401–3.

6. A similar conclusion was reached by Gabriel Vahanian, although along a different line of argument: "Briefly and simply, it [the death of God] corresponds to the serpent's eritis sicut dii ['You will become like God'] in the Biblical myth of Adam's fall." Cf. Gabriel Vahanian, The Death of God: The Culture of Our Post-Christian Era (New York: Braziller, 1957), p. 6.

7. Thomas W. Ogletree, The Death of God Controversy (Nashville, Tenn.: Abingdon Press, 1966).

8. Ibid., p. 22, summarizing Gabriel Vahanian, The Death of God: The Culture of Our Post-Christian Era (New York: Braziller, 1961), pp. 139, 147, 187–88.

9. Ogletree, op. cit., p. 23, summarizing Gabriel Vahanian, Wait Without Idols (New York: Braziller, 1964), pp. 31–32, 46, 231.

10. William Hamilton, "The Death of God Theologies Today," in Thomas J. J. Altizer and William Hamilton, Radical Theology and the Death of God (Indianapolis: Bobbs-Merrill, 1966), pp. 46–47.

11. Ibid., pp. 95, 124.

12. Vahanian, The Death of God, p. 187.

13. Ibid., p. 231.

14. Richard L. Rubenstein, Morality and Eros (New York: McGraw-Hill, 1970), p. 10.

15. Cf., e.g., the statement of Thomas J. J. Altizer: ". . . we know that he [Jesus Christ] is present in his Word, and that Word is a Word reconciling the world to itself. . . . The Christian Word becomes fully incarnate in the concrete actuality of human flesh. . . ." Altizer and Hamilton, op. cit., p. 132. William Hamilton says that what Altizer does is to "call men out of the world into the presence of Jesus," ibid., p. 30. Of Paul van Buren's theology Hamilton says that it calls upon us to "do without God and hold to Jesus of Nazareth," ibid., p. 33.

16. R. Patai, Sex and Family in the Bible and the Middle East (Garden City, N.Y.: Doubleday, 1959), p. 226.

17. Cf. Altizer and Hamilton, op. cit., p. 33.

18. *Ibid.,* p. 40.

19. Dietrich Bonhoeffer, *Letters and Papers from Prison,* ed. Ebehard Bethge, trans. Reginald H. Fuller (New York: Macmillan, 1953), p. 195, as quoted by Ogletree, *op. cit.,* pp. 14–15.

20. Richard L. Rubenstein, *After Auschwitz* (Indianapolis: Bobbs-Merrill, 1966), p. 233.

21. *Ibid.,* p. 227.

22. *Ibid.,* p. 238.

23. *Ibid.,* pp. 237–40 (italics in original). Both concepts and expressions ("ultimate concern" and "ground of being") are borrowed by Rubenstein from Paul Tillich; see Paul Tillich, *Systematic Theology* (London: Nisbet, 1953), I, pp. 14–15, 173, 259, etc.

24. *Op. cit.,* p. 240.

25. *Ibid.,* pp. 240–41.

26. *Ibid.,* pp. 244–45 (italics in original); cf. p. 246 where Rubenstein says that "the statement 'God is Dead' is only significant in what it reveals about its maker."

27. Richard L. Rubenstein, "Homeland and Holocaust: Issues in the Jewish Religious Situation," in Donald R. Cutler, ed., *The Religious Situation, 1968* (Boston: Beacon Press, 1968), p. 56; *Morality and Eros* (New York: McGraw-Hill, 1970), p. 40; "Job and Auschwitz," in *Union Seminary Quarterly,* XXV, No. 4 (Summer 1970), 436–37; private communication to me dated October 21, 1970.

28. See Erich Neumann, *The Great Mother: An Analysis of the Archetype,* Bollingen Series XLVII (New York: Pantheon Book, 1955).

29. See my Hebrew book *Man and Earth in Hebrew Custom, Belief, and Legend,* 2 vols. (Jerusalem: The Hebrew University Press, 1942–43); and my *The Hebrew Goddess* (New York: Ktav Publ., 1967).

30. Raphael Patai, *The Hebrew Goddess,* pp. 27–28. The identity of the female aspect of the deity, the Shekhina, with the Biblical Asherah was recognized by Moses Cordovero (1522–1570), leader of the Safed Kabbalists; see his *Pardes Rimonim,* Sha'ar 'Erkhe HaKinuyim, Ch. 3 (Koretz, 1780), p. 120c.

31. In fact, radical theologians are bogged down in blatant self-contradictions about the resurrection or coming back of the dead God. Consider the following statements which affirm either the irreversibility of the death of God or its opposite:

"The contemporary Christian must accept the death of God as a final and irrevocable event" (Altizer, in Altizer and Hamilton, *op. cit.,* p. 126).

"What can the Christian fear of darkness [i.e., "that terrible 'night' unveiled by the death of God"] when he knows that Christ has conquered darkness, that God will be in all?" (*Ibid.,* p. 21 and p. 15).

"The death of God radical theologians . . . are men without God who do not anticipate his return" (Hamilton, *op. cit.,* p. 6).

"We pray for God to return" (*Ibid.,* p. 47).

"The death of God, therefore, cannot be viewed in any way as a recent historical or cultural misfortune which a revival, be it of religiosity or even of authentic faith, will overcome" (Vahanian, *The Death of God,* p. 6).

"The era of God's death may be only a transition. New social structures and cultural forces may pick up what Western culture has now deserted" (*Ibid.*, pp. 187–88).

Chapter 13

1. See *Muhammad Speaks*, October 2, 1970, p. 32.
2. Cf. C. Eric Lincoln, *The Black Muslims in America* (Boston: Beacon Press, 1961), pp. 218ff.
3. Cf. *ibid.*, pp. 68ff., where he quotes various writings and sayings of Elijah Muhammad and Malcolm X; cf. also Hans J. Massaquoi, "Elijah Muhammad: Prophet and Architect of the Separate Nation of Islam," *Ebony*, August 1970, pp. 78ff.
4. Sir James George Frazer, *Folk-Lore in the Old Testament* (London: Macmillan, 1919), I, 22–23.
5. Or, as Dr. Albert B. Cleage put it in the introduction to his book of sermons *The Black Messiah* (New York: Sheed and Ward, 1968), pp. 7–8: "Many more black Americans, race conscious enough to reject a white Christ, have been reluctant to embrace Islam in view of the role played by Arabs in fostering and carrying on the slave trade in Africa."
6. Dr. Cleage claims that there are "hundreds of shrines to Black Madonnas all over the world, *ibid.*, p. 3.
7. Alex Poinsett, "The Quest for a Black Christ," *Ebony*, March 1969, pp. 170ff.; Vincent Harding, "The Religion of Black Power," in Donald R. Cutler, ed., *The Religious Situation: 1968* (Boston: Beacon Press, 1968), pp. 3ff.
8. Cleage, *op. cit.*, p. 3.
9. *Ibid.*, pp. 238, 243, 39, and 41, respectively.
10. *Ibid.*, p. 238.
11. *Ibid.*, p. 4.
12. *Ibid.*, p. 236.
13. *Ibid.*, pp. 236–37. The Pentecost incident described here is a reference to Acts 2: 1–4, 6, which the author quotes on p. 227.
14. *Ibid.*, pp. 239, 253, 7, 24, and 42, respectively.
15. *Ibid.*, pp. 42–43.
16. *Ibid.*, p. 253.
17. *Ibid.*, p. 274.
18. See Edward B. Fiske, "Color God Black," *The New York Times*, November 10, 1968, p. 6E.
19. Cleage, *op. cit.*, p. 4.
20. *Ibid.*, p. 41.
21. See Hiley H. Ward, *Prophet of the Black Nation* (Philadelphia: Pilgrim Press, 1969), p. 138.
22. James H. Cone, *Black Theology and Black Power* (New York: Seabury Press, 1968), p. 38.
23. *Ibid.*, p. 112 (italics in original).
24. *Ibid.*, p. 68 (italics in original).
25. *Ibid.*, p. 69.
26. *Ibid.*

27. James H. Cone, "Toward a Black Theology," *Ebony,* August 1970, pp. 114–16. The religious aspect of the "Black Power" theme in general is discussed by Vincent Harding in his essay "The Religion of Black Power," in Cutler, ed., *op. cit.,* pp. 3–38.
28. James H. Cone, *A Black Theology of Liberation* (Philadelphia: J.B. Lippincott Company, 1970), pp. 11–12.
29. *Ibid.,* pp. 120, 122, 124, 125. All italics in the original.
30. Cf. Howard Brotz, *The Black Jews of Harlem* (New York: The Free Press, 1964), pp. 9, 10–11. Brotz considers it plausible that W. Fard (or Farrad), who founded the Black Muslim movement in Detroit in 1930, was none other than Arnold Ford, the musical director of Liberty Hall, the headquarters of Marcus Garvey's "Back to Africa" movement, who became a Black Jew and disappeared from New York around 1930; see pp. 11–12.
31. Arthur Huff Fauset, *Black Gods of the Metropolis* (Philadelphia: University of Pennsylvania Press, 1944), pp. 31–40; E. Franklin Frazier, *The Negro Church in America* (New York: Schocken Books, 1963), pp. 63–64.
32. Brotz, *op. cit.,* p. 21.
33. *Ibid.,* pp. 18–19, quoting Rabbi Matthew.
34. *Ibid.,* pp. 20–21, quoting Rabbi Matthew.
35. *Ibid.,* p. 22.
36. *Ibid.,* p. 25.
37. *Ibid.,* pp. 29–34.
38. Sara Harris, *Father Divine: Holy Husband* (Garden City, N.Y.: Doubleday, 1953), p. 15; cf. also *Father Divine: His Words of Spirit Life and Hope,* ed. St. John Evangelist and James Hope (no place or publisher, 1961), pp. 38ff., where Father Divine states that God appears in a "Sonship degree" (namely, in Jesus), and in a "Fathership degree," presumably in himself. There is quite an extensive literature on Father Divine and his Peace Mission Movement. See, e.g., Fauset, *op. cit.,* pp. 91–95; Frazier, *op. cit.,* pp. 56–61; Joseph R. Washington, Jr., *Black Religion* (Boston: Beacon Press, 1964), pp. 122–25. While these studies contain cogent observations on the subject, I have preferred to base my presentation on the primary sources represented by Father Divine's own writings and pronouncements.
39. *Harris, op. cit.,* p. 12; cf. Hadley Cantril and Muzafer Sherif, "The Kingdom of Father Divine," *The Journal of Abnormal and Social Psychology,* XXXIII, No. 2 (April 1938), 157.
40. *Father Divine: His Words of Spirit Life and Hope,* p. 170.
41. Cantril and Sherif, *op. cit.,* p. 157.
42. *Father Divine: His Words of Spirit Life and Hope,* frontispiece.
43. *Ibid.,* pp. 2 and 36.
44. *Ibid.,* pp. 21, 19.
45. *Ibid.,* p. 69.
46. *Ibid.,* pp. 3–5.
47. *Ibid.,* pp. 43, 45.
48. *Ibid.,* p. 114.
49. *Ibid.,* pp. 13, 26ff., 54ff.
50. *Ibid.,* p. 56.
51. See, e.g., E. O. James, *Myth and Ritual in the Ancient Near East* (London: Thames and Hudson, 1958), pp. 113ff.
52. *Father Divine: His Words of Spirit Life and Hope,* p. 144.

53. *Ibid.*, p. 149.
54. *Ibid.*, p. 150.
55. *Ibid.*, p. 151.
56. *Ibid.*, pp. 21, 23.
57. *Ibid.*, p. 153.
58. *Ibid.*
59. *Ibid.*, p. 185.
60. *The New Day*, August 19, 1967, p. 1.

Chapter 14

1. H. J. Rose, *A Handbook of Greek Mythology*, 2nd ed. (London: Methuen, 1933), pp. 205ff.; Roscher, *Lexikon*, s.v. Hercules; Robert Graves, *Greek Myths* (New York: Braziller, 1959), no. 118ff.
2. Marshall Fishwick, *The Hero, American Style* (New York: David McKay, 1969), p. 65.
3. Max Lerner, *America as a Civilization* (New York: Simon and Schuster, 1957), p. 800. There is quite a rich literature on the nineteenth- and twentieth-century mythical folk heroes of America. See, e. g., Sydney Fisher, *The Legendary and Mythmaking Process in Histories of the American Revolution;* Harry Schein, "The Olympian Cowboy," *American Scholar* (Winter 1955); Kingsley Amis, *The James Bond Dossier* (New York: New American Library, 1965); Philip Durham, "The Cowboy and the Mythmakers," *Journal of Popular Culture* I, No. 1 (Summer 1967); Richard C. Carpenter, "007 and the Myth of the Hero," *Journal of Popular Culture*, I, No. 2 (Fall 1967); George Grella, "James Bond: Culture Hero," in Harold Lubin, ed., *Heroes and Anti-Heroes* (San Francisco: Chandler Press, 1968).
4. Lerner, *loc. cit.*
5. *Ibid.*, p. 801–5.
6. *Ibid.*, p. 802.
7. Claude Lévi-Strauss, "The Structural Study of Myth," *Journal of American Folklore*, LXVIII, No. 270 (1955), 435.
8. Rose, *op. cit.*, p. 205.
9. Herbert Marshall McLuhan, *The Mechanical Bride: Folklore of Industrial Man* (New York: Vanguard Press, 1951), p. 104.

Chapter 15

1. 1 Samuel 6:4–5.
2. Isaiah 66:17.
3. Robert Graves, *The Greek Myths* (New York: Braziller, 1959), nos. 14.2, 90.3, 158.2.
4. See Stith Thompson, *Motif-Index of Folk-Literature,* 2nd ed., 6 vols. (Bloomington: Indiana University Press, 1955–58).
5. The above motifs can easily be located in the *Motif-Index* by consulting its index in the sixth volume, s.v. "mouse."
6. Marshall Fishwick, *The Hero, American Style* (New York: David McKay, 1969), p. 216.

7. *Ibid.*, p. 218; see also Richard Schickel, *The Disney Version—The Life, Times, Art and Commerce of Walt Disney* (New York: Simon and Schuster, 1968).

Chapter 16

1. Cf. A. E. Crawley, "Drinks, Drinking," in James Hastings, ed., *Encyclopaedia of Religion and Ethics (ERE)* (Edinburgh, 1912), V, 72–82.

2. See Stith Thompson, *Motif-Index of Folk-Literature* (Bloomington: University of Indiana Press, 1955–58), A153 (Food of the Gods); A153.1 (Theft of Ambrosia); A153.2 (Magic food gives immortality to gods); A153.2.1 (Gods' food gives supernatural growth); A154 (Drink of the Gods); A154.1 (Magic drink gives immortality to gods); D1346.3 (Food of Immortality); D1346.3.1 (Magic honey gives immortality); D1338.1 (Magic drink rejuvenates); D1338.1.1 (Fountain of youth); D1338.1.2 (Water of youth). Georges Dumézil argued in an early work that, as Scott Littleton put it, "there is a common set of Indo-European myths concerning the origin of immortality, its personification as a sacred drink (e.g. beer, *amrta*, ambrosia), and its loss through trickery. His evidence ranges from Greek and Vedic myth to medieval Christian legends of the Holy Grail and modern Ossetic [North-Caucasian] folklore." See C. Scott Littleton, *The New Comparative Mythology: An Anthropological Assessment of the Theories of Georges Dumézil* (Berkeley and Los Angeles: University of California Press, 1966), p. 44.

3. This and the subsequent references to the ancient Greek ideas about honey, ambrosia, and nectar are based on Wilhelm Heinrich Roscher, ed., *Ausführliches Lexikon der Griechischen und Römischen Mythologie* (Leipzig-Berlin, 1884–1937), s.v. Ambrosia, where also all the sources can be found.

4. H. J. Rose, *A Handbook of Greek Mythology*, 2nd ed. (London: Methuen, 1933), p. 264.

5. 1 Samuel 14:27.

6. Exodus 16:31.

7. Edmund Carpenter, "The New Languages," in Edmund Carpenter and Marshall McLuhan, eds., *Explorations in Communication* (Boston: Beacon Press, 1960); as reprinted in Alan Casty, ed., *Mass Media and Mass Man* (New York: Holt, Rinehart & Winston, 1968), p. 38.

8. E. O. James, *ERE*, XI, 632–33.

9. Sources in J. A. MacCulloch, "Incense," in *ERE*, VII, 203–4.

10. Cf. E. A. Speiser, "Akkadian Myths and Epics," in James B. Pritchard *Ancient Near Eastern Texts* (Princeton: Princeton University Press, 1955), p. 95.

11. Genesis 8:20–22.

12. Cf. Exodus 29:18, 25, 41; Leviticus 1:9, etc.; Numbers 15:3, etc.

13. Leviticus 3:11, 21:6; Ezekiel 44:7.

14. MacCulloch, *op. cit.*, pp. 201–5.

15. The same idea was expressed in a more conservative and restrained form by Federal Communications Commission Chairman E. William Henry in an address to the 44th annual convention of the National Association of Broadcasters: "Television viewers, in particular, are led to believe that

cigarette smoking is the key to fun and games with the opposite sex, good times at home and abroad, social success and virility." As quoted in Sam Sinclair Baker, *The Permissible Lie* (New York: World Publishing, 1968), p. 115.

Chapter 17

1. See the old, but still useful and enjoyable study on this subject by Angelo de Gubernatis, *Zoological Mythology* (New York: Macmillan, 1872), 2 vols.
2. See *Time* magazine, February 16, 1970, p. 86; July 12, 1968, pp. 50–51.
3. Tennyson, *Idylls of the King*, "The Passing of Arthur," in *The Works of Alfred, Lord Tennyson*, ed. William I. Rolfe (Boston: Dana Estes, 1892 and 1896), VI, pp. 252–53.

Chapter 18

1. Ovid, *Fasti*, IV: 227–28. It might be mentioned here that the name "Venus" is used to this day in a semi-mythological sense, e.g., as the personification of all the "love-goddesses" that have been produced by Hollywood. A book treating of this theme by Michael Bruno is entitled *Venus in Hollywood* (New York: Lyle Stuart, 1970).
2. "In Her Praise," from *New Poems* by Robert Graves (Garden City, N.Y.: Doubleday, 1963), p. 35. Copyright © 1963 by Robert Graves.
3. By Julius Lester (New York: Dial Press, c. 1968).
4. All three expressions are quoted by Thomas A. Johnson in his report entitled "Harlem Youths Exhibit Loot, Taken 'to Get Back at Whitey,' " in *The New York Times*, April 8, 1968, p. 31.

Chapter 19

1. See the reference to "the orgies of Kybele, the Great Mother," in the *Bacchants* of Euripides, in *Ten Plays by Euripides*, trans. Moses Hadas and John McLean (New York: Bantam Books, 1960), p. 283.
2. See H. J. Rose, *A Handbook of Greek Mythology*, 2nd ed. (London: Methuen, 1933), p. 170.
3. Ovid, *Fasti*, IV: 243–44, as translated by James George Frazer, *The Fasti of Ovid* (London: Macmillan, 1929), III, 195.
4. Cf. Frazer, *The Golden Bough*, 3rd ed. (London: Macmillan, 1932), II, 144–45 and sources there.
5. Frazer, *The Golden Bough*, 3rd ed. (London: Macmillan, 1936), V, 265.
6. *Ibid.*, p. 266.
7. Marshall Fishwick, *The Hero, American Style* (New York: David McKay, 1969), p. 157.
8. Frazer, *The Golden Bough*, V, 272.
9. Philip Shabecoff, "Osaka's Teen-Age Moles Use Way-Down Hangout," *The New York Times*, February 20, 1970.

10. L. de la Vallée Poussin, "Suicide, Buddhist," *Encyclopaedia of Religion and Ethics,* XII, 25–26.

11. See *The New York Times,* June 11, August 5, 17, October 5, 27, December 4, 8, 1963; May 6, 1964; etc.

12. See *The New York Times,* January 5, 1966.

13. Susan Sontag, *Trip to Hanoi* (New York: Farrar, Straus and Giroux, 1968), p. 43; cf. also pp. 41–42; *The New York Times,* November 3, 1965, p. 1., col. 2.

14. Reported in *Der Spiegel,* February 2, 1970, p. 86; cf. also *NOVA,* London, July 1970, pp. 42ff.

Chapter 20

1. Some sex researchers, however, maintain that "there has not been any change in the proportion of non-virginity for the past four or five decades equal to that which occurred during the 1920's." What actually did increase, these authorities claim, was the visibility and public awareness of sex, reflecting "a change in attitudes about sexuality." "Although the same percentage of females have coitus, more of them accept this behavior as proper." See Ira L. Reiss, "Premarital Sexual Standards," in Carlfred B. Broderick and Jessie Bernard, eds., *The Individual, Sex, and Society,* A SIECUS Handbook for Teachers and Counselors (Baltimore: The Johns Hopkins Press, 1969), pp. 110–11. This evaluation is at some variance with other studies in the same volume which discuss, e.g., "The Changing Concepts of Masculinity and Femininity" (pp. 141ff.) in America with the attendant changes in roles, including the greater sexual freedom enjoyed by women.

2. Advertisements in the biweekly *Screw* magazine, as quoted by Edward Grossman, "In Pursuit of the American Woman," *Harper's Magazine,* February 1970, pp. 54–55.

3. Nelson N. Foote, "Changing Concepts in Masculinity and Femininity," in Broderick and Bernard, *op. cit.,* pp. 144, 146.

4. Herbert Marshall McLuhan, *The Mechanical Bride: Folklore of Industrial Man* (New York: Vanguard Press, 1951), p. 99.

5. Grossman, *op. cit.,* p. 68.

6. *Ibid.,* p. 69.

7. Foote, *op. cit.,* p. 151.

8. See Richard C. Carpenter, "007 and the Myth of the Hero," *Journal of Popular Culture,* I, No. 2 (Fall 1967), 80, 85.

9. *Ibid.,* p. 81.

10. *Ibid.,* p. 84.

11. James E. Moore, "Problematic Sexual Behavior," in Broderick and Bernard, *op. cit.,* p. 370.

12. *Ibid.*

13. See Bernard Suran, "The Playboy in Profile," in *Listening: Current Studies in Dialog,* I (Aquinas Institute, Dubuque, Iowa, Winter 1966), as reprinted in Donald E. Hartsock, ed., *Contemporary Religious Issues* (Belmont, Calif.: Wadsworth Publishing, 1968), pp. 82, 83, 85.

14. As cited in Moore, *op. cit.,* p. 370.

15. See Walter M. Gerson and Sander H. Lund, *"Playboy* Magazine:

346 MYTH AND MODERN MAN

Sophisticate Smut or Social Revolution?" *Popular Culture*, I, No. 3 (Winter 1967), 226–27.
16. *Ibid.*
17. *Ibid.*
18. Gerson and Lund, *op. cit.*, p. 220.
19. *Ibid.*
20. See Moore, *op. cit.*, p. 364; cf. also Kinsey *et al.*, *Sexual Behavior in the Human Female*, as quoted in *ibid.*, p. 225.
21. Foote, *op. cit.*, p. 152.

Chapter 21

1. Cf. Teilhard de Chardin, *The Future of Man* (New York: Harper & Row, 1969), p. 185.
2. *Ibid.*, p. 186 (italics in the original).
3. *Ibid.*, p. 187.
4. See Emile Rideau, *The Thought of Teilhard de Chardin* (New York: Harper & Row, 1968), p. 571.
5. See *Mon Univers*, 1924, as quoted in Rideau, *op. cit.*, pp. 572.
6. *Le Phénomène Humaine* (Paris: Editions du Seuil, 1955). English translation: *The Phenomenon of Man* (New York: Harper & Row, 1959). All quotations are from this edition. All italics are in the original.
7. *Ibid.*, p. 273.
8. *Ibid.*, p. 275.
9. *Ibid.*, p. 276.
10. *Ibid.*, p. 286.
11. *Ibid.*, p. 287.
12. Teilhard, *The Future of Man*, p. 126.
13. *Ibid.*, p. 127.
14. Teilhard, "From the Pre-Human to the Ultra-Human" (1950), in *The Future of Man*, pp. 309, 310, 311.
15. Rideau, *op. cit.*, quoting Teilhard, "The Singularities of the Human Species" (1954), in *The Appearance of Man*, pp. 267–68.
16. See Erik Bergaust, *The Next Fifty Years in Space* (New York: Macmillan, 1964), p. 225.
17. *Ibid.*, pp. 231–34.
18. *Ibid.*, pp. 235–36.
19. See *Fate* magazine, December 1964; *Encyclopaedia of Religion and Ethics* s.v. Demons and Spirits.
20. *Encyclopedia Americana*, 1967 edition, s.v. Unidentified Flying Object.
21. See E. J. Ruppelt, *The Report on Unidentified Flying Objects* (Garden City, N.Y.: Doubleday, 1956), as quoted by R. Leo Sprinkle, "Psychological Implications in the Investigation of UFO Reports," in Coral and Jim Lorenzen, eds., *Flying Saucer Occupants* (New York: Signet Books, 1967), pp. 164–65.
22. See, e.g., Frank Edwards, *Flying Saucers—Serious Business* (New York: Lyle Stuart, 1966), pp. 243ff.
23. Cf., e.g., Lorenzen, *op. cit.*, pp. 34ff.

24. Cf. C. G. Jung, *Flying Saucers: A Modern Myth of Things Seen in the Sky* (New York: Harcourt, Brace & World, 1959), pp. 147ff.; Lorenzen, *op. cit.*, p. 35.

25. Lorenzen, *op. cit.*, p. 36.

26. London: Neville Spearman, 1965.

27. R. Leo Sprinkle, *op. cit.*, p. 180.

28. Lorenzen, *op. cit.*, pp. 208ff.

29. Jung, *op. cit.*, pp. 6, 8, 10–12, 14, 152.

30. See Gordon I. R. Lore, Jr., and Harold H. Deneault, Jr., *Mysteries of the Skies* (Englewood Cliffs, N.J.: Prentice-Hall, 1968), p. 158. Cf. also the most recent book on the subject, John A. Keel, *UFOs: Operation Trojan Horse* (New York: Putnam, 1970).

31. See Leon Festinger, Henry W. Riecken, and Stanley Schachter, *When Prophecy Fails* (Minneapolis: University of Minnesota Press, 1956).

32. *Ibid.*, pp. 25ff., 43ff., 103, 140, 169, 180ff., 208, 212ff.

index

Aaron, 195
Abel, 14
Abraham, 133–34, 138, 191, 197, 314
Abraham was black, 194, 197
Achilles, 235, 236; -heel, 6
Adam and Eve, 14, 57, 58, 82, 88, 134, 158, 307, 314
Addis Ababa, 197
Adonis, 51, 55, 56, 164, 169–71, 181, 288, 291
Advertisement, mythical element in, 288. See also Commercials; Television
Aeschylus, 44
Africa, 188–89, 197, 213, 239, 273, 340
African folklore, 223; -peoples, 20, 241
Agathyrsoi, 212
Agenor, 75, 76
Aggiornamento, 144
Aigeus, king of Attica, 234
Aither, 70
Ajax, 248–49. See also White Knight
Aladdin's lamp, 250
Aldridge, John W., 117, 126, 128
Alexander the Great, 12, 77–80, 101–2
Alkmene, 210
Alkyoneus, 213
Allah, 184, 186. See also Black Muslims
Altizer, Thomas J. J., 35, 167, 169, 338

Amazons, 212
Ambrosia, 234–37, 239, 343
America, -ns, 6, 26, 116, 136–38, 165, 191–92, 196, 216, 278, 280, 293, 324–26, 345. See also United States
American folk heroes, 216–17, 342
American Indians, oracles among, 241
American theologians, 136
Ammon, 83
Amor, 265–66. See also Eros
Amorites, 108
Amphytrion, 210
Anamnesis, 23
Anatolia, 272
Ancient Near East, 25, 132, 138, 141, 154, 242–43, 321
Ancient Near Eastern culture, 171, 178; -religions, 13, 93, 164–65, 167, 169, 173, 180, 203, 252
Andersen, Friedrich, 109–10
Androcles, 219
Androgyne, myth of the, 289
Angels, 199, 314–16
Animal gods, 252
Animal-motif in the automobile industry, 252–54
Animal myths in commercials, 251–55
Animal names of restaurants, 254–55

349

Sophocles, 21, 44, 52
Sorcerers, 292
Sorel, Georges, 2–3, 90–92
Soviet genetics, 102; statistics, 103
Soviet Russia, 99–101
Space, outer, 311–12
Spain, 212
Spako, 11
Spanish folktales, 223
Speedy Gonzalez, 229
Sphinx, 228
Spock, TV's Mr., 250, 263
Sprinkle, Dr. R. Leo, 314
Stalin, 101–4
Starship *Enterprise*, TV's, 209, 250
Stereotypes, mythical aspect of, 267, 270, 300
Stoic philosophers, 11, 12, 15
Stone Age, 26. *See also* Old Stone Age
Structural myth, 250–52
Students for a Democratic Society (SDS), 121–23
Stymphalian birds, 211
Styx, 11
Suess, Eduard, 61
Suicide, 275–77, 279–81
Sumerians, 10
Sun, 16; cooling off, 311; golden cup of the -, 212
Superman, 123, 217–18, 226, 230, 262
"Superorganic," 62
Sutton, Willie, 217
Swastika, 109
Sweazy, Dr. George E., 335
Syleus, 213
Syria, -ns, 30–31, 51, 77, 164
Syrian Goddess, 272; -gods, 14
Szulc, Tad, 31

Taboos, 21
Tallensi, 27–28
Tammuz, 56, 163–64, 169, 179, 291
Tanquerey, Adolphe, 138–39
Tantalus, 235–36
Tartarus, 70
Tarzan, 219, 226
Taurus, king of Crete, 76
Tefillin. See Phylacteries
Telepathy, 63
Television, 216, 227, 239, 278, 286, 319, 343; -commercials, 237–38, 240, 245, 247–48, 252, 256–58, 260–61, 288, 300–2; myths on, 240, 264; -serials, 228
TenHouten, Warren, 32
Tennyson, 43, 258
Tertullian, 12
Tethys, 70
Teutonic master race, 324
Thales, 10
Thamus, 163. *See also* Tammuz

Theagenes of Rhegion, 10, 36
Themis, 70
Theogonic tales, 11, 70
Theological approach to God, 159–60, 169, 338
Theology, black, 190; -of Survival, 134–38
Theriomorphic gods, 161
Theseus, 14, 43, 75, 76, 209, 234, 293
Thespios 213
Thetis, 236
Thomas, Dylan, 43
Thomas, Paul, 314
Thoreau, Henry David, 43
Thrace, 162, 211
Tiberius Caesar, 163
"Tiger in your tank," 253–54, 296
Tigris River, 78
Tillich, Paul, 339
Tindall, William York, 43–44
Titanomachia, 70; Titans, 70, 78, 79
Tohu waBohu, 70
Totalitarianism, 323–24
Totalitarian thought, myth in, 321
Totem and Taboo, 52–58
Totem animal, 252; -ic meal, 56
Toynbee, Arnold, 59
Tracy, Dick, 217, 226
Transcendence, of evil, 152–53; of God, 152–53
"Transmythologizing," 154
Tree of Life, 213
Trinity, 95, 167, 180
Triton, 213
Trobrian Islanders, 34
Trotsky, 101
Truth in myth, 3, 18–19, 28–30
Turner, Bishop Henry M., 187
Tussaud, Madame, 224
Tylor, Sir Edward B., 16
Typhon, 15
Tyre, 75, 76

Ultimate Concern, God as the, 174–75, 399
Ulysses, 114
Unidentified Flying Objects (UFOs), 255, 312–19
"Unisex" apparel, 302
United Church of Christ, 188
United States, 1, 31, 92, 104, 134, 143, 187, 197–98, 279, 313, 322
Utnapishtim, 242
Utopia, 91–93

Vahanian, Gabriel, 167–69, 338
Valentino, Rudolf, 286
Valhalla, 102
Vann Woodward, C., 31
Vedic myths, 343
Vegetation gods, 164, 276